The London Olympics and Urban Development

As London sought to use the Olympics to achieve an ambitious programme of urban renewal in the relatively socially deprived East London, it attracted global attention and sparked debate. This book provides an in-depth study of the transformation of East London as a result of the 2012 Summer Olympic and Paralympic Games. Government and event organisers use legacies of urban renewal to justify hosting the world's leading sports mega-event; this book examines and evaluates those legacies.

The London Olympics and Urban Development: The Mega-Event City is composed of new research conducted by academics and policy makers. It combines case study analysis with conceptual insight into the role of a sports mega-event in transforming the city. It critically assesses the narrative of legacy as a framework for legitimizing urban changes and examines the use of this framework as a means of evaluating the outcomes achieved.

This book is about that process of renewal, with a focus on the period following the 2012 Games and the diverse social, political and cultural implications of London's use of the narrative of legacy.

Gavin Poynter is Professor Emeritus at the School of Social Sciences, University of East London, and Chair, London East Research Institute, UK.

Valerie Viehoff is a Research Fellow at the Geography Department, University of Bonn, Germany.

Yang Li is a Senior Research Fellow at Centre for Geo-Information Studies, University of East London, UK.

Regions and Cities

Series Editor-in-Chief
Susan M. Christopherson
Cornell University, USA

Editors
Maryann Feldman
University of Georgia, USA

Gernot Grabher
HafenCity University Hamburg, Germany

Ron Martin
University of Cambridge, UK

Martin Perry
Massey University, New Zealand

In today's globalised, knowledge-driven and networked world, regions and cities have assumed heightened significance as the interconnected nodes of economic, social and cultural production and as sites of new modes of economic and territorial governance and policy experimentation. This book series brings together incisive and critically engaged international and interdisciplinary research on this resurgence of regions and cities and should be of interest to geographers, economists, sociologists, political scientists and cultural scholars, as well as to policy makers involved in regional and urban development.

For more information on the Regional Studies Association (RSA), visit www.regionalstudies.org

There is a **30% discount** available to RSA members on books in the Regions and Cities series and other subject-related Taylor and Francis books and e-books including Routledge titles. To order, just e-mail alex.robinson@tandf.co.uk, or phone on +44 (0) 20 7017 6924 and declare your RSA membership. You can also visit www.routledge.com and use the discount code: **RSA0901**

The London Olympics and Urban Development

The mega-event city

Edited by
Gavin Poynter, Valerie Viehoff
and Yang Li

Routledge
Taylor & Francis Group

LONDON AND NEW YORK

First published 2016 by Routledge

2 Park Square, Milton Park, Abingdon, Oxfordshire OX14 4RN
711 Third Avenue, New York, NY 10017

Routledge is an imprint of the Taylor & Francis Group, an informa business

First issued in paperback 2018

Copyright © 2016 selection and editorial material, Gavin Poynter, Valerie
Viehoff and Yang Li; individual chapters, the contributors

The right of the editor to be identified as the author of the editorial material,
and of the authors for their individual chapters, has been asserted in
accordance with sections 77 and 78 of the Copyright, Designs and Patents
Act 1988.

All rights reserved. No part of this book may be reprinted or reproduced or
utilised in any form or by any electronic, mechanical, or other means, now
known or hereafter invented, including photocopying and recording, or in
any information storage or retrieval system, without permission in writing
from the publishers.

Notice:
Product or corporate names may be trademarks or registered trademarks,
and are used only for identification and explanation without intent to
infringe.

British Library Cataloguing in Publication Data
A catalogue record for this book is available from the British Library

Library of Congress Cataloging in Publication Data
Poynter, Gavin, 1949–
The London Olympics and urban development: the mega-event city/Gavin
Poynter, Valerie Viehoff, Yang Li.
Includes bibliographical references and index.
1. Olympic Games (30th : 2012 : London, England) 2. Olympic host city
selection—Economic aspects. 3. City planning—England—London.
4. Urban renewal—England—London. 5. East End (London, England)—
Buildings, structures, etc. I. Title.
GV7222012 .P69 2015
796.4809421—dc23
2014048553

ISBN: 978-1-138-79494-8 (hbk)
ISBN: 978-1-138-36391-5 (pbk)

Typeset in Times New Roman
by Book Now Ltd, London

Contents

Figures

Tables

Contributors

Editors

Yang Li is a specialist in GIS applications and research, who works at the Centre for Geo-Information Studies, University of East London. He is part of the team preparing the Olympic Games Impact studies for London 2012.

Gavin Poynter is Professor Emeritus, School of Social Sciences, and Chair, London East Research Institute, University of East London.

Valerie Viehoff is a Research Fellow at the University of Bonn. She is an urban and historical geographer and previously worked at London East Research Institute, University of East London. In 2000 she won a silver medal at the Sydney Olympics.

Contributors

Jack Black is currently completing his PhD at Loughborough University on the medial construction and representation of British identity and the role of 'empire' during the 2012 Diamond Jubilee and London Olympic Ceremonies. He also lectures at Nottingham Trent University.

Allan Brimicombe is Professor and Head of the Centre for Geo-Information Studies at the University of East London, and a Chartered Geographer.

Andrew Calcutt worked as a journalist for 25 years and is now Principal Lecturer in Journalism at the University of East London, UK.

Phil Cohen is Emeritus Professor in Cultural Studies at the University of East London, UK, and Visiting Professor in Urban Cultures at the University of Umea, Sweden.

Mike Collins, who died in July 2014, was Head of Research at the Sports Council for 17 years before joining Loughborough University and later becoming Professor of Sports Development at the University of Gloucestershire in the new Chartered Institute for the Management of Sport and Physical Activity.

Antonio Desiderio is completing his PhD in the School of Social Sciences, University of East London, UK.

Beatriz Garcia is a Senior Research Fellow in the Department of Sociology, Social Policy and Criminology at the University of Liverpool and, since 2011, Head of Research of the Institute of Cultural Capital. She was in charge of the assessment of the London 2012 Cultural Olympiad legacy for the Arts Council England and UK Department of Culture, Media and Sport.

Vassil Girginov is Reader in Sport Management and Development at Brunel University London, holding a Visiting Professorship at the Russian International Olympic University and at the University of Johannesburg and recently edited a two-volume *Handbook of the London 2012 Olympic and Paralympic Games.*

Nadia Grubnic is a Senior Lecturer in the School of Health, Sport and Bioscience at the University of East London, UK, where she is also currently completing her PhD on the local political responses to London 2012 in three London boroughs.

Annette Hastings is Professor of Urban Studies in the School of Social and Political Sciences, University of Glasgow.

Andrew Hoolachan is currently completing his PhD in the Department of Architecture, University of Cambridge, on the policy of Localism and its effects on the delivery of sustainable legacies in East London. He has previously carried out research at the University of St Andrews and the University of Manchester and worked in the UK Civil Service for 2 years.

P. David Howe is Senior Lecturer in Anthropology of Sport at Loughborough University. He holds a PhD in medical anthropology from University College London, UK, and has previously worked at University of Brighton and University of Gloucestershire.

Shane Kerr is a Teaching Fellow in Sport Policy and Management at Loughborough University, where he is completing his PhD on the politics of the disability legacy of the London 2012 Olympic and Paralympic Games. In 2012 he won the Coubertin Olympic Awards essay competition with a co-authored work on corporate social responsibility.

John Lock is Chair, Strategic Partnership Board, Sir Ludwig Guttman Health and Wellbeing Centre, and formerly Director of the London 2012 Office at the University of East London.

Judith Grant Long is Associate Professor in Sport Management and Co-director of the Center for Sport Management at the University of Michigan. She previously worked in Urban Planning at the Harvard Graduate School of Design.

Iain MacRury is Professor and Head of Research and Knowledge Exchange at the Bournemouth Media School, Bournemouth University, UK.

Olesya Nedvetskaya completed her PhD on social capital and socio-economic impacts of mega-events at the College of Social Science at the University of Glasgow in 2014. She has professional experience of the public, private and nonprofit sectors in various countries, including as part of the Sochi 2014 Olympic Organizing Committee.

Guy Osborn is Professor of Law in the Faculty of Social Sciences and Humanities at University of Westminster, London, UK

Oliver Pohlisch is a cultural scientist and journalist based in Berlin, currently completing his PhD in Geography at the Johann-Wolfgang-Goethe-University, Frankfurt/Main, on eviction processes in East London's Lower Lea Valley.

Rod Purcell is Senior Lecturer in Social Justice, Place and Lifelong Education at the University of Glasgow with a special research interest in community development.

Andrew Smith is Reader in Tourism and Events in the Faculty of Architecture and the Built Environment, University of Westminster, UK.

Eric Sorensen is a Visiting Professor at London East Research Institute, University of East London, and a former Chief Executive of the London Docklands Development Corporation, 1991–1997.

Richard Sumray was Chief Executive of London International Sport in the mid-1990s and instrumental in gathering support for an East London bid.

Peter Vlachos is Principal Lecturer in Events Management at the University of Greenwich, London, UK. He is a political scientist by training and has over 15 years of experience in events and venue management in the UK and North America

Ralph Ward is Visiting Professor, London East Research Institute, School of Social Sciences, University of East London. He was a government advisor for Olympics and Olympic legacy and previously worked for the London Docklands Development Corporation and the London Development Unit of the UK government.

Linda Wilks is a Visiting Research Fellow at the Open University in the Department of Public Leadership and Social Enterprise. She previously taught Event Management at the University of Hertfordshire and at the University of Greenwich and recently published a jointly edited book *Exploring the Social Impacts of Events*.

Acknowledgements

Our warmest thanks to all the contributors to this text; the chapters reflect the work of colleagues whose research may be located in different academic disciplines but who share a commitment to understanding mega-events and their impacts upon the cities that host them. We would also like to convey our warmest thanks to three contributors whose chapters reflect their professional and personal engagement with East London – Richard Sumray, Eric Sorensen and Ralph Ward.

Academics at the University of East London (UEL) have a long track record of studying the area in which they work not least because many of our students come from local communities and the university is itself part of the story of the subregion's renewal. The hosting of the 2012 Olympic and Paralympic Games initiated the latest phase of urban regeneration in the area and brought East London to the attention of the world. The harnessing of the public investment in the mega-event to a wider programme of urban transformation was a central feature of London 2012. This text attempts to explain and analyse the complex relationship between this global sports mega-event and the urban developments it catalysed.

The book would not have been possible without the discussions with friends and colleagues at UEL, the highly informative seminars and events co-organised by the London East Research Institute and the Centre for Geo-Information Studies and the support of Paul Brickell and Troy Scott in hosting our seminars, the informal meetings of the Post London 2012 Group and the exchanges of ideas with researchers located in universities in many different parts of the world, particularly those in cities that have or seek to host mega-events. We wish to record our deep sadness at the passing of Mike Collins during the period of this book's preparation. Finally, we must also record a debt of gratitude to our families for their help and encouragement over the period it has taken for the book to reach publication.

Gavin Poynter, Valerie Viehoff and Yang Li

Introduction

Gavin Poynter

Rising in the East

Rising in the East was the title of the first book published on the regeneration of East London by researchers then located in the Faculty of Social Sciences at the University of East London. Published in December 1995, contributors examined various dimensions of the first phase of the subregion's transition from the industrial to the post-industrial. In its introduction, Michael Rustin argued that 'the development of East London must be a balanced one if it is to serve the interests of all its citizens . . . a comprehensive approach to development is needed' (Butler and Rustin, 1995:11). His view was prescient. He could not have envisaged that the future 'development' of East London would include hosting the 2012 Olympic and Paralympic Games, but he and other contributors were raising issues that are, arguably, as pertinent two decades later as when they were written.

In the 1990s, East London's renewal was perceived as integral to its role in the development of the Thames Gateway, the expansive corridor that stretched along the Thames estuary from London Docklands to the Essex and north Kent coastlines. Nearly two decades later, the subregion looks to the west rather than the east. It has been reconnected to the city that historically had kept it, literally and figuratively, at arm's length—literally, by the barrier provided by the River Lea and the noxious industries that were established along its banks, and figuratively, because it housed London's poor – the working classes who were at various times, in the nineteenth and twentieth centuries, the subject of the fears and philanthropy of the city's social and political elites.[1]

Reconnection has arisen from state-led interventions that have given rise to the development of docklands and the creation of Canary Wharf, the renewal of essential transport infrastructure and, most recently, the hosting of the 2012 Olympic and Paralympic Games. Regeneration has created pockets of prosperity located alongside areas of persistent social deprivation. The bid to host the world's major sporting mega-event acknowledged this divide, and policies adopted by successive governments over the past decade have sought to harness the public investment associated with the event to achieve the social transformation of the city's east side.

Two decades ago, East London was of interest mainly to researchers who worked there, a handful of eminent historians and planners tasked with producing ideas for its development. Over recent years, however, the subregion has emerged as a place of engagement for those seeking to understand the complex impacts of successive phases of urban renewal, and in particular the changes arising from hosting the 2012 Olympic Games. The attention afforded East London – by political and commercial elites as well as academic researchers – reflects a broader trend. Cities, especially global cities, are seen in the twenty-first century to be central to economic growth and future prosperity. Rapid urbanisation in emerging economies and the renewal of the major urban areas of the west have spawned a vast and diverse literature on the city. In the United States and Britain, cities such as London and New York have reemerged from a period of relative decline following the recession of the 1970s to reestablish themselves as global centres of commerce and consumption—their renewal witnessing population growth, the restoration and gentrification of inner city areas and the concentration of industries and employment in major sectors such as financial and business services.[2]

Renewal has provoked envy and emulation in equal measure as it has highlighted sharply the distinctions in the fortunes between the so-called smart, creative metropolitan centres and the shrinking cities that have been unable to throw off the effects of industrial decline. An important dimension of the emergence of the new metropolitan centres is the competition between them, reflected in the rising number of publications and surveys that compare and rank cities according to a diverse range of economic, cultural and environmental performance indicators.[3] The pursuit of reputational advantage, of image and brand, has spurred city and national governments to compete to host major festivals and mega-events, not least sports mega-events and, in particular, the Olympic and Paralympic Games.

London's hosting of the 2012 Olympiad brought together many strands of contemporary debate about cities. That it sought to utilise the Games to achieve an ambitious programme of urban renewal in its relatively socially deprived east side attracted global attention. London's bid to host the Games gave prominence to the social, economic and cultural benefits that East London would achieve from hosting the event, and, in turn, London 2012 gave shape and meaning to the International Olympic Committee's (IOC) desire to counter the criticism concerning the costs and gigantism of the modern Games. The city's bid and the subsequent preparations for the Games were predicated upon the legacies of urban renewal they would achieve. This book is about that process of renewal, particularly in the period since the 2012 Games, and its focus is the diverse social, political and cultural implications of London's adoption of the framing narrative of legacy.

London's legacy Games

The mega-event is defined by its brief duration and its lasting effects on the host city (Roche, 2000), the 'lasting effects' being the domain of 'legacy'. But legacy may be understood and interpreted in different ways and deployed in different contexts – as, for example, a dominant narrative, as public policy and as a framework for measuring and evaluating the impacts of the mega-event on the host city and nation.

The word's meaning implies gift but requires public and commercial forms of investment for its realisation (MacRury, 2008). Legacy as gift is typically associated with traditional familial relations in which one generation passes its values and material possessions to the next, but in the context of the contemporary discourse of the mega-event, the gift may be interpreted as the provision of public goods. Such public goods often relate to the creation of new spaces such as parklands and other civic amenities as well as the less tangible effects of improvements in the public realm that may give rise to an enhanced sense of civic pride. But the gift has to be paid for typically from a combination of the public purse and private investment, with the latter seeking a return on the capital it provides. Inevitably, the balance achieved between public good and commercial gain is an issue at the centre of the unfolding of the legacy narrative (see Cohen, this volume).

As 'policy', the concept of legacy provides a form of legitimation for the decisions made by political and sports elites to invest in bidding for and hosting the mega-event (Lenskyj, 2008:47–49). The sporting mega-event relies for its success upon the enthusiasm and support for it demonstrated by the citizens of the host city and nation. The close association of a nation's political elite with the event necessarily highlights its relationship with its own citizens. The linking of the mega-event to promises of urban and social renewal is potentially hazardous. The political elite may seek to capture for itself a little of the reflected glory of a successful event and gain credit for the 'lasting effects' achieved by public investment in the urban infrastructure, but it may also experience widespread public criticism and social unrest if the event and its promised longer term legacies are not delivered or if its investment priorities are questioned and contested by citizens.[4]

In the case of London 2012, the scope of the promised legacies arising from hosting the Games expanded between 2005 and 2007 as the final budget (the Public Sector Funding Package) exceeded initial estimates by a considerable margin. In turn, the breadth of the legacy promises provided the context for a complex system of governance to emerge incorporating national, city-wide and local government representatives working alongside the specially created agencies tasked with the delivery of the event and its legacies. London was the first host city of the summer Olympic Games to establish in the pre-event phase an agency with specific responsibility for the legacies of the Games (the Olympic Park Legacy Company which in the weeks before the Games became the London Legacy Development Corporation). In so doing, it also established an approach to an extensive programme of urban regeneration in East London that attracted criticism for its displacement of local democratic planning procedures. In its implementation, therefore, legacy may be understood as a vehicle for legitimising and specifying the diverse social, cultural, economic and environmental outcomes to be achieved by public investment in the event and/or as a managerial discourse that is allied to the imposition of large-scale urban redevelopment by the state in alliance with private enterprise (MacAloon, 2008; Raco, 2013).

As a framework for evaluation and measurement, legacy presents further challenges. The attempt introduced by the IOC and host nations/cities to define and measure impact through the introduction of the Olympic Games Impact Study may provide useful data or an evidence base for evaluating the benefits achieved by public and private investment, but it may also be constructed in ways that preclude important issues such as governance and those qualitative (and often intangible) dimensions of urban change that impact on the host population. It is also difficult, for example, to distinguish the effects of the mega-event on the host city from those developments that would have taken place anyway. Given that, as in London's case, a significant area of the east side of the city had already experienced years of regeneration and numerous plans for redevelopment, the specific impacts of the investment in the Games are but one mode of 'intervention' to be delineated and measured among many. Finally, the mega-event may be planned with considerable precision, its effects being the subject of specific policy objectives, targets and deliverables, but these intended outcomes may be accompanied by the unforeseen, unintended or unplanned not least because of the interdependencies or interactions between the policies and the programmes introduced to achieve them (DCMS, 2011:7; Gratton and Preuss, 2008). These and other dimensions of legacy are addressed by the chapters in this book. Several chapters focus on the specific implications of legacy for East London, while others explore themes that have broader implications for the UK and, potentially, for future hosts of mega-events.

Structure of the book

The book divides into five sections. Part I draws upon the experience of two people who, though working in very different contexts, made significant contributions to London's 'move east'. Eric Sorensen was Chief Executive of the London Docklands Development Corporation between 1991 and 1997. He led the agency tasked with the transformation of 5,000 acres of dockland into Europe's largest new business district. His account provides important insights into the initial phases of reconnecting the east to the city, a process that required significant public investment, entrepreneurial risk taking and voices that were able to persuade reluctant city-based businesses to move from their traditional location to the 'remote' east. Richard Sumray was Chief Executive of London International Sport in the mid-1990s. He provides a different but parallel account of London's move east by reflecting upon the task of persuading city and national leaders that London could host a summer Olympic Games and that the east rather than the west side of the city should be the favoured location. The accounts capture the shift from a city in crisis and one that lacked confidence in its capacity to host a global sporting event to one in which a new business district emerged; the argument for launching a serious bid to host the Olympic and Paralympic Games was won and East London was the location of both initiatives.

While Part I looks back at the preconditions for the east's renewal and the eventually successful bid to host the games, Part II examines different dimensions of the 'lasting effects', in the form of the evaluation of the Games' legacies. Yang Li provides a detailed analysis of the first phases of the IOC/LOCOG

Olympic Games Impact Study, the approach, methodologies and findings. Philip Cohen provides a different perspective on this 'apparatus of evaluation', proposing that it provides a structure in dominance, through which different and contradictory conceptions of the economy of worth or value are played out. John Lock examines the institutions that governed the Games, discussing whether London's success in construction, delivery and its attendance to legacy provides lessons from which other host cities may learn. In particular, he draws attention to the temporal dimension of London's framework of governance that was oriented to the event and to the needs of the part of the city in which many of the events took place. In pursuing this dual purpose, he suggests, effective governance structures have to continue into the long post-Games development period. Finally, Mike Collins and Vassil Girginov provide a different perspective on legacy as the creation of new knowledge through the academic writing that contributed to Routledge's Olympic-focused journal special issues published during 2012 and 2013. Thirty-six special issues were published in 26 journals drawn from different academic disciplines; the chapter assesses the achievements of this unique publishing project.

Part III is about the transformation of urban spaces and places achieved via the hosting of a sports mega-event. Judith Grant Long provides an overview of the experience of host cities over recent decades, and in acknowledging the evidence that records the often 'gloomy' post-Games outcomes, she asks why cities continue to have ambitions to host sports mega-events. The three subsequent chapters focus on the local – the implications of London 2012 for spaces and places in East London. Ralph Ward examines the impact upon the Lower Lea Valley, in particular its transformation from a largely brownfield site to that of the futuristic Olympicopolis imagined by London's Mayor Boris Johnson in mid-2014. The author argues that the transformative effects of the Olympic-led investment may be determined less by what is achieved within the park that hosted the Games and more by the developments on its borders and on the banks of the River Lea. Nadia Grubnic studied the responses of three local authorities – the Olympic host boroughs of Newham, Hackney and Barking and Dagenham – over the course of the seven years prior to the staging of the Games. Her analysis reveals the shifts in policies and perspectives of the councils as they sought to secure lasting benefits from the investment in the mega-event. Her analysis suggests that while the boroughs' achievements varied, they were participant rather than passive stakeholders in 'London 2012'. Finally, Guy Osborn and Andrew Smith provide a compelling analysis of the commercialisation of public space that arises from hosting the Olympic Games. Their analysis identifies the spatial controls that create highly commercialised and privatised areas or brandscapes in the host city; while such controls may be temporary, they may be the subject of 'legislative creep' with effects upon the city that are long-lasting.

Part IV discusses different dimensions of the impacts of the mega-event on the economy and society of the host city. Gavin Poynter traces the pattern of foreign inward investment into East London in the pre- and post-Games phases. He argues that the government's ambition to attract inward investment, one of the main economic ambitions arising from hosting the global mega-event, has been relatively successful, not least because public investment in the games provided private capital with a relatively low risk or secure environment for investment. However, the showcase nature of the event has been matched by the showcase nature of the investment attracted, raising questions, therefore, about the long-term trajectory of the subregion's economy. Peter Vlachos also pursues an economic dimension of the Games' legacies by examining small business' responses in Greenwich to the Olympic events held in this historic part of south-east London. His chapter reveals that small businesses' proximity to a mega-event does not necessarily create the commercial opportunities that the large influx of Games visitors imply; indeed, for the majority of small businesses, the Olympic event in Greenwich was perceived to be a hindrance to their everyday activities.

The four remaining chapters in this section examine different, and perhaps underresearched, aspects of the social to date. Shane Kerr and P. David Howe ask what is meant by a Paralympic legacy, and in so doing they deconstruct the concept of legacy as a precursor to examining the main themes of the public policies that constituted the disability legacy of London 2012. Iain MacRury offers an equally perceptive interpretation of the challenges and contradictions that arise from the branding of the Paralympics with its 'brightness in the wake of 2012 potentially occluding a more comprehensive vision of disability'. Oliver Pohlisch focuses upon another underresearched dimension of the effects of the Games on urban spaces that he calls edgelands – 'peripheral' areas designated as ripe for new development. Such spaces are the subject of a dominant narrative as wasteland when, in fact, they provide a diverse range of activities for local residents. In his study of the Lower Lea Valley, Pohlisch traces the destruction of the edgelands and argues for a more nuanced and gradualist approach to the renewal of such areas. Finally, Andrew Hoolachan discusses the promise of the delivery of a sustainable Olympic legacy in the context of the UK's reform of urban planning through the Localism Act (2010). He critically examines the process of rapid urban change associated with hosting the mega-event and the consequences for a planning framework that emphasises the role of neighbourhoods and local communities in shaping that change.

The final section discusses several dimensions of the cultural impacts and legacies of London 2012. It commences with Beatriz Garcia's comprehensive evaluation of London's attempt to place culture at the heart of the Games. The chapter explores three themes – how the placing of culture at the heart of the Games was defined, how it was delivered and what were the implications of the cultural Olympic programme for the UK's cultural sector. Linda Wilks' research on volunteerism has a similarly broader focus. It draws upon the experiences of London 2012 volunteers to assess the value of the programme for the development of their confidence, knowledge and skills, and while acknowledging the special or spectacular nature of the event, the author suggests that a strong volunteering legacy was achieved. Olesya Nedvetskaya, Rod Purcell and Annette Hastings' research also focused on the volunteers or 'Games Makers', studying in particular the recruitment and selection process as well as volunteers' experiences. In drawing similar conclusions to Linda Wilks about the success of the programme, the chapter also points to the challenges of reconciling the strategic and operational requirements of the events' organisers with the desires and hopes of the volunteers.

The three other chapters in this section examine cultural dimensions within a wider political and historical context. Andrew Calcutt and Antonio Desiderio present challenges to the dominant narratives that informed London's hosting of the Games. Andrew Calcutt's focus is upon the politicians' linkage of the Games with the transforming of East London. He contrasts the enthusiastic pubic response to the festival of sport to the public responses to the Games as a vehicle for economic and lifestyle improvement and suggests that the latter – legacy objectives – never really captured the imagination or support of the city's population, particularly those living in East London. Indeed, the subsuming of the sporting event within the world of politics and public policy revealed the political elites' instrumentalism and its contempt for those it purportedly represents. Antonio Desiderio considers how the dominant narrative enshrined in legislation, city-wide plans and development strategy documents provided a regulatory framework for London 2012 that subjected social change to the needs of capital, thus denying the attributes of plurality upon which effective local democracy relies. Finally, Jack Black's study of the British national press examines how representations of Britain were constructed and reconstructed in the period prior to and during the 2012 Olympiad. He argues that the press coverage reflected an uneasy conception of contemporary Britain, one that sought to reinvent or reimagine its imperial past within a (postimperial) present.

As this brief overview suggests, this book draws upon the research and experiences of its contributors to examine, in particular, the 'lasting effects' or legacies of London 2012, effects that will continue long after the book's publication. It is hoped, however, that this text affirms that the study of the sports mega-event is also a study of the cities and societies that seek to host them and that the chapters that follow make a real contribution to our understanding of this complex interaction.

Notes

1 See Jones, G. S. (1971) *Outcast London: a study in the relationship between classes in Victorian society*. London: Verso; and for a comprehensive insight into East London's industrial and social history, see Marriott, J. (2011) *Beyond the Tower: a history of East London*. New Haven, CT: Yale University Press.
2 See, for example, Zukin, S. (2010) *Naked City*. Oxford: Oxford University Press; and Brownhill, S. (2012) *London Docklands: reflections on regeneration*. London: Routledge.
3 See, for example, Kearney, A. T. (2014) 'Global cities index and emerging cities outlook', available at: http://www.atkearney.com/research-studies/global-cities-index/full-report
4 See, for example, the responses of citizens in Rio de Janeiro to the city's hosting of the 2104 FIFA World Cup and the 2016 Olympic and Paralympic Games, available at: http://www.rioonwatch.org/

References

Butler, T. and Rustin, R. (eds) (1995) *Rising in the East*. London: Lawrence & Wishart.

Department for Culture, Media & Sport (DCMS) (2011) *Meta-evaluation of the Impacts and Legacy of the London 2012 Olympic Games and Paralympic Games: Reports 1 and 2 Summary – Scope, research questions and strategy and methods*. London: DCMS.

Gratton, C. and Preuss, H. (2008) 'Maximizing Olympic impacts by building up legacies'. *International Journal of the History of Sport*, 25(14): 1922–1938.

Lenskyj, H. (2008) *Olympic Industry Resistance*. Albany: State University of New York.

MacAloon, J. (2008) '"Legacy" as managerial/magical discourse in contemporary Olympic affairs'. *International Journal of the History of Sport*, 25(14): 2060–2071.

MacRury, I. (2008) 'Re-thinking the legacy 2012: the Olympics as commodity and gift, twenty-first century society'. *Journal of the Academy of Social Sciences*, 3(3): 297–312.

Raco, M. (2013) 'Governance as legacy and the London model of development', available at: http://www.parliament.uk/documents/lords-committees/olympic-paralympic-legacy/olympicparalymicevidencevolume.pdf (last accessed 6 September 2014).

Roche, M. (2000) *Mega-events and Modernity*. London: Routledge.

Part I

London

Moving east

1 Remaking the east

From Canary Wharf to the Olympic Park

Eric Sorensen

Introduction

The development of Canary Wharf is but one event, a very significant one, in London's changing economy and economic geography. It is the symbol of the 1980s and 1990s' regeneration of the vast Docklands area, and this chapter explores the background, twists and turns of policy and the lessons these could offer.

Setting the policy

Before the 1980s' London Docklands regeneration programme, a more benign and imaginative policy context was set by Peter Shore's (Secretary of State for the Environment, 1976–1979) White Paper 'Inner Cities' of May 1977. Here, for the first time, was the phrase 'inner cities' used in a major government policy statement to capture that deleterious mix of socio-economic trends and patterns we are now so familiar with. Peter Shore, as MP for Bethnal Green and Stepney, had first-hand and detailed knowledge of these economic trends and their impact on communities. He played a major role in reversing orthodox planning policy which had previously focused on the dispersal of London's population and business base and involved an over-rigid zoning of uses.

London was in crisis. The cumulative impact of two decades and more of decentralising London's economy through blocking business investment, providing investment incentives in other regions and encouraging depopulation through the New and Expanding Towns programmes had deprived London, particularly Inner London, of investment and jobs, especially in the newer, higher skilled, higher value-added business sectors. Not for the first time, successive governments had tackled a perceived problem (London being too big and economically dominant) when this was being overshadowed by larger economic forces. London and the whole country were losing out to new investment locations in other parts of the world economy; relocating business capacity in familiar business sectors and inhibiting investment were hardly a recipe for national economic renewal.

The White Paper clearly distinguished between symptoms and causes, between decline of traditional business sectors, decline in jobs especially for the unskilled, increasing physical decay in the urban fabric and the core requirement to rebuild the urban economy, especially in Inner London and in the other major conurbations.

Closure of the docks

For East London, the effect of adverse government policies which had simply failed to address fundamental business sector changes and their impact on complex urban economies was compounded by the collapse of the world's largest enclosed docks system. A vast docks area stretching 6 miles from Tower Bridge to Beckton and built up over some 200 years progressively closed in the short period (1968–1981) as the Port of London Authority (PLA) consolidated its business operations down river at Tilbury. Containerisation offered the PLA and the shipping industry massive efficiency gains. Coincidentally, the first container ships arrived at Tilbury in 1968, the same year as the first major docks closures – East India, St Katherine's and the London Docks by Tower Bridge. The PLA then announced in 1970 their 5 years' phased programme of closures and rationalisation (later amended). Despite its scale, the PLA had never been particularly profitable. It did not control all the Thames wharfage. There had been a long history of difficult industrial relations which was only partly ameliorated by the decasualisation of dock labour in 1966, and the costs of decasualisation fell to the PLA.

Dock closures, their impact on associated businesses and changes in the more general industrial landscape led to very large job losses. For the five East London boroughs (Tower Hamlets, Newham, Southwark, Lewisham, Greenwich), there were some 150,000 jobs lost between 1966 and 1976, 20 per cent of the area's jobs, compared to 13 per cent in London and 2 per cent in the UK over the same period. Local population numbers, particularly in the areas immediately associated with the docks, fell dramatically especially in the later years of the period. Urban wasteland was not hard to find in Inner London in the 1970s, but Docklands was on a different, appalling scale and this stimulated specific interventions by successive governments. Political and strategic reactions to these dramatic economic and social changes were characterised, however, by sharp policy differences, arguments about priorities, wholly inadequate funding commitments and lack of regeneration progress. One key investment must be noted, however: the opening of the second Blackwall Tunnel in 1967.

The search for a regeneration programme

The PLA's 1970 announcement about progressive closure of the docks and the evident lack of investment and urban decline had led one of Peter Shore's predecessors at the Environment Department, Peter Walker, to set up a major Review in 1971 of development options for the 5,000 acres of Docklands. The Greater London Council (GLC), established in 1965, also took a leading interest with the relevant London boroughs in the area's future. Fundamental recurring themes about

Docklands' regeneration were now evident – what does regeneration mean, what business uses are to be fostered, what is to be the employment offer, how to fund and get the necessary infrastructure, whom does regeneration benefit? The development options Review was published in January 1973 and soon became caught up with the GLC election of that year. Though the Review was not dogmatic and offered a range of strategic options, including modest development aspirations and much enhanced open spaces, concern was expressed about the lack of consultation and that the options were not consistent with the business and community heritage of the Docklands area. The GLC led the development of an alternative strategy, and one of the last acts of the Conservative government before Labour won the general election in February 1974 was to agree a more localist approach: the GLC would set up the Docklands Joint Committee (DJC) – the GLC and the five East London boroughs.

Anthony Crosland, now the Labour Government's Environment Secretary, supported the DJC but offered little additional public expenditure support. The DJC produced an investment and development plan (1976) to include a new tube line, the River Line, from Central London to Thamesmead at the Greenwich/Bexley boundary (where the GLC were building a very large housing estate), new east-west strategic roads, new housing but mainly council housing and development of new industrial estates and warehousing. Some significant docks were filled in to provide development sites, with these adding to the vast supply of vacant land.

This plan fitted with traditional East London uses and aspirations, recognised the importance of improving transport infrastructure, but failed to grasp the enormity of the changes faced by the area. There was in effect a political stalemate – little willingness to fundamentally review the area's future and business base as part of changing London and insufficient funding and other support to help make a reality of the DJC's or indeed any other major investment plan. Private sector investors had dipped their toes in the St Katherine's and London docks areas with a trade centre, marina, hotel and some mixed-tenure housing. This reflected the advantages of location, right next to the eastern side of the City of London, but not a willingness to achieve more through a substantial rolling out of public/private investment partnerships. Dismissive attitudes to Docklands regeneration were widespread, indicated by, for example, a *Sunday Times* headline of February 1975: 'Docklands is dying in squabbles and squalor'.

The support arrangements for inner city areas in Peter Shore's 1977 White Paper included Partnership Committees, chaired by ministers to indicate their significance, that were tasked to manage programmes and target support in the most hard-pressed areas. The DJC morphed into a Partnership Committee, but the government still faced a very difficult public expenditure challenge, so the new radical approach to the inner city areas came with little new money and considerable reliance on private investment. Some docks were filled in to provide development sites; some 800 homes were built in the Docklands area in the 5 years between 1976 and 1980, and 1.3 million sq ft of warehousing and other business premises were constructed. Some public transport improvements were also achieved, for example, improvements to the East London Line. Very little progress, however,

was made on land assembly and tackling dereliction, no strategic transport investments were started, arguments continued about the balance between council and
private housing development, which business investments should be backed and
where they should be located.

There is some anecdotal evidence that if Labour had won the 1979 General
Election the Docklands area would have been designated a new town to provide
a substantial investment vehicle which the government could control. Such a proposal was advocated in relevant professional journals in the 1970s. The political
standoff about the strategic future of the area was, by the late 1970s, self-evident.

Radical intervention: the development corporation

The incoming Conservative government, therefore, had little difficulty in exploiting the previous decade's, and even longer period of argument, prevarication and
continuing decline in making the case for radical intervention. Key new Conservative ministers Geoffrey Howe (Chancellor of the Exchequer) and Michael
Heseltine (Environment Secretary) were determined to ensure that the vast decay-
ing areas of Docklands were incorporated into the London economy and that the
private sector would be encouraged to play a leading investment role. New towns
legislation was adapted to enable the setting up of urban development corporations with powers of land assembly, infrastructure investment and planning within
specific designated areas. The draft Order setting up the London Docklands
Development Corporation (LDDC) took 42 days of parliamentary debate in 1981
before being approved; such was the opposition to this intervention. The history
of regeneration over the previous decade could be shown to have been a failure,
however, and that there was an overriding need for these new radical measures.
This argument was clearly accepted by the Parliamentary Committee.

To the LDDC, there were separately added powers for the government to
designate enterprise zone (EZ) areas with incentives lasting 10 years to encourage
business investment – these included business rates holiday, 100 per cent capital
allowances and looser development control regulation. The 1982 EZ in Docklands,
300 acres, covered the northern half of the Isle of Dogs where private business
investment became concentrated and where Canary Wharf landed.

The LDDC had the inestimable advantage of becoming the dominant land-
owner within the designated area. Redundant PLA land holdings were vested in
the LDDC through the Order setting it up, avoiding compulsory purchase and
other lengthy acquisition procedures. Land vesting was also applied to municipal
and publicly owned land such as that held by statutory undertakings. The process
was tempered by arguments about what were operational and nonoperational
(i.e. redundant) sites, but the LDDC soon became the owner of 2,000 acres of
Docklands. Most had low value with little market interest and very poor supporting
infrastructure.

The LDDC, supported by the EZ incentives, nevertheless faced major challenges. It cannot be overemphasised how distant the Docklands and East London
localities were perceived to be by the investors and developers despite the windfall

of development sites flowing from dock closures. The docks and adjoining warehouses had been private and hidden behind large brick walls with very limited access. Access to the East End and public transport was poor with many dock workers living close by. It was a different world from the rest of London, its communities romanticised in newsreels and sometimes hitting the news because of strikes. The strategic differences on how the areas should be regenerated, therefore, reflected different views about the economic and social geography of London. Were the Docklands areas and community's working class, seeking certain kinds of employment, supported by a pervasive public sector? Or, should the opportunity be taken to recognise the loss of much traditional employment and the glue which held these communities together and foster new private sector–led business sectors and open up the local housing markets to owner occupation?

Opening up Docklands: transport investment

The Transport Department and London Transport 'celebrated' the setting up of the LDDC in 1981 by making clear that no further work would be done on planning the new Tube line to East London. Though there was a clear government commitment to Docklands regeneration, Whitehall was and remains a series of departmental baronies where each makes its own decisions about what a government commitment means. There had been related discussions about investment in a mini-tram system, cheaper and more flexible but slower and with much lower capacity. This had first been proposed in the early 1970s' development options Review, and there was now much discussion about the form of mini-tram, street running or with its own dedicated rail pathway. The LDDC advocated an elevated, light rail, computer-controlled railway, encouraged by their success in other countries. Parts of the nineteenth century's elevated rail viaducts still survived, and these could be brought back into use. The government agreed, announced the Docklands Light Railway (DLR) investment in October 1982 with a fixed £77 million cost and planned opening in 1987. Meanwhile a pragmatic connection to the all-important Tube network was provided by the Docklands Clipper, a bespoke bus shuttle service between Mile End and the Isle of Dogs.

The imaginative DLR solution was mirrored by the decision to promote what became London City Airport in the Royal Docks. Here there was space for a short takeoff and landing airport, having both utility and demonstrating how Docklands was changing. Most airports were either state- or municipally owned, but in this case the airport would be a private investment. Following a public inquiry in 1984, the airport opened in 1987. In the late 1990s towards the end of the LDDC, the Royal Docks' space and opportunity offer led to the development of a large exhibition centre, London ExCEL, the first one on that scale in London in nearly half a century.

As with the airport, the Docklands' offer of space to develop attracted the newspaper industry, about to exploit new printing technology and occupying very cramped business space in Central London. Within a few years, newspaper production became Docklands' leading business sector with *News International* in

Wapping, the Telegraph Group in the Isle of Dogs, *Financial Times* at East India and the *Daily Mail* in Rotherhithe/Surrey Docks. Roads were built to serve the EZ and the many other development areas, but strategic road investment would have to wait. The GLC had abandoned its own road investment plans for the area, and the LDDC would struggle to make the case for that scale of disruptive but badly needed investment.

Compared to the disinvestment of the previous years, the ambition, aspiration and actual investments of the LDDC were transformative, and the private sector responded. In the early days, Michael Heseltine personally intervened with the major housebuilders to develop in East London where the owner occupation output was in single figures per year. The private housebuilding programme was very successful and soon output averaged over 1,000 dwellings per year. Many small business units were developed within the EZ. Roads had been built, DLR construction was well under way as was the airport. Historic warehouses next to Tower Bridge were being converted to new uses; new neighbourhoods were being created in Wapping and Rotherhithe. Taken together the regeneration package was imaginative but within the familiar scale of London, until the development of Canary Wharf.

Regeneration themes

What, then, was the essence of this new approach to regeneration? Government commitment was on an unimaginable scale compared to any of the efforts of the previous decade and more. But it was commitment to a vehicle the government controlled in terms of the general direction of its investment with specific approval required of major investment proposals. There was a strong emphasis to attract private sector investment on the back of public sector infrastructure. This inevitably meant deliberately joining the area to the rest of London and recognising that many older business sectors with deep roots in the area had little to offer for investment and jobs. Though there was a willingness to work with the municipalities, indeed cooperation was essential to produce good results, the government and their instrument – the LDDC – drove the regeneration programme.

Second, the relatively rapid transfer of land ownership gave the LDDC very considerable power in managing its own strategic planning, infrastructure investment and onward encouragement of investors and developers. Third, rather than regarding this massive Docklands estate as simply representing opportunities for public housing, traditional logistics and warehousing, and trying to maintain docks-related businesses, the intrinsic assets of the area were to be exploited so as to appeal to investors of all kinds and to bring benefit to the wider London economy. The DLR was designed to be a novel, modern part of London's transport infrastructure, very visible and used to market the new Docklands. Similarly, the new airport, and other new large-space users, exploited the space available, added to transport choices and looked to the future.

Fourth, the docks themselves were not to be discarded, made invisible by being filled in. Waterside had been associated with industrial uses, often noxious or banned from the more salubrious parts of town, with rivers and canals polluted and uncared for. Instead, waterside vistas were to be valued both for their unique amenity offer and with the docks offering an important historical and conservation background to the area. The area became part of the international family of dockland regeneration areas, benefitting from appreciation of history and the high value placed on waterside locations. The same approach was applied to the River Thames where the LDDC promoted a continuous riverside walkway, building this on its own account or making its provision a core part of riverside development planning conditions.

The value attached to the docks themselves was part of a wider effort to appreciate the development history of the area. Despite the long span of development, Docklands was not an area rich in historic buildings of any kind. Industrial innovation, wartime bombing and postwar perceptions of what modernisation meant had resulted in widespread clearance of both houses and older warehousing. In other parts of London, the possibilities of conservation and reuse were more widely recognised. Nevertheless, as part of its exercise to improve the image and attractiveness of the area, the LDDC conserved the remaining historic warehouses, obtained grants to help restore Hawksmoor churches and safeguarded eighteenth- and nineteenth-century terraces.

Fifth, linked to the promotion of waterside amenity was a varied programme of park and public space development, incorporated into a series of development frameworks. The Docklands area was not in any sense homogeneous but rather a series of distinct localities and neighbourhoods with their own histories and communities. The development frameworks offered guidelines about future development but were not prescriptive. Local owners and the community were consulted about the proposals, all designed to raise aspirations and reflecting good principles of access, docks and riverside amenity, with parks and spaces helping to provide overall coherence and knit places together.

Finally, as a relative novelty for a public body, the LDDC spent considerable sums on marketing. The Docklands Crow, the marketing icon, emphasised opportunities so close to the centre, the benefits of investing in the EZ, the new areas being opened up and radically improved. This was part of the tone of the LDDC – conscious of its market, determined to be as flexible as possible to achieve investment and driven by the government's annual physical output targets measuring both enabling infrastructure and consequent investment.

Local politics

The local political context was difficult and led to many missed opportunities for joint cooperation and investment between the three boroughs (Tower Hamlets, Southwark and Newham), parts of whose areas made up the LDDC designated area. A pragmatic political decision had been taken at the outset to draw the LDDC boundaries very tightly around the PLA docks estate together with expansion land in Beckton, Newham. This minimised any argument that the LDDC stood for a wholesale takeover of municipal responsibilities. Though there were about

18,000 largely council flats and houses within the designated area, the boundary omitted large adjacent estates and neighbourhoods. The boundary followed main roads and the river and was, therefore, easily intelligible. But as the infrastructure and regeneration work proceeded, it became obvious that these adjoining estates gained nothing, for example, from the LDDC's extensive programme of estate refurbishment. Over time the physical contrasts between regeneration and little action delineated the boundary.

The hostility of the boroughs' political leadership to LDDC designation was strengthened following the 1983 borough elections when Labour adopted more radical positions on housing, business development and what was in the interests of local communities. This was also the time when the Labour Party split and many leading figures left to form the Social Democratic Party. Though the boroughs had posts on the LDDC board, these were now not taken up by the new borough leaderships, and a general noncooperation approach was adopted. Since the LDDC could largely get on with its programmes and had no responsibilities for mainstream municipal activities such as subsidised housing, education, social and environmental services, this did not slow progress. It would have been far better, however, if a more rounded joint set of programmes could have been developed on behalf of local communities. There were avenues for the government to support the local municipalities in their own related regeneration activities, for example, through the Urban and Industrial Improvement Programmes, if there had been the necessary combined political will. The evolution of political stances and the Tories' third general election win in 1987 encouraged municipal/development corporation cooperation. This facilitated modern education, training and community facilities being provided in the Docklands estate.

The coming of Canary Wharf

Olympia and York (O&Y), led by Paul Reichmann, was an extremely successful North American property company with an undoubted track record in developing large-scale and bold commercial centres. They had developed across the American continent and internationally, but their most well-known developments were in Toronto and New York. In New York, O&Y had bought a portfolio of office towers at the bottom of the market in 1977, at a time when the city itself had been verging on bankruptcy. The subsequent growth of that portfolio added to O&Y's considerable strength so that it could develop in the Battery Park area at the southern end of Manhattan. This southern area was a large landfill site partly created by the excavation of the recently built World Trade Centre also in southern Manhattan (to be demolished in 2001 in the tragic 9/11 terrorist disaster) and owned by a New York City corporation seeking development partners. The arrangements there were broadly similar to the public/private developments fostered by the LDDC.

Meanwhile in London the growing international influence in the financial and related business sectors (notably legal and accountancy firms) concentrated in the Square Mile, the growth of those business sectors and the legacy of poor office stock flowing from previous governments' investment restrictions together provided a fertile context for the Docklands investment offer if other strategic drawbacks, notably constrained accessibility and poor public transport, were tackled.

A Credit Suisse banker, Herbert von Clemm, committed his bank to a major relocation and investment in Docklands. Together with Morgan Stanley, these two powerful banks became the investment base which offered plausibility to an unheard of scale of commercial development in the Isle of Dogs EZ. The project was fostered by G Ware Travelstead, a tireless Texan development promoter, and by 1985, development proposals not unlike those of Canary Wharf today were being marketed to development partners and prospective occupiers.

It was hard, however, to overcome the long-standing resistance of banking and related businesses to leave the city and West End with all their powerful and easily accessed business networks. The transport offer to the east was seen as implausible – the low-capacity DLR link at Tower Bridge and shuttle buses along a crowded road system. The LDDC wished to encourage the development but were also dependent on the commitment of major occupiers to make the development a realistic possibility. The LDDC were committing land and significant infrastructure and in return wished to sign a development agreement committing the developer to building out some 4 million sq ft over a realistic timescale.

In July 1987, O&Y in effect took over the scheme and signed the development agreement. The company's resources, financial standing, construction and development expertise were of a different order. Business links between Paul Reichmann and the Chairman of the LDDC, Sir Christopher Benson, were also important in gaining O&Y's interest (Sir Christopher's English Property Corporation had some years previously been taken over by O&Y). The transport offer by the LDDC and the government now moved to a different gear. The east-west road link options had to be resolved, the scheme designed and built. This became the Limehouse Link (a cut-and-cover tunnel under Limehouse Basin opened in May 1993) with a new road extending to the Royal Docks just to the north of the Canary Wharf site. In retrospect though road links were badly needed, the scale of new road building was oversized and severed straightforward connections between the Isle of Dogs and Poplar immediately to the north.

O&Y financed the DLR extension to the Bank Tube station, opened in 1991. The LDDC and London Transport revived the East London Tube links proposals, though the scale, significance and cost of this meant that it took some time to agree the route of what has become the Jubilee Line Extension from Westminster to Stratford and opened in 2000. Self-evidently, therefore, O&Y relied on the commitment to transport improvements rather than their capacity to convince occupiers to join Canary Wharf. It was a major gamble, and a combination of economic downturn in the late 1980s/early 1990s together with O&Y's failing investments in other parts of their vast development and commodities business caused the consortium construction lending banks to refuse further lending. In May 1992 O&Y went into administration. It was a measure of the government's determination to put the risks of development firmly on the developer, in return for massive infrastructure support, that the development agreement was signed for 4.5 million sq ft with the risk of forfeiture of the site in the event of nonperformance and that the construction of the Jubilee Line was delayed for 18 months to October 1993 as O&Y were unable to pay their £400 million contribution in May 1992.

This is not the place to set out the history of the Canary Wharf development except to say that the banks reconfigured their commitment and refloated the company in October 1993. At that time, about 4.5 million sq ft was ready for occupation and since then the project has steadily grown and does so today. From a few thousand people working in Canary Wharf in 1993, the working population is now 110,000 with, unexpectedly, a parallel growth in shopping so that Canary Wharf has now become a major retail destination. The CrossRail station–related development opens in 2015 with trains running in 2018, substantially adding to the area's offer. New parts of the estate, such as Wood Wharf, are now beginning construction phases, and these will help drive total employment to 200,000 in some 15 years' time.

Why did Canary Wharf happen?

There was no expectation that a commercial development on anything like the scale of Canary Wharf would become the symbol of Docklands' regeneration. A specific combination of economic and development forces acted in a mutually reinforcing way to make possible Europe's largest commercial development. First, the world economy grew rapidly in the middle years of the 1980s, giving investors growing confidence. Second, London's existing office stock was poor and much of it unfit for modern telecommunications. Third, financial and business services were fast-growing sectors in a growing economy with much international investment in London. Fourth, the space and scale of this investment was given a major boost by the government's abolition of restrictive practices in the city and their replacement by new regulatory machinery. This added to the encouragement of international banks and others to invest in city trading and investment organisations. Finally, the demand for modern commercial space was, therefore, high and the LDDC were a willing and positive partner to provide it in Docklands coupled with the EZ investment benefits. It is noteworthy, reflecting the internationalisation of the London market, that Canary Wharf has a strong North American and international influence both in the form of development and its financing.

This vast commercial estate is privately owned, self-contained, with visible security to reassure those who work there. It is a very well designed with meticulous maintenance of squares, parks and gardens. It is a new cityscape for East London but very different from the standard municipal offer. Some found this approach to urbanism initially intimidating and unwelcoming, but the successful growth of the project now provides its own sense of place with a range of entertainment, retail and eating-out facilities on offer.

Conclusion: regeneration for whom?

Regeneration is presented as self-evidently good. Who could reasonably be concerned about the replacement of dying business sectors, of derelict buildings and vacant sites, of inaccessible areas near the heart of a great world city, with successful businesses, modern buildings, choice in housing, job opportunities, good amenities and spaces and excellent public transport. Preparing the area for infrastructure investment and consolidating sites did result, however, in the relocation or loss of many, usually small-scale, local businesses and job opportunities knitted into the historic expectations of the area.

Business and job flight from the area had been endemic for the decade and more prior to the LDDC's arrival. International preferences for business locations in the city, poor premises, relative inaccessibility, the decline of port activity and its supporting businesses, governmental attitudes and policies towards London's fine-grained and interlocking business sectors, all provided a negative backdrop to business development in the area. One statistic tells a typical story: job numbers in Tower Hamlets fell from 145,000 to 75,000 from 1966 to 1981. It was to take some years before the impact of the new business sectors and job opportunities overcame the deleterious impact of historic business decline and job loss in such sectors as warehousing, logistics and food manufacture. In 1984 male unemployment in the Docklands area was 30 per cent compared to 10 per cent for London.

The LDDC was essentially a physically oriented regeneration agency. The lack of a cooperative relationship with the boroughs also inhibited a joint people-based exercise to encourage training provision and training take-up as the business base became increasingly service industry with demand for different IT and other skills. Such training had to be carefully marketed to a local population overwhelmed by the rapid scale of change and suspicious of what was on offer. The LDDC fostered a local business club to provide a mutually reinforcing network and to improve knowledge about requirements to foster business development. An Information Technology Centre was set up, one of a network of 140 around the country, offering training in computing and information technology. Construction and similar specialist centres were also established. By 1988 the LDDC had set up a more systematic matching of employer requirements and training provision. Skillnet provided this brokering function, but funding provision from the Employment Department was lacking and it was not possible to fill all the training gaps emerging.

One key lesson was that training support was, and is, targeted at particular groups, for example, young people leaving school with poor qualifications. What was lacking was a more widespread and deeper governmental approach, addressing a wide variety of employability and training needs in local communities. What was needed was a training offer over many years of significant scale combined with a bespoke employment-related service which together matched the scale and varied outcomes of the massive physical regeneration programme.

2 East or west?

The story of the London 2012 bid

Richard Sumray

Introduction

By 1994, London had already lost two internal bids to host major events – the 2000 Olympic and Paralympic Games and the 2002 Commonwealth Games – to Manchester. It appeared that the lack of a strategic authority, a perception of London not being able to deliver a credible bid or organise multisport Games on the scale of these, and poor transport services and links were paramount reasons. Eighteen years later, London delivered what has generally been perceived as one of the most successful and enjoyable Olympic and Paralympic Games ever hosted, with an enduring legacy in many areas. The transformation was complete and the perceptions about London profoundly altered. Much is recorded about the years after 2003 when the government decided to support a bid from London but little of the 9 years before then when the building blocks were put into place. This chapter focuses upon those years.[1]

Shortly after Manchester lost its bid to host the 1996 Olympic and Paralympic Games in 1990, two groups from London declared an interest in leading bids for the city. One was led by Seb Coe, the other by senior members of the London Council of Sport and Recreation then responsible on behalf of the Sports Council for the development of sport in London. These potential bids developed separately until the British Olympic Association (BOA), which at that point ran a bidding contest between British cities interested in hosting the Games, announced that it would only accept one bid from London. Agreement was reached to join forces 3 months before the bids were formally presented, leaving only a short time to bring together two very distinct proposals. The major difference was where the proposed Games would be centred. One focused on existing and renowned venues principally in the west of London, the other on regeneration to the east of London in the Docklands area in new venues. The latter was eventually chosen.

The proposal put forward to the BOA in April 1991 stated that the Games would centre on the East Thameside area, also known as London Docklands, with the Olympic village across the river at Port Greenwich. The reasons we gave for locating the Games in that area were that we wanted to stage as many events as possible in one small and secure area close to a village site and because the region, which a few years before had been an area of growing dereliction, was one of the largest regeneration projects in the world. There were unparalleled opportunities to build new communities with large-scale leisure facilities and create the transport infrastructure to cope with the massive developments taking shape. The Olympic Games would leave a legacy of fine international and local sports facilities as well as thriving new villages. In this sense, the Games would act as a catalyst for the regeneration of Docklands and the East Thames region. Interestingly, the proposed venue for cycling was in the Lee Valley Regional Park near the East-way Road Cycling Circuit. There was, however, too short a time to put together a coherent proposition in the timescales available. Manchester had a first bid for 1996 and 4 years' preparation to build upon and the BOA vote was conclusively in favour of Manchester as the chosen city to bid for the 2000 Games. It was comprehensively beaten in what became a close vote between Sydney and Beijing.

At the end of 1993, another possibility emerged and that was to make a bid to host the 2002 Commonwealth Games. At that point it seemed as if those Games were going to grow in scale with the advent especially of more team sports. With its many stadia, London seemed to be potentially an ideal city for the Games to be held. In 6 weeks a credible bid was put together, led this time by the London Council of Sport and Recreation working with Wembley plc. It was based in West London with the athletes' village at Brunel University and Royal Holloway, University of London. With its significantly reduced size and scale compared to the Olympic Games, it could not be developed as a Games for regeneration, and existing venues needed to be utilised, the majority of which were in West London. Again, Manchester easily won the bid – it had adapted the two unsuc-cessful Olympic bids and its success could be seen as a legacy from them. Within a short time it became apparent that the Commonwealth Games were not going to expand as envisaged, and, consequently, Manchester was the more suitable host city. Those Games would not have been able to be the same showcase in a city as large as London.

Preparing a London Olympic bid

With the loss of two bids, those of us heavily involved reflected on what London needed to do to be more successful. First, it was to go back to basics and start to put some building blocks into place. It was decided to establish a new organisation whose principal objectives would be to bring major sporting events to London, building up more gradually to the Olympic and Paralympic Games and to ensure that these events were used to develop the sports concerned at all levels. London International Sport Ltd (LIS) was formed and incorporated in 1996. Its members comprised the key London-wide organisations that needed to be involved – the Association of London Government, London Tourist Board, London Chamber of Commerce, London First, London Sport and London Federation of Sport with the Government Office for London and the Sports Council, London Region, as observers. Despite being very small, it became part of the landscape of pan-London organisations made necessary because of the absence of a strategic authority for London. Contact was made with a number of governing bodies of sport, including the British Athletics Federation (BAF) which was considering making a bid for London to host the World Championships in Athletics.

Up to this point, the way the BOA chose a city to bid to host the Olympic Games was through conducting a bidding process itself. Thus, a city even if it did not stand a chance on the international stage of winning could be chosen. When Sydney was selected to host the 2000 Games in 1993, three British bids in a row, one for Birmingham and two for Manchester, had been unsuccessful. The BOA did not want to make another bid unless the prospects for success were greater, and in informal discussions, over the following years, it became apparent to them that the only city that stood a realistic chance of being successful was London. Having maintained informal contact with the BOA over the years, in October 1996 I met with Craig Reedie, the then Chairman, and suggested to him that, first, the BOA should change its process for selection of a British city and accept that London should make the next bid without competition and that, second, LIS was ready to work with the BOA on a potential bid for 2008 or 2012. Craig Reedie agreed to put these propositions to the National Olympic Committee where they were accepted in principle, but the Committee also wanted to be sure that London was ready to support a potential bid. He decided to host a dinner to which the most important decision makers in London would be invited at the suggestion of LIS to determine if London was a city in which the BOA could realistically base a bid. This dinner was held at the beginning of March 1997 and assurances were given by the London representatives there of support for a possible London bid. Contacts made with the Department of National Heritage and shadow ministers by LIS had also indicated broad government support. Consequently, the BOA agreed to begin working with LIS.

At a meeting later that month, LIS proposed and the BOA agreed to the establishment of four Commissions to progress the work. They covered the Olympic village, sports venues, transport and the environment. I chaired them all and the BOA was represented on them through David Luckes who was appointed at that time to work specifically on an Olympic Games bid. The task of the first two Commissions was to seek appropriate locations for the village and venues looking at available land and extant venues that could meet the specifications. The London Planning Advisory Committee (LPAC), a body established following the abolition of the Greater London Council with a strategic planning brief for London, was tasked with assessing all possible options in the London area for an Olympic village.

Initially the work was started on the basis of London making a bid possibly for the 2008 Games. With the 1996 Games being hosted in the United States and the 2000 Games in Australia, if a European city failed to host the Games in 2004, a successful European bid for 2008 was very much on the cards. On the other hand, a European win in 2004 would make it very unlikely that a 2008 bid from London could be successful. In the summer of 1997, Athens was awarded the 2004 Games and it became clear and quickly agreed that work should be geared towards 2012.

Until December 1999, a fixed point for any bid from London was the designation of Wembley as the national stadium for athletics. There had been a contest to determine where the next national stadium for football should be located, and at the end of 1996, Wembley had been chosen. Within London two possible sites emerged to compete with those outside the capital; they were Wembley and Stratford. At that time, Wembley had the slightly better transport links and a great deal of history, and the Sports Council made the decision to replace the then national stadium with a new one at the same location. It was decided at the same time that the stadium should also be the home of athletics. It meant, in effect, that any bid for the Olympic Games had to factor in Wembley as the likely venue for the opening and closing ceremonies as well as for the athletics.

The implications of Wembley's role shaped the evolving work of the Commissions for the first 2 years. During that period, despite recognition that a regeneration bid would have to emanate from East London, an Olympic bid based in West London seemed more likely and the initial work of LPAC was geared towards that area. In early 1997, the village sites that seemed the most likely were Northolt Airport, Ruislip Golf Course and Copthall Farm to the west of London, Wormwood Scrubs and the Kings Cross Railway Lands nearer the centre and Greenwich Peninsula to the east, the latter included because of the prospective Jubilee line extension. The brief given to LPAC by the Village Commission was that any village needed to be within a 30-minute journey time to Wembley, could accommodate 15,000 athletes and officials and ancillary uses (a minimum of 50 hectares) and could be available for construction no less than 3 years before the Games took place. Various other factors were taken into account in assessing their relative merits, including access to other principal venues, ease of development, access to the West End and airports and security.

Up to the end of 1999, with Wembley being a fixed point, the task was to assess the possibilities of a bid based in West London, one based in East London and an amalgam of the two. The most important interrelationship during that period was between the Village and the Transport Commissions, the latter being tasked to look at the most appropriate village locations in respect of the transport implications while taking into account the possible host venues. By 1998, it was clear that a mixed bid from an amalgam of East and West London would simply not work. Transport links were too difficult to achieve in the necessary timescales, and no such bid would be credible enough to stand a chance of being successful.

Although the brief described above to LPAC was generally adhered to, LPAC with the Commission's agreement also looked at other sites where, for example, major regeneration benefits would accrue and where special transport improvements might be made. These sites were generally to the east but also included, among others, the Kings Cross railway lands. That they were to the east was not a surprise; parts of East London including the London boroughs of Hackney, Newham and Tower Hamlets were among the most deprived in the country as well as containing some of the youngest and most ethnically diverse populations in Europe. The view I held at that time, having in particular assessed the impact on the regeneration of Barcelona of the 1992 Games, was that a London Games should, if at all possible, focus on where regeneration was most needed and that was clearly in East London. Anticipated transport developments were also factored in and included the Jubilee line extension, the Paddington to Heathrow

Express, road schemes in East London, improvements to the North Circular Road and the Channel Tunnel Rail Link to St Pancras. There were future possible projects to be taken into account as well, including Thameslink 2000, Crossrail and the Chelsea–Hackney line.

LPAC had looked at 37 sites by June 1998, and, of those, 12 warranted further appraisal as they met some or all of the criteria. They included Stratford Railway Lands, an area of up to 120 hectares of potential development land, including operational rail land whose principal owner was London and Continental Railways. It was noted that the area lacked sports facilities but that there was potential for major sports facilities to be developed at the nearby Hackney Wick Stadium. At that point, a planning framework was being developed by the relevant London boroughs and landowners for a comprehensive programme of renewal and regeneration encompassing commercial, leisure residential and environmental-led development. Other possibilities included Ebbsfleet and Joyce Green Hospital, both outside London. Some sites had been discounted because they were on green belt land.

In April 1997, having raised the issue with Derek Casey, the Chief Executive of the English Sports Council, I discovered that the plans for Wembley Stadium included the reduction of over 20,000 seats when in athletics mode from the then planned capacity of 80,000 seats for football. It had been anticipated that an additional 10,000 temporary seats could be made available around the top of the stadium, but the proposal for a retractable roof made that impossible. No city bidding for the 2004 Games had a main stadium capacity of less than 65,000, and the International Olympic Committee (IOC) had stipulated in 1995 that for the opening and closing ceremonies a capacity of 75,000 would be required. In his response, Mr Casey stated that the criteria for the National Stadium when in athletics mode must be no less than a seating capacity of 55,000. He indicated that, as the design was not at that stage confirmed, the capacity may be able to be altered and that he believed that the English Sports Council had taken a potential Olympic bid into full consideration.

Over the summer of 1997, the International Association of Athletics Federations (IAAF) stipulated that it required a spectator capacity for a World Championships in Athletics of at least 65,000. In 1996 the BAF had stated that it was very keen to make a bid to host the World Championships in Athletics in London in 2001 at Wembley. Following delays commissioning work at Wembley and internal problems at the BAF, the bid was put back to 2003, but arrangements began to be made for a bid team to be put into place.

Correspondence over the following months failed to elicit any further clarifications or movement. In effect, although designated as the National Athletics Stadium, it appeared that Wembley would not have sufficient capacity for possibly two of the three major athletics events the stadium would potentially be converted to be used for – the Olympic Games and the World Championships in Athletics. In addition, it also became apparent that no site had been designated to be the warm-up track for athletics, and it was not easy to decide where that should be located. It was also unlikely that it could be a permanent fixture, thus leaving no legacy for athletics with the main stadium only being temporarily converted for the major athletics events hosted.

After fruitless correspondence, I suggested the BOA, a more established organisation, should pursue the case, and this they did writing to the English Sports Council in January 1998. The response from Derek Casey to the BOA suggested that the likely outcome would be a seating capacity of 65,000–70,000 for athletics with an understanding that a related issue would be the ability to increase capacity for the opening and closing ceremonies. What followed was mixed messages about the capacity the designers were working towards. In January 1999, Derek Casey responded to a letter from me by confirming that the acquisition of Wembley Stadium by the English National Stadium Development Company from Wembley plc had taken place, that minimum capacity when in athletics mode would be 65,000 and that the design team had been asked to make provision to increase this capacity to the required number of 75,000 in the event of a successful Olympic bid. Only 65,000 spectator capacity was included in the lottery funding agreement, however. Contradictory statements about capacity were also given at the Culture Media and Sport Select Committee in April 1999.

Further correspondence and meetings between the Minister of Sport and the BOA led to the Minister, Tony Banks, confirming that the design was capable of being upgraded to accommodate up to 80,000 people in athletics mode in the event of a successful Olympics bid. When shown the design, however, no information on the upgrading was given by the architects. At a presentation by Wembley National Stadium Ltd (WNSL) in October 1999, options were finally put forward to increase the capacity to 80,000, but it was clear to the BOA that the sightlines would be degraded as a consequence. An independent technical report was commissioned from Ellerbe Becket who confirmed many of the BOA's concerns. Responses from WNSL were not believed to be satisfactory, and, in a surprise announcement on 22 December 1999, the Secretary of State for Culture Media and Sport announced that athletics would not be part of the new stadium at Wembley which would focus on football only. This was a game changer as far as the shape of an Olympic Games bid was concerned and had a profound impact on the bid for World Championships in Athletics.

Even before that point, the work of the principal commissions had begun to focus more on East London. The government's proposals and legislation to establish a Mayor and a Greater London Authority with elections in 2000 created a different environment in London and reflected a revived interest in finding overarching London-wide solutions rather than dealing with more parochial issues. Reading the runes, it appeared that any elected Mayor would be more likely to favour a bid based in an area where regeneration was a top priority rather than in West London that in comparison was 'overheated'. It was also during 1999, recognising the ongoing problems with Wembley, that I started, on behalf of LIS, to have meetings with political leaders, senior local authority officers and regeneration and community groups to assess the appetite for a Games to be hosted in East London. In addition, following the work already carried out by LPAC, the Commission had asked for further sites in and around East London to be assessed. In total, 51 sites were examined. Those that emerged as possibilities included Hackney Marsh and Temple Mills (just north of the Stratford Railway Lands), Fairlop Plain and Beckton Gas Works/Beckton Gateway/Albert Dock Basin. The first of these was particularly interesting, and a subgroup of the Commission was sent to have a look at the area and report back. That report was made shortly before the Wembley announcement and indicated that an Olympic village in that area was feasible with caveats and could also be linked with the Chelsfield proposals for housing in the northern part of the Stratford Railway Lands.

By the beginning of the new millennium, the potential to host major sporting events in the capital had increased dramatically, albeit with setbacks along the way. Mayoral elections were only a few months away, and it was generally recognised that, with a strategic authority for London, the capital's credibility would improve. Wembley was proceeding on the basis of football only, and the World Cup bid for 2006 with Wembley at its heart was in full swing. An intensive search was underway for a stadium to host the World Championships in Athletics and a decision made to bid for 2005 rather than 2003. The BOA with support from LIS and the Commissions was preparing a substantial document to submit to the government on the feasibility of making an Olympic bid. It had originally been intended to be presented at the end of 1999 but was put back because of Wembley. LIS started to convene a series of meetings with politicians and senior officials from local authorities and other organisations in East London to look at the shape of a possible Games, particularly centred on Hackney Wick and the Eastway Cycle Track with links to Stratford, and gauge support for it in that part of London.

The immediate imperative was to find a venue for the athletics. Initially, it seemed as if Twickenham would be the obvious choice, but potential local opposition and the costs of transport improvements in an area not deemed to be a priority soon took it out of the reckoning. The other sites on the shortlist were Hillingdon House Farm, Crystal Palace and in the Lee Valley where there were two possibilities – Hackney Wick and Picketts Lock. Crystal Palace was not supported by most sporting bodies, and there were considerable access problems. Hackney Wick was a developer-led proposal where the developer who owned the dog track there wanted it demolished and replaced by a stadium. There was support from Hackney and other local authorities, but there were problems with land acquisition because of its diverse ownership, the costs involved in its purchase and concerns about what the state of the whole area would be like in 2005. It was also being considered as the Olympic village site for a 2012 bid. Hillingdon House Farm where there was an existing but nonfunctioning athletics track was favoured by UK Athletics. There were issues with the Green Belt and with road congestion, and it was not an area marked out for regeneration. Most importantly, the local authority late in the day was not prepared to make the quick decision that was necessary. Picketts Lock was a site owned by the Lee Valley Regional Park Authority (LVRPA) occupied by a leisure centre at the end of its useful life and in need of major refurbishment. There was strong local political support and, at the urging of LIS, the LVRPA offered to commit capital to the scheme. There were problems with but potential solutions for accommodation for athletes and transport for spectators. In March 2000, Picketts Lock was chosen, and this decision strengthened an East London Olympic bid option especially when in April the IAAF chose London to host the 2005 Championships (see Figures 2.1 and 2.2).

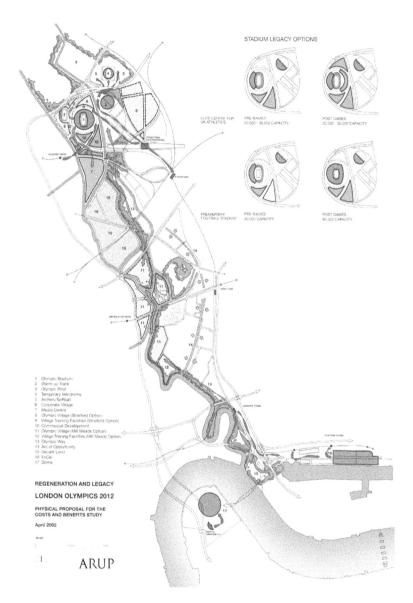

Figure 2.1 Regeneration and legacy – London Olympics 2012: physical proposal for the costs and benefits study (April 2002).

Source: Department for Culture, Media and Sport.

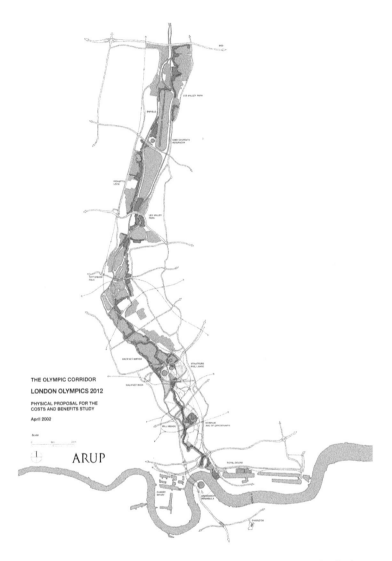

Figure 2.2 The Olympic corridor – London Olympics 2012: physical proposal for the costs and benefits study (April 2002).

Source: Department for Culture, Media and Sport.

The east prevails

In May 2000, Ken Livingstone was elected as Mayor of London. He had already declared support for an Olympic Games bid if the Games was going to be based in East London. LPAC became part of the Greater London Authority, and the London Development Agency (LDA) was established incorporating the relevant sections of English Partnerships that had begun to become involved in the discussions. There were many issues the new Mayor had to get to grips with, and sport was not at the top of his agenda. Nevertheless, despite the loss of the 2006 World Cup bid that summer and delays over Wembley because of escalating costs, a very successful Olympic and Paralympic Games in Sydney raised the level of interest in a London-based Games. A presentation on progress towards a bid was made by the BOA and LIS to senior civil servants in the spring of 2000, where the shift towards East London was described. At that point though, both the BOA and civil servants considered that the West London options should be considered further. During the spring and summer of 2000, architects on the Village Commission began to sketch out what a Games in East London might look like and included the Stratford Railway Lands alongside Hackney Wick and Temple Mills.

Most of the work in the autumn was orientated towards East London. One of the early pieces commissioned by the LDA was a report on the property and development implications of proposals to site an Olympic village on land at Waterden Road, Hackney Wick and Temple Mills, Stratford from the property management consultancy Gerald Eve. Its conclusions were that, although difficult and not easily fitting into the then master plan proposals and their timescales, such a proposition was not impossible and further work was required. Given the uncertainty over what the athletics stadium at Picketts Lock might become, a stadium based around the Stratford Railway Lands started to be considered as well, albeit with opposition from London and Continental, the owners of much of the land. The leader of the London Borough of Newham expressed strong support for both the village and stadium to be in Newham. Meetings were held with those likely to be responsible for the Millennium Dome and the managers of ExCel, and there were discussions about developing a white water canoeing course near Broxbourne. The Transport Commission, with changed membership due to the establishment of Transport for London, highlighted the potential synergy between Crossrail, the proposed Chelsea to Hackney line, other developments in East London and a Games centred there.

Towards the end of 2000, after revisions incorporating the changes in London and lessons from the Sydney Games, David Luckes from the BOA completed the 400-page report which had been compiled over the preceding 18 months, covering the 18 themes stipulated in the IOC's Bidding Guidance to Candidate Cities for the 2008 Olympic Games. On location it was balanced between West and East London and gave no views as to any preference there might be. This document was presented to government ministers at the beginning of 2001 and was used in the presentation we made to the Mayor. The government's response was positive, but it did not want to do much more before the General Election or the IOC's announcement of the result of the 2008 bid, due in July. Ken Livingstone reaffirmed his commitment to the bid, provided it was based in East London. Further meetings were held with leaders in East London that were mostly positive although there was opposition from the Hackney Wick Partnership Board that wanted employment rather than housing in its area. The spectre of Wembley being constructed so that it could be converted to athletics for the Olympic Games was also raised again by Sir Rodney Walker who had been made the new chairman of WNSL.

Following the General Election in May 2001, a new ministerial team at the Department for Culture, Media and Sport was created, and preparations were made for the first meeting of the Olympic Key Stakeholders Group. In the meantime a group of mainly architects had met and were putting into place a concept for East London based on its regeneration as a 'Water City'. Another working group emanating from the Village Commission started work on an overall brief for the work required in East London. I held a meeting with the Chairman of West Ham United Football Club and he expressed an interest in principle in moving West Ham to a stadium based at Stratford. The first meeting of the Key Stakeholders Group took place in June, and the proposal to conduct a cost–benefit analysis was raised by senior civil servants as was the need to resolve the East/West issue.

Before the second meeting at the end of July, the decision that Beijing should host the 2008 Games had been made, leaving the door open for London to make a bid for 2012. The LDA had also commissioned Insignia Richard Ellis (IRE) to carry out two pieces of work – looking at the available sites and cost implications, why the Games should be in East rather than West London and, in respect of East London, what would be involved in terms of land take, blight, costs, planning constraints, and what would happen to the particular sites if a bid was not mounted.

Between the second and third meetings of the Key Stakeholder Group at the end of November 2001, IRE finished its report 'Investigation of possible locations for the staging of the Olympic Games in London 2012', and the tender brief for the cost–benefit analysis was drawn up. London had also been withdrawn from hosting the World Championships in Athletics in 2005 with potentially serious implications for an Olympic bid as the alternative proposal put forward – Sheffield – had been ignored by the IAAF. The IRE site investigation looked at potential locations for the main stadium, the Olympic village, an indoor arena and the media centre and in particular the colocation of the first two. Seven sites were shortlisted of which only Northolt was in West London, and of these, only Stratford, Bow, Hackney Wick and Beckton, all in East London, were deemed to be at all feasible, with Stratford and Hackney Wick supported. The final brief for the cost–benefit study issued shortly afterwards stipulated that the Olympic village, main stadium, warm-up track and many of the other facilities should be located in the Stratford area. Arup, with IRE as a subconsultant, was commissioned in January 2002, paid for by the government with a contribution from UK Sport and the LDA, on behalf of the Mayor, to carry out the study (see Figures 2.1 and 2.2). The dye was cast. If a bid was to be made, it would be based in East London. It would be a bid for regeneration and legacy. The rest is history.

Note

1 Editors' note: The chapter is in narrative form; its author was a major contributor to the establishment of a credible bid for London to host the 2012 Olympic and Paralympic Games. In recognition for this work, Richard was awarded a Member of the Order of the British Empire (MBE) in January 2006.

Part II

Evaluating London's Olympic legacy

3 Measuring and assessing the impacts of London 2012

Yang Li

Introduction

The legacy of an Olympic Games is often conceived in many different contexts. In order to achieve a lasting legacy, it is critical to measure and assess the impact of the Games from a range of perspectives. The International Olympic Committee's (IOC) impact study provides a record of the specific nature of the London 2012 Olympic Games and its host context and a database of information that is common to all Olympic and Paralympic Games. Through such impact studies, the IOC will build up a detailed and tangible information base on the effects and legacy of each Games. In turn, this will allow the IOC to fulfil two of its principal objectives as enshrined in the Olympic Charter:

- to encourage and support a responsible concern for environmental issues, to promote sustainable development in sport and require that the Olympic Games are held accordingly;
- to promote a positive legacy from the Olympic Games for the host cities and host countries.

In June 2007, the IOC issued the first Technical Manual on Olympic Games Impact (OGI) Study. This is the governing document for the study; it sets out the rationale, scope and technical requirements and incorporates materials from the International Paralympic Committee (IPC). London was the first Summer Games host city to be mandated to carry out the study. OGI is based on a set of 120 defined indicators spread across the three internationally recognised areas of sustainable development: economic, socio-cultural and environmental. Though this is not a predictive study of potential impacts, the indicators allow the observation of trends and outcomes of hosting the Games. Indicators can be categorised into context and event indicators. An indicator is referred to as a context indicator if what it measures relates more to the environment in which the Games will be staged, its general context, a broader scale that is indirectly related to the Games. An indicator is referred to as an event indicator if what it measures is directly related to the Games or it is highly probable that the staging of the Games will have an impact upon what is to be measured by that indicator.

The indicators draw upon data for a maximum period of 12 years, commencing 2 years prior to the host city election and continuing through to 3 years after the Games. For London this means 2003 to 2015. It is recognised that longer term impact evaluations would be valuable, but the IOC's contractual limit on OGI is 3 years post-Games. In the IOC's Technical Manual, there are 20 mandatory and 14 optional environmental indicators, 25 mandatory and 18 optional social indicators, 28 mandatory and 15 optional economic indicators.

There are four stages of the London OGI study, which are Initial Situation, pre-Games, Games-time and post-Games. The Initial Situation study was carried out in 2008 by the UK Data Archive. The report provided baseline data for indicators which helped to set the scene in the context of the city, region and country prior to becoming a host city. The pre-Games study was carried out in 2010 by a University of East London (UEL) and University College London collaborative team. The report provided detailed data and assessment for the period 2003 to 2010 and presented an understanding of the trends and any observable impacts for the city, region and country arising from being a host city. The Games-time study was carried out in 2012 by the UEL team. The report provided a documentation and evaluation of indicators for the period 2003 to 2012, which is an update of the pre-Games study and preparation for the post-Games study. The post-Games study is being carried out by the UEL team and will be extended to 2015. It will assess the long-term impact and legacy of the London 2012 Games.

Methodology

Geographical categories

The IOC Technical Manual allocates each indicator into one of three geographical categories: country, region and city. These have been defined in a London 2012 context as shown in Table 3.1. Additionally, two further categories have been identified for those indicators which do not neatly fit into any of the three standard categories.

Taking into account the local situation of the London 2012 Games along with data availability and continuity, determined by the London Organising Committee of the Olympic Games (LOCOG) in discussion with IOC and the IPC, the London 2012 OGI study concentrated on 12 environmental indicators, 24 socio-cultural indicators and 22 economic indicators. These cover the preparation and staging of the event. The post-Games study is expected to further update and analyse context indicators within the framework of a long-term legacy perspective, while archive event indicators remain as they are.

Indicators

The indicators which are assessed in the London 2012 OGI study are set down in Table 3.2.

Table 3.1 Definition of geographical areas for OGI indicators

IOC Technical Manual categories	London 2012 categories	London 2012 interpretation
Country		UK
Region		Greater London – the 32 boroughs of London plus the city of London
City	Local	Host boroughs – comprising the six London boroughs of Barking and Dagenham, Greenwich, Hackney, Newham, Tower Hamlets and Waltham Forest
	Site	Venues: Olympic and Paralympic competition and non-competition venues, for example, indicator En26 – Capacity of Olympic Facilities
	Programme	Indicators which relate to London 2012 programme as a whole, for example, indicator En20 – Greenhouse Gas Emissions of Olympic Games; indicator Ec34 – Structure of OCOG expenditure

Source: Based on Brimicombe and Li (2013).

Table 3.2 London 2012 OGI study indicators

Code	Indicator name	Event (E)/ context (C)
Environmental indicators (12)		
En03	Water Quality	C
En04	Greenhouse Gas Emissions	C
En05	Air Quality	C
En06	Land-Use Changes	C
En07	Protected Areas	C
En10	Public Open-Air Leisure Centres	C
En11	Transport Networks	C
En18	Solid Waste Treatment	C
En20	Greenhouse Gas Emissions of Olympic Games	E
En26	Capacity of Olympic and Paralympic Venues	E
En29	Olympic-Induced Transport Infrastructure	E
En33	New Waste and Wastewater Treatment Facilities	C
Socio-cultural indicators (24)		
So06	Poverty and Social Exclusion	C
So07	Educational Level	C
So08	Crime Rates	C
So09	Health	C
So10	Nutrition	C
So12	Sport and Physical Activities	C
So13	School Sports	C

(Continued)

Table 3.2 (Continued)

Code	Indicator name	Event (E)/ context (C)
So14	Available Sports Facilities	C
So16	Top-Level Sportsmen and Women	C
So18	World and Continental Championships	C
So19	Results at Olympics and World Championships	C
So20	National Anti-Doping Controls	C
So25	Political Involvement in the Organisation of the Games	E
So27	Votes Connected with the Olympic Games	E
So28	Consultation with Specific Groups	E
So29	Opinion Polls	E
So30	Participation of Minorities in Olympic Games and Paralympic Games	E
So31	Homelessness, Low-Rent Market and Affordable Housing	C
So32	Olympic Educational Activities	E
So34	Cultural Programme	E
So38	Volunteers	E
So44	Perceptions about People with Disabilities in Society	C
So45	Support Network for People with Disabilities	C
So48	Accessibility of Public Services	C

Economic indicators (22)

Code	Indicator name	Event (E)/ context (C)
Ec01	Employment by Economic Activity	C
Ec02	Employment Indicators	C
Ec03	Size of Companies	C
Ec06	Public Transport	C
Ec07	Accommodation Infrastructure	C
Ec08	Accommodation Occupancy Rate	C
Ec09	Tourist Nights	C
Ec10	Airport Traffic	C
Ec17	Hotel Price Index	C
Ec18	Real Estate Market	C
Ec22	Foreign Direct Investment	C
Ec24	Structure of Public Spending	C
Ec26	Public Debt	C
Ec27	Jobs Created in Olympic and Context Activities	E
Ec30	Size and Quality Management of Contracted Companies	E
Ec33	Structure of OCOG Revenues	E
Ec34	Structure of OCOG Expenditure	E
Ec35	Total Operating Expenditure (Olympic activities)	E
Ec36	Total Capital Expenditure (Olympic activities)	E
Ec37	Total Capital Expenditure (context activities)	E
Ec38	Total Wages Paid (Olympic activities)	E
Ec44	Employability of People with Disabilities	C

Source: Based on Brimicombe and Li (2013).

Table 3.3 Impact coding of indicators for a Games effect

Relevance	The considered degree to which the data informs the causality of a Games effect vis-à-vis legacy promises	H M L	High Medium Low
Rating	The level of impact that is judged to have taken place over the data period, given relevant context	G Y R	Green (positive impact) Yellow (small or indeterminate impact) Red (negative impact)
Confidence	The level of confidence with which the conclusions concerning impact can be derived from the data	H M L	High Medium Low

Source: Based on Brimicombe and Li (2013).

Table 3.4 London 2012 legacy promises

1   To make the UK a world-class sports nation: elite success, mass participation and school sport
2   To transform the heart of East London
3   To inspire a new generation of young people to take part in local volunteering, cultural and physical activity
4   To make the Olympic Park a blueprint for sustainable living
5   To demonstrate that the UK is a creative, inclusive and welcoming place to live in, to visit and for business
6   To develop the opportunities and choices for disabled people

Source: Based on information retrieved from DCMS (2008).

Impact coding

The OGI study carries out an objective and scientific analysis of the impact of Olympic Games. Each indicator is coded for a Games effect to reflect the analysis outcome. The coding system is designed as set down in Table 3.3.

This coding of impact is in relation to the legacy promises for the London 2012 Olympic and Paralympic Games and is set down in Table 3.4.

Sustainability scoring

The data collected for the indicators provides a wealth of detail on the current state of and trends in economic, environmental and socio-cultural aspects of the context for the London 2012 Games and its locality. However, to provide an over-all assessment and analysis of sustainability performance, this wealth of detail needs to be transformed into standardised scores.

There have been a range of such definitions adopted in relation to the sustainability of the 2012 Games, which highlight the difficulty of achieving a unique definition (CSL, 2010, 2012). This is well known; the Brundtland definition (World Commission for Environment and Development, 1987), while capturing the essence of sustainable development, has proved amenable to many different applications and

Table 3.5 Sustainability scoring of indicators for an overall performance

Indicator characteristic	Scoring		Rationale and comments
Relevance	High	1	This weighs the final indicator score so as to take account of the possibility to discern a Games effect from the data and to reduce the score of indicators where, from the data, there is little likelihood of discernible causality.
	Medium	0.5	
	Low	0	
Rating	Green	+1	This weighs the final indicator score in terms of the direction of impact and excludes indicators where there seems to be no significant impact. Summing indicator scores will mean that the balance of positive and negative impacts will determine the sign of the final sustainability score.
	Yellow	0	
	Red	−1	
Confidence	High	1	This weighs the final indicator score to take account of the reliability of the data in determining impact and to reduce the rating score of indicators where there is low confidence in the rating.
	Medium	0.5	
	Low	0	

Source: Based on Brimicombe and Li (2010).

interpretations. Sustainability is assessed in terms of the achievement of benefits from three perspectives: environmental, socio-cultural and economic. This is the approach that has been adopted in the London 2012 study with the definition of a suite of indicators and the assessment of performance on each of these indicators. The selection of indicators within these three categories has paid close attention to the London 2012 legacy promises in particular as the best guide to the desired impact of the Games from a sustainability perspective.

Impact coding provides a ranking of three characteristics of each indicator (relevance, rating and confidence) as detailed in the previous section. Following the model established by the Vancouver 2010 Pre-Games Impact Study, sustainability scores have been assigned to these rankings. The overall sustainability scores for each indicator is then weighted by the three corresponding scores. The scoring system is recorded in Table 3.5.

Metadata

In order to use or share data sets legally and correctly, it is necessary for users to understand the data content and its provenance through additional information. Metadata are information about the content of a data set and are provided so that data users can judge the value, reliability and suitability of data sets. Metadata ideally consist of a series of standardised attributes, such as definitions, means of measurement and coding, data sources and data quality by which users can assess fitness for use in a particular application and the conceptual compatibility of the data for integration and use with other data sets.

The data for each indicator, sometimes from more than one source, are stored in spreadsheets and used to produce the assessment results. We at UEL have

Table 3.6 The Dublin Core

Label	Definition
Title	Name given to the resource
Creator	Entity primarily responsible for making the resource
Subject	Topic of the resource
Description	Account of the resource
Publisher	Entity responsible for making the resource available
Contributor	Entity or entities responsible for making contributions to the resource
Date	Point or period of time associated with an event in the lifecycle of the resource
Type	Nature or genre of the resource
Format	File format, physical medium or dimensions of the resource
Identifier	Unambiguous reference to the resource within a given context
Source	Related resource from which the described resource is derived
Language	Language of the resource
Relation	Related resource
Coverage	Spatial or temporal topic of the resource, the geographical applicability of the resource or the jurisdiction under which the resource is relevant; the relevant time period
Rights	Information about rights held in and over the resource

Source: Based on 'The Dublin Core metadata element set, BS ISO 15836:2009'.

introduced the recording of a consistent metadata set within the spreadsheets for each indicator. This allows any user in a subsequent OGI stage to be oriented to a data set and to understand and trace its provenance.

To create useful metadata, it is essential to follow national or international standards so that data users can understand them. There are a number of widely used standards, such as CEN/TC 287 Geographic Information Metadata, FGDC-STD-001-1998 Content Standard for Digital GeoSpatial Metadata, and the Dublin Core Metadata Element Set (ISO 15836:2009). Compared with other metadata standards, Dublin Core Metadata Element Set is generally applicable and of low implementation cost due to the simplicity of such a light metadata. The London 2012 study has, therefore, implemented Dublin Core as the standard to follow in generating metadata for OGI.

The Dublin Core Metadata Element Set is a vocabulary of 15 properties for use in resource description. The name 'Dublin' comes from its original 1995 invitational workshop, which took place in Dublin, Ohio; and 'Core' because its elements are broad and generic, usable for describing a wide range of resources from numerical data to web content. The components of Dublin Core are outlined in Table 3.6.

Open data

UK Open Data and Transparency policy offers up data within government to the public. UK open data are free and downloadable online. Official statistics in UK open data are subject to a Code of Practice published by the UK Statistics Authority (2009) to ensure their quality, consistency and usability. The Code is consistent with the United Nations Fundamental Principles of Official Statistics (United Nations Statistics Division, 2006) and the European Statistics Code of Practice (Eurostat, 2005). Most official statistics are derived from centrally compiled administrative data sets created by government departments, state agencies and other public organisations.

The London 2012 OGI study was predicated on the use of accessible secondary data. No primary (survey) data collection was feasible within the available study period and budget. Open data, therefore, offers major data sources for this OGI study due to UK open data policy and web dissemination of data tables (Brimicombe & Li, 2012). When data are specific to the work of the Olympic Delivery Authority (ODA) and LOCOG, these data were collected directly from LOCOG. This is clearly not the case with other host cities, for example, in Vancouver, Sochi and Rio, large amounts of primary data collection become necessary because fundamental data on the environment, economy and society were not readily available at sufficient granularity. The performance of London 2012 can continue to be monitored on an annual basis from open data updates which act as a barometer to legacy outcomes. This is a testament to the accessible time-series data infrastructure that has been created in the UK which for most data sets can be a decade.

Assessment

The analysis of change and assessment of impact in terms of a discernible Games effect are based on IOC definitions of indicators in the Technical Manual and the extent to which available data matched the specification. Impact codes and sustainability scores of each indicator are derived from detailed data analysis and reasoned judgements in interpreting the analysis result.

On the basis of impact coding and sustainability scoring, each indicator was assessed as shown in Table 3.7. To achieve an overall sustainability score for each indicator, sustainability scores of the relevance, rating and confidence scores are calculated. A positive overall sustainability score derives from a positive rating score, indicating a positive impact. The closer the score is to +/−1, the greater the relevance and confidence scoring for the indicator. Thus, the composite (i.e. overall) sustainability score provides a robust assessment of the use of this data to derive the likely impact of the Games on an aspect of sustainability. These sustainability scores are then averaged for each subset of economic, socio-cultural and environmental indicators as well as across the whole indicator set.

Generally, this indicator set is a strong one for London 2012 Games. By average scores for all indicators, both relevance and confidence are high at 0.86 and 0.91, respectively. There is clearly positive impact as the average score of impact rating is 0.57 (where +1 is the maximum possible score, −1 is the minimum possible score, 0 is the status quo). Overall the sustainability score is calculated as 0.5 for the Games.

The subset of socio-cultural indicators is particularly strong with scores of 0.98 and 1.00 on confidence and relevance, respectively. The subset of economic indicators also performs strong on confidence (with a score of 0.95) but relatively less strong on relevance (with a score of 0.77). Conversely the subset of environmental

Table 3.7 Impact coding and sustainability scoring

Code	Indicator name	Relevance	Rating	Confidence	Sustainability
Environmental indicators					
En03	Water Quality	H	G	H	1
En04	Greenhouse Gas Emissions	M	Y	M	0
En05	Air Quality	M	Y	M	0
En06	Land-Use Changes	M	Y	M	0
En07	Protected Areas	M	G	M	0.25
En10	Public Open-Air Leisure Centres	M	G	M	0.25
En11	Transport Networks	H	G	M	0.5
En18	Solid Waste Treatment	H	Y	H	0
En20	Greenhouse Gas Emissions of Olympic Games	H	Y	M	0
En26	Capacity of Olympic and Paralympic Venues	H	G	H	1
En29	Olympic-Induced Transport Infrastructure	H	G	M	0.5
En33	New Waste and Wastewater Treatment Facilities	H	G	H	1
Average for environmental indicators		**0.79**	**0.58**	**0.67**	**0.375**
Socio-cultural indicators					
So06	Poverty and Social Exclusion	H	Y	H	0
So07	Educational Level	H	Y	H	0
So08	Crime Rates	H	G	H	1
So09	Health	H	Y	H	0
So10	Nutrition	H	Y	H	0
So12	Sport and Physical Activities	H	Y	H	0
So13	School Sports	H	Y	H	0
So14	Available Sports Facilities	H	Y	H	0
So16	Top-Level Sportsmen and Women	H	G	H	1
So18	World and Continental Championships	H	G	H	1
So19	Results at Olympics and World Championships	H	G	H	1
So20	National Anti-Doping Controls	H	G	H	1
So25	Political Involvement in the Organisation of the Games	H	G	H	1
So27	Votes Connected with the Olympic Games	H	G	H	1
So28	Consultation with Specific Groups	H	G	H	1
So29	Opinion Polls	H	G	H	1

(Continued)

Table 3.7 (Continued)

Code	Indicator name	Relevance	Rating	Confidence	Sustainability
So30	Participation of Minorities in Olympic Games and Paralympic Games	H	G	H	1
So31	Homelessness, Low Rent Market and Affordable Housing	H	Y	H	0
So32	Olympic Educational Activities	H	G	H	1
So34	Cultural Programme	H	Y	H	0
So38	Volunteers	H	G	H	1
So44	Perceptions about People with Disabilities in Society	H	Y	H	0
So45	Support Network for People with Disabilities	M	Y	H	0
So48	Accessibility of Public Services	H	G	H	1
Average for socio-cultural indicators		**0.98**	**0.54**	**1**	**0.542**
Economic indicators					
Ec01	Employment by Economic Activity	M	Y	H	0
Ec02	Employment Indicators	H	Y	H	0
Ec03	Size of Companies	H	G	H	1
Ec06	Public Transport	H	G	H	1
Ec07	Accommodation Infrastructure	H	G	H	1
Ec08	Accommodation Occupancy Rate	M	Y	M	0
Ec09	Tourist Nights	M	Y	H	0
Ec10	Airport Traffic	M	Y	H	0
Ec17	Hotel Price Index	M	Y	H	0
Ec18	Real Estate Market	H	Y	H	0
Ec22	Foreign Direct Investment	M	Y	H	0
Ec24	Structure of Public Spending	H	G	H	1
Ec26	Public Debt	M	G	H	0.5
Ec27	Jobs Created in Olympic and Context Activities	H	G	H	1
Ec30	Size and Quality Management of Contracted Companies	M	Y	M	0
Ec33	Structure of OCOG Revenues	H	G	H	1
Ec34	Structure of OCOG Expenditure	H	G	H	1
Ec35	Total Operating Expenditure (Olympic activities)	M	G	H	0.5
Ec36	Total Capital Expenditure (Olympic activities)	H	G	H	1
Ec37	Total Capital Expenditure (context activities)	H	G	H	1

Ec38	Total Wages Paid (Olympic activities)	M	G	H	0.5
Ec44	Employability of People with Disabilities	H	G	H	1
Average for economic indicators		**0.77**	**0.59**	**0.95**	**0.523**
AVERAGE FOR ALL INDICATORS		**0.86**	**0.57**	**0.91**	**0.5**

Source: Based on Brimicombe and Li (2013).

indicators does well on relevance (score of 0.79) but relatively less well on confidence (with a score of 0.67).

However, the scores are not high on impact rating. The average score of impact rating is 0.58, 0.54 and 0.59 for environmental indicators, socio-cultural indicators and economic indicators, respectively. Encouragingly, the assessment shows there is no indicator having negative impact, while 33 of 58 indicators have positive impact. Based on the sustainability scores of impact rating, confidence and relevance, none of overall sustainability scores is negative, while positive results can be seen across three subsets. The average of overall sustainability scores is moderate for socio-cultural indicators and economic indicators (0.542 and 0.523, respectively) and is relatively low for environmental indicators (0.375).

Furthermore, indicators can be regrouped so that particular areas can be assessed with insights and various patterns being exposed. For example, indicators could be regrouped into context and event categories for each subset. In average, event indicators have a higher impact rating than context indicators across the three subsets. Event indicators in the socio-cultural subset are particularly strong followed by the economic subset. Event indicators in the environmental subset are relatively less strong. This might be because most event indicators have immediate or short-term impact, and in contrast, many context indicators have long-term impact. In the pre-Games impact study, initial assessments were carried out on some regrouped indicators, such as environmental outcomes indicators, environmental activities indicators, social outcomes indicators, sport outcomes indicators, economic outcomes indicators and tourist outcomes indicators. In the post-Games impact study, in-depth assessments will be excised on further regrouped indicators.

In summary, no negative impacts were found to arise from the preparation and staging of the Games, primarily because of the scale of any effects in relation to the rest of London. Some positive impacts were found, but for many impacts, the indicators were inconclusive, because it was too early for positive legacy to arise in many areas. Overall the sustainability score also gives a positive outcome, which implies that the possibility exists for the London 2012 Games to provide further positive contributions to sustainability (Table 3.7).

Conclusion

In this study, data have been collected, integrated, explored, analysed and presented on 58 indicators. The inclusion of indicators from the IOC Technical Manual is decided by the host city in discussion with the IOC. The choice of OGI indicators depends on what is deemed to be relevant for the particular host city.

The data are largely secondary data from UK open data sources, except for some data specific to the Olympic construction and operation which have been collected by the ODA and LOCOG and provided to us. For all indicators, we have striven to construct a time series from 2003 to the present. We are in a fortunate position that so much current and historical data about government and the public sphere are made available online. This is a testament to the accessible data infrastructure that has been created in the UK.

The advantages of using secondary data are that reports such as this can be compiled much more quickly and can be readily used to study trends. However, there are some disadvantages that need to be addressed. The already compiled data may not precisely focus on the effect that needs to be studied or may not be available at the right geographic level. There may be changes in the way statistics are collected and published, leading to a discontinuity in the time series. There is also a time delay in the publishing of official and administrative statistics, typically 18 to 24 months.

Assessments of any Games impact are based on the IOC definition of indicators in the Technical Manual, the available data to match that specification and the collective backgrounds of the research team. The impact assessments are driven by deep data exploration, in-depth data analysis and reasoned judgements. No negative impacts were found as a result of preparing and staging the 2012 Games; some positive impacts were found, but many indicators were inconclusive. Such inconclusiveness is not a criticism; it may stem from data issues, but also from the diverse policy landscape of the UK, London and East London. East London has been the beneficiary of regeneration from European Regional Development Funds and government investment in the development of Thames Gateway. The public investment in London 2012 complements and adds significantly to the programme of urban renewal and development that has taken place over recent decades. In this context, disaggregating the effects of the Games' impact from those of other regeneration projects is a complex affair. In relation to data issues, crime rates reported in the British Crime Survey and police-reported crime have been falling consistently since 1997, and this national trend is overlaid by host boroughs, metropolitan police and home office efforts to make the 2012 Games a 'safe and secure Games for all'. This study period has also seen the banking crisis and a full-blown recession with a period of austerity now upon us. Thus, what is presented in this study is partway through a sequence of studies. While the content of this report presents trends for a range of indicators that provide information to stakeholders, no firm conclusions on impacts and legacy should be drawn at this stage.

While this study has updated and analysed 58 indicators across the environmental, socio-cultural and economic spheres, there are some good news aspects of delivering the 2012 Games which are not captured through any of the indicators in the Technical Manual. For example, not captured are the innovations that have been made in procurement and supply change management in the construction of the venues, athletes' village and the Olympic park. OGI should have the flexibility to introduce a small number of ad hoc indicators that reflect local innovative practices (and their impact) so as to inform studies conducted by future host cities.

References

Brimicombe, A. J. and Li, Y. (2010) 'Olympic Games impact study – London 2012 pre-Games report', available at: http://www.uel.ac.uk/geo-information/documents/UEL_TGIfS_PreGames_OGI_Release.pdf

Brimicombe, A. J. and Li, Y. (2012) 'Open data and the monitoring of the sustainability of a London 2012 legacy'. *Researching and evaluating the Games conference.* London: Department for Culture, Media and Sport.

Brimicombe, A. J. and Li, Y. (2013) 'Olympic Games impact study – London 2012 Games-time report', available at: http://www.uel.ac.uk/geo-information/London_OGI2/documents/GamesTime_OGI_Report.pdf

Commission for a Sustainable London (CSL) (2010, 2012) *2009 annual review.* London: CSL 2012.

Department for Culture, Media and Sport (DCMS) (2008) *Before, during and after.* London: DCMS.

Eurostat (2005) *European statistics code of practice: for the national and community statistical authorities.* European Statistical System: Eurostat.

UK Statistics Authority (2009) *Code of practice for official statistics.* London: UK Statistics Authority.

United Nations Statistics Division (2006) 'Fundamental principles of official statistics'. Resolution adopted by the General Assembly on 29 January 2014.

World Commission for Environment and Development (1987) *Our common future.* Oxford: Oxford University Press.

4 The Olympic compact

Legacies of gift, debt and unequal exchange

Phil Cohen

Introduction

This chapter opens by looking at the meta-evaluative framework developed for London 2012, rejecting the model of causality operationalised in impact studies and an audit culture based on a bureaucratic concept of performance, suggesting an alternative framework grounded in a comparative anthropology of value.

The chapter argues that the Olympic compact – the deal struck with key constituencies of interest in the host city in order to justify and win popular support for the bid, especially in terms of its legacy – must be understood as a complex totality or 'structure in dominance' produced at the intersection of moral, market and political economies of worth. The tensions and contradictions between these different economies, their various forms of mediation, is what gives each Olympics its distinctive identity as a 'values tournament'. The principles of variation in the compact are traced by briefly comparing London 2012 with Beijing, Sydney, Atlanta, Barcelona and Berlin 1936.

Impacted truths: the Olympic audit culture

One consequence of the emphasis on 2012 as the 'legacy Games' is that a large apparatus of evaluation was built around assessing its immediate and long-term impact on East London and the wider metropolitan and national society.[1,2] If you ask a professional story teller what it means to give an account of an action and its consequences, she will say that it involves making a report about something that has happened principally in order to attribute responsibility for it; in other words, it is a form of narrative explanation centred on human agency. If you ask your bank manager what an account is, she will probably reply that it is a record or statement of your financial affairs, of how much you are currently worth, and yours is overdrawn. The Olympic legacy story entails a merger of these two principles of accountancy; it is part of a historic shift away from the notion of a final audit, the day of judgement where a person or organisation is called to account by a higher moral authority, and towards the notion of audit as a process of continuous self-assessment where behaviour is monitored in the light of some internalised principle or norm of social accountability. This frequently takes the form of applying a system of double-entry book keeping to judge actions in terms of personal cost or benefit, profit or loss, thus creating a kind of audit trail of the inner working of the psyche considered as an agency of self-interest and rational choice. It is a key way in which market ideology penetrates and reorganises the moral economy of the self.[3]

This is an essentially private process – and one, therefore, subject to all the ruses of self-deception, so how can it be made available to public scrutiny? The answer lies in the notion of performance.[4] In the second half of the twentieth century, the original meaning of the term as 'a dramatic presentation or display especially of conspicuous or irritating behaviour' (*Oxford English Dictionary*) increasingly gave way to its opposite usage, as a 'measure of efficiency in the way somebody carries out a routine or prescribed task'. The social sciences have played a vital part in engineering this discursive shift, in so far as they make use of dramaturgical metaphors for representing patterns of social interaction as 'role playing', but they also furnish instruments for measuring social attitudes and behaviour in terms of their conformity or deviance in respect of statistical norms.

Biometrics, anthropometrics, psychometrics, sociometrics, geometrics, chrono-metrics, econometrics – it is no coincidence that these systems of metrication should have been developed in application to bodies regarded as requiring disciplined or coordinated effort: labouring bodies, military bodies, civic bodies, children's bod-ies and, above all, athletes' bodies.[5] The various techniques evolved to capture the behaviour of these differently embodied subjects under conditions specified by each discipline have one thing in common: they create a grid of standardised measurement codified into common, quantifiable indices of 'performance'. It is this principle of performativity created by the machinery of metrication itself which enables these bodies to be tested, compared and judged, and differential values assigned to them in terms of their efficiency and/or effectiveness – in other words, to be measured both for their productivity or output and their 'outcome'.[6] Metrication became an integral part of a panoptic system of governance, furnishing a new regime of mass observa-tion in which the theatrical and the bureaucratic orders were merged: performance as dramatic display/visual exhibition and as measurable productivity/outcome become integrated into a single apparatus of control.[7]

This new system of evaluation enabled ever more precise benchmarks of suc-cess and failure to be constructed – the tiniest difference in performance being sufficient to draw the line between success and failure. They also enabled a whole array of disparate practices to be tested and treated as commensurable objects of calculation, even as they foreclosed value judgements about their ultimate worth. Instead what comes to be valued is the test itself for what it discloses about those subjected to it. As Strathen puts it, 'the report on the output is predicated on the form of evaluation which it itself produces'.[8] She defines this as an instance of auto-poesis – it is about how a closed system generates its own self-enabling rationality. The evaluation process, thus, sets its own endogenous norms of attain-ment. Audits evaluate the auditees' capacity to be put to the test of the audit.

We can see this process at work very clearly in the official framework of evaluation that has been put in place for the 2012 Olympics. The concept of a 'logic chain' is central to the methodological protocols which the framework is concerned to establish:

> Every evaluation must show through a customised logic chain how the project's delivery is expected to proceed from initial objectives to final outcomes. Some of these outcomes will relate to pre-determined project objectives set out in the project plan, while others will be outcomes that would be logically expected even if they are not included in or even aligned with the project objectives.
>
> (DCMS, 2009, p. 17)[9]

> Logic chains need to be developed in the early stages of the evaluation based on expectations given the activities proposed and experience of similar projects. As the evaluation progresses, the logic chains should be refined, populated with evidence and, where needed, amended to better match the observed interactions. A final logic chain should be produced at the end of the evaluation reflecting the evidence and understanding gained in the evaluation process.
>
> (DCMS, 2009, p. 37)[9]

What is being evaluated, then, is a developmental logic intrinsic to the way an Olympic project is delivered, a sequential chain comprising 'objectives, inputs, outputs and outcomes', which precisely describes the trajectory of the audit itself and its particular form of narrative explanation. Auditability is built into the way a project is conceived, planned and executed from the outset and what is being measured is just that. Then when it comes to assessing the value added by an initiative, its 'additionality', the principle of evaluation turns itself inside out; the value ascribed to a project by those whom it is intended to benefit – its internal economy of worth – is largely ignored and instead an external principle of counterfactuality is introduced, to guesstimate what the state of affairs might have been had the project never happened. This is not, however, a genuine exercise in the sociological imagination – these studies are not going to tell us what Stratford might have been like had London failed to win the Olympics – but rather a way of bracketing a project's effects off from the influence of externalities over which it has no control, and whose impact cannot be easily quantified. Paradoxically focusing on what did not happen becomes a way of ignoring the wider implications of what did.

The Olympic audit is organised around the notion of impact. Who is impacted? Where is the impact felt? When is the impact felt? This is the holy trinity of research questions around which the evaluation of 2012 revolves. Impact studies operate with a unilinear model of causality: they are supposed to measure the effect of agency interventions on target populations and rarely take into account the reciprocal action of these populations on the agency itself. In an Olympic context they underwrite the notion that the essential story is about how the Games have changed the host community, rather than how that community itself has changed the Games. In modelling the purely immanent self-referential dynamic of the agency, the impact study reduces the human actors to mere puppets, and the communities who are supposed to be the beneficiaries into either passive supports or obstacles to the realisation of governmental aims and objectives, without any autonomous agency of their own.

Impact-driven auditry is a hard data discourse which carries most weight with 'hard-nosed' politicians, policy makers and sports administrators on account of its replicable and largely statistical procedures; it gives the appearance of an objective and reliable narrative.[10] It also enables one Games to be compared to another in terms of a set of common performance indicators, so enabling a panoptic survey of past Olympiads to be conducted from a properly 'Olympian', i.e. global, perspective.[11] It is here that a forensic social science dedicated to the continuous monitoring of programmes of social intervention designed to regulate and modify public behaviour establishes its pre-eminence in the art of how to manage knowledge as a process of public impression making.[12]

Yet there is a ghost in the machinery of the audit culture which continually undermines its credibility: its meaning. For as soon as the audit has to stake its evidential/knowledge claims in the public arena, it becomes enmeshed in narratives which articulate some higher order principle of interpretation: it becomes a story about aspiration or achievement, justification or blame, praise or disappointment. It is to this wider narrative framing we must now turn.

The Olympic compact and its economies of worth

Shortly after the announcement of London's successful bid, the organisers made an announcement saying, simply 'THANK YOU LONDON'. They did not thank the International Olympic Committee (IOC) for awarding them the prize, they thanked the inhabitants of the host city, whose support for the project they had spent so much time, money and advertising effort in enlisting. In the first flush of self-congratulation, so brutally foreclosed by the bomb attacks the following day, the first thought of the bid campaigners was to express a debt of gratitude to the people who had, seemingly, gifted them this opportunity.

The announcement was in response to the fact that one of the key tests for the legitimacy of a city's candidature is the level of support for the bid among the citizenry as measured by focus groups, polls and press coverage. This is the one brief semi-plebiscitary moment in what is otherwise a massively top-down command and control operation. But who had really passed the test and needed to be thanked? Clearly it was the PR people who successfully massaged public opinion and sold the Olympics to Londoners. But thanking the People has a special payoff in so far as it carries the implication that there is some kind of compact with them based on a relation of mutual indebtedness and that this principle of balanced reciprocity is a pact sealed by the Olympics. This is clearly what the 2012 Olygarchy wanted to believe to be the case, even though it does not remotely correspond to the actual state of affairs and indeed is the reverse of the real power relations that obtain. For in reality the London Organising Committee of the Olympic Games and the Olympic Delivery Authority (ODA) were the dispenser of patronage and funds through which they procured the services and allegiances of businesses, community organisations and others who stood in a more or less clientelist relation to them. Against this background, the hoped-for benefit in thanking Londoners for backing the bid was not only the enrolment of their further support for the project but their commitment to the belief that they were equal partners in a shared enterprise going forward to 2012, when they clearly were not.

Is there more to this than populist mystification? What is in play in the Olympic compact are a number of different economies of worth, different discourses and measures of value, and these generate distinct and often contradictory definitions of legacy. It is in this sense why the Olympics remain a 'values tournament' even in a so-called post-ideological age.

We start by distinguishing between *moral* economies and *market* economies. We usually think of moral economies in terms of pre-capitalist forms of exchange based on the notion of just price, the practice of mutual aid and the regulation of social arrangements to ensure that the poor do not perish. But moral economies had a wider brief: they were part of a system of customary arrangements for transferring land, property and other assets, primarily from fathers to sons. Legacies were in the gift of the head of household, and assets – both material and symbolic – were regarded as *heirlooms* or *heritage* to be held in trust by one generation for the next. The disposition of the legacy was a way of ensuring that the issue of ancestry and descent continued to cast a long shadow over the lives of both heirs apparent and the young pretenders to their 'throne'. For all the conflicts it engenders, this moral economy also ensures continuity of cultural heritage between the generations. Whatever the legacy materially consisted in, and for the poor it might be little enough, it represented an emotional bond of kinship between donor and recipient, a permanent reminder of the life they had shared together. The Olympic compact draws discursively on this sense of legacy as commemoration and conservation of the past to project the Olympics as a *gift legacy*, as a bequest to be held in trust for future generations.

Moral economies are anathema to capitalism which is primarily concerned with the liquidity and marketability of assets. It is a mode of production and consumption of wealth whose circulation and distribution is primarily through the market. Inherited wealth and position come to be regarded with as much suspicion as poverty. Hierarchy and deference give way to meritocracy, gift exchange becomes part of the struggle for competitive advantage, and the bonds of community and kith and kin are replaced by impersonal contractual relations. Legacy is no longer a heritage from the past, but from the donor's standpoint an *investment in the future*, and from the recipients a *dividend*, its worth measured by the financial benefit or competitive advantage it promises to bring. Under this imprimatur, the Olympic legacy is now a site of rational calculation not of sentimental attachment between benefactor and beneficiary. We might call this a *payback legacy*, since it is about servicing debts and settling accounts.

Yet moral economies do not simply wither away. They are subsumed under the new dispensation, sometimes become marketised and sometimes provide legitimations for capitalism that capitalism cannot give itself. For example, wealthy entrepreneurs and industrial magnates like Lakshmi Mittal erect monuments to their wealth *and* generosity by financing iconic buildings or establishing charitable foundations, just as they buy art both as an investment *and* as a sign of their superior cultural taste. They want to be remembered for these public endowments and not for less creditable legacies – the shady business deals they may have done or the people whose lives they may have embittered in the course of building their financial empires. At the same time, the concept of *endowment*, taken back into the moral economy from which it derives, offers an alternative form of payback legacy, and this, as we will see, has important implications for the future of the Olympic park.

Moral economy under capitalism retains the horror of personal financial indebtedness. It may be OK to owe the bank, although the stigma of bankruptcy remains in middle-class society. Solvency is still the straight and righteously narrow path to salvation. Hell is not one self but other people you owe money to. We may no longer have debtors' jails, but the spectre of creditors and bailiffs at the door still evokes fear and loathing in the suburbs. In public culture, the threat of such negative reciprocities has led to risk-averse prudentialism and the precautionary principle. But there is a double standard in operation here. It is fine to cancel symbolic debts, the only price paid being a bad conscience, but material debts must be honoured at all costs, even if means closing down hospitals and schools.

The paradox, of course, is that lending and borrowing is the life blood of financial capitalism. Since the 1980s, living on the never-never has been encouraged not only by banks but by both Labour and Tory governments who thought consumer credit was the easiest way to stimulate economic growth. Moral and social status, the issue of legitimacy and illegitimacy become reduced to creditworthiness.

When speculation in what turned out to be bad debts resulted in banks – and nearly the whole, seemingly solid, apparatus of financial capitalism going into melt down, requiring a state bail-out on an unprecedented scale – capitalism's own credit rating fell to almost zero. A generation to come will still be living with this legacy of debt, a payback which has involved the time-honoured practice, derived from the (im)moral economy, of robbing Peter to pay Paul. It is the spectre of public debt that hangs over every Olympics, including 2012.

All this makes it imperative to keep precise records and accounts; this is possible because, in contrast to legacy-as-gift, legacy-as-payback generates transactions that are time-delimited and indexed to the transfer of specified material assets. This is linked to the growth of an audit culture whose mode of operation in the Olympics we have just discussed. But it is now possible to see that in this context we are dealing with not one legacy but two, one based on gift exchange and its moral economy and the other on debt servicing in the market economy. Each has its own avatars in the hurly-burly of Olympic legacy politics.

In the first case, we are dealing with the narrative legacy of the Games, which is generated through the free circulation and exchange of information, the swapping of stories, to create a shared memoryscape around each Olympiad, comprising a cultural heritage transmitted from generation to generation. It is a process which strengthens solidarities within and rivalries between the Olympic movement's various interpretive communities, and these exchanges are not, by definition, time-delimited; they

Table 4.1 Moral and market economies

Moral economy	Market economy
Heritage	Payback
Heirloom	Dividend
Gift reciprocity	Debt servicing
Name and reputation	Credit rating
Blood relations	Impersonal legal contract
Emotional labour of dis/ownership	Cultural/social/intellectual capital
Heir/pretender	Stakeholder/partner
Hierarchy/deference	Meritocracy
Mutual aid	Competitive advantage
Memoryscape	Audit
Symbolic assets/liabilities	Material assets/liabilities
Endowment	Asset stripping
Elastic time frame	Delimited time frame

focus on symbolic or invisible assets and liabilities and the act of owning or disowning the Olympic heritage. This is a system of open-ended reciprocities in which no debt or obligation is being incurred.

At the same time, this narrative legacy, which is in its own right an invisible asset, may become marketised, commodified in the form of memorabilia produced by the Olympics heritage industry, exploited by civic imagineers to promote sports tourism and the hospitality industries and be generally used to confer competitive advantage to the host city in the global cultural economy. The payback legacy concerns the concrete plans for what is to happen after the Games and concentrates on the disposal of material assets and liabilities – to whom are they to be bequeathed or sold off and under what conditions – and how debts of various kinds are to be negotiated within a time-delimited frame. It constitutes the basic plot of the 2012 legacy narrative.

Both types of legacy are necessary to the framing of the Olympic compact. Table 4.1 provides an inventory of the distinctive features that characterise the dual economy of worth. I have already hinted that one of the ideological sleights of hand performed by the compact is to pass off debts as gifts and redescribe what should be gifts as commodities whose exchange generates debt. In what follows we shall look in more detail at this interaction to understand how the hidden or deep legacy of 2012 has come to be constructed.

The triangulation of values

In winning prizes, athletes imagine themselves to be paying back a debt they owe to all those who have helped them develop the special gifts or talents with which they have been endowed, whether by nature, nurture or God. It follows that if they lose, they are deemed to have failed to honour this debt, as we say they 'have let the side down', and can only redeem their position by redoubling their efforts to succeed. Part of their script, written for them by the moral economy of sport, is to affirm pride in representing the team or the nation, literally embodying their hopes, and to act as ambassadors for their sport. So letting the side down often carries an added burden of debt and guilt.

Of course, sporting success also brings fame and fortune – it turns athletes, sometimes almost overnight, into celebrities; they find themselves in the media spotlight, courted by all and sundry and offered lucrative sponsorship deals by multinational companies and advertisers. The market value of their reputational status can be accurately logged on their bank accounts. The impact on their lives can be traumatic, and many sporting memoirs focus on the difficulty of managing the conflicting demands of public persona and private life. But these individual biographical dilemmas also speak to a structural issue.

The Olympics are a values tournament because they are produced at the intersection of rival economies of worth.[13] I have referred so far to this phenomenon as a 'dual economy', but I think a 'mediatised economy' is perhaps a better term, because it suggests that its hybrid character does not just emerge spontaneously through some internal process of syncretism but is produced through the intervention of a third force which plays an active role in giving the transactions a distinctive character. That function may be increasingly performed by the mass media in reconstructing the Games as a global sporting spectacle in which the values of commerce and community are magically reconciled. But a key role is still played by 'moral entrepreneurs', i.e. by lobbying groups and organisations that draw on a moralising discourse of stakes and claims over public amenity linked to the notion of sport as a civilising process.[14] Today, the leading moral entrepreneurs of the Olympic movement are the architects of the host city bids who stress the gift legacy. It is left to the Olympophobes in unholy alliance with the free marketers to organise moral panics around payback issues.

The other intervening variable between moral and market economies is supplied by *political economy*. This term refers to the governance of the body politic by the state through its ideological, legislative and coercive apparatus of intervention into economic life. In the present context, I am going to use it to refer to the various governing bodies of sport and the Olympics, their relationships to both state and market, to the key players in the regeneration process and to political lobbyists who become active around particular sport and regeneration agendas. It is at this level that the underlying tensions within the Olympic compact that are voiced in a somewhat indirect and displaced fashion by the moral enterpreneurs take on a more concentrated and condensed form and become subject to specific strategies of mitigation.

This principle of triangulation around Olympic compact, forged through specific coalitions of interest, in turn leads to the formation of a number of distinct cultures operating along different local/global axes:

1   *Olympic enterprise culture* – promoting the Games as an economic project. The legacy issue is how the various forms of capital generated by the Games are to be realised and distributed to meet different kinds of debt, whether in the form of dividends (viz. health dividends) or as paybacks for public and private investment.

2   *Olympic endowment culture* – concerns the gift legacy and how the assets of a Games are to be managed within a particular structure of conveyancing. How far is it possible to maintain a balance between the rival heirloom claims of local community stakeholders and the dividend claims of those whose political stake is institutional?

3   *Olympic hospitality culture* – each host city develops a visitor economy around the Games and has to manage the conflicting demands of commerce and communitas – for example, to balance conflicting priorities of security and conviviality. Here the tensions between gift and debt legacies come most visibly to the surface, for example, the use of hospitality as a form of bribery.

Market ideology

Today, the Olympic movement's determinant – but not always visible – economy of worth is provided by the worlds of commerce, industry and the marketplace. It is not just that professional sport is big business and dominated by global interests and mega-events, but that a 'winner takes all' market ideology has become the referential model for the norms and values of competitive achievement promoted through sport. This same ideology also provides a model of regeneration that emphasises 'gold plated' urban development and investment in premium sites with the effect of gentrifying the Olympic zone and its immediate hinterland. Finally, under the rubrics of this grammar, a Game's governance is judged in terms of efficiency of delivery, cost-effectiveness and the competitive advantage it confers on the host city or nation in the global marketplace. Whatever the balance of public/private investment in a particular Games, economistic criteria remain the preferred measures for evaluating and comparing their outcomes.

The 1996 Games staged in downtown Atlanta, in the heart of the black ghetto, are usually told as a cautionary tale about what happens when market ideology prevails and the private sector runs the show, riding rough shod over the needs of deprived host communities.[15] Certainly measured as a return on capital investment, the Atlanta Games could be counted as a profitable success, but despite some local environmental gain in the legacy park, the regeneration benefits were minimal. In London 2012, market ideology was carefully sublimated in the rhetoric of aspirationalism, but it was nevertheless the major driving force in the delivery strategy of the ODA. Whether it will be subsumed or displaced by other economies of worth in the post-Games legacy politics remains to be seen, although the signs are not propitious.

Moral economies

In an Olympic context, moral economies come in two flavours. There is the justification which insists on the unique character of the Games as an inspirational project centred on an international community of elite athletes who are supposed to embody the Olympic values of excellence, resilience, collaboration and integrity. An Olympiad, from this standpoint, is a moveable feast of sublime athleticism, providing a hall of fame which drives athletes on to enter their personal zone of peak performance and, as members of the Olympic family, serve as charismatic role models for the youth of the world, encouraging them to get fit and play fair. This economy of worth draws on familial – and indeed still largely patriarchal – norms and places a high value on intergenerational solidarity. Sport here is treated as having a purely intrinsic value, as having no purpose other than to be fully itself in embodying these values. In terms of regeneration, host cities are regarded as heritage sites and the legacy of each Games a contribution to an ongoing epic narrative. I propose to call the moral entrepreneurs who carry this flag 'Olympo-patriarchs' to indicate their loyalty to the ideals of de Coubertin as the founding father of the Games. Many of them are certainly to be found within the ranks of the Olygarchy, but they also typically oppose the 'modernising' of the Games, which they regard a betrayal of the gift to the world handed down by the good Baron. In the recent history of the Games, the Athens Olympiad judged itself a success in these terms under the rubric of the Games returning to their ancient site of inspiration, although on other grounds (e.g. regeneration and governance), it is widely regarded as a failure, if not a fiasco. In London 2012, there were a few ritual nods in the direction of Olympic traditionalism, for example, in Lord Coe's speech at the torch ceremony at Mount Olympus, both otherwise it was conspicuous by its absence.

Second, there is what might be called a Para-Olympic economy of worth, and which is indeed best exemplified by the Paralympic Games. Here neither fame nor fortune, nor national pride are the key drivers, but the desire to participate in an event that represents a community of athletic practice to itself. The value added is simply the strengthening of the bonds between athletes and with the spectators and the creation of an inclusive and convivial culture of hospitality. Sport is again valued for its intrinsic properties, which are here associated with a culture of *virtuosity* combining technical accomplishment with the aesthetic appreciation of grace, beauty and sublime performance, the instrumental and expressive aspects of sport being considered equivalent forms of the pursuit of moral excellence.[16] For Para-Olympians, the regeneration value of a Games is twofold. The Games are judged by the quality they add to the urban environment, the architectural value of the infrastructure and the role of the cultural Olympiad in promoting greater appreciation of both art and sport. The material assets are considered as heirlooms to be handed over to the host community or its political representatives in the form of an endowment to be held in trust for future generations. The central task of governance is to facilitate this process and also create a framework for convivial exchanges between visitors and residents of the host city. In no Olympics has this grammar of worth been the dominant organising force, although it has sometimes articulated aspirations. In London 2012 it inspired some oppositional groups and was present in some media presentations of the Paralympics, including the opening ceremony on the theme of Enlightenment.[17]

Olympo-Patriarchs and Para-Olympians find themselves on opposite sides in most debates, the former suspecting the latter, not without reason, of radically egal-itarian sympathies, while they in turn are viewed, again with some justification, as the conservative defenders of an outdated aristocratic ideal. Nevertheless, the two camps are united in their contempt for the free marketeers, in their espousal of the amateur tradition in sport and in appreciation for the extraeconomic, aesthetic aspects of regeneration. There is thus something of a love/hate relationship between the two sets of moral entrepreneurs. The Olympic naysayers are often portrayed as curmudgeonly misanthropes and lumped together with the Olympophobes, but their objections are based on rational argument not irrational knee-jerk prejudice against sport in all its forms; the vehemence of their protests is grounded in their strong identification with the more idealistic elements in the Olympic Charter. So the conservative defenders of de Coubertinism sometimes have a sneaking sympathy for these protesters even if their actions are abhorrent. In London 2012 they joined the naysayers in denouncing the lockdown measures, albeit for very different reasons: what for one was proof positive that Britain had become a police state was for the other an assault on the festive spirit of Olympic communitas.

Mediatised economies

Many accounts of Olympic legacy politics tend to stop at this point and focus only on the direct triangulation of the compact. But there have been very few Olympiads in which conflict between moral and market economies is directly registered at a political level in a crisis of governance. One exception was Rome in 1956 where doping and the whole issue of professionalism in sport came to the fore; the moral economists closed ranks and mobilised against the corruption of sport by big money and the collusion of the IOC in the process. More usually, Olympic compacts are heavily mediated, opening up a complex field of alliances, conflict and compromise in which both moral entrepreneurship and political lobbying play a key role in establishing the different measures of value assigned to sport, to regeneration and to the governance of the Games. The legacy compact comprises a complex structure whose synergies are always partly conditioned by the forms of subsumption it entails.

There are six intermediate regimes of value whose grammars have variously played a part in the setting of Olympic agendas, and I will discuss each briefly in turn.

Media spectacle

Today the corporate media provide a stage on which the values of Olympic sport are enacted in a special dramaturgy of fame. It is the sports journalists who stand in judgement over the performance of the athletes, the gossip columnists who write the stories that secure or demolish individual reputations, the editorialists who deliver the final verdict on the Games. The value of sporting achievement is here defined and measured solely in terms of the fame that accrues. This puts a premium on public impression management and techniques of self-promotion; although it is never explicitly registered in a host city bid, it also informs much of the marketing and lobbying strategy associated with it, notably in the 'imagineering' of the host city and nation and the sports tourism which organises the pilgrim routes to the Olympic venues. The close integration of hospitality and enterprise culture has given the media a key role in the political economy of the spectacle and in marketising the Olympics. But, at the same time, the growth of social media has pulled on aspects of the moral economy, embedding sport and popular festivity in new circuits of evaluative response outside the control of the corporate media.[18]

The Los Angeles Games are generally credited with inaugurating the Olympics as a global media spectacle, with the introduction of Hollywood production values not only into the opening ceremony but in the impresario style of management adopted by the Games organisers and the way Reagonomics was used to reimagineer the Olympics. For the moral entrepreneurs of these Games, the synergy between the values of media and market as evidenced by Hollywood and also in a 'sim city' style of urbanism perfectly matched the subsumption of civic enterprise under the national-popular ideology of the American Dream.[19]

In London 2012, the iconic stories, the ones that may define what the London Games come to mean to posterity, were inevitably focused on the sensational issues that made good – or bad – news headlines: the scandals and panics about site security, the absurdity of the branding restrictions, the London cabbies' protest against the Olympic road network, and the classic moral panic about an epidemic in street crime associated with an influx of professional gangs from Romania, Lithuania and South America. Yet 2012 was also the social media games. In the age of the blogosphere, the conduits of gossip and rumour were no longer confined to the Olympic village or regulated by the official mediascape; athletes were busy tweeting and twittering to their fan bases who could tweet and twitter back, while visitors were able to instantly record and relay their reports via smartphones to friends and relatives back home. Breaking news was thus no longer the monopoly of the accredited press in the international broadcasting centre, and any analysis of the media coverage of 2012 has to include a sampling of this unofficial journalism which co-constructs its own version of events.[20]

Biopolitical

The biopolitical economy of worth is centred on the athleticised body whose internal organs and external performance are constantly monitored as measures of its health or efficiency, defined in bioenergetic terms as 'economy of effort'. This is a model body which has become increasingly marketised with the growth of medical, cosmetic, prosthetic and 'keep fit' industries organised around its maintenance and regeneration. But it also remains firmly embedded in a moral economy where it supports various pedagogies and therapies of self-improvement and, by this bias, connects to the aesthetic, ethical and emancipatory aspect of the Para-Olympian programme. In contrast, subsumed within a patriarchal frame, biopolitical regimes promote sport as a 'civilising process' for the dangerous and delinquent classes with the aim of installing deferential and decent minds in docile bodies. Articulated to national/popular ideologies, biopolitics construct an image of an organic polity purged of its 'pathological' elements. This has provided a strategy for choreographing mass support for totalitarian regimes through the media of sport and spectacular political rallies, as, for example, in the Spartakiads of the Stalinist era and the contemporary North Korean 'Arirang'.[21]

The 1936 Berlin Games, designed as a propaganda platform for National Socialism, racialised patriarchal Olympic values by subsuming the agonistics of athletic competition under the fascist vision of 'ubermensch' and the triumph of the will, while the ceremonies and stadium architecture gave an Aryan gloss to the de Coubertin's invented Hellenic traditions.[22] In London 2012, the keynote message 'Inspire a generation' – an exhortation addressed primarily to Olympic athletes as embodiments of athletic excellence – gave a traditional Olympic inflection to biopolitical values of organic solidarity, but, at the same time, the rhetorical appeal to uniting people across gender, age, race and class articulated elements of the Para-Olympian ideal.[23]

National-popular

The national-popular is a strategy for organising class and ethnic identifications into an alliance of subaltern groups against the dominant power bloc by drawing on progressive elements of popular culture and 'nationalising' them.[24] Sport in general and the Olympics in particular have been an important platform on which this is stage-managed. The aim is to encourage mass participation in sport as a way of combating disenchantment and withdrawal from the public realm and regenerating the body politic. The strategy is inherently unstable and may be pulled in either a populist or nationalistic direction, in the first case being subsumed under a civic agenda, in the second under a biopolitical regime.

In London 2012, the national-popular was directly articulated to market ideology in the headliner 'everyone's a winner', was given a strong multicultural inflection in the ceremonies and the cultural Olympiad, as well as a civic emphasis in the imagineer's portrayal of London as a host city embodying the British virtues of resilience, fortitude and a readiness to welcome strangers.

Civic

The Olympics are increasingly judged as a civic enterprise and for what they contribute to public utility and the common good. Under this rubric, sport has a purely extrinsic value and is judged by what it delivers in terms of promoting forms of rational recreation associated with community cohesion and civic pride. The governance value is defined and measured in terms of bureaucratic indicators of public well-being. All host city bids now pay lip service to this criterion, but the extent to which it is actually applied depends on the degree to which municipal authorities can exercise democratic control over outcomes as against the power of the central and state government.

There is an in-built tension between the notion of well-being as an index of community cohesion and its appropriation by the state as a platform for promoting its own version of national/popular unity. In the case of Beijing, local power was minimal as the inhabitants of the 'hutong' immigrant quarter, demolished to make way for the 'Birds Nest' arena, discovered to their cost. The priority for the Chinese authorities was to use the Olympic facilities to demonstrate the country's advent to full modernity, not preserve the city's urban fabric or heritage, and they did not mind jeopardising their carefully contrived media image in the process.[25] In the case of Barcelona, in contrast, it was the city which called the shots and controlled the regeneration process so that its local working class as far as possible remained in place, while the rhetoric of Catalan nationalism gave the governance of the Games a populist emphasis that effectively neutralised opposition.[26] In London 2012, the civic agenda pushed by the five Olympic boroughs predictably sought to maximise local benefits while minimising costs and emphasised legacy as dividend, a material payback for the symbolic debt owed by the nation to East London for hosting the Games.

Multicultural

The promotion of equal opportunities in and through sport and the combating of all forms of prejudice and discrimination are now central planks in the Olympic Charter and hence have to be built in to any compact with the host communities. The Olympic movement is formally committed to create a level playing field for all nations to compete in the Games. In practice, the language of multiculturalism is used to promote and legitimatise a number of quite different agendas: national-popular, civic and market ideologies are all now strongly multiculturalised and tend to decentre issues of 'race' equality in favour of integrationist and pluralist scenarios. Multicultural capitalism, the niche marketing of ethno-commodities, is a key aspect of how globalisation subsumes and exploits the local enterprise culture, and the Olympic hospitality and heritage industries have played an important role in that process. Multiculturalism within a patriarchal frame produces an elite cosmopolitanism in which hybridity rules OK but when given a Para-Olympian twist can become grounded in more visceral norms of multiculturalism via popular music and body language.

In London 2012, the multicultural agenda was headlined in the image struck of 'the world in a city', and the theme of cultural diversity was marketed as a unique selling point of the bid. A direct link was made between the city's economic dynamism and its demographic, implying that the wealth created in the city, the West End and Canary Wharf, where the financial services, creative industries and other branches of the knowledge economy are concentrated and where minority ethnic communities are still greatly underrepresented in the professional workforce, was somehow derivable from the rich mix of poor people in London's east end.

Environmental

Since the start of the millenium, the environmental agenda has steadily gained in importance within the Olympic movement, and now every host city bid claims to be putting on a greener Games than ever before. As a measure of sporting value, the green agenda supports physical activities that bring participants into a harmonious relationship with the natural environment and the great outdoors and advocates measures to reduce the ecological footprint of sports stadia and other facilities. But its main impact, inevitably, has been on regeneration and governance. Sustainability is now supposed to permeate every aspect of delivery and legacy, and, in so far as it does so, it cuts across and to some extent unsettles the historical compromises that have been reached between the other economies of worth. The green economy of worth is highly moralised – the very notion of sustainability involves ensuring that a generation leaves no bad debt in terms of pollution and depletion of resources behind and holds the planet earth in trust for its successors. It can also have a strong civic emphasis in local programmes to reduce carbon emissions, promote alternative sources of renewable energy *and* become marketised through the development of green industry and social enterprise.

Environmental agendas can thus mediate between the rival claims of moral and market economies, but they can also become highly politicised in their own right. In the Sydney Games, native Australian demands for civil rights, including land rights, were articulated to public concerns about the city's ecological footprint; however the close imbrication of national-popular and multicultural themes in the Olympic compact effectively subsumed environmental concerns within a civic agenda which stressed the local benefits of the Games in promoting Sydney as a world city and left the native Australian community once more out on a limb. Their bush cultures might be lauded for their sustainability, but their claims on the political economy were regarded as lacking in 'street cred'.[27]

London 2012 claimed that it was the first truly sustainable Games, and a great deal of effort was expended in using recycled and low-carbon construction material, wind turbines, solar energy and rainwater runaways in transforming the Olympic park. However, the fact remains that mega-events by definition generate a global visitor economy that leaves a large carbon footprint. In ecological terms, the legacy of London hosting the Olympics and Paralympics is equivalent to adding a city the size of Cardiff to the UK.

The key issue for judging the outcome of London 2012 is whether market ideology has been subsumed under civic enterprise, and if so is this merely a discursive manoeuvre, or has it produced substantive effects on both delivery and legacy as well as on the measures of value assigned to sport, regeneration and governance? Alternatively, was the civic project of East London's regeneration merely a cover story for the marketisation of its assets? It is already clear that the synergy between the national-popular and multicultural agendas achieved through the media spectacle created a rhetorical platform on which biopolitical and environmental themes could be segued into a seamless web of assertion about the primacy of legacy values; however, the actual connections being made on the ground between the sports venues, the regeneration of Stratford and its hinterland and the post-Games governance of the Olympic park seem to indicate that the core values of the 2012 Olympic compact, although they are still being driven by the market, are being mitigated by a civic agenda, for example, in relation to the need for affordable social housing.

Table 4.2 maps the key features of the Olympic economies of worth I have been discussing in terms of their legacy values.

Table 4.2 Legacy values

	Sport value	Regeneration value	Governance value
Market	'Winner takes all'	Gold-plated developments	Max benefits/min costs
Moral economies			
Patriarchal	Olympic family elite	Heritage sites	Intergenerational solidarity
Para-Olympian	Virtuosity	Aesthetic and heirloom sites	Culture of hospitality
Mediatised economies of worth			
Spectacle	Media reputation	Urban imagineering	Host city brand
Biopolitical	Healthy mind/body	Evolutionary growth	Organic polity
National-popular	Mass participation	'Everyone's a winner'	Class alliance
Civic	Rational recreation	Community cohesion	Bureaucratic accountability
Multicultural	Equal opportunity	Cosmopolitanism	Interethnic solidarity
Environmental	Great outdoors	Green industry	Sustainable community

The Olympic compact as a structure-in-dominance

An Olympic compact is a discursive field of manoeuvre governed by specific relations of ideological force or soft power. It can best be described as a 'structure in dominance', a concept first developed by Louis Althusser as a theoretical approach to understanding social phenomena as complex totalities without reducing them to a single underlying principle of structural causation and allowing each element a relatively autonomous effect on the whole.[28] Rejecting multicausal explanations that simply weigh factors according to their empirical visibility, the model proposes a conceptual distinction between the dominant features of a social phenomenon, whose immediate effects may be variously hierarchised and have to be empirically established in each case, and their overdetermined features which derive from present-absent structures of social contradiction that remain relatively constant. In the model of the Olympic compact outlined here, it is possible to make similar distinction between the *axis of synergy* – in which affinities, affiliations and alliances between different interests are conjuncturally negotiated (and battle lines drawn) – and *the axis of subsumption* which configures the structural field of these interactions and overdetermines their outcome. Using this model, it is possible to distinguish four relatively autonomous elements of the compact:

1 the discourses and image repertoires that thematise a compact and give it rhetorical coherence;
2 the nexus of power relations between economies of worth;
3 the grand narratives that articulate delivery and legacy evaluation;

4 the critical and oppositional discourses that problematise the compact but elements of which may also be incorporated within it.

This model offers a framework for the comparative evaluation of Olympic compacts in terms of the modes of articulation of elements, as is diagrammed in the profiles (Figure 4.1).

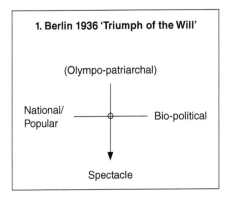

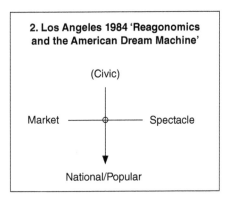

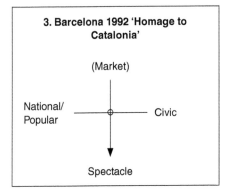

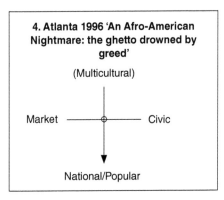

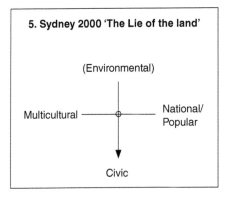

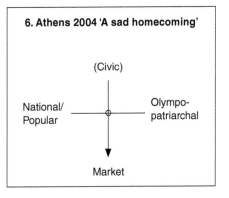

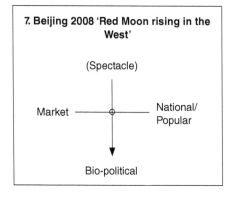

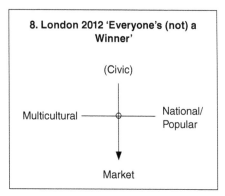

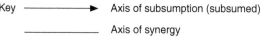

Figure 4.1 Olympiad profiles 1936–2012.

Conclusion: the Olympics as a values tournament

It has frequently been argued by commentators on the recent history of the Olympics that whatever topical or local variations in the Olympic compact struck by different host cities, there has been a convergence in the interpretation of 'Olympic values' since the end of the cold war and the advent of the globalised mega-event. It is a version of the end of ideology thesis: capitalism is the only game in town, whether the town in question be Beijing, Athens or London, Rio or Tokyo. This is to ignore the contradictions and variations within capitalism itself and to overestimate the homogenising power of globalisation and the diversity of local responses – including resistances – to it.[29]

Max Weber coined the term 'values tournament' to describe events in which different value systems might enter into competition through various forms of ritual contest.[30] The term has had some currency in the analysis of mega-events, including the Olympics, and has been further developed by anthropologists in analysing the impact of globalisation on customary forms of symbolic exchange.[31]

Values can be defined in many different ways. To a market economist, they measure the extent to which something is desired and how much people are willing to forego to get it. Value is measured by market price, and everything – and everyone – has their price. So we can ask: did the Olympics give value for money in delivering the goods to all those who in various ways bought into it? To a Marxist political economist, value is to be measured by the amount of labour that goes into the making of something, which is not fully represented in what its producers are paid; the exchange value of commodities, including that of labour, conceals the mechanisms of exploitation through which 'surplus value' or profit is extracted. From this standpoint, the 2012 Olympics represented a gigantic machinery for exploiting the workforces engaged in their preparation, enabling the companies which employed them to sustain their profitability and stay in business at a time of world recession; in terms of consumption, the Olympics are viewed as a bread-and-circus act distracting workers from the real issues, a form of popular escapism, pure and simple, at best a way of conducting the class struggle by other, more diplomatic means, at worst a poor excuse to declare a truce.

Although value is a central category in political economy, it is not confined to it. To a sociologist, values represent what groups consider to be worthwhile, what represents for them the 'good life' or what they judge to be fitting or normative: these might be values of altruism, cooperation and generosity, or individualism, competition and parsimony, but in every case, they are enacted through specific social practices. For an anthropologist, value always involves some kind of symbolic investment in an object, person or event that gives it special, often ritual, significance.[32] So here the Olympics may be judged in terms of how far they promote the dominant values of the market place or enable alternative economies of worth to flourish. Finally, for the linguist and semiotician, value is always diacritical, marking the advent of meaning through the play of difference, while for the narratologist, it marks that moment in the telling of story where the narrator reflects on the import and consequences of the actions or events described and the role of the story itself in defining their meaning. Within this interpretive framework, what counts is the reputational identity and status of a host city as relayed through various media.

Value is also important for moral philosophers. When the term 'value judgement' is attributed to some proposition about the world, it usually implies that it is biased or in some way departs from the gold standard of scientific objectivity and truth. This is especially likely to be the case where aesthetic or moral judgements are in question and where issues of personal taste or ethics are at stake. 'I think Hadid's Aquatic Centre looks a giant tongue hanging out' is not likely to be taken as an accurate or fair description of this building, but as a statement of distaste for a certain kind of modernist architecture.

The theory of judgement remains a fraught matter of academic disputation, but most philosophers agree that judgements of any kind are always based implicitly on values rather than on some rational calculation or dispassionate weighing of the evidence.[33] In similar vein, the idea promoted by the Olympic audit culture that the two can be divorced is a nonsense, because some higher order principle of evaluation is always at stake. What counts as a benefit within one economy of worth may be put down as a cost within another. What counts from one standpoint as the creation of new public amenity for Londoners represents from another as the destruction of a fragile but valuable ecosystem and local community resource.

The implication of this perspective is that far from there being a consensus about a single fixed outcome of an Olympics, there is an ongoing struggle between different strategies or criteria of evaluation, especially where these are espoused by particular interest groups including oppositional groups. In the era of 'Legacy Games', the Olympic compact is continually being renegotiated as bargains are struck over the distribution of resources and amenity between local authorities, community groups, central government and other stakeholders. Although the initial compact sets the limits and conditions of these subsequent negotiations, their outcome is far from a foregone conclusion. As far as London 2012 is concerned, there is still a lot to play for in terms of securing benefits to the communities of East London. But that, as they say, is another story.[34]

Notes

1 For a critique of audit culture, see the contributions to Strathern, M. (Ed.) (2000) *Audit cultures: anthropological studies in accountability, ethics and the academy.* London: Routledge.

2 Ibid.

3 See Rose, N. (1999) *Governing the soul: the shaping of the private self.* New York: Free Association Books.

4 See McKenzie, J. (2001) *Perform or else: from discipline to performance.* New York: Routledge.

5 See Solnit, R. (2003) *Motion studies.* London: Bloomsbury. For an account of how aesthetic and scientific studies of the body-in-movement converged, see also Budd, M. (1997) *The sculpture machine: physical culture and body politics in the age of empire.* Houndsmill: Macmillan. For a critique of contemporary 'body politics', see Heller, A. *et al.* (Eds.) (1996) *Biopolitics: the politics of the body, race and nature.* Aldershot: Avebury. Cherniavski, E. (2006) *Incorporations: race, nation and the body politics of capitalism.* Minneapolis: University of Minnesota Press.

6 See Rabinbach, A. (1992) *The human motor: energy, fatigue and the rise of modernity.* Berkeley: University of California Press.

7 For a discussion of the relation between techniques of observation, measurement and governance as regimes of capitalist modernity, see Crary, J. (2002) *Techniques of the observer.* Cambridge, MA: MIT Press.

8 See Strathern, *Audit culture*, p. 22, and also her *Commons and borderlands.* Wantage: Sean Kingston.

9 Department for Culture, Media and Sport (DCMS) (2009) 'London 2012 Olympic and Paralympic Games impacts and legacy evaluation framework'. Final report. Prepared by PricewaterhouseCoopers LLP for the DCMS.

10 There is an irony to the fact that impact studies, with their robust image of measuring extrinsic effects, should be the methodology of choice for evaluating auto-poesis and that an approach which started out life as a means of empowering local communities to defend themselves against large-scale redevelopment should now be the main way regeneration agencies manage conflict and achieve consensus. See Obliggiato, J. (2005) *From community empowerment to conflict management: a short history of impact studies.* London: Gower.

11 For an economistic approach to host city comparisons, see Preuss, H. (2009) *Staging the Olympics: a comparative guide 1972–2008.* Cheltenham: Edward Elgar. A more urbanistic strategy of comparison is offered by the contributors to Gold, J. R. and Gold, M. M. (2007) *Olympic cities: city agendas, planning and the World Games 1896–2012.* London: Routledge. For an overview, see Hiller, H. (2003) 'Toward a science of Olympic outcomes: the urban legacy' in C. Kennett *et al.* (Eds.), *The legacy of the Olympic Games 1984–2000.* Lausanne: International Olympic Committee. For a general overview of legacy studies, see Dyreson, M. and Mangan, J. A. (2010) *Olympic legacies: intended and unintended.* London: Routledge, and also Smith, M. (2009) *When the Games come to town.* London: LERI University of East London.

12 See, for example, ESRC/LOCOG (2010) *Olympic Games impact study – London 2012 pre-Games report.*

13 For what follows I have drawn on the framework proposed by Boltanski, L. and Thevenot, L. (2006) *On justification: the economies of worth.* Oxford: Princeton University Press. The French regulation school approach to economic sociology has

been criticised for its overreliance on discourse analysis. Graeber's (2001) *Towards an anthropological theory of value*. New York: Palgrave, has the advantage of grounding a critique of value theory and evaluation processes in a wider analysis of their political and ideological conditions of existence.

14 The term 'moral entrepreneur' was first coined by Howard Becker in *Outsiders* (London: Free Press of Glencoe, 1966) and was developed further by Stanley Cohen in his study of public responses to 1960s youth cultures: *Folk devils and moral panics* (London: Routledge, 2002).

15 See Rutheiser, C. (1996) *Imagineering Atlanta: the politics of place in the city of dreams*. London: Verso.

16 This perspective is sometimes described as 'aretism' to contrast it with the agonistic model of achievement-oriented competitive sport. For the Ancient Greeks, the meaning of *arête* was close to the Roman notion of *virtu*, a moral or spiritual quality which any citizen might possess but which was demonstrated by political actions which made them stand out from the crowd. As such it lacked the elitist and aristocratic connotations which 'excellence' has taken on within Olympo-Patriarchal culture. See Arendt's *The human condition* for a general discussion of this term, and for its take-up within the Olympics debate, see Hollowchak, M. and Reid, H. L. (2011) *Aretism: an ancient philosophy for a modern world*. Lanham, MD: Lexington Books.

17 For further discussion, see Phil Cohen's (2013) *On the wrong side of the tracks*. London: Lawrence & Wishart, pp. 284–310.

18 See Sugden, J. and Tomlinson, A. (Eds.) (2012) *Watching the Olympics – politics, power, representation*. London: Routledge.

19 On Los Angeles as a pre-eminent city of the American dream, see Soja, E. (1996) *Third space: journeys to Los Angeles and other real-and-imagined places*. Oxford: Blackwell; and also Davis, M. (1990) *City of quartz: excavating the future in Los Angeles*. London: Verso.

20 See the contributions to Tremaine, M. (Ed.) (2007) *Blogging, citizenship and the future of the media*. London: Routledge.

21 For the role of national-popular ideology in the Olympics, see the contributions to Tomlinson, A. and Young, C. (Eds.) (2006) *National identity and global sports events*. New York: State University of New York Press. See also the contributions to Foster, S. (Ed.) (1995) *Choreographing history*. Bloomington: Indiana University Press.

22 See Hilton, C. (2006) *Hitler's Olympics: the 1936 Berlin Olympic Games*. London: The History Press.

23 See *On the wrong side of the track?*, pp. 162–204.

24 See ibid., chapter 8 for further discussion of the role of the national-popular in the 2012 ceremonies.

25 See Brownell, S. (2008) *Beijing's Games: what the Olympics mean to China*. Beijing: Rowman & Littlefield.

26 See Hargreaves, J. (2000) *Freedom for Catalonia: Catalan nationalism, Spanish identity and the Barcelona games*. New York: Cambridge University Press.

27 See Cashman, R. (2006) *The bitter-sweet awakening: the legacy of the Sydney 2000 Games*. Sydney: Walla Walla Press.

28 See Althusser, L. and Balibar, E. (1970) *Reading capital*. London: New Left Books.

29 For a critique of globalisations and ethnography of its locally situated meanings, see Knowles, C. (2014) *Flip-flop: a journey through globalisation's back roads*. London: Pluto Press.

30 See Weber, M. (1958) *From Max Weber: essays in sociology*. New York: Oxford University Press; and the discussion in Sykes, K. (2001) *Arguments in anthropology: an introduction to the critical theory of the gift*. London: Routledge.

31 See Guttmann, A. (1992) *The Olympics: a history of the modern games*. Urbana: University of Illinois Press. Appadurai, A. (1981) *The social life of things: commodities in cultural perspective*. Cambridge: Cambridge University Press.

32 For a comprehensive discussion of different theories of value, see Graeber, D. (2001) *Towards an anthropological theory of value: the false currency of our own dreams.* Basingstoke: Palgrave. See also Appadurai, A. (1986) *Commodities and the politics of value in the social life of things.* Cambridge: Cambridge University Press.

33 On the debate about the moral and epistemological bases of judgement, see Rorty, R. (2007) *Philosophy as cultural politics.* Cambridge: Cambrige University Press; and MacIntyre, A. (2007) *After virtue: a study in moral theory.* Notre Dame, IN: University of Notre Dame Press.

34 This is the subject of ongoing ethnographic research and community arts projects being undertaken by Living Maps in and around the Olympic park, which will be reported in *A Hollow Legacy?* (edited by Phil Cohen and Paul Watt) to be published by Palgrave Macmillan in 2016. Further information from http://www.Livingmaps.org.uk.

5 Governance

Lessons from London 2012

John Lock

Introduction

Governance of the Olympic and Paralympic Games is complex, diverse and very large scale. It is intended to review here how London 2012 approached governance challenges, characteristics of London's arrangements, questions arising and what can be understood which may be relevant to the organisation of future Games and their legacies.

Governance covers the legal requirements of the two sets of Games. It covers the arrangements for creating and managing Games-ready venues and facilities, from athlete accommodation to mass catering, to the technologies which underpin event management, to global TV distribution. It covers city management in terms of transport, visitor accommodation, health services, policing and so on. It covers national and international systems such as security and visitor management at ports of entry. Governance recognises the requirements, firstly, of the International Olympic Committee (IOC) and the International Paralympic Committee (IPC) and then of the administrations of the host city and nation in terms of how they conceive of the task of delivering the Games. In other words, some elements are mandated, but others are not. Governance of legacy is principally a local choice. In the UK, the approach to legacy followed other decisions; eventually it was decided that the Mayor of London should be responsible for London, initially through the London Development Agency (LDA) though this was later abolished and succeeded by the Olympic Park Legacy Company (OPLC) and then the London Legacy Development Corporation (LLDC), and the government for the rest of the UK (e.g. Weymouth where the sailing events were to be held). The government Olympic Executive had a coordinating role across the whole panoply of delivery.

To state the obvious, no two countries are the same, no two host cities are the same. 2008 and 2012 are close in time, but Beijing/China and London/UK are not close in nature, politically, geographically, economically, socially or culturally. Notwithstanding common and comparable arrangements for every Games required by the IOC and IPC, Games governance necessarily changes from one host city to another. In certain respects, a particular Games could provide a model for other Games; in others, it will be more helpful to consider each Games as generating experience and knowledge which may inform future Games. Replicability is likely to be particular, not over-arching. The context-specific focus of one or other Games may well affect forms of governance and also test their effectiveness differently.

London 2012 seems set to be thought of as the Games which raised the bar in terms of planning and delivering a positive legacy. Evaluation of their governance has a standardised dimension in the sense of the IOC and IPC views of its success in meeting their requirements. Governance arrangements should also be assessed in terms of their delivery of legacy if legacy is now a significant factor. This perspective may assign a lower value to outcomes that the IOC/IPC valued if the London Games comes in due course to be regarded as unsuccessful in delivering legacy. The contrary is also true.

London, therefore, did not constitute a particular model of governance, or of legacy, which Pyeongchang or Tokyo or bidders for subsequent Games can or must simply copy. However, the London thematic stress on legacy it appears, will serve to intensify the seriousness with which those cities and their nations choose or are required by the IOC/IPC to respond to the question of how they will achieve legacy.

Previously, it can be asserted that cities dealt more with the 'aftermath' of the Games than they planned 'legacy', for example, planning long-term city change arising from how impacts of their Games were channelled. Olympic venues and zones returned to prior uses leaving little trace (Los Angeles), gained other immediate uses (Munich, Atlanta), were left idle (Athens) or a more iterative approach was adopted which over time worked out solutions (Sydney). Barcelona is an exception to this – city change was anticipated and has occurred. London though has made the connection between Games and legacy far more explicit. It has also segued governance arrangements between the two.

What the London Games seems to have done, therefore, is to change the relative importance of legacy – to become a significant determinant of how a city approaches bidding to host a Games and to make legacy a more salient component of how people internationally think about what constitutes success. Legacy and governance are now intertwined themes. We can, therefore, think of governance in four stages: deciding to bid and bid preparation (open-ended), delivering the facilities and arrangements necessary to hold the Games (7 years), Games-time (around 7 weeks for both Games and the change-over period), legacy (open-ended).

The governance of legacy

The governance of legacy is now a question appropriate to successive Games and open to comparative study. A number of bidding rounds and Games will need to occur before legacy governance is validated as a long-term or permanent matter. We can at this point though identify that legacy has become an additional, significant factor which governance at local, city and national levels have to consider. If a reminder of that were necessary, the loud, mass and violent public reaction to public spending on the 2014 FIFA Brazil World Cup indicates that value and outcome can be questions reaching beyond the sum of sport occurring with global visibility. Governance here is in part about who is responsible; it is also about who is able to be responsible. A common aspect of the Sydney and London Games was local government (Auburn in Sydney and the five host boroughs of Greenwich, Hackney, Newham, Tower Hamlets and Waltham Forest in London) making it clear publicly that they felt sidelined from decisions which would have direct, long-term effects on their areas long after the Games and long after national governments had lost interest. A difference though is that in London the local authorities did become considerably more involved which appears to have had a clear facilitating effect in terms of a broad common view of legacy and its delivery in East London at least.

Owen (2002) examines local community and municipal opposition to the form of implementation of the Sydney Games, not least more centralised planning, more relaxed planning regulation and more involvement of the private sector in government processes. Owen states that local activism secured benefits from the Games which presumably would not otherwise have been forthcoming. In London, the host boroughs were necessarily engaged in questions like planning permissions and local security arrangements. They were at the outset, though, outside the curtilage of key decisions about legacy having had only limited engagement in the bid process. In some discrete aspects, the preparation of the Candidate File for the IOC was open to wider engagement, but its core formulation was tightly controlled in the space between government, the Mayor of London and key British sports bodies.

The London Organising Committee of the Olympic and Paralympic Games (LOCOG) was chaired by Lord Sebastian Coe. Board members comprised UK government, Mayor of London's office, British Olympic Association, British Paralympic Association, British members of the IOC, former Olympic athletes, as well as other members with special expertise. Among the latter were the elected Mayors of Hackney and Newham and the Council Leaders of Tower Hamlets (later an elected mayor) and Waltham Forest. There were local authority members of the London 2012 bid board as well. There was no local authority membership of the board of the LDA which undertook the first stages of Olympic park development before the Olympic Delivery Authority (ODA) was set up by Act of Parliament to deliver the facilities and venues needed for the Games, particularly the Olympic park. The LDA was an agency of the Mayor of London.

Four local authority members, though, sat on the ODA Planning Committee reflecting the fact; although the ODA was a statutory planning body with development control powers, it required the four boroughs adjacent to the park to participate directly to ensure this worked as well as possible. The Mayor of London did have an appointee on the ODA board. LDA's role in terms of initiating work on legacy was subsumed in the OPLC, whose shareholders were the Mayor of London and UK government. OPLC's board did have local authority representation from the four boroughs adjacent to the Olympic park. OPLC was succeeded in 2012 by the London Legacy Development Corporation (LLDC), a mayoral development corporation owned by the Mayor of London. It has the planning and land-owning powers of the ODA which OPLC did not. The local authority inputs remain; UK government no longer plays any direct role.

Initially, the consistent memberships across the main bodies comprising governance structures were UK government and the Mayor of London. As the debate about legacy began to move from the headlines in the London bid to more specific questions related, for example, to economic and housing land uses, the Olympic Park Regeneration Strategy Group (OPRSG) was established which comprised two government ministers – the Olympics Minister and the Secretary of State for Communities and Local Government – the Mayor of London and the Mayor of Newham on behalf of the five (later six with the inclusion of Barking and Dagenham) host boroughs. OPRSG oversaw a process of multilevel dialogue between government at local, regional and national levels which resulted in the creation of a Strategic Regeneration Framework. The SRF (2009) established the principal of 'convergence' that 'within 20 years the communities who host the 2012 Games will have the same social and economic chances as their neighbours across London'. Since its publication, there have been four reports on the convergence indicators set out in the SRF. Convergence is also a principle enshrined in the London Plan, the Mayor of London's statutory planning framework for London. Only by combining their efforts did the host boroughs in London get into formal governance structures.

Two years after the Games, it is becoming clearer that this participation had successes and limits. Lord Toby Harris, Chairman of the House of Lords Select Committee on Olympic and Paralympic legacy, addressed a seminar the day before the government's response to his Committee's report on legacy (House of Lords Select Committee on Olympic and Paralympic legacy, 2013) was published. He spoke of the 'incredible degree of cooperation' by an 'alphabet soup of organisations' which was essential to make the Games work. There was top-down pressure obviously, he acknowledged, but in the UK not a monolithic state proceeding by undemocratic fiat.

This might be characterised then as a huge flotilla of contributing bodies whose combining self-organisation and self-determination enabled the ensemble to proceed towards a common point. The common point arrived at – a successful Games – was via a set of mutually recognised principles or pressures, including an unmoveable deadline, a (re)fixed budget, security aims, numbers of people to be transported and so on. The mutual recognition points are important – bodies acknowledge what other bodies have to achieve and pool effort to enable all to do what they have to. There may be arguments, but they are temporary because the fixed deadline requires a resolution and that resolution has to relate to the common arrival point; the risk of anything else is too great. Political control of the mayoralty of London changed in 2008 and of the UK government in 2010. Neither change made a significant difference to the conduct of preparation for the Games.

Harris also commented that once the deadlines are removed, as they are after the Games, unless they are replaced with a second set of principles tied in some irresilable way to legacy, then the focus on legacy is likely to be characterised by organisations, capacity, finance, attention, etc. steadily peeling away leaving only those with a directly engaged responsibility or aspiration. This has happened to an evident degree. The UK government effectively pulled out of legacy over the period 2012–2013, not least because the Mayor of London wanted to exercise clear responsibility albeit without the question of long-term resourcing being in any way answered. Once LLDC has spent the transformation budget allocated to the park, it will only have such resource as the Mayor of London can find over and above income from land which it has to develop to repay the Treasury and the Lottery for funds used to pay for the Games. In the current context of public sector finances, few would be optimistic about this. It is worth noting that these repayments came about from an agreement between the Mayor of London and government as part of the discussion about bridging the funding gap which opened up once it became clear that the original London 2012 cost estimates were far too low. The local authorities were not party to this and would have opposed it as self-evidently it meant that most gains from post-Games land development – in a scenario where land value would almost certainly be higher as a result of reme- diated land, park environment, enhanced transport links, etc. – would not fully accrue to the local area. This is revealing in a context of the national interest in terms of repayment supervening on the city area interest in terms of regeneration, notwithstanding the national, regional and local recognition of regeneration as the driving rationale for hosting the Games.

On the basis of its evaluation, government declared the Games a great suc- cess which signalled its exit save for the fig-leaf of a small outpost in the Cabi- net Office headed up by Lord Sebastian Coe who had led LOCOG. It had no budget and a skeleton staff with no responsibility for the further management of or funding of legacy actions. There was no senior government minister with responsibility for legacy across the government. Simultaneously, LOCOG was wound up and the ODA reduced to a rump with the transfer of its land use plan- ning functions and powers to LLDC. The majority of the special structures which superintended preparation for and delivery of the Games nationally disappeared or are disappearing. Those specific to the Olympic park continue with ongoing local authority involvement at board level. London's legacy governance arrange- ments are in effect at sub-city level, whereas Games governance arrangements operated at local, regional, national and international levels (the latter in respect of the IOC and IPC and security collaborations). Though Lord Coe and others talked of the Games as 'inspiring a generation' and LOCOG operated its international education and national Inspire Mark and volunteer programmes, all apparently very successfully, any substantive continuation action seems to have evaporated in terms of national imperative or structure.

Reflecting this shrinkage in focus and governance, there was also a radical decline in the public sector resource to invest in legacy in the long term. LLDC's immediate destiny is to focus on getting new development to occur at a set of iden- tified locations around its designated area. Treasury and Lottery repayments will mean that surpluses generated leave the area despite the fact that this is, according to both the original London bid and the SRF, the focus for enhancement through legacy. Once the Crossrail railway is opened in 2018/19, UK government investment in infrastructure in the area will tail off further (noting that the financing of Crossrail has anyway come in significant part from London not HM Treasury). From 2010, when the Coalition government came into power, the 'austerity' programme has removed very large sums from local authority budgets with an immense squeeze on revenue funding in particular. The Coalition has abandoned previous policy towards regeneration of Thames Gateway, including East London. It should be acknowledged that these choices might have been different had the credit crunch not occurred. However, it can also be observed that government did not see national backing for legacy as an unavoidable priority, either in London or more widely.

London made a very rapid start on legacy with the partial reopening of the Queen Elizabeth Olympic Park one year after the opening day of the Olympic Games. The strategic legacy momentum after five years could well be the extent to which, within a statutory planning framework, predominantly private sector activity at new development locations creates jobs, housing and amenities. There is an obvious question as to who benefits from this and whether the legacy governance structures, even with formal local authority involvement, are strong enough to channel outcomes to tackle disadvantage as the convergence principle advocates.

A conclusion from this must be that while inclusion in governance is necessary to exert influence over decision making and policy, that inclusion and efficacy of governance can be systematically vitiated without adequate resource and powers. Sitting at the table is essential, but just sitting at the table is not the same as delivering legacy. Further, although democratic local involvement was achieved by the engagement of local authorities which continues, bodies such as LDA, LOCOG, ODA, OPRSG, OPLC and LLDC are different in kind from the kinds of regeneration partnership which preceded them over the period from 1980 to 2006. After intense public argument about the nature and behaviour of the London Docklands Development Corporation, particularly during the 1980s, a style of regeneration partnership working emerged that started with the City Challenge programme and continued through successive rounds of programmes of the Single Regeneration Budget, New Deal for Communities, Neighbourhood Renewal and so on. This was highly engaged with surrounding community interests. Not inevitably good, not always successful, but nonetheless this style of working maintained a sense of 'doing with' not 'doing to' and had local residents and business affected by change round the table, as it were.

The Games did not work in this way. This was partly for unavoidable reasons, for example, it is necessary to put up the security which surrounds a large and dangerous building site such as the Olympic park. However, for a local population used to the idea that they had a voice in the continuing dialogue about regeneration, the Games were experienced as dislocating in some quarters. There were and are large community information exercises. There have been very large statutory planning consultations and such consultation will continue development by development. However, that is not the same as having a voice and an influence on decision making by partnership-based bodies meeting in public. Once the time-bound

Olympic ball starts rolling, backed by legislation, quite a lot of dialogue about where it is going and what will follow becomes cosmetic. The fact that the London Games were popularly seen as a success and the reopening of the park was also successful undoubtedly has ameliorated this so far. It has yet to be demonstrated though, for simple time reasons thus far, that post-Games development will deliver the local jobs and genuinely affordable housing that are expected. If they do, the argument will presumably die away. If they do not, the likelihood is of this failure being attributed to local interests and needs not being able to get sufficient purchase on the whole process from the outset.

It is important to enter a caveat here: this is *not* to say that legacy is a failure seen at autumn 2014. This is a conclusion neither intended nor implied. The Games promoted infrastructure development in East London and elsewhere that would otherwise have occurred later or perhaps not at all. Collaboration between Westfield Shopping Towns and the ODA kept the Stratford City shopping development on track in 2008 when the credit crunch caused Westfield to mothball temporarily most other developments in its global portfolio. This opened the door through collaboration between Westfield, its tenants, Newham Council and the government agency Job Centre Plus for some 3,000 of the *c.*10,000 jobs created on opening in 2011 to go to jobless local residents. Job attainment measures continue. The sports, leisure and amenity legacy of the Olympic Park is real, with substantive local and international impacts. It is growing and the signs are that major events will continue to come to the park for the foreseeable future with delivery partners committed to ensuring wider public benefit. If the park successfully attracts occupants such as University College London, the Victoria & Albert Museum and Saddlers Wells (dance), as is planned, then these are assets from which prospectively real value in the long term can be gained locally through intelligent collaboration. There are, therefore, many real, positive and prospectively lasting legacy impacts already in view after just 2 years.

The issue though remains how the overall scale of value which arises from legacy is shared and whether or not legacy governance is strong enough to influence local flows of benefit on a large scale. Otherwise, legacy governance will be attempting with fairly meagre powers and resources to mediate a landscape of change which is highly dynamic, very competitive and very unequal. This prompts the observation that legacy as a large-scale phenomenon in one or more large cities cannot realistically be separated out from national policy and city capacity to manage change.

It is also worth observing that much of the cost of hosting the Games is infrastructure. Games-oriented governance tends to scrutinise schedule, then cost. The deadline of Games-time trumps everything else. However, the cost of infrastructure is great. Having a 'good Games', as London did, with its volunteers being one example of notable success, is clearly a value for money outcome from the investment. Much value though ought also to accrue in legacy for the payback to be at a scale which really justifies the investment. Various London observers noted that what was put in place for the London Games could all have been done at lower cost without the Games – there would, for example, have been no post-Games transformation process to fund – and probably quicker. The London process did not overall concretise the general promises of legacy during the planning phase, i.e. create a solid baseline of expectations which could be monitored. Pre-Games governance of legacy in that sense was not as strong as it might have been, notwithstanding real legacy achievements which are materialising. It did not, for example, manage a transition of the successful volunteer effort into a post-Games programme. Rather, volunteering was split between several agencies, and while still there (LLDC and Longon borough of Newham both have sizeable ongoing commitments to support volunteering), as a national phenomenon it is a shadow of what was marshalled in 2012 which many consider a serious and avoidable waste of civic potential. Master planning of the Olympic park did create a framework which put high-level numbers on housing and jobs, which have been revised and will be revised again by what actually happens. It is possible to conclude that if legacy had been spelled out at the outset of the bid as a detailed proposition rather than a general rationale (regeneration of East London) susceptible to wide interpretation, it would have been easier to frame in governance terms, more consistently owned through each stage of the process and more strongly articulated in terms of long-term outcomes.

Lessons from London 2012

A growing literature on the London Games and governance is emerging, which enables this London experience to be put into context. MacRury and Poynter (2009) point to governance as central to the objective of achieving urban transformation through the agency of the Games and provide a typology of approaches in past Games. They identify governance as critical to the resolution of possible tensions between the aims of delivering the Games in specific locations and at specific times and ensuring that lasting local benefit results. Without effective governance from planning through to Games-time to post-Games legacy delivery, urban transformation is unlikely to occur optimally. Without the structures of the host boroughs as a group and the OPRSG, local influence on decisions affecting legacy would have been smaller and principally confined to the ODA Planning Committee where local authority members were in a minority.

Noting the sheer scale of the modern Games, Jennings (2012) explores the governance of risk in bidding for and hosting the Games and looks at the roles of decision makers and organisations both historically and contemporaneously. Jennings makes the same point as Raco (2012) that the Games should not be seen as outside of the wider context but as an inextricable part of it. Raco makes the case that governments, in their search for risk offset, hand very large contracts to very large private companies which exert considerable influence within public decision-making structures. In this sense, even in open, democratic societies, there is much which is not open to easy public scrutiny; the Games exemplify that governance is a mixed economy with mixed access. The delivery capability of large private companies gets those which win contracts inside the decision-making processes. Their roles can influence what is affordable or achievable in construction terms, for example. The same is true of those which become corporate sponsors. They may not participate in decision making in the same way, but the protection of their interests most certainly is a driver of how the Games are delivered. Commercial interests affect the course of decision making, sitting within some sections of Games/legacy governance while being largely or entirely insulated from others.

Commissioned by government and drawing on interviews with politicians, executives and public officials, Norris *et al.* (2013) set out a 'lessons learned' view of the London Games addressing them from the perspective of how government conducts programme and project management. (On those specific issues, it is salutary that Anthony King and Sir Ivor Crewe in their book *The Blunders of Our Governments* (2013), which is a relentless and excoriating critique of the competence of successive UK governments and senior ministers, praise the London Games as 'the one indubitable domestic success of [Prime Minister] David Cameron's first three years in office'.) Norris *et al.* draw out conclusions, for example, relevant to city and national governance, the management of major sporting events and the operation of public–private partnership. The report of the House of Lords Select Committee on Olympic and Paralympic Legacy (2013) comments on the requirement for strong legacy governance to be in place for as long as significant legacy development occurs and for there to be clear and appropriate political responsibility.

In this light, the lessons from London in terms of governance will derive from understanding how London's governance operated and what specific characteristics it had, positive or negative. Aspects of this may be replicable, while others may simply highlight something which will play out differently in other cities. Exchange of knowledge in terms of what is replicable can be assumed to proceed relatively straightforwardly, either through formal IOC/IPC mechanisms or intercity/intergovernment visits or repeated use of delivery agents such as private companies. The drivers are also perhaps relatively clear and include compliance with IOC/IPC requirements such as branding, sports regulations and risk offset in terms of construction timescales.

Key questions prospectively focus more on political concerns, cultural issues and different or competing values. From a governance perspective, they will derive from how policy and decision making addressed 'who the Games are for?', 'how benefit was identified and determined to be achieved, or not?' and 'who had influence and who didn't?'. The London 2012 emphasis on legacy makes this more interesting as questions pertain to longer timescales and become more contextual. When the point of the Games is 'having a good Games', the timescale is the point at which the decision to bid is made, the bid period, the decision and the 7-year run into Games-time – perhaps a decade in all. When the point of the Games is both to have a good Games and to harness the impact of a mega-event to site-specific urban transformation, say, that timescale might triple or quadruple. It might warrant a longer pre-bid planning period as well as an extended post-Games development period. This, in turn, warrants a hard look at governance, powers and resources marshalled formally over long management periods, not just the classic Games-period from bid success to closing ceremony.

Governance as a concept orients towards the city and its proposed needs, then to the IOC/IPC, then back to the city. Thus, while governance has obvious and large elements related specifically to the Olympics and Paralympics, in other ways it is ineluctably connected to city and national systems for doing things. Games governance places large demands on these systems, but they predate the Games period and continue after it. The Games sit within an approach to governance and can thus reveal aspects of how it works. Examining how this happened in London can inform how future bid cities think through their own processes.

Conclusion: the agenda of value

A focus on legacy rather than Games building or Games delivery is obviously not confined to London. Barcelona (1992) is the exemplar, but Munich (1972) led to a planned incorporation of the Olympic park into the city as a new city district. Facilities constructed for Atlanta in 1996 became permanent elements of the city – Georgia Tech took over the aquatics centre, while the remodelled stadium became known as Turner Fields and was home to the Atlanta Braves baseball team.

London though is at a different scale and scale is an issue, as described above, in terms of the urban area in scope, the size of financial input, the size of flows of benefit from redevelopment and the capability of governance to influence who benefits. Atlanta's population is about 450,000, Munich's 1.3 million, Barcelona's 1.6 million. London's almost 8.2 million. The cost of the London Games, though not as much as Beijing or Sochi, was significantly greater than Munich, Barcelona or Atlanta. The Atlanta Games were the last held in a city that is essentially regional. Every Summer Games since Sydney in 2000 have been held in the city in the host nation that is the largest or the capital or both. Tokyo in 2020 continues that trend, noting that the other close contenders – Istanbul and Madrid – also fit the pattern. Obviously, the Games have often been held in large or capital cities, but not at anything like the scale of Games as they are now. Scale and the politics of scale are now central governance questions. The Games have been controversial in the past – 1936 in Berlin, the Munich bomb, the Montreal and Moscow boycotts, for example. However, controversy has derived from issues particular to the moment. Scale is different – it is now an unavoidable question for every Summer Games and possibly, after Sochi, every Games winter and summer.

London 2012 is the point where governance, legacy and scale intersect. This did not apply in Munich, Barcelona or Atlanta – all were coherently local in their way. Munich was not thought of differently because of the Games (leaving aside the tragedy of the bombing); their outcome created local benefit specific to the city. Barcelona was a Catalan project, not a Spanish Games, at least in the minds of the city's leadership and population; the Games were very much part of the reassertion of identity post-Franco. Atlanta was a city business project, not a US national project; the object was to promote Atlanta. In Beijing the question of legacy perhaps did not really arise in the London sense, despite controversy about clearing parts of the city for the Games. It was understood that the Beijing Games were very much a national identity project, a giant coming-out party for an emerging global power. In London, an undisputed world city, the declared logic of the Games was the regeneration of East London; they were a legacy project from the outset. And they occurred at a scale in a part of London where it continues to be argued that large-scale investment is required to drive large-scale change, as it has been for decades. Albeit different, one component of Rio's Games has a similar logic – city improvement. Tokyo is different; the host city for 2020 appears to have won IOC approval by presenting itself as the safe pair of hands with much in place and the cash to make the Games work. However, the Tokyo Games are intended to renew infrastructure, notably a new national stadium, and promote further development of the Tokyo Bay area and islands there which have been a long-term development target since they were demilitarised. The long lists of self-declared bid cities for 2024 and 2028, predominantly large cities and capital cities across five continents, contain many that would need to think of the Games in terms of city development for their case to work.

Questions about London's legacy and its governance, therefore, have a potential reach forward into city governance across the world, informing how bid cities frame the governance appropriate to themselves in terms of legacy and scale. The London experience suggests four areas of question.

1   In a governance nexus inevitably dominated by city–IOC–government– delivery agency relationships, how are other voices heard? How successfully can they influence policy and decisions pertaining to legacy?
2   How is legacy defined? What is it, what will it do? Who is it for? How is it appropriate to its proposed beneficiaries? How will this be measurable? How does it work over time?
3   What decision-making processes and structures own legacy, from bid inception to preparation for Games-time to Games-time itself and well beyond?
4   Is this an area or city or national level question? Do the decision-making processes and structures, at all appropriate levels, cumulatively have the capacity, resource, power and longevity to succeed?

These very much comprise an agenda of value: what value is generated, who controls it, who gets it? Who wins, who loses? This interest in value is increasingly inextricably connected to considerations of scale, cost and impact. The London 1948 Games were the first to have more than 50 nations present. The 1968 Mexico City Games passed 100 for the first time. Athens 2004 passed the 200 mark. The Olympic and Paralympic Summer Games doubled in size in a generation on this measure. Controversy over the cost of the Olympics is not new. Montreal after the 1976 Summer Games was saddled with debt for three decades and is far from the only example. By contrast, the 1984 Los Angeles Games were successful financially, the first since 1932. However, value has not been as *unavoidably* high profile an issue as it now appears to have become with apparently every Games inevitably costing a huge sum to mount. With virtually every nation in the world participating across some or all of 26 sports, it appears to have become impossible for the Games to be 'modest'. London Games, proposed in 2008 by London

Mayor Boris Johnson as 'cosier' and 'more intimate' than Beijing, were implemented with exemplary project management and delivered to (a revised) budget. Although cheap by comparison with Beijing and Sochi, they still cost over £9 billion to put on.

Issues of cost and success have always been questions of governance for cities and the Games. Governance has always been political. In the context of a new focus on scale and the gigantic costs of Beijing and Sochi, what London points to is an attempt by Games governance to manage that debate by adding legacy to the credit side. What has resulted is experience – still playing out – which contains real and genuine success, but also reveals how the value questions do not evaporate.

References

House of Lords Select Committee on Olympic and Paralympic legacy (2013) *Keeping the flame alive: the Olympic and Paralympic legacy*. London: The Stationery Office Limited. Available at: http://www.publications.parliament.uk/pa/ld201314/ldselect/ldolympic/78/7802.htm

Jennings, W. (2012) *Olympic risks (Executive politics and governance)*. London: Palgrave Macmillan.

King, A. and Crewe, I. (2013) *The blunders of our governments*. London: Oneworld.

MacRury, I. and Poynter, G. (2009) *London's Olympic legacy: a 'Thinkpiece' report prepared for the OECD and Department for Communities and Local Government*. London: London East Research Institute, University of East London. Available at: http://www.uel.ac.uk/londoneast/documents/20101008-CLG-OECD-2012.pdf

Norris, E., Rutter, J. and Medland, J. (2013) *Making the Games: what government can learn from London 2012*. London: Institute for Government. Available at: http://www.instituteforgovernment.org.uk/sites/default/files/publications/Making%20the%20Games%20final_0.pdf

Owen, K. A. (2002) 'The Sydney 2000 Olympics and urban entrepreneurialism: local variations in urban governance'. *Australian Geographical Studies*, 40(3): 323–336.

Raco, M. (2012) 'Taking the politics out of the Games – privatisation and the London Olympics', *The Occupied Times*, available at: http://theoccupiedtimes.org/?p=5850

6 Rehashing and new knowledge about the Games

A bibliometric analysis and assessment of Routledge's special Olympic journals issues

Mike Collins and Vassil Girginov

This chapter is dedicated to the memory of Mike Collins, an academic with fierce intellect and integrity, a mentor and friend and a great human being.

Introduction

Haggerty (2011) wrote, 'mega-events such as the Olympics have become vehicles for different forms of transformation. To date, however, such events have largely escaped mainstream academics scrutiny. With the Olympics arriving at the heart of London this situation is apt to change.' A home-based Olympic Games was an obvious opportunity for the British academic community in particular to study and publish new theoretical and empirical material of the Games and the Olympic movement and its values. Indeed, more material than ever before has appeared in scores of books, reports and hundreds of articles. Some might say, what apart from particular London-based material was there to be added to the already huge Olympic bibliography? According to Girginov (2014), London did make particular claims, to be the first Games, to:

- use the event to make six major promises for mass social change;
- integrate the Olympic and Paralympic programmes;
- operationalise Olympic inspiration through a 'kitemark' awarded to 2,700 UK projects;
- provide Inspiration programmes for children in 20 developing countries;
- measure the event's carbon footprint over the whole project timescale;
- have its Organising Committee certified by a British Standard for its sustainability programme (BS 8901) and subsequently to become an International Standard (ISO 20121) for events;
- have its Organising Committee capture the complete knowledge-creation process;
- offer the debut for 3D television (230 hours);
- permit women from all countries to be represented in all sports;
- to be fully digital – via Sociolympics;
- to have a government-commissioned meta-evaluation (Grant Thornton *et al.*, 2013; Her Majesty's Government for the Province of Nova Scotia, 2013).

In recognition of the unique opportunity presented by the 2012 Olympic and Paralympic Games, global publishers of books and journals on sport – Routledge – invited 48 Olympic-focused journal special issues from a wide range of disciplines to be published during 2012 and 2013. This project was part of a broader strategy designed to create unique synergy between the global public and academic interest generated by the London Games, the publishing and knowledge-disseminating capabilities of Routledge, and the 2012 International Convention on Science, Education and Medicine in Sport (ICSEMIS), the world's largest scientific gathering which takes place every 4 years before the Olympic Games – the UK event happened in Glasgow on 19–24 July 2012, with some 2,700 scholars from 78 countries. The main objectives of this strategy were twofold: to generate new knowledge and to raise the status of Olympic and sport studies in general. Routledge has been at the forefront of promoting critical Olympic scholarship for over 40 years. Its first Olympic-related publication dates back to 1969 (Abrahams, 1969) and has since expanded considerably to include more than 2,000 dedicated books and journal articles. Its second major initiative was to commission two volumes, each of 21 chapters on *Making* and *Celebrating the Games* (Girginov, 2013, 2014).

This chapter critically reflects on the new knowledge and the multidisciplinary legacy of academic writing that has been generated in publishing the 36 journal special issues from 26 journals and the process behind the project. First, this was an original and unique project. Most commentators agree that Olympism is a complex phenomenon requiring a multidisciplinary and interdisciplinary approach, but so far the academy has failed to study the Games in a concerted and coordinated fashion. Second, journal publishing is a complicated business, and logistical issues had to be addressed: some journals are published in association with professional or learned societies, and contractual and editorial arrangements vary. Third, however outwardly attractive an Olympic topic may seem, every special issue is a risk in attracting authors and readers, which may explain in part why 24 journals (all but three outside sport) did not take up the challenge. All journals retained complete editorial freedom to decide on the thematic orientation and the format of their special issue, and Routledge and the coordinating editor provided only swift responses and logistical support. The project was widely promoted via several international conferences between 2009 and 2012, via global professional email lists, ICSEMIS congress communications and a dedicated online platform – *Routledge Online Studies of the Olympic and Paralympic Games* (www.routledgeonlinestudies.com), which had achieved 4,469 downloads by December 2012. In 2012, from 200 projects submitted in a national competition, the Research Councils UK presented *Routledge Olympic Special Issue* (ROSI) with a bronze award for an exceptional contribution to research.

The following five sections summarise how the ROSI project operated and what it achieved. The first explains the approach to the analysis; the second discusses the bibliometrics of the collection; the third examines four interrelated questions concerning what makes it possible for scholars to engage with the Olympics, how issues enter and exit the Olympic gaze, what new ideas have been introduced as a result of the research reported. The fourth discusses areas of potential and neglect and the readiness of academia to respond to old and (re-)emerging issues. The conclusions look at challenges for Olympic publishing and research, the International Olympic Committee (IOC) and host cities.

Approach to the analysis

Analysing the content of 26 very distinct academic journals and 266 articles from a range of academic disciplines across the arts, humanities and social sciences, united loosely by the word 'Olympic', presented methodological challenges. It was not possible to apply well-tested methods such as systematic review or meta-analysis to understand a particular trend or issue within the wide collection of special issues. However, we were able to do basic measuring of authorship, methods and topics, as set out below. For each paper we identified the authors and their gender, discipline, country and institution (usually but not always an institute of higher education), which qualitative or quantitative methods were used, the main topic and four keywords to describe it, and whether, in our judgement, it made an empirical, theoretical or discursive new contribution to knowledge.

Since ROSI was to promote new critical scholarship, it was decided to focus the analysis on knowledge creation, both as a means (i.e. routine-procedural, concrete knowledge) and as a goal (i.e. declarative-generative knowledge that is abstract and intellectual). It is generally believed that the apex of generative-declarative knowledge is newly created knowledge (Kaufman and Runco, 2009). Knowledge, however, is not an enduring object with constant properties, but rather something which is constantly recreated in particular contexts. Thus, it has to do with understanding; as Piaget (1976) argued, 'to understand is to create'. The main generative mechanism in knowledge creation comes from exercising judgement – researchers drawing new distinctions about an issue as part of a dialogue with a particular group, community or society (Tsoukas, 2009).

Since the themes of the special issues in this collection spanned a wide range of fields, from pedagogy to psychology, management, politics and biosciences, there was little scope for focusing on discipline-specific knowledge. Instead, the analysis borrowed from Hacking's (2002) historical ontology approach. We were conscious that the analysis engages with a subject area with long history and contested interpretations and that the studies under consideration were published at a particular moment in time leading up to the London 2012 Olympics.

Hacking (2002) outlined three main approaches to historical ontology, each concerned with a different central issue. The first examines how the historical possibilities arise for scholars to take interest in a 'thing'. The second approach is concerned with how objects enter and exit the scientific gaze, i.e. become topical, and the third focuses on things that come to birth as a result of the activities of scientists. Ribes and Polk (2012) proposed a fourth approach, which is interested in how objects of scientific research change over the course of being studied. Combining these four approaches provided a structure to the analysis. More specifically, it addressed the following questions:

1   How did possibilities emerge for the academic community to take an interest in Olympic matters?
2   How did objects enter and exit the Olympic gaze?
3   Which topics and issues emerged as a result of research by these Olympic scholars?
4   Which Olympic-related phenomena changed over the course of being studied?

Bibliometric results

Volume

These issues covered 3,190 pages of varying sizes and formats and contained 266 articles including relevant editorials. Four journals had two special issues and one, the *International Journal of Sports History*, three (Table 6.1). The shortest was two pages (two articles) in the *Royal United Services Institute Journal* on security and private investment in London, and the largest (201 pages) in S*port Ethics & Philosophy* (13 articles). These were prepared by 478 writers, 32 per cent women. The female share is very comparable with 29 per cent during three decades of *Leisure Studies* (though 40 per cent in the third decade) and 31 per cent across 18 years of publishing of *Managing Leisure*. Of these, 42 per cent were from non-sport disciplines and backgrounds, who had not published regularly on sport or Olympism (Table 6.7). The sports-related journals had been going for an average of 17 years, with only three relatively new titles; the 12 nonsport journals were twice as old on average at 34 years, with only two new titles.

Special focuses

As Table 6.1 shows, of specific topics, only one – Paralympism – appeared in both a sport and a nonsport journal. Other than legacy, only sports tourism was also given two separate issues. The most microscopic attention was given to diagnosing, treating and preventing anterior cruciate ligament injuries, one of the most common and debarring sports injuries, in *Research in Sports Medicine*. It was good to see the introduction of fields like archiving, photography, journalism, architecture and planning. Many, of course, used 2012 opportunistically and probably will not repeat their adventure, even around Rio de Janeiro in 2016. So, it was pleasing to see journals like *Archives, City, Mass Communication & Society* and *The Royal United Services Institute Journal* entering the Olympic fray. Twelve editors were from a nonsports background and some invited guest editors who knew about the field.

Origins

As Table 6.2 illustrates, authors came from only 26 countries, but 78 per cent from four Anglophone countries – UK 37 per cent, USA 19 per cent, Australia 13 per cent and Canada 10 per cent. People were obviously clustered by discipline

Table 6.1 Routledge Special Issue Collection on the Olympic and Paralympic Games (2011–2013)

Field (noncontributing) journal name	Volume	Issue	Issue title	Impact factor
Culture (3)				
International Journal of Heritage Studies	19	2	Examining the Olympics: Heritage, Identity and Performance	
Journal of the Royal Society of Archivists	33	1	Community Engagement and the Olympic and Paralympic Games	
Celebrity Studies	3	3	The Olympics	
Visual Studies	27	2	Olympics Special Issue	
Education (2)				
Educational Review	64	3	Olympism and Education: A Critical Review	0.66
International Journal of Disability, Development and Education	59	3	The Paralympic Games	0.59
Engineering (3)				
Environment (3)				
Media (1)				
Mass Communication & Society	15	4	Olympics, Media, and Society	0.83
Policy and Planning (5)				
City	16	4	Un-linking the Rings: Cities and the Olympic Games	
The Royal United Services Institute Journal	157	2	Olympic Security	
Tourism (2)				
Journal of Policy Research in Tourism, Leisure & Events	4	2	The Unintended Policy Consequences of the Olympics and Paralympics	
Journal of Sport & Tourism	16	4	Sport, Tourism & the Olympic Games	
Journal of Tourism and Cultural Change	10	2	Tourism and the Olympics	0.18
Leisure (1)				
Leisure Studies	31	3	Leisure, Culture & the Olympic Games	0.56
Managing Leisure	17	2–3	Management of Excellence	

Sport (3)

Journal	Vol.	Issue	Article	
European Sport Management Quarterly	12	4	Managing the Olympic Experience: Challenges and Responses	0.88
International Journal of History of Sport	29	16	The Media Is the Message: Proclaiming National Purpose and Pursuing International Approbation	0.38
International Journal of History of Sport	30	4	From Beijing to London: Delivering Olympic & Elite Sport in Cross-cultural Context	0.38
International Journal of History of Sport	30	7	London Olympic Games: European Perspectives	
International Journal of Sport Policy and Politics	4	3	Olympic & Paralympic Policy	0.38
International Journal of Sport Policy & Politics	5	2	Assessment of UK Sport Policy in Comparative Context	
Journal of Sports Sciences	29	Suppl.	Sport Nutrition	
Journal of Sports Sciences	30	3	Sport Science and the Olympics	1.93
Measurement in Physical Education & Exercise Science	16	2	World Record Prediction and Human Limit in Track and Field and Swimming	
Qualitative Research in Sport and Exercise	4	3	Paralympics and Disability Sport	
Reflective Practice	13	3 & 4	Coaching for Performance: Realising the Olympic Dream	
Research in Sports Medicine	20		ACL Injury: Incidences, Healing, Rehabilitation and Prevention	
Sport, Ethics and Philosophy	6	2	Olympic Ethics and Philosophy	
Sport in History	32	2	Britain, Britons and the Olympic Games	
Sport in Society	15	5	Bearing Light: Flame Relays and the Struggle for the Olympic Movement	
Sport in Society	15	6	The Olympic Movement and the Sport of Peacemaking	
Sports Technology	3	4	Aerodynamics in Olympic Sports	
Sports Technology	5	1–2	Paralympic Sports Technology	

Source: authors' own work/data.

Table 6.2 Countries of origin of academic writers

UK	158	Germany	5	Serbia	2
USA	79	Japan	5	Republic of South Africa	1
Australia	55	Czech Republic	4	Republic of Ireland	1
Canada	42	Sweden	4	Denmark	1
People's Republic of China	11	New Zealand	4	Russia	1
Italy	9	South Korea	4	Sweden	1
Norway	8	France	4	Singapore	1
Belgium	7	Cyprus	3	South Korea	1
Greece	6	Brazil	3	Argentina	1
		Netherlands	3	Not known	2

Source: authors' own work/data.

and often worked with erstwhile colleagues and/or their PhD tutors or students. Likewise, editors chose individuals they knew well and believed, rightly on the evidence, would deliver, which tends to cluster writing (for a sophisticated analysis of sports scholarship in the US, see Quatman and Chelladurai, 2008). Of the top four countries of origin, 128 higher education institutes (HEIs) were represented by five or more writers; otherwise only Leuven, the German Sports University (Cologne) and the Norwegian School of Sports Sciences (Oslo) appeared.

In the UK, it was not surprising to see Loughborough in first place, but Royal Holloway's entry was due to seven people collaborating on several aspects of improving performance in wheelchair sports, and Hartpury College's on three authors working together reflecting on coaching (Table 6.3). There were a few people from outside HEIs, from local or central government, and private companies or consultancies. 51 per cent of the papers had single authors, 25 per cent had two, 15 per cent three and a handful more – one Australian paper on preventive practice for anterior cruciate ligament injuries had nine, from six HEIs!

Coverage of Games and allied issues

As Table 6.4 shows, 26 per cent focused on a particular Summer or Winter Games, and only 7 per cent focused on London 2012, perhaps because much of this had to be written 12–18 months before the Games; Bejing was second.

Disciplines

Sixteen sports-related disciplines and 30 nonsports disciplines were presented, of which 11 and 10, respectively, had more than four people, as shown in Table 6.5. The higher average of sports science authors per article shows up here. Both cases showed an eclectic mixture, again substantially affected by the journals that chose to take part and the clustering of scholars; perhaps one of the most interesting teams was one from four US universities joining to study the effect of parent–child functioning and TV watching on disabled and nondisabled children, comprising a pediatric medic (interested in statistics), a child physiologist, a sociologist and a public health specialist.

Table 6.3 Higher education institutes (HEIs)

UK		USA		Australia		Canada		Others	
Loughborough	17	U Chicago	5	U Sunshine Coast	8	Ottowa	5	Leuven	10
U Central Lancashire	17	U Florida	5	Griffith U	7			Norwegian School of Sport Sciences	6
U Birmingham	14	U Pittsburgh	5	U Queensland	7			German Sport U	5
Leeds Metropolitan U	8			U Sydney	5				
U C London	6								
Canterbury Christ Church U	6								
Sheffield Hallam U	5								
Royal Holloway	5								
U Wolverhampton	5								
U Bath	5								
Hartpury College	5								
Total HEI	52		16		38				22
Non-HEI	17		6		8				4

Source: authors' own work/data.

Table 6.4 Focus on particular Olympic Games

Summer venues		Winter venues	
Earlier	5	Turin 2006	2
Sydney 2000	3	Vancouver 2010	4
Athens 2004	8	Sochi 2014	2
Beijing 2008	19	Youth Games 2010	2
London 2012	19		
Rio de Janeiro 2016	3		

Source: authors' own work/data.

Table 6.5 Disciplines in sport and nonsport special issues with more than four adherents

Sports		Nonsports	
Biomechanics/engineer	42	Journalism/media	25 (12 for sport)
Sociology	36	Geography	15
Physical education	32 (5 adapted)	Photography/film	15
Management	31	Engineering	12
Biochemistry/nutrition	29	Sociology	10
Sports history	24	Design/architecture/art	6
Psychology	23	Political science	5
Philosophy	16	Planning/urban studies	6
Sports medicine	12	Cultural studies	7
Coaching studies	12	History	7
Sport tourism	12		

Source: authors' own work/data.

Research methods

In this sample, qualitative methods predominated, especially documentary analysis (53 per cent), questionnaires and interviews (Table 6.6).

Table 6.6 Research methods in Olympic special issues (where specified/derivable, excluding editorials)

Qualitative						Quantitative	
Document analysis	140	Ethnography	3			Experiments	10
Interviews	22	Questionnaires*	15			Modelling	5
Focus groups	2	Observation	7			Factor analysis	1
Discourse/debate	21	Photographs/film	10			Statistical modelling	2
Semiotics	1	Literature review	8†				
Descriptive stats	4						

Source: authors' own work/data.

Note:*Four of these studies used questionnaires sent out by email; one study used a 'life histories' approach; †one claimed to be systematic.

How, historically, did scholars come to engage with the Olympic theme?

From the first modern social history of the Ancient Olympic Games (West, 1749) to the present, many scholars have been interested in the subject, and much knowledge has been created. The conditions for engagement have varied significantly over the centuries and fall into three types – Games-, governance- and publishing-related – that have stimulated the academic community to take an interest in Olympic matters.

Games-related conditions

London marked a departure from the traditional model of a single-themed Games focusing on athletes (e.g. Athens 2004), regeneration (e.g. Barcelona 1996), the environment (e.g. Sydney 2000), or harmony, technology and peace (e.g. Beijing 2008). London made two concrete offers. The first was inward-looking and promised to deliver a lasting social, economic and sporting legacy for Britain. The second was outward-looking and promised to inspire the youth of the world to engage with sport, which by extension was London's way of saying 'thank you' to the Olympic Movement for awarding the Games to the UK.

Governance-related conditions

Never in the history of the Games has the government of the host country made a commitment to use the event to deliver six substantial promises:

- economic (supporting new jobs and skills, encouraging trade, inward investment and tourism);
- sporting (developing a world-class sport system, providing more sports facilities and encouraging participation in schools sports and more widely);
- social and volunteering (inspiring others to volunteer and encouraging social change);
- international image (presenting UK as creative, inclusive and welcoming place to live and do business);
- regeneration (reuse of venues, new homes, improved transportation in East London and at other sites);
- for people with disabilities (changing societal perceptions about disability and creating equal opportunities for participation in life; DCMS, 2007).

Delivering this commitment entailed setting up complex governance mechanisms and structures to steer collective actions, beyond what the IOC had previously required of host Organising Committees.

Publishing-related conditions

Routledge is a world leading academic publisher with a portfolio of more than 1,700 academic journals. No other publisher has the same capacity and breadth in its publishing programme. The company headquarters are in the UK, which allowed for better coordination with the ROSI's executive editor, journal editors and authors. Of the 26 journals participating in the project, 74 per cent had UK-based editor/editors of the special issue. Another important condition that emerged was Routledge's 3-year engagement as a sponsor of the ICSEMIS congress, thereby enabling active worldwide promotion of the project. One innovation with considerable future possibilities for engaging with academia on Olympic themes was to make some 70 articles (or 15 per cent) of the content freely available online.

These three interrelated conditions framed London 2012 not just as a sporting event but as a social, political, economic and cultural phenomenon with far-reaching implications. They also naturally stimulated the curiosity of researchers to interrogate issues related to the organisation, management, political and legal regulation of the Games, their media coverage and their beneficiaries. Table 6.7 compares the previous involvement of the nonsport journals with Olympic matters prior to the launch of ROSI. With over 150 years of their combined existence, the 12 nonsport journals published 33 articles dedicated to Olympic matters, more than half from the relatively new *Journal of Sport and Tourism*. Although the five-fold growth around 2012 cannot be solely attributed to the ROSI project, it is clear that the combined conditions enhanced the possibility of scholars from various nonsporting backgrounds in engaging with the Olympic theme. So, where disciplinary attachments could be verified, 31 per cent of authors came from nonsport departments or institutions, exactly the sort of academic 'diaspora' one would hope to engender through such an initiative.

Table 6.7 Nonsport journals' record of publishing dedicated Olympic articles

Journal	Established	Olympic articles to 2012	Special issue articles
Celebrity Studies	2010	0	5
City	1996	4	5
Educational Review	1948	0	9
International Journal of Disability, Development & Education	1954	2	6
International Journal of Heritage Studies	1994	1	8
Journal of Policy Research in Tourism, Leisure & Events	2009	4	6
Journal of Royal United Services Institute	1857	2	2
Journal of the Society of Archivists	1955	0	3
Journal of Sport and Tourism	1993	18	8
Journal of Tourism & Cultural Change	2003	0	8
Mass Communication & Society	1998	2	9
Visual Studies	2002	0	15
Total articles		33	84

Source: authors' own work/data.

Topics that entered and exited the Olympic gaze

Warning *et al*. (2008) mapped the disciplines of the Olympics, identifying 13 thematic clusters including critical feminism, critical reformers, sport policy and international relations, ideals and questions, drugs, the revival of the Games, athletic performance, legal aspects, organisational performance, the history of women's involvement, the Ancient Games, the North American perspective and Olympism.

Although the period under consideration is very short for making any grand conclusions about the total emergence or exit of topics, the ROSI collection nonetheless allowed some interesting observations to be made. Nine of Warning *et al.*'s (2008) clusters were present in various forms in several journals. But critical feminism, advocates of Olympic reform, nineteenth-century revival, drug abuse and legal aspects received no treatment. Previously well-worn topics that were lightly represented were gender (only four articles), race/ethnic issues (three articles), and only four items treated the hot topic of the previous two Summer Games – environmental impact – and one the Ancient Games.

More specifically, we consider that several topics successfully entered the Olympic gaze. The focus of the *European Sport Management Quarterly* special issue was on managing the Olympic experiences, which is a topic of critical importance to the Olympic movement in times of changing multi-polar systems of international regulations and a deep crisis of Western economies. This is because, as the guest editors noted, 'both of these phenomena have important implications for Olympic management, in relation to understanding the issues of delivery of an event with universalist pretensions in culturally varied contexts, and in respect to the need to deliver value in times of economic difficulty' (Chatziefstathiou and Henry, 2012:313). Since almost all of this writing preceded the event, ideas on how management performed had to await volume 2 of the *Routledge Handbook* (Girginov, 2014), Grant Thornton *et al.*'s (2013) meta-evaluation, the government's self-congratulatory commentary (UK Government and Mayor of London, 2013) and the House of Lords' (2013) more qualified gloss on legacy. It was, of course, very difficult for researchers to get into the host Organising Committee/ governmental machines at the time of greatest pressure; as Girginov (2014) pointed out, the government was loud about its own information, but often silent on contentious or difficult topics.

One area of increasing focus in management is the policy for and process of managing elite performers, and an increasing area of deliberate political investment of public monies (12 papers came from 16 countries in *Managing Leisure*, three looking at professional UK Rugby, US soccer and Korean bike racing, seven at sport-specific policies and two at forecasting results), and of ensuring at least commensurate results and accounting for them. Another is the growth of sports media studies, reflecting the rise of its parent field, in looking at both the production and reception/interpretation of messages and images; volume 29.16 of the *International Journal of the History of Sport* focused on the three Asian Games in Tokyo, Seoul and Beijing and how they mixed east and west meeting with local messages, some received and other fighting against long-held stereotypes.

The topic of *Visual Studies* was on 'seeing the Olympics: images, spaces, legacies'. The editors and the contributing authors introduced a different perspective on the Olympics as an international sporting spectacle. Using a style of photo-essays almost entirely absent from mainstream Olympic studies, this special issue provided 'a series of shifting lenses on this complex global event, extending the visual repertoire for representing the Olympics and providing new insights into its significance, local and global' (Coles *et al.*, 2012:117).

The *Journal of Tourism and Cultural Change* explored 'Tourism at the Olympic Games: visiting the world'. This special issue shifted the academic preoccupation with tourism solely as a consumptive practice of late capitalism to a much less understood and explored topic. As editors Ploner and Robinson (2012:99) suggested, 'at the level of the tourist experience, the Olympic Games produce a kaleidoscopic range of intangible engagements with place, time and spectacle, fresh negotiations with ideas of nation and the cosmopolitan, invoking collective memories, touching on emotions and generating a sense, however fleeting, of global *communitas*'.

Both the *Journal of Sport Studies* and *Measurement in Physical Education and Exercise Science* submitted to scrutiny the link between sport science and the Olympics. The success of the Olympic spectacle relies to a large extent on record-breaking performances by athletes. The eight articles in volume 5 of *Sports Technology* provided new information for designing Paralympic equipment, while the supplement to volume 29 of the *Journal of Sport Science* contributed to a new IOC (2011) statement on sports nutrition. But Balmer *et al.* (2012) questioned human abilities and argued that in some sports/disciplines further general growth in performance will need to rely on technological or technical innovations. This issue posed a range of ethical issues for sport scientists and event organisers.

At the heart of the Olympics is the notion of excellence of body and mind, as expressed through the exploits of competitors and its inspirational power to draw young people to sport and better citizenship. *Celebrity Studies* submitted for consideration the controversial role of modern elite athletes when they get elevated to celebrity status and whether they serve the cause of Olympism or the reproduction of an achievement culture and commercial consumption.

Two journals – *Educational Review* and *Sport, Ethics and Philosophy* – albeit completely independent and from different perspectives submitted the topic of whether Olympism as an educational philosophy is fit for children and schools. While the *Educational Review* was concerned with Olympism in curricula and the experiences of children and athletes, *Sport, Ethics and Philosophy* questioned the values of the IOC's latest project the Youth Olympic Games.

Of course, the legacy issue had appeared in the literature for some years, at the beginning as a matter of good after-use of venues, then of environmental sustainability, and – more recently and in response to the London bid – of social sustainability in terms of increased mass and elite participation and local residents and traders feeling fairly treated.

What were researcher-generated Olympic topics?

A notable contribution of the ROSI was to the further construction of the topic of Olympic legacy. While concerns with mega-events' legacy have existed before this project, what the 24 (11 per cent) articles in this collection achieved was to interpret Olympic legacies as no longer an abstract concept, but to legitimise it as specific ways of being and acting. Two articles raised the issue of the level of security precautions after the New York and London terrorist attacks and after Beijing's precedent, one even speaking of 'lockdown London.' Such matters will become automatic considerations in future mega-events. Through introducing such new categories of legacy, various contributions questioned the Olympic Games as a project for social change as well as the behaviour of individuals and institutions to live up to the proclaimed legacies of the Games, particularly the engendering of more participation in sport, where Veal *et al.* (2012) reemphasised the lack of evidence that the Games do so. Neither Sport England's *Active People Survey 7* nor the House of Lords' report (2013) nor the English Health Survey (2013) demonstrated an 'Olympic bounce'.

What were changing Olympic phenomena?

ROSI made some distinct contributions to the fourth analytical question, which Olympic-related phenomena themselves changed over the course of being studied. First, *Sport, Ethics and Philosophy* examined the changing nature of the fundamental Olympic values, the format of competition and the key factors contributing to this change. More specifically, the special issue engaged with one of the more recent innovations within the Olympic Movement – the Youth Olympic Games – which for the first time included mixed gender and nationality competitions. It questioned where the new slogan 'Excellence, Friendship, Respect' sprang from and its relation to earlier formulations. As guest editors McNamee and Parry (2012:104) observed, 'this mutation reminds us that the Olympic Games, and the Olympic movement more generally, is not a static phenomenon, but one that changes through time, and requires continued attention and analysis'.

Second, the special issue of *Journal of Sport & Tourism* as well as other papers in various journals not only helped generate a new topic of investigation but also documented the changing interpretations of Olympic legacy and their implications for policy makers, educators and managers. Weed *et al.* (2011) pointed out that the Games were, to borrow a term from economics, an 'exogenous shock' to English tourist policy, which in London then took a battering from local policies to discourage workers and traders from travelling in the Olympic fortnight, when some regular tourist flows had already been diverted (as in most world-city Olympics) by threats of congestion and high prices, which did not eventuate.

Third, in the first of the two special issues of *Sport in Society – Bearing Light: Flame Relays and the Struggle for the Olympic Movement* – guest editor John MacAloon offered a fascinating study of the Olympic Flame Relay which was instituted in 1936 to celebrate the Berlin Olympics, spanning 25 years, from the

Los Angeles in 1984 to the IOC pronouncement in 2009 that there would be no more global relays. As MacAloon (2012:575) pointed out, 'this extended ethnological research offers a rare case study of continuity and change in a leading transnational and transcultural ritual form. It also further exposes the managerial revolution, with its characteristic language of "world's best practice", that has succeeded the commercial revolution in international Olympic affairs'.

Conclusion

The ROSI collection has demonstrated the heuristic value of conducting large-scale international and multidisciplinary studies on a complex phenomenon for better understanding the Olympic Games and their relations with modern societies. Similar to Gilbert West's (1749) *Dissertation on the Olympick Games*, which was concerned not simply with the history of the Ancient Games but with understanding the cultural and political world of the ancient Greek Olympic Games, the current collection also confirmed that the modern Games, London 2012 in particular, have been seen both as a subject of research and as a prism for the study of society. The analysis has shed light on important critical ontological questions dealing with the historic conditions for the engagement of scholars with the Olympic theme as well as the key themes dominating research and the shifting focus of academic gaze.

What are the challenges arising from this wide collection of papers?

For publishing – the initiative was innovative and demonstrated that publishers can make significant contributions to promoting multidisciplinary and interdisciplinary studies in a particular field through focused publication programmes. Although such initiatives should not be seen as substitute for research projects per se, they can nonetheless provide considerable impetus in generating new knowledge and can be selectively replicated with regard to other events, or just to promote a field.

For Olympic/Paralympic research – given the fixed timescale, how can proper measurement of longer term legacies be successfully instituted when the earliest they can have an IOC-legislated effect is on the Games after next? Can more research be done to gather the opinions and responses of schoolchildren, host city residents and citizens? And can there be follow-up on earlier studies? Only two, one empirical and one opinionative, appeared in this collection.

For the IOC – what are the sport development and social legacies of the Games to be? Does it want the Olympic machine to continue growing in economic power, political influence and organisational complexity, foreclosing its hosting by all but the 'safe hands' of mega-cities, when the generative effect is clearly greater on cities of a more modest size?

For host cities – can top-down, mandated and bottom-up responsive-to-people planning be reconciled?

Routledge deservedly can be pleased with the outcome of the initiative in terms of the number of nonsport journals and authors taking part, at some new topics, and the stimulation of many new ideas. The authors certainly are.

Acknowledgements

The authors would like to register their thanks to Jonathan Manley, Kate Nuttall, Zita Balogh and Leen Van Broeck from Routledge for their commitment and support to the project. Our sincere thanks are extended also to all journal editors, special issues guest editors and the hundreds of contributors for sharing their work and enhancing our knowledge of Olympism.

References

Abrahams, H. (1969) 'The Commonwealth at the Olympics'. *The Round Table*, 59(233): 44–50.

Balmer, N., Pleasence, P. and Nevill, A. (2012) 'Evolution and revolution: gauging the impact of technological and technical innovation on Olympic performance'. *Journal of Sports Sciences*, 30(11): 1075–1083.

Chatziefstathiou, D. and Henry, I. (2012) 'Managing the Olympic experience: challenges and responses'. *European Sport Management Quarterly*, 12(4): 313–315.

Coles, P., Knowles, C. and Newbury, D. (2012) 'Seeing the Olympics: images, spaces, legacies'. *Visual Studies*, 27(2): 117–118.

DCMS (2007) 'Our promise for 2012. How the UK will benefit from the Olympic Games and Paralympic Games', available at: https://www.gov.uk/government/publications/our-promise-for-2012-how-the-uk-will-benefit-from-the-olympic-games-and-paralympic-games

Girginov, V. (Ed.) (2013) *Routledge handbook of the 2012 Games (Vol 1): making the Games*. London: Routledge.

Girginov, V. (Ed.) (2014) *Routledge handbook of the 2012 Games (Vol 2): celebrating the Games*. London: Routledge.

Grant Thornton, Ecorys, Loughborough University, Oxford Economics (2013) *Meta-evaluation of the impacts of the London 2012 Olympic and Paralympic Games*. London: Department of Culture, Media and Sport.

Hacking, I. (2002) *Historical ontology*. London: Harvard University Press.

Haggerty, K. (2011) 'Review of securing and sustaining the Olympic city: reconfiguring London for 2012 and beyond', available at: http://blog.ashgate.com/2011/04/05/security-and-the-Olympics (last accessed 28 September 2013).

Health and Social Care Information Centre/National Statistics (2013) *Health social care & lifestyles: summary of key findings*. London: NatCen Social Research.

Her Majesty's Government/Mayor of London (2013) *Inspired by 2012: the legacy from the London2012 Olympic and Paralympic Games London*. London: Cabinet Office.

House of Lords Select Committee on Olympic and Paralympic Legacy (2013) *Keeping the flame alive: the Olympic and Paralympic legacy*. London: The Stationery Office.

International Olympic Committee (2011) 'Concensus statement on sports nutrition 2010'. *Journal of Sport Sciences*, 29 (suppl 1): S3–S4.

Kaufmann, G. and Runco, M. (2009) 'Knowledge management and the management of creativity' in T. Rickards, M. Runco and S. Moger (Eds.), *The Routledge companion to creativity*. London: Routledge.

MacAloon, J. J. (2012) 'Introduction: the Olympic flame relay. Local knowledge of a global ritual form'. *Sport in Society*, 15(5): 575–594.

McNamee, M. and Parry, J. (2012) 'Olympic ethics and philosophy: old wine in new bottles'. *Sport Ethics and Philosophy*, 6(2): 104–107.

Piaget J. (1976) *The grasp of consciousness*. Cambridge, MA: Harvard University Press.

Ploner, J. and Robinson, M. (2012) 'Tourism at the Olympic Games: visiting the world'. *Journal of Tourism and Cultural Change*, 10(2): 99–104.

Quatman, C. and Chelladurai, P. (2008) 'Social network theory and analysis'. *Journal of Sport Management*, 22(3): 338–360.

Ribes, D. and Polk, J. B. (2012) 'Historical ontology and infrastructure' in *Proceedings of the 2012 iConference*. Toronto, CA, ACM, pp. 252–264.

Tsoukas, H. (2009) 'Creating organisational knowledge dialogically: an outline of a theory' in T. Rickards, M. Runco and S. Moger (Eds.), *The Routledge companion to creativity*. London: Routledge.

UK Government and Mayor of London (2013) 'Inspired by 2012: the legacy from the London 2012 Olympic and Paralympic Games'. A joint UK Government and Mayor of London report. Available at: https://www.gov.uk/government/uploads/system/uploads/attachment_data/file/224148/2901179_OlympicLegacy_acc.pdf

Veal, A. J., Toohey, K. and Frawley, S. (2012) 'The sport participation legacy of the Sydney 2000 Games and other international sporting events hosted in Australia'. *Journal of Policy Research in Tourism, Leisure and Events*, 4(2): 155–184.

Warning, P., Ju Mae, R. C. and Toohey, K. (2008) *Mapping the discipline of the Olympic Games: an author co-citation analysis*. SMU Economics & Statistics Working Paper 15. Sydney University of Technology.

Weed, M., Stephens, J. and Bull, C. (2011) 'An exogenous shock to the system? The London 2012 Olympic and Paralympic Games and British tourist policy'. *Journal of Sport & Tourism*, 16(4): 345–377.

West, G. (1749) *Odes of Pindar, with several other pieces in prose and verse. Translated from the Greek. To which is prefixed a dissertation on the Olympic Games*. London: J. Dodsley.

Part III

Creating spaces, reconstructing places

7 The Olympic Games and urban development impacts

Judith Grant Long

To gauge the extent of mounting concern over the urban development impacts of the Olympic Games in host cities, one need only search the internet using the keywords 'Olympic' and 'legacy'. Therein one can find impact assessments by journalists, academics, pro- and anti-Games interest groups, as well as organisations linked to the Olympic Movement. Though these assessments vary in scope, perspective and quality, they invariably make claims about post-Games use of venues, and their findings tend to fall into two categories: positive or negative (Ong, 2004; Hillier, 2006; Tomlinson and Young, 2006; Broudehoux, 2008; Mangan, 2008; Zimbalist, 2010). On balance, most recent analyses are not bullish on Olympic legacy. For example, Sydney's Olympic Park is characterised as a 'white elephant', overbuilt and underutilised by virtue of its location too far removed from the urban core. Athens' massive building campaign for the 2004 Games lies in a state of 'modern ruins', a tangible symbol of the Greek financial crisis. Beijing's bold vision for its Olympic Green, though painted against a backdrop of extraordinary construction activity, has delivered uneven post-Games impacts: its landmark Bird's Nest stadium is still absent a long-term tenant, and its new nickname 'Empty Nest' reminds us that the culture of sports is not yet fully globalised.

Yet in spite of this recent history of underperforming Olympic real property assets, prospective hosts march forward with ambitious plans to leverage the Olympic Games in the name of capturing urban development benefits. The recent Games in London were tethered to a massive urban development plan for the Lower Lea Valley, in what may be the most ambitious, considered and studied legacy effort of the modern Olympics. Though it is too early to gauge the post-Games impact, the tactic of bundling the post-Games legacy within such a large and long-term project will make it difficult to disentangle any specific impacts attributable to Olympic investments, should anyone be much concerned about this relationship 20 or 30 years from now. Looking ahead to Rio de Janeiro in 2016, hosting sports mega-events is an important element of its urban development and infrastructure development planning, as well as to Brazil's foreign relations and trade policy. Although it is also too soon to gauge the impact of the Olympic Games on Rio, this case has captured the attention of legacy researchers because of potential efficiencies in post-Games use made possible through its hosting of a sequence of high-profile mega sports events over a very short period of time. In this manner, Rio's 'golden decade of sports' – a period that started with the Pan Am Games in 2007, followed by the World Military Games in 2011, the FIFA Federations Cup in 2013, the World Cup in 2014 and culminating in the Olympic Games in 2016 – promises to be a uniquely important test of best practices in post-Games use.

What explains this continued enthusiasm and ambition among prospective host cities despite the gloomy snapshot of post-Games outcomes? One interpretation is that when reckoning the benefits and costs associated with hosting the Olympic Games, the long-term costs of keeping a set of underutilised sports event facilities on the books are not very important. From this perspective, the costs associated with building venues and infrastructure are treated as operating costs rather than capital costs – despite the International Olympic Committee's (IOC) accounting structure that requires separating the two – and are subsequently treated as 'sunk' after the Games are over. These arguments suggest that the Games would be produced regardless of the large costs paid by host city governments (Senn, 1999; Lenskyj, 2008). Since there are significant economic and political benefits associated with the Olympic Games that accrue disproportionately to a small set of elite private and public actors, and since these actors are in a position to influence the political process in host cities, the result is the continued production of the Olympic Games even in the face of rational concerns over cost–benefit efficiency. Put simply: If Sydney, Athens and Beijing knew then what they know now, they are likely to still have chosen to host the Olympic Games. Thus, society's collective interests might be best served, in the near term, by developing strategies to improve post-Games outcomes, rather than aiming to dismantle the system of interests that currently sustains the Olympic Movement.

Another explanation for the actions of host cities is that they are able to capture – along with their states and/or nations – real and significant benefits associated with hosting the Games and that these benefits would exceed the costs, or at least break-even, in a cost–benefit analysis. Most hosting strategies make the case that there is a demonstrated increase in global brand recognition that comes with hosting the Olympics, which confers benefits in terms of foreign policy, international trade and related areas. (Although some argue that many of these benefits can be captured by participating in the bid process rather than ultimately being selected as host city, as evident in the number of bids from prospects that appear less qualified than the general pool; Rose and Spiegel, 2011; Maennig and Richter, 2012). Next, host cities are motivated by economic benefits, particularly the promise of new jobs and tax revenues that accompany the Olympic Games through activities such as pre-Games construction and planning, Games-times visitors and tourism and the private investment associated with post-Games use. In addition, most Olympic legacy plans target a set of social and environmental benefits. Primarily these social benefits revolve around increased access to athletic opportunities, a heightened interest in the progression to elite-level sports and investment in local-scale sports facilities that allow capturing of public health benefits. Environmental benefits include targeted opportunities for remediation and demonstrating cutting-edge green technologies at Olympic sites and venues. Finally, host cities identify a series of physical benefits that they hope to achieve either directly through the provision of sports facilities, athletes' villages and related infrastructures, or indirectly through the private investment that might be stimulated by these public investments.

The focus of this chapter is on the urban development impacts of hosting the Olympic Games, discussing the evolving role of urban development aspirations in the bid process and mapping the trajectory of 'Olympic sprawl' that has occurred alongside. This interest is based on two countervailing trends. On the one hand, urban development is an increasingly important rationale for cities bidding to host the Olympic Games and other sports mega-events. On the other hand, urban development impacts are poorly understood and have only recently been the subject of research that seeks to build our understanding of its particular complexities. While these issues are more fully discussed later in the chapter – including the role of the IOC in giving shape to the legacy concept – the current situation can generally be characterised as follows: host cities are increasingly reliant upon urban development rationales to galvanise support for their bids, but do so with little theoretical guidance about causes and effects, leading to suboptimal outcomes. As evidence, most host cities adopt legacy rhetoric in their bids that aims closer to Barcelona than Montreal on the spectrum of post-Games outcomes, but the experiences of the past decade suggest that the pathway to successful Olympic-led urban development is not yet mapped. As a response, the goal of this chapter is to contribute to our understanding and analysis of urban development impacts.

The evolving role of urban development impacts

Among Olympic host cities, Barcelona is generally considered the model for creating a favourable legacy borne of positive urban development impacts. For many readers interested in Olympic studies, Barcelona 1992 was the first time that a host city sought to marry urban aspirations with the provision of sports venues and infrastructure. However, it was Rome 1960 that in fact marked this important shift in the history of the Olympic Games from the perspective of urban development. Rome was the first host city whose vision of accommodating the Olympics was entrenched in an ambitious urban development agenda. Prior to Rome, the Los Angeles 1932 and Berlin 1936 Games included the first versions of purpose-built Olympic sports complexes, but these were not explicitly part of a broader urban agenda. Subsequent to Rome 1960, however, almost every host city combined broader urban aspirations with those of building Olympic infrastructure. Tokyo 1964, Mexico City 1968, Munich 1972, Montreal 1976, Moscow 1980 and Seoul 1988 each included substantial, centralised sports complexes, most combined with large athletes' villages and ceremonial parks in close proximity as the keystone of their bids in combination with visions for urban expansion and regeneration in targeted parts of the city. As the hallmark of post-Montreal efficiency, the 1984 Olympic Games in Los Angeles called for the reuse of infrastructure already built for the earlier Games held there in 1932.

In Barcelona, planners advanced our thinking of how hosting the Olympic Games could be integrated into longer term urban development plans, choosing a decentralised set of venue clusters positioned in strategic locations around the city, including its port. It was an effort that mimicked earlier successes leveraging mega-events to grow the local economy and transform parts of the city – namely the 1929 Barcelona International Exposition held in the newly developed Monjuic area including the Estadio Olimpic in 1936, as well as the 1888 Barcelona Universal Exposition which aided the development of the Parc de la Ciutadella. Planning efforts for 1992 included four decentralised clusters, connected by new transportation infrastructure to disperse the impacts of the Games throughout the city. The plan included new facilities and the athlete's village at the Port Olimpic, anchoring regeneration of this strategically located former industrial port. Despite the successes of Barcelona 1992, however, most host cities have chosen to return to variations on the central complex model, including Atlanta 1996, Sydney 2000, Athens 2004, Beijing 2008 and London 2012. Interestingly, the plan for Rio de Janeiro 2016 mirrors that of Barcelona 1992 very closely: if one were to compare the conceptual plan included in the bid submitted for Rio 2016, the images are strikingly similar, including emphasis on transforming parts of the port. Perhaps the organising committee for Rio 2016 was hoping to position a favourable reading by the IOC by evoking the image of its best example of a desired Olympic legacy and, once the bid was won, to channel the positive legacy borne of this configuration by so closely mapping its spatial strategy.

In most host city bid packages, it is the urban development framework that guides the delivery of the Olympic legacy, often serving as a locus of a set of desired economic, social, environmental and physical benefits. Upon first glance, the reasons for focusing on urban development as the organising mechanism for delivering Olympic legacies are fairly clear: the post-Games use of venues and infrastructure is dependent upon factors that fall within the traditional concerns and regulatory context of urban development, such as location, land acquisition, programme or use, capacity, public spaces, security, transportation access and so forth. By extension, the nature, magnitude and distribution of economic and social benefits are also tied to urban development decisions. For example, decisions about whether to build a new venue versus renovating an existing facility will affect economic impacts such as the number of jobs created as well as the value of construction, both of which affect tax revenues. Often decisions about the location of venues carry significant social implications, ranging from the relocation of existing residents and business to make way for new construction as well as the access of underserved populations to new sports venues when the Games are over.

The small but growing literature that examines urban development impacts focuses mainly on how host cities have worked through the tensions that arise from the provision of Olympic facilities (Chalkley and Essex, 1999; Burbank *et al.*, 2002; Essex and Chalkley, 2003; Kissoudi, 2008; Gold and Gold, 2011). Since these host cities are typically large in size and have sophisticated governance structures, their local planning institutions are accustomed to working through these kinds of development issues, albeit with outcomes expressed as a function of their particular political, economic and cultural contexts. Much of this literature has been developed in Australia and the UK during the run-up to Sydney 2000 and to London 2012. This work is generally imbued with a capacious definition of urban development impacts, and its contributions lie along the trajectories of urban theories as they intersect with economic, social and environmental concerns. Themes include the economic analyses and the impact on regional economic indicators, political analyses such as the formation and effectiveness of protest movements, sociological studies that investigate changes in the culture of sports and participation, and so forth. More planning-oriented research examines the relocation of existing populations or the use of eminent domain or other regulatory strategies to make land available for Games-related development. Importantly for this chapter, the extant literature is less concerned with expressly physical and spatial outcomes, often providing little analysis beyond description.

This current thinking on urban development outcomes misses some important nuances that mark the increasing influence of Olympics Games – and other mega sports events – in host cities. A closer examination reveals that host city plans have evolved beyond their original function as a mechanism for delivering the broader benefits of the Games, to a more elevated and far-reaching role as a locus of urban aspirations. Several factors explain the heightened import of planning that takes its cues from the needs of the Olympics. On a practical level, prospective host cities must have a mega-event strategy in place to be able to respond to the increasing scale and complexity of planning for the Games, to the longer time-frame of the host city selection process and to the reality that multiple bid cycles may be necessary to win the designation, which in turn requires demonstrating experience with other mega-events. There is very little research that evaluates the role of mega-events in city planning processes.

The IOC has also played an important role in strengthening its influence in the planning process in host cities. Its host city selection process requires applicant cities to lay out their plans for delivering a positive legacy after the Games. The origins in the IOC's legacy policy lay primarily in serving its own interests while secondarily serving those of its host cities. The IOC is motivated to facilitate positive experiences for its host cities to ensure a strong pool of candidate cities, since competition among candidates increases the extent of its political and economic influence. The financial debacle that followed in the wake of ambitious building plans in Montreal 1976 had the effect of dampening demand for prospective hosts for years after. Thus, the legacy policy was targeted to both managing the urban aspirations of host cities, so as to reduce financial risk and to literally cement a positive impression of the Games among residents of the host city and the rest of the world.

As regards monitoring Games impacts, the IOC now requests host cities to track a set of indicators – including some designed to measure urban impacts – over the pre-Games, Games-time and post-Games periods and to publish their measures in the Olympic Games Global Impact report – later shortened to the Olympic Games Impact report – 2 years after the Games end. The first of these reports was to be prepared following Bejing 2008, although it has not yet appeared at the time of this writing. The preliminary reports for London 2012 highlight the urban impacts mainly in the form of a list of what was built in the East London site, starting with the remediation of 250 hectares of former industrial land, followed by the build-ing of new sports venues and the athletes' village and other Olympic facilities, including the creation of 100 hectares of greenspace and otherwise transforming a site that was 'fragmented in terms of urban form and use' as part of a longer term vision for regeneration (Department for Culture, Media and Sport, 2012).

Over and above the unique strategies associated with hosting mega-events and the influence of the IOC, it is important to understand that the process of planning for the Olympic Games is different from other large-scale urban development projects and involves a unique cast of participants. Plan making for the Olympic Games typically lies outside of the local planning process in its formative stages. It is often led by a coalition of private interests that includes local power brokers, with representatives from the business, sports and political communities, and may be fronted by a high-profile former Olympic athlete. Generally, these exploratory efforts are privately funded. These fledgling bid committees tend to be very good at acquiring the necessary information and advice on inventorying the existing stock of venues, identifying sites for necessary new construction and thinking about ways to move people around.

As part of this early-stage planning, bid committees also selectively and infor-mally engage representatives from the local, regional and national governments. If forward momentum is sufficient to attract additional private funding, expert bid preparation consultants may be hired to aid the preparation of a conceptual plan. By the time the bid has garnered sufficient local political approval, then the plan must wend its way through local planning review, as well as that of higher levels of government since public guarantees are also required as part of a formal host city bid. Moreover, since the designated host city may not alter the plans presented in the bid document without approval from the IOC, this review is important in paving the way to future approvals, since these approvals are not always required until the host city designation is won.

Since planning for the Olympic Games lies outside of the traditional local planning process in its formatives stages, some argue that this leads to urban development that is more visionary, more regional in scope and more accelerated. Certainly much of the conceptual planning for an Olympic bid happens early on and engages actors who might not normally have a seat at the plan-making table or otherwise be inclined to have an interest in local planning issues. It is this free-dom from the local planning process and the involvement of a coalition of special interests that leads to claims of planning that is more visionary, more regional in scope and is also relieved of many of the usual burdens of implementation, such as identifying sources of public funding, the crisscrossing of political boundaries and the complexities of land acquisition. Doubtless good and creative ideas have sprung forth from this process, although their ultimate success must be framed in the local planning context.

More compelling is the notion that the planning undertaken to support a bid to host the Olympic Games can lead to an accelerated pace of development. In almost every Olympic bid document, a statement can be found suggesting that a certain piece of infrastructure was to be built eventually, but was fast-tracked to help accommodate the Games. There is merit to the notion – though it is hard to measure – that a sense of momentum can be created around planning for a project like the Olympic Games, capturing the collective imagination and eventually speeding up the implementation process by attracting public and private funds, eliminating red tape and smoothing the path to political approval. However, this notion of accelerated planning can be a self-fulfilling prophecy. In almost every host city, and in almost every regard, the programme of land uses introduced by the Games is in excess of short-term local demand. Large-scale sports venues created capacity sufficient for decades to come. The new housing units introduced by the athletes and media villages were typically far in excess of annual absorption rates. Infrastructure might be designed for Games-time peak capacities and, if intended to spur future growth, was typically provided years in advance of its associated development. In this sense, the Olympic Games created excess supply in its core programme of land uses, some of which took years to clear the market. Thus, the validity of positioning this accelerated development as leading the market is a matter of perspective.

Viewed critically, the rationale for the increasing aspirations of Olympic urban plans may have its roots in subverting the politics of local development. Bundling Olympic development projects within a larger urban development initiative serves the purpose of helping locals connect the dots between near-term needs for the Games and the long-term needs of the host city. By embedding the Olympic needs as a precursor to the larger development, one can pick the idiom: the stick before the carrot, the cart before the horse, the tail wags the dog. This bundling is often structured as a means to aiding the local approval process for both projects and may, in some cases, insulate the Olympic projects from direct voter approval. Skeptics may further argue that this approach is less concerned with the realisation of the long-term project and is primarily concerned with delivery of Olympic benefits to its special interests. Given the lengthy build-out timeline of any urban development plan large enough to include Olympic-scale facilities as a component, it may well be that by the time concerns emerge about its slow pace, the Olympic investments will be long forgotten.

The increasing scale of urban development impacts

At the same time as urban development aspirations are playing a heightened role in the motivations of prospective host cities, the increasing scale of the Olympic Games is making it more difficult to understand, analyze and influence their impacts. By almost every measure, the obligations associated with hosting the Games have multiplied. In the century following the 'rebirth' of the Modern Olympic Games, the number of sports represented on the Olympic programme expanded from nine in Athens 1896 to 28 in London 2012; over the same period, the number of medal events grew from 43 to 302. As more countries joined the Olympic Movement, the number of athletes participating rose from 241 to over 10,500. In tandem with this growth, the number of coaches, referees, judges and operational staff increased; alongside the 'Olympic family' made up of officials from the IOC, the International Federations (IFs), the National Olympic Committees (NOCs) and the local Organising Committees of the Olympic Games (OCOGs), as well as a ballooning contingent of sponsors, media and broadcast professionals and local volunteers. Rounding out the programme are live spectators: over nine million tickets were sold for the Olympic Games in London 2012.

As a key metric of urban development impacts, a form of 'Olympic sprawl' now accompanies this burgeoning Olympic programme, leading to changes in size and composition of infrastructure required to accommodate the Games. Over the past century, building for the Summer Games has evolved from a single stadium to large complexes encompassing multiple venues, as well as housing for thousands of athletes and members of the media, ceremonial parks, broadcast and press centres, all connected by transportation facilities capable of moving hundreds of thousands of spectators each day. For the first Olympiad in Athens 1896, only seven venues were needed, including renovation of an ancient stadium and other existing facilities such as the Athens Tennis Club and the Bay of Phaleron for swimming events. Over the past 50 years, the number of sports venues used by host cities averages just over 30 facilities, with 38 venues in use for Barcelona 1992, 29 venues for Sydney 2000 and 31 for London 2012 (Table 7.1).

Table 7.1 Comparison of Olympic Games: size, programme and venues

Host city	Year	Number of athletes	Medal events	Number of venues
Athens	1896	241	43	7
Paris	1900	997	95	14
St. Louis	1904	651	91	5
London	1908	2,008	110	12
Stockholm	1912	2,407	102	12
Not held due to World War I	1916	–	–	–
Antwerp	1920	2,626	15	17
Paris	1924	3,089	126	14
Amsterdam	1928	2,883	109	15
Los Angeles	1932	1,332	117	22
Berlin	1936	3,963	129	25
Not held due to World War II	1940	–	–	–
Not held due to World War II	1944	–	–	–
London	1948	4,104	136	25
Helsinki	1952	4,955	149	24
Melbourne	1956	3,314	145	17
Rome	1960	5,338	150	34
Tokyo	1964	5,151	163	33
Mexico City	1968	5,516	172	25
Munich	1972	7,134	195	32
Montreal	1976	6,084	198	27

(Continued)

Host city	Year	Number of athletes	Medal events	Number of venues
Moscow	1980	5,179	203	28
Los Angeles	1984	6,829	221	31
Seoul	1988	8,391	237	31
Barcelona	1992	9,356	257	43
Atlanta	1996	10,318	271	29
Sydney	2000	10,651	300	30
Athens	2004	10, 625	301	35
Beijing	2008	10,942	302	37
London	2012	10,500	302	31
Rio de Janiero	2016	n/a	n/a	34

Source: author's own work, drawn from author's database and data from IOC official reports.

In providing Olympic infrastructure, host cities are contractually obligated first and foremost to the technical requirements of a set of main stakeholders. These include the IOC, particularly its executive board, the IFs who govern individual sports and their subdisciplines, the NOCs who sponsor and represent the athletes from their country and the local OCOGs who govern the delivery of the Games and manage relationships among these parties, including the host city and other levels of government for a specific Olympiad. These stakeholders, particularly the IFs, can determine whether existing facilities pass technical muster and, in so doing, have a good degree of influence on the amount of new construction required and the cost of venues. Depending on how ticket and broadcast revenues are shared, different stakeholders can seek to influence the spectator capacity of a given venue, rendering existing facilities with small fixed-seating capacities as unusable for the Games. The IOC, for its part, is aware of the increasing scale of the Summer Games and the impact on host cities. Colloquially referred to as concerns over 'gigantism' in IOC documents, the IOC has led efforts to reign in the scope of the Olympic programme. For example, the IOC has limited the number of sports to 28, the number of events to approximately 300 and the number of athletes to approximately 10,500. If form follows function, then ideally limiting the scope of the programme should result in a smaller footprint. Again, the IOC, with input from the IFs and NOCs, provides prospective host cities with some guidance about the expected number of venues, capacity requirements and planning dimensions, based on the 28/300/10,500 formula. For example, in the late 1990s, the guidelines for the minimum surface area of the Games estimated a total footprint of approximately 671 hectares or 1660 acres (Table 7.2).

The import and impact of this theoretical minimum footprint in part depends on the size of the host city and the extent of its 'city proper'. In Barcelona, a comparatively small city with a surface area of 10,360 hectares in the city proper, this 671-acre footprint represents approximately 7 per cent of its total area. In a large city, such as Beijing with a surface area of 75,109 hectares, the footprint shrinks to a comparatively miniscule 1 per cent. Of course, what is required is often different from what is built. This minimum Olympic 'template' is a net of elements such as the large-scale public spaces and ceremonial green spaces that are often

Table 7.2 Minimum estimated land area requirement

Outdoor competition facilities	Athletics, baseball, velodrome, equestrian sports centre, football, hockey, softball, tennis, beach volleyball	81 hectares
Indoor competition facilities	Small halls, medium halls, large halls	32 hectares
Special competition facilities	Rowing and canoeing stadium, slalom canal, swimming pool complex, shooting centre, archery complex, Olympic port	445 hectares
Training facilities	Various	20 hectares
Accommodation facilities	Olympic village, family town, referees and judges, observers, media village, youth camp	82 hectares
Service facilities	International broadcast centre, main press centre, OCOG headquarters	11 hectares
Total		671 hectares

Source: Abridged from Millet (1997), based on IOC technical manuals.

included as part of the main complex designs, nor do they include parking areas or allowances for transportation facilities. In Beijing, the total footprint of the 2008 Olympic Games is estimated at approximately 3,400 hectares – or 5 per cent of its total land area – including 1,215 hectares for the Olympic green, 680 hectares for the Olympic forest park and 80 hectares for the Olympic village. Albeit an imperfect metric, since some facilities are located within the city proper and others are not, it remains clear that if the average footprint of the Olympic Games and its attendant infrastructure averages around 5 per cent of its host's total surface area, it is a significant use of urban land. Of course, location can trump scale, particularly when Olympic facilities are sited in areas with more important and strategic long-term uses.

Recalibrating the urban development impacts of the Olympic Games

An important means to reducing the cost and complexity of the Olympic Games is to rethink the size and composition of its infrastructure. Sports venues are the primary determinant of the scale of the Olympic footprint (Table 7.1), in an equation where the number of venues is a function of the number of sports, disciplines (branches of sports), events and participants. The constraint of the 3-week duration often makes it necessary to provide multiple versions of a single-venue type – proposals to extend the length of the Games have not succeeded. For example, several indoor facilities (including gymnasiums, arenas and halls) are required to accommodate events such as gymnastics, fencing, judo and weightlifting. Similarly, more than one pool is typically needed to accommodate the four disciplines within the sport of aquatics: swimming, diving, water polo and synchronised swimming. For football, several stadiums are required to host the qualifying and tournament matches, although these matches tend to be distributed regionally to existing stadiums in nearby cities and thus constitute an exception to the 'one city' rule along with the venues for sailing competitions. The type of sport to be accommodated also influences venue provision, particularly as the Olympic programme has diversified to accommodate new sports and disciplines such as BMX cycling, canoe/kayak slalom and beach volleyball.

Whether these sports venues are overlaid onto existing facilities, built new or provided temporarily also influences the scale and cost of hosting the Games. Among recent host cities, the average number of existing venues used is just over 50 per cent, though in most cases these existing venues required modifications to accommodate Olympic events. Some cities were in a better position to make use of existing facilities. For Los Angeles 1984, more than 75 per cent of the venues used were already existing and attributed to the fact that Los Angeles was a previous Olympic host with some facilities still intact, as well as a region rich with newer large-scale sports facilities and an organising committee very sensitive to the financial woes facing Montreal after hosting the Games in 1976. Though to be fair, despite significant financial difficulties building its main complex, Montreal otherwise made use of a large number of existing facilities, in a proportion almost matching Los Angeles 1984. In contrast, other host cities built far more new facilities than their counterparts, including Seoul 1988, Sydney 2000, Athens 2004 and Beijing 2008. In the case of Asian cities, including Tokyo 1964, cultural preferences for sport produced a different set of existing facilities as a baseline.

Temporary facilities are also gaining favour, particularly for outdoor, grass-based sports with lower spectator demand, such as archery, shooting and equestrian events. They are attractive primarily because of their cost basis, estimated at approximately one-half to one-third less than building new. Theoretically, the use of temporary facilities also allows host cities to make choices about matching the need for permanent venues with local sports preferences. Less direct, but perhaps more important, temporary facilities eliminate the spatial opportunity cost of occupying urban land for low-demand land uses. Beijing 2008, London 2012 and Rio de Janeiro 2016 all make use of temporary facilities. Rio plans to use 34 competition venues, of which five are intended to be temporary and 18 are already existing, though many were built for previous mega sports events over the past decade, including the Pan Am Games in 2007 and FIFA World Cup in 2014.

Viewed from the perspective of host cities, then, reducing the urban development impacts of delivering the Olympic Games is very much a function of the scale of its infrastructure, particularly the sports venues. As the cost of providing these 'Olympic infrastructures' spirals to unprecedented levels, widespread criticism has emerged concerning that host city spending outpaces – and in some cases replaces – public investment in traditional projects such as highways, schools and hospitals. Public perceptions about the cost of the Olympic Games are confused by the peculiarities of Olympic accounting, where most Games are announced to 'break-even' from an operations perspective. That is, Games-time revenues through ticketing, sponsorships and broadcast revenues typically exceed Games-time operations expenses such as accommodation, food and beverage, transportation and security. Capital expenditures are far greater than the Games-time operating budget and include spending on sports venues, Olympic villages and media facilities and are accounted for separately from the reckoning that determines the financial success or failure of a particular Games. Moreover, these costs are the sole responsibility of host cities, and host governments must guarantee their provision as part of the host city contract.

Host cities might reduce the urban development impacts of delivering the Olympic Games by more carefully monitoring the Olympic programme for policies that imply a larger number of venues or an increasing number of specialised venues. Host cities might also coalesce to have their interests represented in Olympic programme deliberations and to share information and knowledge more directly. Reducing urban development impacts also requires careful choices about new venues over existing or permanent venues over temporary. The IOC, for its part, also has a strong interest in recalibrating the infrastructure required of host cities, since the viability of its mission, and its political power, is predicated on a strong candidate pool. Over the past 20 years, the quantity of host cities bidding for the Games has not markedly decreased, but the composition of cities in the bid pool now includes a larger proportion of cities located in emerging markets as well as smaller cities, as more established world cities forgo the opportunity to serve as Olympic host cities, in part based on increasing financial and political risk. To support the long-term viability of the Olympic Games, efforts to recalibrate the scale of this Olympic development and to reduce the obligations of host cities with regard to the provision of Olympic infrastructure should be an ongoing priority of the IOC and the global urban policy community.

References

Broudehoux, A. (2008) 'Spectacular Beijing: the conspicuous construction of an Olympic metropolis'. *Journal of Urban Affairs*, 30(2): 175–190.
Burbank, M. J., Andranovich, G. and Heying, C. H. (2002) 'Mega-events, urban development, and public policy'. *Review of Policy Research*, 19(3): 179–202.
Chalkley, B. S. and Essex, S. J. (1999) 'Urban development through hosting international events: a history of the Olympic Games'. *Planning Perspectives*, 14(4): 369–394.
Department for Culture, Media and Sport (2012) *Report 5: Post-Games evaluation: meta- evaluation of the impacts and legacy of the London 2012 Olympic Games and Paralympic Games*. London: Department for Culture, Media and Sport.
Essex, S. and Chalkley, B. (2003) 'Urban transformation from hosting the Olympic Games', available at: http://olympicstudies.uab.es/lectures/web/pdf/essex.pdf
Gold, J. R. and Gold, M. M. (2011) *Olympic cities: city agendas, planning, and the world's Games, 1896–2016*. London: Routledge.
Hillier, H. H. (2006) 'Post-event outcomes and the post-modern turn: the Olympics and urban transformations'. *European Sport Management Quarterly*, 6(4): 317–332.
Kissoudi, P. (2008) 'The Athens Olympics: optimistic legacies – post-Olympic assets and the struggle for their realization'. *The International Journal of the History of Sport*, 25(14): 1972–1990.
Lenskyj, H. J. (2008) *Olympic industry resistance: challenging Olympic power and propaganda*. Albany: State University of New York.

Maennig, W. and Richter, F. (2012) 'Exports and Olympic Games: is there a signal effect?'. *Journal of Sports Economics,* 13(6): 635–641.

Mangan, J. A. (2008) 'Prologue: guarantees of global goodwill: post-Olympic legacies – too many limping white elephants?'. *The International Journal of the History of Sport,* 25(14): 1869–1883.

Millet, L. (1997) 'Olympic villages after the Games' in M. de Moragas, M. Llinés and B. Kidd (Eds.), *Olympic villages: a hundred years of urban planning and shared experiences.* Lausanne: International Olympic Committee.

Ong, R. (2004) 'New Beijing, great Olympics: Beijing and its unfolding Olympic legacy'. *Stanford Journal of East Asian Affairs,* 4(2): 35–49.

Rose, A. K. and Spiegel, M. M. (2011) 'The Olympic effect'. *The Economic Journal,* 121(553): 652–677.

Senn, A. (1999) *Power, politics, and the Olympic Games.* Champaign: Human Kinetics.

Tomlinson, A. and Young, C. (2006) *National identity and global sports events: culture, politics, and spectacle in the Olympics and football World Cup.* Albany: State University of New York.

Zimbalist, A. (2010) 'Is it worth it?'. *Finance and Development,* 47(1): 8–11.

8 Barriers and borders

London's legacy development ambitions and outcomes

Ralph Ward

Introduction

One of the most striking features of the 2012 Games was London's ability to carve out a bespoke new site for the Olympic park less than 5 miles from the city of London. That such an established, expensive, large and growing World City could find 300 hectares of land near its centre capable of siting a compact Olympic Games seems extraordinary. More remarkable perhaps was that this massive development was achieved not simply with a relative lack of controversy but was broadly welcomed by the local population (BRMB, 2012). This chapter explores the development ambitions for East London which lay behind the London 2012 bid and how far these ambitions might be realised.

A legacy-driven location

This location was fundamentally a legacy-driven decision. The site certainly worked well for the event itself, with its rail accessibility and its proximity to the established sights and hotels of the city. But as a location for such a massive development with an inflexible brief and deadline, it was a heroic choice. The challenges – the undergrounding of electricity pylons for the first time, the largest ever compulsory acquisition of over 5,000 separate land interests, contamination problems whose scale and nature were unknown – presented enormous risks to the delivery of the Games to time and budget.

These risks, however, were acceptable to a Mayor of London who was attracted to the Olympics precisely by the scale of change and investment that it would bring to East London (HMG, 2012) – particularly as the associated cost risk was being born by the government. East London is both the most deprived part of London and the part of London designated in the London Plan as its primary location for housing growth in particular (GLA, 2012). Mega-events can find themselves bolted on to the outskirts of the city, where the available and relatively inexpensive land tends to lie, as with the Sydney, Athens and Rio Olympics and the Seville and Lisbon Expos. The Olympics are hoped to provide the infrastructure and generate the market interest that will sustain a new urban extension. In practice, we find that breathing life after the event into these new destinations can be a slow and difficult process. A brief stint as a mega-event site is not a magic wand to overcome strategic weakness.

London has its extensive peripheral areas of brownfield land languishing along the river to the east of the city, which for over 30 years has offered a default location for large-scale development. City Airport, Canary Wharf, the O2 Dome and the Excel exhibition centre, all went east not because the location worked particularly well for them but because the land was there. All were accompanied by impressive urban regeneration narratives for their surrounding areas which generally have yet to be realised, with the exception of Canary Wharf. The singular lesson of London 2012 is it created a site that its organisers and advocates knew really did have a legacy future, rather than being an attempt to invent a legacy future out of land that happened to be available.

The site London chose is in the Lower Lea valley. The valley of the River Lea, London's second river, is a large industrial 'corridor' which developed in the nineteenth century as the city's first industrial and manufacturing zone, linked by the river to the London Docks. It was famous for the technological innovations it fostered but was also notorious for the noxious industrial processes – chemical works, brewing, dyeing – that it attracted, which used the river to discharge their waste.[1] Development was dense, uncontrolled and haphazard. The area developed a desperate reputation memorably described by Charles Dickens in his essay 'Londoners over the border' (1857).

To a degree, it is a reputation that it has not wholly thrown off. It remains an industrial enclave, disconnected from the wider city, known and used only by its remaining business occupants. As London's manufacturing role declined, so the area has fallen into increasing dereliction and underuse. But low land values, complexity of land ownership and the continued scattered presence of industrial activity have combined to deter renewal of what, in principle, is a singular waterside location. Its once central role in London's economy became increasingly replaced by a reputation as a romantic, 'liminal' backwater (Sinclair, 2011).

Regeneration ambitions

Not surprisingly therefore, in view of this potential, the 'regeneration' of the Lea Valley has been a long-standing urban policy goal. In the 1980s, it featured in the spatial strategy for London prepared by the London Planning Advisory Committee (LPAC, 1988)[2] and in the 1990s in the government's subsequent Regional Planning Guidance for London (RPG3; Government Office for London, 1996) and Thames Gateway Strategy (1995). Stratford was designated as a City Challenge location in 1997, and in desperation, perhaps, London Thames Gateway Development Corporation (LTGDC) was created in 2003 to attempt to 'unlock it'.

In parallel, strategies have been developed at a more local level, including Newham Council's 'Arc of Opportunity' (2002) and the Water City initiative still being promoted by a partnership of local community and commercial organisations. These both have embraced huge ambitions but have had very limited success beyond the immediate environs of Stratford. Stratford possessed both excellent transport connections and a large area of publicly owned land next to the existing town centre (known as the Stratford 'rail lands', the site being one of UK's premier rail engineering works up till the 1960s). This land offered by some way the most viable and practicable development opportunity in the valley. When, in support of its Thames Gateway strategy, the government agreed in 1994 to fund the construction of an international station at Stratford on the projected Channel Tunnel Rail Link in an attempt to 'kickstart' regeneration in the area, the rail lands were transferred to the successful Rail Link bidder London and Continental Railways (LCR). LCR agreed to develop an international station and to procure a major commercial centre on the site (a development now known as Stratford City). It is salutary that even now it is not commercially feasible for international trains to stop at Stratford, and the infrastructure is mothballed.

As the Stratford City project plan evolved in the late 1990s, there was no hint of an Olympic bid or an Olympic park at Stratford. Stratford City was seen as the realistic limit of plausible renewal for a long time to come, the combination of multiple land ownership, infrastructure and contamination, barring further moves west. The Stratford City plan for a huge shopping centre, a residential community of some 4,000 dwellings and a new business quarter of over 4 million sq ft was itself revolutionary for the area and barely credible, given the area's poverty, unfashionable reputation and weak consumer market.

Enter the Olympics

Stratford first emerged in 1999 as a potential location for the Olympic village, rather than the Games as a whole. At the time a new national stadium intended for both football and athletics was under construction at Wembley in north-west London, and it was assumed that this would naturally form the centrepiece of any putative future London bid. A report for the British Olympic Association prepared in 1999 by LPAC (1999) recommended Stratford as the preferred site for the village principally because of its accessibility to Wembley but also in support of the area's long-standing regeneration ambitions.

Stratford as a comprehensive location for the Games emerged as the plan to use the new Wembley Stadium for Olympic athletics evaporated for technical and cost reasons. At the same time, a Mayor had been elected for London as part of its new governance arrangements[3] who was prepared to back the concept of a London bid on condition that it was sited in Stratford and could function as a vehicle to attract new investment to the east of the city (Institute for Government, 2013:13).

This introduced the possibility that the money and muscle unique to an Olympic project could be deployed to address the hitherto intractable territory beyond Stratford City. Even so the initial feasibility study was cautious. Undertaken by Arup, who lay behind the rerouting of the Channel Tunnel route through Stratford in 1994 and were then masterplanning Stratford City for commercial developer clients, their proposal for a 'specimen' games posited a relatively modest land take excluding the need for engineering, for example, to underground the pylons that crossed the site (Arup, 2002:i–ix).

As the bid took shape, regeneration legacy became increasingly central to London's Olympic proposition and its prime selling point to the city and the country and to the International Olympic Committee. The size of the park grew as the site was planned in greater detail, and the demand grew for a more comprehensive and impressive Olympic park that gathered together more of the events and hence venues in one place. In principle, the land for this was available, albeit adding to the cost and complexity of the development, and the larger area increased the scale of the ultimate urban renewal.

At the strategic level, the outcomes expected of this ultimate urban renewal were not elaborated in any detail. It was enough that the Games would finally bring this land into the public realm and into modern productive use, in a way that would establish a new, high-quality image for the area and a stronger development market. How it would actually be used was a detailed issue left to the planners. The outcome that was given most prominence was the creation of a large new open space, billed incorrectly as the largest new park in Europe for over a century. This focus on creating a new open space seems somewhat paradoxical, since open space is something that the immediate vicinity is well supplied with, e.g. in the form of the Lee Valley Regional Park and Victoria Park.

These physical transformations were embellished with a broader social and community dimension. Stratford lies at the centre of the most deprived part of London and surrounded by communities whose levels of employment, income, educational attainment, quality of health and life expectancy are the lowest in the country. A celebrated legacy of the Olympics was to be its social and community impact; in the words of the bid, 'transforming the heart of east London for the benefit of all communities who live there'. Exactly how this could come about was not clear. Nevertheless, these social and community ambitions grew, culminating in a policy agreed at all political levels to adopt a long-term goal that the social conditions of East London, inferior to those in the rest of London, should have converged to the London average over a period of 25 years.[4] In the words of David Cameron in his first speech to the House of Commons as Prime Minister in 2010, 'let's make sure the Olympics legacy lifts East London from being one of the poorest parts of the country to one that shares fully in the capitals growth and prosperity' (PoliticsHome, 2010).

That goal remains, and a note on progress, albeit only five short paragraphs, was included in the 2014 government legacy report (HM Government/Mayor of London, 2014:43). The emphasis of the East London legacy now tends to focus on the growing success of the immediate built legacy of the park.

Planning for legacy

An outline layout for the development of the site, post-Olympics, was first prepared in 2004 prior to the bid. This early planning was a requirement imposed by the Olympic boroughs[5] which at the time were responsible for planning control (subsequently taken over by the Olympic Delivery Authority, ODA). It demonstrated that the plans and layout for the event itself would provide a sensible and practicable basis for legacy development afterwards and that the ODA was serious about its legacy intentions and provided an initial idea of what the site might ultimately be used for. It proved very durable and has formed the basis of all subsequent Legacy Masterplan Frameworks until recently, when the Olympicopolis concept emerged of using more of the site for cultural institutions (see below).

These and subsequent legacy proposals centred on housing, clustered in five housing areas (what came to be called 'neighbourhoods') located around the site on the tranches of land which remained when the temporary arenas and facilities required for the Games had been removed. Forecast figures of dwellings were very approximate at this early stage, but the bid talked of some 6,000 dwellings. The priority given to housing was surprising given the commercial potential of the site, particularly with Crossrail[6] starting to attract serious political backing. Nevertheless, the housing flavour remained, probably driven by a number of factors: the pressing need for housing in London and in East London in particular, where much of London's forecast population growth is targeted to take place in the London Plan; the desire not to undermine or compete against established plans for the development of Stratford City and the international quarter in particular; and the uncomplicated and relatively predictable development process involved in housing and the reliability of the resulting receipt income, which is part of the overall legacy budget. Housing also appeared to offer a more overt local community benefit which chimed with the social ambitions of legacy, although how much of the proposed housing was to be 'affordable' and how many people from existing local communities might actually eventually get to live in one of them has remained a controversial issue that sparks sporadic debate.

Boosting employment was seen as a goal for the remainder of the Lower Lea Valley rather than the park. The Valley, as we have learnt, is almost wholly in employment use, albeit fairly run down, and London's planning policy over the last few decades has sought to find a balance between the pressures of renewal which tends to be housing-led and its implications for the loss of low-value industrial uses which often support small manufacturing business and local jobs. The Lower Lea Valley Opportunity Area Planning Framework (GLA, 2007) sought to resolve this issue in the context of the Lea Valley and Olympic park, by broadly favouring housing on the Olympic park and the retention of business uses down the rest of the Valley.

The legacy strategy did, however, propose the retention and conversion of the giant Broadcasting, Press and Media Centre (the IBC/MPC) for business purposes. Despite the enormous size of the building and its location at the least commercial extremity of the Olympic park, improbable hopes were cherished that the building might continue to operate as a centre for digital communications business, led by the private sector and exploiting the technology embedded in it, and somehow linked with the technology sector then establishing itself a few miles away at so-called 'Silicon Roundabout' in Shoreditch. The fact that these improbable hopes have been realised began to prompt a rethink about how the park as a whole might be used after the Games.

Olympicopolis

'Olympicopolis' was the term used by Mayor Boris Johnson in mid-2014 to describe a development strategy which seeks to create a new cultural zone for the city. It is inspired by the cultural legacy of the Great Exhibition in 1851, the so-called 'Albertopolis' which resulted in a cluster of institutions being built in South Kensington, including the Victoria and Albert Museum and the Royal Albert Hall. In mid-2014 the London Legacy Development Corporation (LLDC) was in negotiation with the Victoria and Albert Museum over the development of space for new cutting-edge design, and with the Sadlers Wells theatre, University College London and the Smithsonian Institute over new satellite developments in the Olympic park.

Possibly, the successful conversion of the IBC/MPC, together with interest expressed in 2011 from the Welcome Foundation to take over the whole park to establish a life science centre, finally alerted the Greater London Authority (GLA) to the potential strategic value that the site possessed as somewhere for business and cultural investment that was seeking a London location that was new and distinctively contemporary. For the first time, a significant transformation in the status and role of East London looks plausible. To establishment London, East London has always been 'over the border' as Charles Dickens put it in 1867, and not a serious destination for cultural or state institutional investment (unless the O2 transatlantic entertainments complex and the Excel exhibition centre qualify, isolated and becalmed on Greenwich Peninsula and Royal Docks, respectively). Neither Canary Wharf nor Stratford City offers much more than stacks of offices, shops and branded restaurants. The Olympic park appears to have broken this prejudice, although, at the time of writing, it is still talk and may not materialise. Stratford's reputation as a respectable London location is still fragile, Olympics notwithstanding. Even one of the pioneers of the policy of 'moving London east', the late Sir Peter Hall, wrote shortly before his death an article where he expressed caution about the wisdom of the 'tendentious, real estate driven' process represented by the 'explosion of the Central Business District' and the potential offered by the Olympic park if its development took a different direction:

> In a 2012 anniversary a few weeks ago 5000 runners high fived Sir Chris Hoy in the Queen Elizabeth Olympic Park as kids splashed around in water fountains. Perhaps they had heard whispers, subsequently reported in newspapers, that Boris Johnson [Mayor of London] was talking to the American Smithsonian Museum about opening an outpost there. It would join other institutions – the Victoria and Albert Museum, the Sadlers Wells theatre and [yes] University College London – in a new cultural quarter, potentially bringing 10,000 jobs to Stratford. A triumph for the Mayor and his Legacy Corporation, you might say: the most outstanding after use of an Olympic Park in modern history.

But he went on to comment:

> Academics at UCL's Bartlett School of Planning are apprehensive about finding themselves relocated to Stratford.
>
> (Hall, 2014:32) (Sir Peter, of course, was Bartlett Professor of Planning at University College London)

The challenges of delivering legacy

A seamless transition from Games to legacy 'mode' was a deliberate goal of planning for London 2012. The Games layout was designed to be suitable for legacy; efforts began almost as soon as the bid was won to resolve the future of the arenas and buildings that were to be retained; and the creation of a management body to take ownership of legacy was put in motion well in advance of 2012.

Nevertheless, tensions exist between Games and legacy planning. The Games have a clearly defined brief and an absolute deadline; legacy is flexible and open-ended. Although the ODA earnestly proclaimed its legacy credentials (ODA, 2007), the inevitable need to deliver the Games for 2012 at all costs pushed 'too difficult' issues into the convenient longer grass which legacy offered. Unable to find a legacy tenant for the stadium, for example, the ODA solved the problem for itself by building a short-life structure to be taken down after the Games to leave a more modest low-level athletics stadium in its place. When, once the stadium was built, it was decided that it should be retained, the Olympic Park Legacy Company (OPLC, the forerunner of the LLDC) found itself having to unearth that elusive tenant that even the ODA had been unable to find. The intended commercial future for the IBC/MPC was put at risk by the Olympic decision to locate it in the commercially least favourable corner of the site, presenting OPLC with a further problem. Both facilities have survived and are likely to prosper though this would not have occurred without the considerable efforts of the LLDC and, in the case of the stadium, substantial additional cost to the taxpayer.

These examples raise the question of whether a single organisation responsible for Games and legacy might be preferable to the separate organisations established in London. Arguably, institutional continuity would have ensured that legacy considerations were fully assessed when Games decisions were made and might also have encouraged more of the vast Games budget to be available for direct legacy objectives. The way in which the environmental conditions – access for people with disabilities, for example – simply falls away outside the excellent facilities in the park comes as a surprise to visitors. Legacy has no comparable budget to that designated to the Games to address issues such as these.

On the other hand, the integration of delivery and legacy within one organisation might be seen as compromising the ODA's focus on the Games and risking critical delivery failure. Separate organisations also allow legacy strategy to change direction, as is happening in London, something that might be more difficult to achieve where internal bureaucratic inertia needed to be overcome. The creation of the LLDC has introduced new boundaries which extend beyond the

Olympic park into the Lower Lea Valley. This enables it to engage more directly with the difficult issues of integrating the new site with its old surroundings and exporting any Olympic effect into its wider hinterland.

Beyond the Olympic park – the impact on the wider Lea Valley and East London

'My aim', said Mayor Ken Livingstone in 2007, 'is to build on the area's unique network of waterways and islands to attract new investment and opportunities, and to transform the Valley into a new sustainable, mixed use city district, fully integrated into London's existing urban fabric. The Valley will host the 2012 Olympic and Paralympic Games and is one of the most exciting and challenging urban regeneration opportunities in Britain, with the potential to accommodate up to 40,000 new homes and provide 50,000 new jobs' (OAPF, 2007:1).

The figures for homes and jobs quoted here relate not just to the park but to a much larger area embracing the Valley as a whole. Proponents of London 2012 found it tempting to meld the confident but unexceptional housing outputs of the park with more wistful expectations for the wider development area. This temptation proved particularly strong in London given the prominence attached to the Games' regeneration rationale and the vague geography involved. The arguments behind these bigger expectations largely rest on the simple fact of the proximity of the areas concerned, rather than any more substantive theory centring on, say, infrastructure and improved accessibility. In practice, proximity is not a good guide particularly in London, where the juxtaposition of areas of high land value, significant wealth and development potential and areas of extreme poverty and brownfield inertia are a feature of the city.

Stratford

The relationship between the Olympics and its immediate neighbour, Stratford City, is a nuanced one. The two projects have followed parallel but largely separate paths, both in terms of design and construction, and they sit, in summer 2014, side by side oddly independently, the dull blocks of the shopping mall presenting their back to the idiosyncratic collection of space and buildings that comprise the Olympic site, now called the Queen Elizabeth II Park. (The impression is perhaps exaggerated by the absence thus far of the precinct of commercial offices, the international quarter, which will stand between the mall and the park.)

In two respects, however, their development was joined at the hip: the Stratford City housing zone in part provided the athletes village for the duration of the Games, and the main route and entrance to the Games from Stratford rail station ran through the shopping centre. The implementation of two such large developments simultaneously and side by side presented logistical challenges, exacerbated by the special security requirements attached to the Olympics, but also by the ownership convulsions which Stratford City underwent just as the Olympic bid was taking shape. For a period the GLA/London Development Agency even considered seeking to purchase the Stratford City site to ensure the Games plan was deliverable, and indeed the ODA had to build the village when the failing housing market forced the original commercial partner to withdraw. But the commercial synergy ultimately encouraged Westfield to proceed, and Stratford City was actually opened several months in advance of the Games. A study has estimated that it enabled Westfield to 'bring forward [the] development around 5–7 years earlier than would otherwise have occurred' (Volterra, 2011).

What one might call 'new' Stratford – the combination of the Queen Elizabeth II Park and shopping centre – is separated from the established Stratford town centre by the railway. If and how new and old will gel is uncertain. Fears that the commercial pull of the new development would extinguish the old shopping centre, however, as yet have not materialised; its location en route to the rail and bus interchange from a wide hinterland to the south has maintained its footfall. In fact, the old core of Stratford is experiencing striking commercial pressure for housing, with one 30-storey tower under construction opposite the station and two more in receipt of planning consent and expected to commence in late 2014. The immediate hinterland of Stratford, notably Stratford High St, linking Stratford westwards towards the river Lea and the city, has also undergone an extraordinary housing transformation which began much earlier, soon after the Olympic bid was won in 2005. A series of residential blocks and two budget hotels have replaced the collection of nondescript commercial buildings in generally poor condition that used to occupy the frontage.

The Olympic fringe and the Lower Lea Valley

The integration of the park with its surrounding area (bar Stratford City) was always going to be difficult, certainly physically. The park is enclosed on almost all sides by water, road and rail infrastructure with very few points of access. These form a barrier which interrupts the rhythm of the urban structure on both sides. This was not addressed in the park masterplanning, and a striking contrast exists between the manicured nature of the park and the rough and ready character of much of its surroundings. Because the site was carved out of a former industrial area, much of it remains as it was beyond its boundaries, oddly reminiscent of the Olympic park's own pre-Olympic days. One can walk out of the park for a few metres and it is a memory, bar distant views of the main stadium (one reason perhaps why it was decided belatedly to keep it). Land speculation is already a feature of the fringe and how the area will evolve is hard to judge. The GLA has produced a strategic planning policy document, and in mid-2014 the LLDC was producing a local plan to create a policy basis to try and manage the change.

Sensitivity developed in government as the park was taking shape that a 'cliff-edge' (as it was called) was being created between the expensive environment of the park and the deprived character of its surrounding areas. The Games it was said were threatening to 'show up', and not 'show off', East London.[7] A modest budget of £25 million was found to share between the 'host' boroughs[8] to fund additional public realm works beyond the park. Little of this money actually found its way to the immediate fringe or the Lea Valley, the majority being spent on high-profile locations on main routes to Stratford.

In parallel with the development of the Olympic park, the government sponsored LTGDC to work in concert with the ODA to promote and facilitate development in the remainder of the Lea Valley. In practice, the budget made available was insufficient to make much impact on the area, and unlike its predecessor the London Docklands Development Corporation and the ODA, it received no dowry of land to factor into a regeneration programme. The LTGDC was closed when responsibility for legacy transferred wholly to the Mayor. The Lea Valley, however, was one location where the Olympic programme did extend to new transport investment which has improved the accessibility of the area, potentially with an impact on the marketability of the land. An extension of the Docklands Light Railway from Stratford to Canning Town was built, which has created a string of new local stations down the Valley.

The development market for new housing in particular is beginning, in mid-2014, to get active down the Lea, and a scatter of substantial new schemes is now under construction on a number of sites where land happens to be available. Judging by the marketing material associated with them, it is the area's more fashionable and 'liveable' post-Olympic image that is central to their appeal. But the development of the area continues to lack a coherent sense of direction, with housing and industrial land lying side by side. It is not clear how far the ad hoc nature of these developments will displace or be displaced by the industrial character of the valley. In 2014, discussions took place that could extend the boundaries of the LLDC to embrace the whole of the Valley. This would seem essential if the full potential of the area is to be realised.

Wider East London

The legacy ambitions attached to the Games were subregional if not regional. They were expected after all to 'transform East London', although more recent commentary sensibly does not stray far beyond the park itself. (The government-sponsored meta-evaluation interim final report speaks for the first time of 'an area of influence up to 2km around the Park'; DCMS, 2012:171.) While at the time of the bid the geography was never defined in any detail, it was widely taken to mean that the Olympics might be expected to have an impact on the extensive areas of brownfield land along the Thames estuary, notably the Royal Docks, Barking Riverside, Greenwich Peninsula and Woolwich, much of which still awaits development.

It is the case that a series of substantial projects is under consideration in the Royal Docks in particular, although this is itself not new. The issue is whether they come to fruition and prove a success. As the official meta-evaluation report suggests, even then it is difficult to attribute this to the Olympics (DCMS, 2012:176). Crossrail is now under construction; its two eastern extensions will serve Stratford, the Royal Docks and Woolwich and may be a more significant influence. Crossrail adds passenger capacity which will trigger the next phase of development at

Canary Wharf, which in turn will have an impact on the local area and property market. In this situation, the Olympics can only be understood as part of a mix rather than a definitive influence in its own right.

Conclusions

The interesting legacy questions for London 2012 are whether the Olympics has made a difference to the trajectory of regeneration and development in East London; if so, what kind of difference and by how much. Answering these questions is difficult; in practice there is a limit, which unfortunately is reached fairly quickly, to what conventional evaluation methodology can tell us with any confidence. The official 'meta-evaluation' undertaken by consultants on behalf of the UK government was frank on this point:

> while change is already apparent, the true legacy impact of the Olympic Park and its associated venues will not be fully realised for a number of years. One of the over-riding conclusions from the LDA's 2012 Games Legacy Impact Evaluation Study was that with regard to the Olympic Park and Lower Lea legacy, it is simply too early at this interim stage to assess whether the scale and quality of the activities implemented were reasonable and effective or what impact they have had in transforming East London over and above what would have been achieved anyway.
>
> (DCMS, 2012:176)

At the same time, it is difficult to spend almost £8.5 billion[9] on transforming a relatively small area (circa 300 hectares) without there being some positive results. There is no question that the area of land now occupied by the Queen Elizabeth II Park is introducing uses into East London which will diversify and strengthen the local economy and generate future-facing economic activity that historically would not have entertained this part of London as a suitable location. Its growth, allied to the quality of the environment created, has the potential to diversify the local economy, in a way that the 400 small businesses employing some 5,000, which occupied the land prior to the Olympics, did not.

How far this sense of a new place can be established in East London generally is fundamentally a function of what else is done in other parts of the area, rather than of the Olympics and the park. The eye-watering public cost of creating the park as a location for new development (some 16 times the funding for the development of the Greenwich Peninsula) suggests that exporting the Olympic effect may take some time. Conversely, the impact of Crossrail factored in may make the calculus very different. Perhaps a useful indicator of ultimate Olympic success should be the opening of Stratford international station and the commencement of international rail services. The office development component of Stratford City has been christened 'The International Quarter' in anticipation. We shall see.

London did not know how it would use the Olympic site after the Games. The London Plan at the time talked banally about 'a new mixed use quarter for London'

(GLA, 2004). There was, however, a clear belief that this was a site that could and would deliver radical market-led change, and London appears to be being proved right. The Olympics provided funding that otherwise would not have been found to liberate this potential, and the success of the Olympics, extraordinarily, has turned Stratford into London's feel-good location. London could probably not have asked for more.

Notes

1 The industrial history of the Lea is recounted in a series of books by Dr Jim Lewis. The broader sweep of East London history is contained in *Beyond the Tower* by Professor John Marriott. Dr Jim Clifford has researched the environmental history of the Lower Lea Valley in detail and produced a range of articles on the subject. See http://libripublishing.co.uk/index.php?main_page=index&cPath=1
2 The LPAC was formed by London boroughs to provide strategic planning advice following the abolition of the GLC by the Conservative government in 1986.
3 Until the creation of the London Mayor and GLA in 2000, London had been without an elected administration following the abolition of the GLC in 1986. During this time London lacked the necessary political structure to host an Olympic bid. Enthusiasts for a London bid, led by the British Olympic Association, moved rapidly in 2000 to secure the new Mayor's support.
4 The 'Convergence' report published by the five 'host boroughs' in 2009 summarised the statistical gaps that existed between their socio-economic conditions and the rest of London.
5 Planning control was subsequently taken over by the ODA which was established after London won the bid to host the 2012 Games.
6 Crossrail is a fast new underground line connecting West, Central and East London which is under construction following decades of gestation. It will significantly reduce journey times and opens in 2018.
7 A comment attributed to Dr Tim Williams, then the Chief Executive of the London Thames Gateway Partnership, which was a promotional consortium of east London local authorities.
8 A modest figure for 'public realm improvements' provided by the Department of Communities and Local Government, following pressure from five East London boroughs hosting Olympic events. It was some way below the figure sought by the boroughs and contrasted sharply with the government funds provided for the Olympic park. Used at the local authorities' discretion, projects included the remodelling of Cutty Sark Gardens in Greenwich and cosmetic street frontage improvements to the A12, the main road route to Stratford from Central London.
9 A figure contained in Table 6-2 of the Interim final meta-evaluation report (p. 165), which assembles total land and development costs for the first time.

References

Arup (2002) 'London Olympics 2012 costs and benefits', available at: http://www.arup.com/_assets/_download/download368.pdf (last accessed 6 June 2014).
BRMB (2012) 'Inspiring a generation: a taking part report on the 2012 Olympic and Paralympic Games', available at: https://www.gov.uk/government/uploads/system/uploads/attachment_data/file/78316/Taking_Part_Olympic_Report.pdf (last accessed 10 August 2014).
Department of the Environment, Transport and the Regions (1995) *RPG9a: the Thames gateway planning framework*. London: London Stationery Office.

Dickens, C. (1857) 'Londoners over the border'. *Household words* (Vol. XVI), available at: http://pubhistory.co.uk/CanningTown/CharlesDickens.shtml (last accessed 16 August 2014).

Government Office for London (1996) 'Regional planning guidance RPG3', available at: http://regulations.completepicture.co.uk/pdf/Planning/Strategic%20guidance%20 for%20London%20planning%20authorities.pdf (last accessed 20 May 2014).

Greater London Authority (GLA) (2007) 'Lower Lea Valley opportunity area framework 2007', available at: http://legacy.london.gov.uk/mayor/planning/docs/lowerleavalley-pt1.pdf (last accessed 20 May 2014).

Greater London Authority (GLA) (2012, June) 'The London plan, revised early minor alterations', available at: http://www.london.gov.uk/sites/default/files/LP%20REMA% 20June%202012_0.pdf (last accessed 6 June 2014).

Hall, P. (2014, August) 'Mayor's business districts inflates'. *Planning Resource.*

HM Government/Mayor of London (2014, Summer) 'Inspired by 2012: the legacy from the Olympic and Paralympic Games. Second annual report', available at: https://www.gov. uk/government/uploads/system/uploads/attachment_data/file/335774/140723_Inspired_ by_2012_-_2nd_annual_legacy_report_-_accessible.pdf (last accessed 14 July 2014).

Institute for Government (2013) *Making the Games.* London: Institute for Government.

London Borough of Newham (2002) 'Arc of opportunity, Lower Lea Valley, Stratford to Thameside', available at: http://apps.newham.gov.uk/environment/udp/spgPdfs/ Lower%20Lea%20Framework.pdf (last accessed 1 June 2014).

London Planning Advisory Committee (LPAC) (1988) *Strategic planning advice for London.* London: LPAC.

LPAC (1999) *Site options for the Olympic village.* London: LPAC.

Olympic Delivery Authority (ODA) (2007) *Sustainable development strategy.* London: london2012.com.

PoliticsHome (2010) 'David Cameron's first speech to Commons as PM', available at: http://www.politicshome.com/uk/article/9253/david_camerons_first_speech_as_pm. html (last accessed 20 July 2014).

Sinclair, I. (2011) *Ghost milk.* London: Penguin.

Volterra (2011) *Stratford city: the inheritance before the Games.* London: Volterra.

9 The Olympic host boroughs

Local authority responses to the London 2012 Games

Nadia Grubnic

Introduction

This chapter analyses three local authority responses to the opportunities and challenges arising from their role as host boroughs to the 2012 Olympic and Paralympic Games. Two boroughs, Newham and Hackney, were designated as host boroughs from the outset of London's Olympic bid; the third, Barking and Dagenham, despite its geographical proximity to the venues designated for the Games, was not accorded host status until 2011. While sharing several characteristics of their region – including areas of acute social deprivation arising in large part from the protracted process of decline of traditional manufacturing industries – the boroughs had several differences, not least in relation to their demographics. Their initial responses to East London being designated as the site for the city's bid to host the Games also differed. However, as the following analysis suggests, over the period of what might be called the pre-event phase, there was a convergence of interests and responses to the opportunities presented, particularly as the narrative of the positive urban legacies to be sought from the Games gained traction through the policies developed by central government.

The chapter draws on interviews conducted over the period 2007 to 2014. These involved local government politicians and officers as well as representatives of national government and the agencies tasked with the delivery of the Games and its urban legacies. It also draws upon official documentation and the observations of the author derived from public meetings and other 'local' events that took place in the pre-event phase. The chapter examines the changes in the perceptions and policies adopted by the three local authorities over three phases. The first phase (2003–2005) covers the period immediately preceding the submission of London's bid to host the Games. The second focuses upon the years immediately following the bid's success (2005–2008), a time when central government and the agencies tasked with organising the event were seeking to translate a bid designed to win the competition to host the Games into a blueprint for their delivery, and the final phase (2008–2012) covers the period during which the major construction of the Olympic venues and their associated infrastructure took place. This was also the period during which the programme of urban transformation, the Games' urban legacy, took shape. The hosting of a sports mega-event such as the Olympics has often been associated with the marginalisation of local democratic institutions, with the 'local' being the subject of urban transformation rather than having a real influence over its direction. The chapter concludes with some reflections on this issue and, in particular, on the role of the local authorities as 'stakeholders' in the governance of the Games.

Phase 1: bidding for the Games (2003–2005)

In phase 1 the three local authorities were in very different starting positions in terms of their initial perceptions of the bidding process, receptiveness to the idea of being *part* of such discussions and in their respective *visions* of what a successful bid leading to the hosting of the Games in their area might bring in terms of a range of benefits and opportunities. In Newham there was a strong political will (even to bid) as evidenced by several key respondents from both inside and outside the borough when reflecting on this period. For example, a key respondent (Senior Newham Officer 1 [SNO1]) interviewed in 2007 argued that 'part of the aim was to change Newham's image even if the decision was "no"'. There was strong leadership and support from the elected Mayor, and there was evidence of key figures from the borough taking a proactive role in the lobbying process from as early as 1999 (London Bid Advocate, 2013). In terms of thinking about and planning for delivery in the event of a successful outcome (which was far from a foregone conclusion at such an early stage in the preparation for the bid), delivery structures had been planned in advance in order to mobilise the borough quickly in the event of the bid being successful. A possible reason for Newham's position and planned responses was the existence of 'aspirational' policy goals for the borough which the Games were then identified as a catalyst for achieving or accelerating. For example,

> to establish a clear sense of place and identity for Newham, attracting investment and promoting a diverse choice of high quality cultural, leisure and recreational activities.
>
> (London Borough of Newham [LBN], 2001)

The actions of Newham leaders in this phase strongly suggest a perception of the Games as a tool for urban transformation, a view reflected in an interview with SNO2 in 2007 in which he referred to using the Games as a vehicle for 'branding, to achieve social inclusion and other pre-existing goals'. Equally there was a sense of not only 'buying into' the official narrative once this had been created by central government and the bid writers but perhaps of having been ahead of national government in this respect. An illustration of Newham's policies and programmes consistent with this view was the 'Summer of Sport' events held from 2004 onwards with the twin goals of consulting and engaging with local communities as well as promoting the benefits of the 'Olympic project'. These were large-scale, aspirational, 'confident' events that served the purpose of promotion as well as fulfilling the official role of public consultation.

By contrast, the initial approach in Hackney was acknowledged, even by those who went on to lead the work for the borough, as a 'slower start' (Senior Hackney Officer 1 [SHO1], 2007). This can be seen in the degree of political support for bidding or identifying the possible links between the Games and the council's existing policy priorities which, although it could be argued were still concerned with 'transformation', presented a different understanding of this compared to Newham. Explanations for this difference in priorities and perspectives between Newham and Hackney include the track record of poor administration by the latter (Audit Commission, 2001), which made it a higher priority for Hackney to seek to turn this around and change perceptions. Second, some socio-economic shifts were already starting to occur irrespective of the prospects offered by the Games in terms of both the economic and employment aspirations of Hackney's residents, suggesting that the political desire to accelerate transformation in the borough was not as strong as in Newham. Lastly, the idea of 'difference' within a place (in which areas of relative affluence exist near to areas of severe social deprivation) began to emerge quite early on in Hackney's policies and marketing strategies although, at this stage, this idea was not yet fully linked to the 'Olympic project' but was more to do with the borough's policy focus on the distinctive needs of different areas and neighbourhoods (SHO2, 2013).

In terms of engagement in the prebid talks, Hackney was present but not as vocal or proactive as Newham. Although having a similar political structure (with an elected Mayor since 2002) which could have facilitated dialogue at the most senior level, it did not appear to be high on Hackney's agenda. There was some evidence of cooperative thinking and working, however, as seen in the borough's 'sport-based' talks with potential host boroughs in case the bid was successful, but these took place at a lower level than that of the senior council officers (SHO1, 2007). There were certainly no plans in place for the creation of 'Games-focused' structures to capitalise on a winning bid. A further key difference between Newham and Hackney was the existence in the former of more vocal opposition to the idea of a potentially successful bid. This arose from the greater likelihood of businesses and other groups in Newham facing the potential threat and disruption of Compulsory Purchase Orders and other forms of 'relocation' if the plans proved to be successful.

By comparison to Newham and Hackney, the London borough of Barking and Dagenham was clearly an outsider in both geographical and political terms in phase 1. Its main strategic alliances were with the (London) Thames Gateway. As interviews revealed (Senior Barking and Dagenham Officers [SBDO] 1 and SBDO2, 2007; SBDO3, 2013), there was a difference of opinion among members of the council as to whether the possible benefits from getting involved with the 'Games project' would actually detract from existing and planned regeneration initiatives. Decision makers were, of course, *aware* that a bid was being discussed, but their responses suggest ambivalence towards the concept of a 'local' global sporting mega-event and the possible 'good' it might bring. This ambivalence related, at least in part, to geopolitical factors – the borough not seeing itself as close enough to the planned location to really accrue any tangible benefits as well as its officers and councillors 'identifying' more closely (politically and strategically) with places towards outer rather than inner London.

In summary, the three boroughs were in very different positions during phase 1 – they had different priorities (although the ideas of change, improvement and transformation could be seen to some degree in each of their broad policy goals). Second, their perceptions of the Games and the potential benefits they might bring were also very different and related to how 'visionary' their leadership was and how central they might eventually be to the proposed location of the Games, particularly the Olympic park as the main stage/centrepiece. Finally, their respective geographical positions were also reflected in the political/decision-making perspectives held, with Newham seeing itself clearly in a leadership role, Hackney on the 'fringes' and Barking and Dagenham very much the 'outsider'.

Phase 2 (2005–2008): 'from hopefuls to hosts'

In phase 2 the relative positions of the three boroughs remained broadly similar with Newham still the 'frontrunner' in terms of initiatives and policy responses. However, towards the end of this phase, some interesting shifts and changes could be observed. At the start of phase 2 (in 2005 immediately post-decision), Newham was typically 'quick off the mark' most visibly in the creation of its 'Olympic Unit' and the publication of its 'Vision' document just days after the success of the bid (LBN, 2005b). There was a governance/delivery mechanism in place and a smooth transition in marketing and policy terms from the borough being branded as part of a 'candidate' city team to that of being a 'host'.

During phase 2, Newham clarified its message and 'offer' with a focus on the policy goals of transformation and improvement. For example, in an interview with SNO1 in 2007, he shared his belief that 'Newham is already seen differently and will never be the same again'. The promotional materials as well as policies produced at this time deployed 'image' as a key theme. Tangible and intangible goals and potential gains were defined to include jobs, transport, sport and housing (LBN, 2005a). The presentation of these in a 'cross-cutting' way was closely tied to the policy style of the then new Labour government. Newham was able to act swiftly and decisively largely because of the confidence of the Mayor and key officers in preparing for a positive outcome to the bid, a confidence also mirrored at officer level (interview with SNO3, 2007). This ambitious and transformation-driven approach championed by Newham was captured in the council's strapline 'a place people choose to live and work' (Sir Robin Wales; LBN, 2006) and could also be seen in other aspects of its social policy such as housing. This concept of 'place' was deployed on different levels – in a very *real* way with a focus on the tangible physical improvements sought for the borough (such as improved connectivity through the development of Stratford station) and on a symbolic level with the sense of a future *imagined* Newham being part of the council's policy goals, possibly with very different kinds of people being attracted to living and working there.

Newham's perception of itself as a 'leader' within this process – both of the other host boroughs and as an equal to other (national) key decision makers – seemed to be confirmed early on in this phase, with the Mayor taking up a position on the Olympic Board. Equally illustrative of Newham's increasingly confident self-image was the tone and style of the Tessa Sanderson Academy which on reflection probably turned out to be more an exercise in showing Newham 'had arrived' and had a raised profile rather than being effective in sports development terms (observation at academy launch event, October 2006, interview with SNO3, 2007).

By 2007, however, there were rumblings of discontent within the council (possibly linked to the broader impacts of the recession commencing at that time), and there was a questioning of the effectiveness and 'value for money' of the Olympic Unit which was subsequently downsized (SNO3, 2008). The downsizing occurred at the time when national government and the newly established delivery organisations, the Olympic Delivery Authority (ODA) and London Organising Committee of the Olympic Games (LOCOG), were set up to lead in the delivery of the Games, thus, arguably, diminishing the role and significance of the 'individual' host boroughs. From the comments of Newham's leaders, there was a move towards a more collective or collaborative approach with the other host boroughs. Rather than Newham and its leadership thinking it could 'do it all alone', there was a turning point within phase 2 when Newham's leadership undertook a more measured approach. There was a growing recognition that the benefits promised by the bid might not be delivered, community benefits could be 'sacrificed' to bigger (national) agendas and that a move to a more collective approach – through the Host Boroughs Unit (created in 2007), a small team representing the five East London Olympic boroughs – would make good pragmatic policy sense. This could be seen in a shift in policy statements from the council including, for example, an admission in a 2006 legacy strategy document that 'a realistic view might be that we will have only limited success in influencing the quality of the legacy 2013' (LBN 2006:8) and in a presentation given by SNO4 in May 2007 which noted that there was a broadening of outlook with the concept of 'Broader legacy' being focused on the concept of the 'image of East London' as opposed to centring on Newham alone. Lastly, the leader of the Host Boroughs Unit at that time later reflected that it had been an 'effective grouping' and gave its members a channel through which to approach new organisations such as the ODA (Senior Host Boroughs Officer, 2013).

Although Hackney did not seize the potential opportunities as quickly or perhaps wholeheartedly, this phase could be seen as one of growing confidence as policy goals in relation to the successful bid (as well as a reflection on the best ways to achieve them) crystalised. While Hackney continued with a less proactive and ambitious approach in the early days of phase 2, this appearance may not tell the whole story. For example, unlike Newham there were no initial changes in terms of governance or delivery structures – the Hackney 2012 unit was not established until 2007. However, the political context was changing rapidly. Hackney had been recognised as an improving council (Audit Commission, 2009; interview with SHO2, 2013) and different policies were emerging as a result. In defining potential benefits to be gained from involvement in the 'Olympic project', broad-ranging goals were developed that came to include employment, housing and sport, but there were also, at the same time, two very specific areas of focus – the borough's commitment to establishing the Olympic park's Press and Media Centre as a permanent post-Games facility and, second, to use it in local legacy terms to generate employment and infrastructure improvements (SHO1, 2007). This selective approach might have been due to the council and its leadership having more of an interest in legacy rather than the prestige associated with the mega-event itself (SHO2, 2013) and linked to the borough's position and centrality (politically and spatially). It did not expect the 'lion's share' of venues and facilities and was, therefore, able to act in a more 'measured' and targeted way. It could be seen as a very strategic policy decision to focus the borough's 'demands' with the hope of improving chances of success. Hackney's style of working was also emerging as being quite different to that of Newham, typically adopting a more 'partnership-centred' approach. This could again have been down to practical issues such as proximity, but equally there is evidence of Hackney council having a more collaborative approach in the past (for example, the Joint Sports Development Framework developed in 2005). They were the 'legal' hosts for the Host Boroughs Unit (initially the 'Five Boroughs Unit') and saw this as a more effective mechanism for lobbying and 'extracting' benefits from other stakeholders.

Publications produced by Hackney in this phase also give an indication of the changing perception of itself and the promotion of this new confident 'image' to the rest of London and beyond. The sense of 'place' as represented through the theme of 'neighbourhoods' emerged more strongly and had the dual purpose of changing perceptions and attracting business (SHO2, 2013). This could be seen clearly in the 2007 'Gold' marketing campaign as well as the 'Streets Ahead' inward investment publication. Both presented the positive promotion of Hackney and situated the borough as 'central to London's 2012 plans' (Invest in Hackney, 2007).

The actions of Barking and Dagenham in this phase were interesting because it was still not an official host borough and at times found itself in a challenging and controversial political context. Policies produced at the time reveal a concerted effort to outline potential benefits that could be gained from the Games (perhaps proportionately more than Hackney at the time), as presented, for example, in its 'Gateway to the Games' publication (LBBD, 2006). In reality the most likely gains at this stage may have been to have training venues located in the borough, but broad cross-cutting policy goals did emerge. An Olympic Unit was established in 2006 and certain parallels can be drawn with Newham in the sense that Barking and Dagenham assumed a leading role among Gateway boroughs. The Gateway remained the main strategic 'base' for the borough. Interestingly this network then replicated some of the policies and structures of the Host Boroughs Unit (for example, in the 'Next Stop 2012' strategy produced by the Gateway boroughs in 2008).

Barking and Dagenham's main 'offer' in relation to the Games was to package the borough as a tourism/day destination linked to the 'rediscovery' of local heritage (and again possibly reflecting Newham's 'Be a Local Tourist' campaign). In other aspects too, similarities can be seen to Newham in terms of the aspirational language used in policies and interviews. For example, a key respondent referred to the council's primary focus of 'raising the profile of the borough' (SBDO 2,

2007). Internally, in terms of broader policy goals, there was a continuation of the pursuit of large-scale regeneration initiatives, such as the work on improving town centres and pushing forward the Barking Riverside development. However, a key moment for the borough during this period was the challenging political situation in 2006 when the British National Party (BNP) became the official opposition.

In terms of policy content and aims, all three boroughs sought to secure employment opportunities for local people (although the definition of 'local' came to be contested). Newham and Hackney created their own job brokerage schemes with Hackney also focusing on the legacy role of the media centre for this. Housing was a key concern for Newham and Hackney, and both had acute housing need (for different reasons) though Newham had very different housing policies to all the other host boroughs. Sporting legacy was a further common theme in terms of physical legacy, and all mentioned the target of raising participation and promoting talented young sportspeople. Finally, all emphasised achieving benefits to local business, improved transport/infrastructure (including the enhancement of Stratford station, the extension of the underground to Hackney and tourism).

The developments happening in this phase need to be seen in the context of an increasingly complex national picture in which, following the celebrations arising from winning the bid, the reality of needing to deliver to unmoveable International Olympic Committee (IOC) deadlines and on its own bid promises led national government to create new structures and organisations with whom the host boroughs would have to work and liaise. There was also a 'top-down' push for cooperation between the boroughs from national government to facilitate this liaison to help deliver the ambitious legacy promises made in the initial bid which served increasingly to legitimise in public debate the government's commitment to a significantly higher Olympic budget than appeared in the original London bid book (Senior Civil Servant, 2011).

The need for the host boroughs to be 'heard' in this new governance structure – to articulate/demand/represent and ideally deliver on local political goals – presented a significant challenge. Despite Newham's Mayor being on the LOCOG board, Newham moved closer to its fellow host boroughs towards the end of phase 2, recognising the potential benefits of a more collective approach. Conversely, Hackney seemed to be moving in a different direction. Although still coming from the perspective of seeing the benefits of a more collective approach, in phase 2 very clear objectives were defined and pursued with energy and determination from this point until the start of the Games. Barking and Dagenham remained aligned with the other Thames Gateway boroughs but also began to seek greater involvement with the 'Olympic project', particularly as its internal political challenges arising from the presence of the BNP, began to be resolved.

Phase 3: from competing visions to convergence (2008–2012)

In the final phase (2008–2012), there were further shifts in the experiences, responses and relative positions of the three boroughs. One illustration of this was in their representation at the Beijing Games in 2008. The Mayor and some key figures were present from Newham, but by far the strongest representation was from Hackney who sent the biggest party and hosted several quite high-profile events (such as the breakfast meeting/promotion which featured Tessa Jowell and had a big emphasis on 'celebrity' links and place promotion; participant observation, August 2008). This could be seen as indicative of Hackney's growing confidence in terms of identity, goals and positioning. Barking and Dagenham was not represented, but nevertheless established international links with particular Chinese districts and exchanged visits and advice. Although working in different ways, all three boroughs begun to adopt a 'global view' by the start of phase 3.

Newham continued to establish a position closer to the other host boroughs, moving away from the official national narrative with many of the official statements from the council (in policies, presentations given by officers of the council and on the council website) clearly redefining and repositioning the forthcoming Games as *one* of their key regeneration projects alongside developments such as Westfield (which was to open in 2011). This was, in effect, a 'downsizing' of the significance of the forthcoming mega-event and the council's reliance on it to accelerate the delivery of its goals. However, it was also Newham's way of managing and offering a particular representation of events when faced with the reality of the enormity of the mega-event 'on their doorstep' as well as the 'fear' that expectations of legacy outcomes (promised to residents and voters) might not be possible to deliver because of the complexity of emerging governance structures and the worsening economic climate.

Throughout this phase the Mayor did not relax in his leadership, nor did he move away from his very personal leadership style. However, there was a change in what exactly was being sought from the Games and their legacy as well as how this might be achieved. More 'realistic' goals were emerging due to wider national as well as local scrutiny. Although largely 'sold' (to the wider public and the IOC) on the promise of regenerating the whole of East London, research (e.g. Raco, 2004; NEF, 2008; Poynter, 2009) began to warn that disadvantaged communities might be the least likely to benefit from Games, for example, in terms of 'affordable' housing and 'local' jobs and that politicians representing them might become marginalised. While some critics have suggested that the Olympic investment was likely to shift the borough's demographic profile in favour of more new middle-class residents, something implicitly if not publicly supported by the borough, there was also a strengthening of the resolve to gain *local* benefits or tangible outcomes such as jobs as well as securing the future of the Olympic stadium and its legacy for Newham (SHO2, 2013 reflecting on LBN).

Hackney could be characterised as developing strongly in phase 3 not only as seen in the borough's presence and 'style' of promotion in Beijing in 2008 but more broadly in its 'consolidation' of image and representation of identity – global, cultural and artistic. By the end of this phase, despite Hackney's 'late start', progress was being made towards achieving its priority policy goals. A more assertive and confident style of negotiation emerged in the way in which leaders lobbied strongly to ensure that the Olympic Press and Media Centre and its potential jobs legacy was delivered 'as promised' and that the decision was taken to extend and improve the rail infrastructure through the borough, particularly the East London Line, in the summer of 2008. This may be seen as a dual approach; as well as being the location for the Host Boroughs Unit and fully adopting the collective policies designed to achieve convergence between these boroughs and the rest of London in terms of the life chances of their residents, the borough also pursued its own very specific goals.

Other aspects of the Hackney 'brand' were also being developed such as the plans to expand the fledgling 'Tech City' located in Shoreditch, and although the borough would not directly benefit from housing developments taking place in the Olympic park post-Games, its involvement in the 'Olympic project' seemed to be having a 'spillover effect' on Hackney's housing policy. New development schemes using promotions such as 'Hackney – the new place to be' represented a huge turnaround in the borough's image and marketability from what it was a decade before (SHO2, 2013). In some ways, Hackney (or parts of it) 'arrived' and were 'on the map' even before the mega-event actually took place – in terms of achieving established policy goals, creating shifts in image and perception and certainly in creating a turnaround in council performance (measured by indices such as educational attainment). Although the infrastructure improvements and the location and legacy role of the media centre were not easily won, they had been confidently fought for. Examples of this new identity could be seen by the end of phase 3 in the successful 'Personal Best' volunteering programme and being the venue for BBC Radio 1's 'Hackney Weekend' in June 2012, an event that reached a global audience (Hackney Today, 25 June 2012).

For different reasons, phase 3 was also the most positive period for Barking and Dagenham. The key change was officially becoming a host borough in 2011 (joining the legacy narrative), a move that was strongly supported by the (new) national coalition government. It provided evidence of Barking and Dagenham 'buying into' (or perhaps being *allowed* to buy into) the national agenda and official narrative and reflected the reversal in electoral fortunes of the BNP in the national and local elections of 2010.

Being 'invited' or 'included' at this late stage may have been of symbolic importance more than a 'guarantee' of any tangible benefits, but it did complement national and local versions of the legacy narrative. In coming to the table late, Barking and Dagenham may not have fully capitalised on the local job opportunities that the other host boroughs, particularly Newham, had access to during the construction phase. However, there were some tangible benefits to be realised in terms of the upgrading and construction of leisure facilities (which allowed the council to deliver on an existing policy priority of investment in this area). The borough defined their likely gains as being 'a greater share in the opportunities that the 2012 Games will bring' (LBBD, 2013). Two of the outputs from Barking and Dagenham at this time – the 'Our Games' publication (LBBD, 2012) which continued the theme of local pride and focused on historical and cultural sites and 'London's Newest Opportunity' (LBBD, 2012) which showcased economic opportunities in the borough – can be viewed in the light of the borough's new position (in relation to the Games but also more broadly as a changing and more 'accepted' place).

Phase 3 coincided with the crucial construction stage in which conflicts and challenges would emerge, but these did not happen so much *between* the host boroughs as they did between the boroughs and central government and the public agencies responsible for organising the Games. Such negotiations were exemplified by Hackney's concern to secure the permanent presence of a key Olympic venue (the Press and Media Centre) as a post-Games legacy. Newham continued to expect to achieve the most from the Games but presented a slightly different view of the mega-event as being but one major project among *other* regeneration initiatives such as Westfield (although whether this would have happened at such a pace without London 2012 remains a matter for debate). Both Newham and Hackney looked set to realise many of their policy aims in relation to London 2012 although the road towards achieving them was not without obstacles, while Barking and Dagenham had come to the table late but sought to capitalise on the situation not least in relation to restoring its public image. Finally, the shift in perspective could most clearly be seen in the five (then six) host boroughs signing up to the Strategic Regeneration Framework in 2009, a strong expression of their collective outlook and their commitment to their borough residents achieving the same quality of life and living standards as the rest of London.

Conclusion

The focus of this chapter has been local responses to London 2012. Four main conclusions can be drawn. First, across the three phases there was a move towards a common framework of convergence as a local policy goal and the utilisation of joint structures such as the Host Boroughs Unit as a way of achieving this outcome. It is highly likely that this coming together of the boroughs was due to the complex policy landscape and governance structures that emerged to deliver the Games and its promised legacies and was spurred by fears that the promises made by the national government would be 'downsized' in the harsh reality of the global recession that began to emerge in 2007.

Second, each local authority's view of itself and what it could hope to deliver for its communities, as a result of its involvement in the Games, underwent subtle but important changes. Newham moved away from what it once labelled 'Our Games' to a more collective approach. Barking and Dagenham, despite its late entry to the process, gained from the Games and its legacy narrative, re-establishing its political image and its relationship to the city of London in contrast to its earlier association with the relatively anonymous and amorphous Thames Gateway. Hackney grew in confidence from a position of relative inactivity to positively enhancing its 'brand' and achieving several specific neighbourhood policy goals.

Third, of the three boroughs studied, Hackney 'gained' most from London 2012. It started slowly but worked solidly towards achieving a few specific but nevertheless ambitious 'wins'. It is hard to disentangle exactly how much of a contribution London 2012 made to Hackney's changing fortunes and 'image' as perceived internally by residents and externally by potential visitors and investors because evidence suggests changes were afoot already. The council was turning its performance round from 'failing' to 'improving' – pockets of gentrification indicated a (subtle) shift in demographics and class structure and enclaves of art and tech businesses were indicative of new industries already emerging; the Games reinforced and, arguably, accelerated these trends.

Finally, the evidence suggests that three of the local 'stakeholders' of London 2012 were not excluded or entirely marginalised by their being recipients of or close to the location of the mega-event (also see Evans, 2013). The local authorities were, albeit to different degrees, participant rather than passive. Figuratively and materially, they were reconnected to the city. Paradoxically, this reconnection is, however, likely to accelerate many of the trends occurring elsewhere in the city, including their gentrification, especially in parts of Hackney and Newham.

References

Audit Commission (2001) 'London borough of Hackney corporate governance reinspection', available at: http://archive.audit-commission.gov.uk/auditcommission/sitecollectiondocuments/InspectionOutput/InspectionReports/2001/HackneyLBC04.pdf (last accessed November 2010).

Audit Commission (2009) 'London borough of Hackney organisational assessment', available at: http://archive.audit-commission.gov.uk/oneplace/infobyarea/region/area/localorganisations/organisation/pages/default-region=51&area=350&orgId=1235.aspx.html (last accessed November 2013).

Evans, G. (2013) 'Materializing the vision of a 2012 London Olympic Games' in V. Girginov (Ed.), *Handbook of the London 2012 Olympic and Paralympic Games (Vol 1): making the Games.* London: Routledge.

Hackney Today (2012, June 25) 'Holla Day: the BBC Radio 1 Hackney weekend put the borough in the international spotlight on 23 and 24 June – and it did itself proud'.

Host boroughs (2009) 'Strategic regeneration framework: an Olympic legacy for the host boroughs', available at: http://www.gamesmonitor.org.uk/files/strategic-regeneration-framework-report.pdf (last accessed 11 April 2015).

Invest in Hackney (2007) 'Hackney streets ahead – Hackney: a business destination', available at: http://www.renaisi.com/an-inward-investment-strategy-for-hackney/ (last accessed 10 January 2008).

London Borough of Barking and Dagenham (2006) 'Gateway to the Games', available at: http://www.webarchive.org.uk/wayback/archive/20101006020218/http://www.barking-dagenham.gov.uk/2-news-events/olympics/pdf/prospectus.pdf (last accessed 3 June 2015).

London Borough of Barking and Dagenham (2012a) 'London's newest opportunity', available at: https://www.lbbd.gov.uk/business/growing-the-borough/londons-newest-opportunity/overview (last accessed 3 June 2015).

London Borough of Barking and Dagenham (2012b) 'Barking and Dagenham – host borough for the London 2012 Games', available at: http://moderngov.barking-dagenham.gov.uk/ieDecisionDetails.aspx?ID=1994 (last accessed 11 January 2013).

London Borough of Newham (LBN) (2001) *Past, present future: visitor strategy.* London: London Borough of Newham.

London Borough of Newham (LBN) (2005a) *Vision statement*. London: LBN.

London Borough of Newham (LBN) (2005b) *Minutes from meeting of the Cabinet Board for the 2012 Olympics*. London: LBN.

London Borough of Newham (LBN) (2006) *Making Newham Olympic and Paralympic winners*. London: LBN.

New Economics Foundation (NEF) (2008) 'Fool's gold: how the London 2012 Olympics is selling East London short and a 10 point plan for a more positive local legacy', available at: http://b.3cdn.net/nefoundation/c20cafb222715b6594_glm6b8ert.pdf (last accessed 3 June 2015).

Poynter, G. (2009) 'The 2012 Olympic Games and the reshaping of East London' in R. Imrie, L. Lees and M. Raco (Eds.), *Regenerating London – governance, sustainability and community in a global city*. Abingdon, UK: Routledge.

Raco, M. (2004) 'Whose gold rush? The social legacy of a London Olympics' in A. Vigor, M. Mean and C. Tims (Eds.), *After the gold rush: a sustainable Olympics for London*. London: IPPR and DEMOS.

Thames Gateway London Partnership (2008) 'Next Stop 2012', available at: http://www.24dash.com/news/communities/2008-08-15-next-stop-2012 (last accessed December 2013).

Interviews (chronologically)

Senior Newham Officer 1 (SNO1), 5 March 2007.
Senior Newham Officer 2 (SNO2), 5 March 2007.
Senior Newham Officer 3 (SNO3), 23 March 2007.
Senior Barking and Dagenham Officer 1 (SBDO1), 23 March 2007.
Senior Barking and Dagenham Officer 2 (SBDO2), 23 March 2007.
Senior Hackney Officer 1 (SHO1), 13 April 2007.
Senior Newham Officer 4 (SNO4), 8 May 2007 (discussion and presentation).
Senior Newham Officer 3 (SNO3), 30 July 2008.
Senior Host Boroughs Officer (SHBO), 22 June 2011.
Senior Civil Servant, 7 October 2011.
London Bid Advocate, 12 June 2013.
Senior Newham Officer 3 (SNO3), 25 June 2013.
Senior Hackney Officer 2 (SHO2), 1 November 2013.
Senior Barking and Dagenham Officer 3 (SBDO3), 14 February 2014.

Participant observation by author

6 October 2006 – launch of Tessa Sanderson's Sports Academy, Stratford, LB Newham.
8 May 2007 – Newham Unit for the 2012 Games – vision & legacy', presented by SNO4.
23 August 2008 – Hackney breakfast event in Beijing 'Hackney: a host for 2012'.

10 Olympic brandscapes

London 2012 and the seeping commercialisation of public space

Guy Osborn and Andrew Smith

Introduction

Various authors identify how mega-events correspond to, exacerbate or even usher in broader ideological shifts. Hayes and Karamichas (2014:249) suggest that sport mega-events are 'peculiar, recurrent, time-space compressions where global norms and the ideological operations that sustain them are made visible and identifiable'. One recurrent theme in the literature is that mega-events are essentially neoliberal projects driven by the perceived need for greater urban entrepreneurialism or competitiveness and that they are indelibly linked to the commoditisation of culture, time and space (Smith, 2012). Our approach here is focused on one aspect of neoliberalism, namely the commercialisation of public space and the relation between the public and the private. Through this analysis, we identify a nuanced form of Olympic legacy and the processes through which this legacy is realised.

Banarjee (2001:9) contends that 'we are experiencing a steady withering of the public realm', and some authors have observed that this (contested) process is a feature, and even a legacy, of the Olympic Games. Indeed, Sanchez and Broude-houx (2013:133) understand the Rio Olympic Games as 'state-assisted privatisation and commodification of the urban realm'. Since the Los Angeles Games of 1984, complaints about the over-commercialisation of the Olympic Games have intensified. In this chapter we argue that the Games have not only become more commercialised, but that commercial orientation has made the Olympic Games an agent of urban commercialisation. In doing so, we evaluate the emergence of this underexplored legacy of the Games. The chapter begins with a review of the conceptual framework we have used to explain how the Olympic Games affect urban space. Our work then focuses on the 2012 London Games and culminates in a more specific case study, London's Hyde Park, which we use to illustrate key issues.

Brandscapes

A key aim of the chapter is to understand how the Olympic Games affect public space in both the short term (during) and in longer term (after). It is evident that space is reconfigured during the Games, but we are also interested in the aftermath when the Games themselves have long since departed. Particular focus is placed on processes of commodification, and the notion of a 'brandscape' provides a useful conceptual frame within which to understand these processes. According to Wood and Ball (2013:62), brandscapes represent 'the current apex of hyper-consumption in neoliberal capitalism'. Branding has become the key vehicle for creating value in the twenty-first century, and, given the dominance of consumer culture, this is something that now also pervades urban places too. As branding is meant to generate seductive 'affect' (Wood and Ball, 2013), rather than merely awareness or interest in products, corporations have sought to create experiences in which consumers can be fully absorbed. As Mikunda (2002) notes, this type of thinking has led to the creation of 'brand lands' where companies exhibit their products in purpose-built visitor experiences designed to invoke sensual and emotional connections. This phenomenon[1,2] is related to the rise of the experience economy, a new stage of capitalist production, where the value of goods is enhanced through embedding products in experiences (Pine and Gilmore, 1999). Following the tendency of capitalism to reinvent itself and colonise (and commoditise) new spheres, the spatially concentrated idea of a 'brand land' has become more pervasive. As Klingmann (2007:81) notes, 'while the spatialisation of brands was first realised in the formation of isolated flagship stores and malls, it has over the course of the last two decades reached another level as a ubiquitous formula of market culture that permeates urban centres, edge cities and residential communities alike'. This is what Klingmann (2007) identifies as 'brandscapes', where entire urban districts become branded products. From a commercial perspective, there are obvious advantages of 'exteriorising' or 'placing' brands in this way, not least the fact that 'if a corporation is connected with the emotive qualities of a place, customers will identify more strongly with the brand' (Klingmann, 2007:83).

The rise of brandscapes is a feature of contemporary cities, best illustrated by outdoor malls such as Liverpool 1. Their relevance to mega-events is, however, less obvious, although when one considers the reliance of the Olympic Games on funding from media rights, sponsors and licencing, the connection becomes clearer. Host cities are now obsessed with protecting their own commercial interests and those of the companies that help fund these events. This has led, for example, to regulations that restrict what people can carry into, buy and consume in venues. The scope of control extends to the city streets where vendors are restricted from selling or advertising certain products and services in designated areas (James and Osborn, 2013a). Outdoor advertising around Olympic venues is also strictly limited to official sponsors, and host cities increasingly allow iconic urban landscapes to be appropriated by corporate sponsors[3] (Hagemann, 2010).

The contemporary obsession with the 'look and feel' of Olympic venues – and the streets and concourses that surround and envelop them – corresponds with the main objective of brandscapes – to immerse and seduce consumers. For the Olympics, 'look and feel' design guidelines have been in existence since the 1964 Games in Tokyo (Edizel *et al.*, 2013) and iteratively embedded since. A further link between the Olympic Games and brandscapes is the perceived need to provide highly regulated, safe environments that are exclusive to 'the right sort of people'.[4] According to Wood and Ball (2013), the success of brands is premised on security and saniti-sation. Given the obsession with safe and 'clean' venues in Olympic cities, we can start to see the parallels between the Games and brandscapes more clearly. Branding is all about control, and this is also an obsession of Olympic organisers, with many Olympic cities criticised for their tight restrictions on access and behaviour.

Wood and Ball (2013) point out that the contemporary brandscape is partly bio-political: consumers can be understood as prosumers because they reproduce the brands by wearing or embodying them. This is also true of Olympic cities, with spectators asked not to wear items promoting companies not officially spon-soring the event. The bio-political aspect of the Olympic Games also extends into the wider city, where citizens and visitors wear Olympic merchandise such as t-shirts displaying the event logo and where volunteers and officials are highly visible because of their branded uniforms and trainers.

In summary, there are clear connections between the Olympic Games and brandscapes. Indeed, we think it is helpful to think of contemporary Olympic cities *as* brandscapes, albeit temporary ones. This is explored further in the next section where we identify the different layers of the London 2012 brandscape.

Layers of the 2012 Olympic brandscape

There is a large amount of research detailing the way Olympic cities (over)regu-late public order, terrorism and safety (Fussey *et al.*, 2011, 2012). In this chapter, we argue that Olympic securitisation can also be understood as the securitisation of the brandscape.[5] From the outset, organisers of London 2012 were obsessed with branding: 'we need a powerful brand to help us achieve our ambition . . . [o]ur emblem is simple, distinct, bold and buzzing with energy. Its form is inclusive yet consistent and has incredible flexibility to encourage access and participation. It can communicate with anyone from commercial organisations to kids playing sport' (Miller, 2008:44). The 'spatialisation' of this brand was planned and con-trolled meticulously. To illustrate this, one only needs to consider the requirements relating to advertising and trading in the vicinity of events around London 2012:

> We are regulating advertising and trading in open public spaces for three reasons:
>
> - to ensure all Olympic and Paralympic events have a consistent celebratory look and feel to them;
>
> - to prevent ambush marketing within the vicinity of venues;
>
> - to ensure people can easily access the venues (DCMS, 2011:7).

Here we see city dressing, branding and health and safety all bundled up into one approach. However, the compatibility of these objectives is questionable. Does the protection of intellectual property (IP) and sponsors' rights fit with trying to protect the 'celebratory feel' of an event zone? To help us understand this tension and to consider how the 'look and feel' of the brandscape is implemented in public spaces requires a legal perspective. We need to analyse how these spaces are regulated and policed and the interrelationship between public and private space, however fluid this relationship might actually be (Blomley, 2005). As Bottomley and Moore (2007) note, what delineates these public and private spaces is not so much ownership, as *use*. In terms of regulation, Layard uses a 'law of place' to understand this, acknowledging 'that the site of regulation may shift from the national, local or individual level to a more amorphous scale, delineated on an ad hoc basis by developers, local authority officials or regulators' (2010:414). Layard's account of how this creates legally delineated geographical units can be used to examine London 2012, where a number of what we have termed 'layers of control' were applied in particular spaces.

Venues

There are a number of layers or zones of control that make up the Olympic brandscape. For any sporting event, and certainly for the Olympic Games, the site of the sporting activity itself is a crucial space. Access to this area is subject to the terms and conditions dictated by the property owner and/or event organiser. Admittance is usually via ticket, and as such the relationship is governed via the law of contract, an area of private law.[6]

Purchasers of tickets for London 2012 were bound by the terms and conditions of ticket purchase. These controlled the resale and transfer of tickets. It was a criminal offence to sell a ticket for London 2012 without the authority of the London Organising Committee of the Olympic and Paralympic Games (LOCOG) under the London Olympic Games and Paralympic Games Act (LOGPGA) 2006, section 31. The restrictions contained within these terms and conditions also facilitated brandscape control. Clause 19.2 detailed a list of prohibited and restricted items that could not be brought into the venue. Many of these were unsurprising, with ticket holders prohibited, for example, from bringing weapons into the venue. Restricted items also included food and beverages, alongside items such as flags of countries not competing in the Games. Other restrictions were clearly intended to protect the rights of sponsors: with restriction on 'Objects bearing trademarks or other kinds of promotional signs or messages (such as hats, t-shirts, bags etc) which LOCOG believes are for promotional purposes' (LOCOG, 2012: Clause 19.2.3). In addition to restricted and prohibited items, Clause 19.3 also regulated what it termed 'forbidden behaviour'. This included not only activities that put public order or safety at risk or that disrupted a session, but also political and religious protest, ambush marketing and unauthorised use of recording equipment. These contractual restrictions relating to intellectual property were in addition to, and reinforced, other restrictions as detailed in the sections below.

Live sites

The International Olympic Committee (IOC) note that Live Sites can 'provide a forum for people to come together in peace to celebrate the excitement of the host city during an Olympic Games' (IOC, 2005:86). In London, various Live Sites were constructed, where people without event tickets could watch Olympic action on big screens. These took a number of forms, but we argue the larger, closed versions established in Hyde Park and Victoria Park functioned as venues and extensions to the brandscape. Entry was regulated by the terms and conditions set by the event organisers in a similar fashion to a conventional ticketed venue. As such, and in common with many entertainment events, if you did not want to be bound by these terms you did not have to enter, but agreeing to them was a condition of entry, and you would be refused entry if you did not intend to be bound by them.[7] The London Live Sites are a good example of the commercialisation of public spaces. Although they were located in public parks, space was enclosed by a private event organiser who then dictated how the space was used.[8] Therefore, we see these as an extension of the brandscape, where a new venue offering a different experience is created outside the traditional venues and events.

Exclusion zones

In line with a trend observed since the Los Angeles Games (1984), and particularly post-Atlanta, London 2012 intellectual property and associated rights were heavily secured. The Olympic symbol and related properties attract specific protection under the *Olympic Symbol etc (Protection) Act 1995*.[9] In addition, the LOGPGA created a special set of statutory rights, including the London Olympic Association Right (LOAR) which gave LOCOG exclusive rights to authorise sponsors and licencees to create an association with London 2012. This was justified by the need to preserve prestige and prevent rights being undermined (LOCOG, 2010). Protection was wide-ranging, as Montagnon (2012:389) noted: 'The LOAR's breadth and lack of specificity attempts to get over the unpredictability of ambush marketing and cover every eventuality'. These rights are in addition to the pre-existing protections that exist in IP law, contract law and tort and have been described as 'super-', 'quasi-' or 'uber-' IP (James and Osborn, 2013b).

Under the *London Olympic Games and Paralympic Games (Advertising and Trading) (England) Regulations* 2011/2898, certain types of activity, including street trading and advertising, were not permitted in specified areas (termed event exclusion zones) over a specified period (the event periods). In tandem with the LOGPGA 2006, section 19, under the Regulations almost any display or activity that created a link to the Games was prohibited, could be removed or destroyed and in certain cases a conviction could have resulted in a fine of up to £20,000 (James, 2013). Similarly, street trading in public places around the venues was heavily regulated, existing licenses were suspended and new ones had to be applied for. These provisions privileged global sponsors over local businesses (James and Osborn, 2012), something that seemed to contradict official London 2012 rhetoric about significant economic impacts for local businesses. This could have been one of the most lucrative periods in a trader's life, yet people were potentially prevented from trading on their proximity to Olympic events and had to reapply for a licence to trade during the Games. These arrangements seem even more heavy-handed when one considers that substantial protection already existed (James and Osborn, 2013b). The zones themselves, the spaces where these restrictions applied, were also highly contested and subject to a consultation in advance of the Games (DCMS, 2011).[10] Although the exclusion zones were not visible/tangible, in some instances they were materialised because they tended to correspond with transport routes. For example, in Greenwich the zones were marked by physical barriers used to corral spectators into the equestrian venue. This added to the frustration of local businesses who were not only restricted from benefitting from the Games symbolically, but who now had to endure physical restrictions preventing passing trade from Olympic spectators.

Wider spatial controls

> In the months before the Olympics, the police sent what JRT describes as a 'symbolic message' to the area's residents to stay away from public spaces, seemingly driven by an underlying fear – intensified by the previous summer's riots – about young people from Newham scaring visitors and upsetting the drive for the 'perfect Games'.
>
> (Newham Monitoring Project, 2013:4)

Outside of the layers described above, there were a number of wider spatial controls that helped reinforce London's Olympic brandscape; these included, for example, temporary road closures and the shutting of certain stations to assist logistics. Some public buildings and spaces (e.g. Kensington Gardens) were used to host Olympic Houses. These provided headquarters for participating teams, but functioned as brand lands in that they served as experiential nation-branding vehicles. More controversially, and to reinforce the security of the host city, some public spaces were used as sites for anti-aircraft missiles.

Public space in London is already heavily regulated, and the Olympic measures brought in merely exacerbated existing spatial controls. Much to the dismay of civil liberties groups, many parts of London are subject to obscure laws preventing certain behaviours or activities. These zones, often unmarked or poorly signposted, prevent leafleting (under Clean Neighbourhoods and Environmental Act 2005) and dogs (Dog Control Orders Regulations 2006) as well as perhaps more overtly problematic non-activities such as 'being' in a particular public space. Spatial controls include dispersal zones, sanctioned by the Anti-Social Behaviour Act 2003, which gives the power to order two or more people leave specified areas and to ban their return for up to 24 hours. The area close to the Olympic park in Stratford, including the town centre, the main transport hubs and the 'West Quadrant' was designated as such 3 months before the London Games began (Blowe, 2012). While there is evidence that these dispersal order powers have had some positive effects, they antagonise unnecessarily, and their discretionary and subjective nature exacerbates conflict (Crawford and Lister, 2007).

Legacies: creep and seep

Olympic brandscapes are temporary phenomena, but they may have longer term effects. These can be understood through processes that have previously been identified as 'legislative creep' (James and Osborn, 2012). In the context of the Olympic Games, legislative creep is essentially an iterative process by which the next edition of the Games learns from previous legal mappings and redraws its legal framework in the light of this experience. These restrictions are temporal and limited – they last for a period of time during the event and then cease shortly afterwards, although they then become part of the exemplar for future Games and similar events (James and Osborn, 2011). What is perhaps more interesting, and less overt, however, is whether there are any longer term effects in spaces where the events took place. We would argue that alongside creep across Olympic Games, there is a process of seep, whereby new regulations and behaviours become embedded in a host city. This is a more subtle form of legacy left by an edition of the Games. In the following section, we outline an example from the London 2012 Games where aspects of the Olympic brandscapes have seeped into an important public space.

London's lesser known Olympic parks

The 2012 Games extended London's brandscape both temporally and spatially. Temporally, we think the 2012 Games have left a shadow by commodifying spaces and by providing justification and precedent for the commercialisation of public space in the future. In other words, brandscapes are one of the lesser acknowledged legacies of the 2012 Games. Spatially, we have seen the emergence of brandscapes in places previously thought to be outside consumer culture, including public parks. This is something acknowledged by Weber-Newth (2013) and Duman (2012) in their analyses of Olympic 'adizones'. This was the name given to 50 state-funded public gyms installed in UK parks owned by local authorities to help deliver Olympic legacies for local communities. As Adidas provided 50 per cent of the maintenance costs, and because the company was a Tier One sponsor of the 2012 Games, these zones were heavily branded using the Adidas and London 2012 logos. Accordingly, Weber-Newth (2013) sees them as 'a lucrative branding space for corporate symbols' and as 'a symbolic extension of the Olympic Park'. Using our terminology, these zones represent a spatial and temporal extension of the Olympic brandscape. This marketing may actually have more impact, not merely because of its physical longevity. Adidas may benefit more from the edgy and authentic nature of this form of advertising, which makes the brand seem less corporate, adding to its resonance (Weber-Newth, 2013).

The case of Hyde Park

The issues and ideas explored in previous sections can be illustrated via one focused site – Hyde Park in London. This is one of London's oldest, largest and most famous parks, and it was allocated a major role in staging the 2012 Games. Hyde Park was the venue for the long-distance swimming races and hosted the Triathlon events. Reflecting the previous discussion, the Park also hosted a large, fenced Live Site, and there were other parts of the Park where normal public access was restricted during the Games. The designation of Hyde Park as an Olympic venue made perfect sense for the organisers of the Games, but it is harder to equate with the established mission to protect both the environment of the Park and public access.

Hyde Park provides a valuable public space in Central London. It is a Royal Park, but also one where public access is protected via historic legislation. A 1537 Act of Parliament conferred the land on which Hyde Park is situated to Henry VIII who wanted to use it as hunting grounds. Public access was granted in 1637. The Park remains Crown Estate (owned by the monarch), but following section 22 of the Crown Lands Act of 1851, the government is responsible for managing the Park and is obliged to guarantee public access for recreational purposes. The Park is managed by The Royal Parks, an executive agency of the Department for Culture, Media and Sport. The Mayor of London also has some degree of control in that s/he now appoints the Royal Parks' Strategic Board. The Park is also regulated by the City of Westminster, the local authority in which most of the Park is situated. In line with various planning policies, Westminster Council grants planning permission for interventions. The Park was made a Conservation Area (Grade 1 listed) in 1980 and is Metropolitan Open Land. These designations also affect decisions made about changes to the Park, including whether or not to permit large-scale events.

The use of Hyde Park as a venue for high-profile events is nothing new. Indeed, the world's first mega-event of the modern era – The Great Exhibition – was staged in the Park in 1851. More recently, the Park has regularly hosted large music concerts in the summer months and other smaller events throughout the year. The driver for the greater emphasis on events is financial. The Royal Parks are funded by a national government grant which is being reduced over time, with Parks required to generate more of their own funding. The Royal Parks now generate over half of their own income and their latest *Annual Report 2012/13* suggest approximately one-third of this is from events (The Royal Parks, 2013a). Proposals to generate more revenue sit awkwardly with the wider mission to conserve the environment of the Park for the benefit of its diverse audiences. The current Business Plan (The Royal Parks, 2013b) identifies that 'tensions remain between those who believe that too much commercialisation threatens the intrinsic qualities of Parks and those who accept that . . . more income must be generated'.

The Hyde Park brandscape during the 2012 Olympic Games

During the Olympic Games, large sections of Hyde Park were inaccessible to the public, and there were activities and installations that would not normally be permitted. The central area around the Serpentine lake was designated as an event venue, with a large grandstand and reserved area for ticket holders installed on the north bank (Figure 10.1). Only those with tickets could access this area during the Games. The scale of the works required for the temporary venue meant that this area was inaccessible for 3 months during 2012. Another large part of the Park was inaccessible for 2 months; a fenced Live Site (sponsored by BT) was constructed with a large screen, stage and supporting infrastructures (Figure 10.1). The City of Westminster (2012:6) report granting planning permission for this Live Site acknowledged: 'the temporary structure and fencing will encroach into the open parkland character of Hyde Park which will significantly alter its character and appearance. However it is considered that the exceptional circumstances of the London 2012 Games justifies an exception to normal policy'.

The Live Site was free to access and attracted 800,000 visitors (The Royal Parks, 2013a). However, the area is perhaps best understood as a brandscape rather than a benevolent attempt to provide an alternative viewing experience for ticketless people. There were strict entry and behavioural controls seemingly imposed more for commercial rather than security reasons. People could not bring in their own food or water into the Live Site, which forced them to consume refreshments offered by commercial outlets. The Site not only hosted hospitality outlets but installations promoting the major sponsors, for example, 'Cadbury House'. Other parts of the Park also became commercialised brandscapes during the Games. A large London 2012 Superstore was constructed at the south of the site, and other commercial installations were permitted close to the Live Site entrance (Figure 10.1). These sold 2012 merchandise, mainly London 2012 and Adidas clothing, that helped the physical brandscape to become an embodied one in the bio-political way we describe above. The Superstore was not merely a retail outlet; it also contained 'sponsor event zones' dedicated to Coca Cola, Adidas and Swatch.

The overall effect of this tranche of installations and regulations was to create an area which extended London's commercial brandscape (centred around Oxford Street) into Hyde Park (see Figure 10.1). Despite the large size of the Park at around 350 acres, this brandscape infiltrated into almost all areas of the public space; and rather than being something that existed merely for the duration of the event, it affected the Park all summer. Precious public space in Hyde Park was 'festivalised' during the event and more people visited than usual. However, the space was also heavily commercialised, and 'normal' uses were restricted to protect the commercial interests of organisers and sponsors. Large parts of the Park became inaccessible without payment, and other parts became valuable branding tools for corporations. The changes were permitted and justified because they were viewed as temporary incursions that helped London to stage a prestigious one-off event, but there is evidence that the changes introduced during the 2012 Games have had more permanent effects too.

The legacy of the 2012 Games for Hyde Park

According to The Royal Parks (2012), the 2012 Games were a great success and they claim the Parks 'achieved an important reputational legacy' from their designation as host venues. Two million people visited and the Parks made money

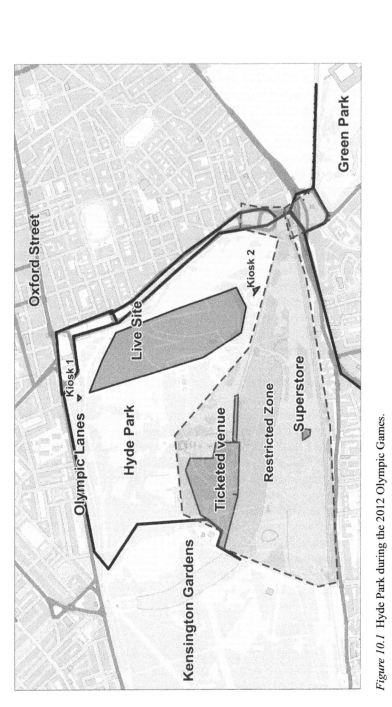

Figure 10.1 Hyde Park during the 2012 Olympic Games.

Source: Based on an Ordnance Survey Map, ©Crown Copyright/database right 2012. An Ordnance Survey/EDINA supplied service.

Note: Here 20yy is replaced with the year in which the maps are produced.

from the extra events staged, although this was offset by a drop in other income (The Royal Parks, 2013a). Only a short period of time has passed since the 2012 Games, so it is impossible to provide a definitive account of how the event has changed Hyde Park. However, it is possible to link the Games to various processes linked to the 2012 Olympic brandscape.

The most obvious legacy is that the Park seems to be used for major events more regularly than before. According to The Royal Parks (2013c), 'an increasing number of approaches for new events' have been received. Rather than the Olympic projects representing merely an exceptional incursion, it now seems likely that the Park will be increasingly used for other major events, many of which are highly commercialised. For example, in September 2013, Hyde Park hosted the World Triathlon Championships, an event that involved imposing many of the same installations and restrictions seen during the Olympic Games. A grandstand was built, a merchandise village was installed and the Park was covered in hoardings promoting the event sponsors. A year previously, The Royal Parks signed a five-year contract with AEG Live – one of the world's leading event companies – that allows the company to stage six summer concerts a year. This effectively turns the Park into another AEG venue every summer, providing an outdoor and more centrally located alternative to Wembley Arena and the O2 (also owned by AEG).

Since the Olympic Games, levels of commercialisation and regulation in the Park seem to have been stepped up, with licenses now required for commercial fitness trainers and dog walkers. In addition, and controversially, the Park now plans to charge people who play organised sport (e.g. softball/football) for the right to use certain parts of Hyde Park. Although these changes are not directly linked to the Games, they are linked to the wider commercialisation agenda. The Royal Parks now pursues 'Corporate Objectives' which include 'continuing to deliver better value for money and exploring commercial opportunities' (2013b:3). The role of the Games in these processes is subtle, but significant. As explained above, the Games have acted as a vehicle to normalise these controversial changes and provide a high-profile precedent. The perceived success of the Games generated both the expertise and the mandate to facilitate further commercialisation of The Royal Parks. This makes it easier for The Royal Parks to both stage more events in the future and to impose the sorts of restrictions and regulations seen during the 2012 Games. We think this represents the seepage of some of the Olympic brandscape controls into an urban public space long after the Games and their controversial regulatory framework have departed.

Conclusion

The Olympic Games undoubtedly leave many positive legacies for the cities that host them. However, as we have identified, there are also more subtle and potentially pernicious legacies that are underacknowledged. One of these is the commercialisation of urban space. The Olympic Games can be linked to wider processes whereby public space is being increasingly secured, controlled and managed for the benefit of private organisations and private companies. In this chapter, we have used the notion of brandscapes to encapsulate these processes and to link them to the Olympic Games. During the Games, parts of host cities are transformed into brandscapes where strict controls are introduced that restrict access and govern what can be done in designated urban spaces. There are even efforts to control the atmosphere, and the idea that typical brandscapes exhibit seductive and bio-political characteristics (Wood and Ball, 2013) fits well with the kinds of spaces created to stage the Games. Our work not only identifies these as being features of formal event venues, it suggests that event brandscapes areas are spreading into other parts of the city too. Indeed, mega-events like the Olympic Games seem to be responsible for the creation of new types of space in host cities. Rules and conditions used to regulate venues are now becoming part of the way cities are regulated more generally. In this sense we can see why some commentators see the stadium as a spatial prototype for both temporary and long-term changes in cities – 'projecting its functional, economic social and regulatory conditions into public space' (Hagemann, 2010:724). Our research also suggests that these brandscapes are not merely temporary phenomena; their effects seep into the cities that host the Olympic Games. This seep represents a subtle Olympic legacy; the Games do not cause public space to be commercialised, but act as a convenient vehicle that condones and normalises commercialisation. While it is too early to state categorically that London's brandscapes were enduringly extended by staging the Games, some initial evidence suggests that there is such a legacy emerging. Following this chapter, and Smith (2014), more work is needed to examine the long-term effects of the temporary structures and systems increasingly adopted for the Games.

While we argue that the processes above have negative effects, it is worth reflecting critically on whether they are as problematic as they may first seem. Branding and brandscaping are now ubiquitous, and some would argue that there is some inevitability about the processes we have described. Research into the effects of branding at music festivals suggests young people are fairly laid back about the incursions of corporate branding into new spaces. Many are unaware of the branding that surrounds them, and those that are see corporate funding as necessary ways of keeping events running (Tickle, 2011). As research into attitudes towards shopping malls has shown (Tyndall, 2010), brandscapes still offer a type of public space. Furthermore, we must not underestimate people's capacity to ignore or subvert efforts to control our emotions and our behaviour, something reaffirmed in an events context by Frew and McGillvray's (2008) analysis of the Munich Fan Fest at the 2006 FIFA World Cup.

This chapter contributes to the literature on the Olympic Games by exploring the notion that the Games are not only becoming more commercialised, they are now an agent of urban commercialisation. While this is mentioned in other texts, the processes through which this occurs are rarely explored in any depth. Our work also contributes to the emerging literature on the London 2012 Olympic Games by extending analyses away from East London and Stratford, to look at the way the Games affected other parts of London too. The chapter is an example of a multidisciplinary study involving an experimental collaboration between authors from the legal and urban studies fields. We would argue that future Olympic legacy research needs to adopt these kinds of multi- or interdisciplinary approaches in order to capture the complexities involved.

Notes

1 Perhaps this is best illustrated via reference to developments such as those of 'Nike Towns' or other flagship stores.
2 It is in these spaces where the urban brandscape becomes intertwined with the 'mediascape' – the wider mediation of the brandscape – defined by Kolamo and Vuolteenado (2013:504) as 'the channels and concentrations of media publicity through which the tournament brand was communicated by the staged representations of urban spaces that in themselves were constituents of the branded cityscape'.
3 This has been termed 'interdictory space' (Flusty, 2001).
4 That said, the space is not immune from the gaze of the criminal law. If we take UK football as an example, encroaching onto the pitch, throwing missiles and racist chanting within the stadia are all subject to very specific legislation via the *Football Offences Act 1991*, and broader criminal law and public order provisions would still apply (Greenfield and Osborn, 2001).
5 During London 2012, these sites were generally not ticketed, although for some of these sites, such as the Live Site in Hyde Park, you were able to apply for tickets in advance that guaranteed access.
6 This fits with Hagemann's (2010:730) interpretation of FIFA Fan Fests that is as 'a piece of public space is temporarily cut out of the urban context, fenced and given over to the control of a private event organiser who is then allowed to economically exploit in and regulate the ways in which it will be used'.
7 Essentially the Olympic Association Right.
8 Contentiously, some of these zones were extended in response to the view that zones were not wide enough to achieve their aim; see, for example, the extension at Weymouth discussed by James and Osborn (2013a).
9 These 'brand experiences' were typical – albeit temporary – 'brand lands' (Mikunda, 2002).
10 The Live Site and Event Zone imposed obvious access and behaviour restrictions during the Games, but there were also some more subtle spatial controls employed in and around Hyde Park. The main roads to the north and east of Hyde Park (Bayswater Road and Park Lane) were designated as Games Lanes reserved for the exclusive use of athletes, officials, media and sponsors during the Games. An extended area of the Park and its perimeter was also designated a zone with 'Advertising and Street Trade' restricted by the Olympic Act.

References

Banarjee, T. (2001) 'The future of public space: beyond invented streets and reinvented places'. *Journal of the American Planning Association*, 67: 9–24.

Blomley, N. (2005) 'Flowers in the bathtub: boundary crossings at the public–private divide'. *Geoforum*, 36(3): 281–296.

Blowe, K. (2012) 'Police announce Olympic Dispersal Zone', available at: http://www.blowe.org.uk/2012/05/police-announce-olympic-dispersal-zone.html (last accessed 4 March 2014).

Bottomley, A. and Moore, N. (2007) 'From walls to membranes: fortress polis and the governance of urban public space in twenty-first century Britain'. *Law and Critique*, 18(2): 171–206.

City of Westminster (2012, May 10) Planning and City Development Committee: Report of Strategic Director Built Environment.

Crawford, A. and Lister, S. (2007) *The use and impact of dispersal orders*. New York: Joseph Rowntree Foundation.

Department for Culture, Media & Sport (DCMS) (2011) 'Regulations on advertising activity and trading around London 2012: a consultation'. London: DCMS.

Duman, A. (2012) 'AdiZones: rewriting the 2012 Olympic legacy as permanent branding' in I. Guillamon and H. Powell (Eds.), *The art of dissent*. London: Marshgate Press.

Edizel, O., Evans, G. and Dong, H. (2013) 'Britain welcomes the world: dressing up London' in V. Girginov (Ed.), *Handbook of the London 2012 Olympic and Paralympic Games (Vol Two): celebrating the Games*. London: Routledge.

Flusty, S. (2001) 'The banality of interdiction: surveillance, control and the displacement of diversity'. *International Journal of Urban and Regional Research*, 25(3): 658–664.

Frew, M. and McGillivray, D. (2008) 'Exploring hyper-experiences: performing the fan at Germany 2006'. *Journal of Sport & Tourism*, 13(3): 181–198.

Fussey, P., Coaffee, J., Armstrong, G. and Hobbs, D. (2011) *Sustaining and securing the Olympic city: reconfiguring London for 2012 and beyond*. London: Palgrave.

Fussey, P., Coaffee, J., Armstrong, G. and Hobbs, D. (2012) 'The regeneration games: purity and security in the Olympic city'. *The British Journal of Sociology*, 63(2): 260–284.

Goodchild, S. (2014, February 12) 'Fitness trainer sued for using Royal Park'. *Evening Standard*.

Greenfield, S. and Osborn, G. (2001) *Regulating football: commodification, consumption and the law*. London: Pluto Press.

Hayes, G. and Karamichas, J. (2014) 'Conclusion: sports mega-events: disputed places, systemic contradictions and critical moments' in G. Hayes and J. Karamichas (Eds.), *Olympic Games, mega-events and civil societies*. London: Palgrave.

IOC (2005) 'Technical manual on ceremonies', available at: http://www.gamesmonitor.org.uk/files/Technical_Manual_on_Ceremonies.pdf (last accessed 4 March 2014).

James, M. (2013) *Sports law*. London: Palgrave.

James, M. and Osborn, G. (2011a) 'Response to regulations on advertising activity and trading around London 2012: a consultation'. Submission to DCMS.

James, M. and Osborn, G. (2011b) 'London 2012 and the impact of the UK's Olympic and Paralympic legislation: protecting commerce or preserving culture?' *Modern Law Review*, 74(3): 410–429.

James, M. and Osborn, G. (2012) *Legislative creep: unpacking Lex Olympica, Sport and EU Annual Conference*. Lausanne: Swiss Graduate School of Public Administration.

James, M. and Osborn, G. (2013a) 'The Olympic laws and the tensions and contradictions of promoting and preserving the Olympic ideal' in V. Girginov (Ed.), *Handbook of the London 2012 Olympic and Paralympic Games (Vol. 1): making the Games*. London: Routledge.

James, M. and Osborn, G. (2013b) 'Guilt by association: Olympic law and the IP effect'. *Intellectual Property Quarterly*, 2: 97–113.

Klingmann, A. (2007) *Brandscapes: architecture in the experience economy*. Cambridge: MIT Press.

Kolamo, S. and Vuolteenaho, J. (2013) 'The interplay of mediascapes and cityscapes in a sports mega-event: the power dynamics of place branding in the 2010 FIFA World Cup in South Africa'. *International Communication Gazette*, 75(5–6): 502–520.

Layard, A. (2010) 'Shopping in the public realm: a law of place'. *Journal of Law and Society*, 37(3): 412–441.

London Organising Committee of the Olympic and Paralympic Games (LOCOG) (2010) *Brand Protection London 2012's UK statutory marketing rights.* London: LOCOG.

London Organising Committee of the Olympic and Paralympic Games (LOCOG) (2012) 'London 2012 terms and conditions of ticket purchase', available at: http://www.kingdomsg.com/files/8813/0250/9663/Ticket_terms_and_conditions_of_sale_and_spectator_policy.pdf (last accessed 4 March 2014).

Mikunda, C. (2002) *Brand lands, hot spots and cool spaces: welcome to the third place and the total marketing experience.* London: Kogan Page.

Miller, T. (2008) 'London 2012 – meeting the challenge of brand protection'. *International Sports Law Review*, 4: 44–47.

Montagnon, R. (2012) 'Olympic bias'. *Journal of Intellectual Property Law & Practice*, 7(6): 389–390.

Newham Monitoring Project (NMP) (2013) 'Monitoring Olympics policing during the 2012 Security Games', available at: http://netpol.files.wordpress.com/2013/12/monitoring-the-security-games-final-report.pdf (last accessed 12 May 2014).

Pine, B. J. and Gilmore, J. H. (1999) *The experience economy: work is theatre and every business a stage.* Boston: Harvard Business Press.

Sánchez, F. and Broudehoux, A. M. (2013) 'Mega-events and urban regeneration in Rio de Janeiro: planning in a state of emergency'. *International Journal of Urban Sustainable Development*, 5(2): 132–153.

Smith, A. (2012) *Events and urban regeneration.* London: Routledge.

Smith, A. (2014) 'Borrowing public space to stage major events: the Greenwich Park controversy'. *Urban Studies*, 51(2): 247–263.

The Royal Parks (2012, November 2012) 'Royal Parks Board minutes', available at: http://www.london.gov.uk/moderngov/documents/g4701/Printed/20minutes/20Wednesday/2025-Jul-2012/2009.00/20Royal/20Parks/20Board.pdf?T=1 (last accessed 3 June 2015).

The Royal Parks (2013a) Annual report and accounts 2012–2013, available at: https://www.gov.uk/government/uploads/system/uploads/attachment_data/file/246635/0372.pdf (last accessed 4 March 2014).

The Royal Parks (2013b) The Royal Parks Business Plan 2012–13, available at: http://www.royalparks.org.uk/about-us/publications/business-plans (last accessed 4 March 2014).

The Royal Parks (2013c, June 18) 'Royal Parks Board Minutes', available at: https://www.gov.uk/government/uploads/system/uploads/attachment_data/file/246635/0372.pdf (last accessed 3 June 2015).

Tickle, L. (2011, July 18) 'Music festivals: the sound of escapism: the Guardian', available at: http://www.theguardian.com/education/2011/jul/18/music-festivals-research (last accessed 4 March 2014).

Tyndall, A. (2010) 'It's a public, I reckon: publicness and a suburban shopping mall in Sydney's Southwest'. *Geographical Research*, 48(2): 123–136.

Weber-Newth, F. (2013) 'Landscapes of London 2012: adiZones and the production of (corporate) Olympic space'. *Contemporary Social Science*, (ahead-of-print): 1–15.

Wood, D. M. and Ball, K. (2013) 'Brandscapes of control? Surveillance, marketing and the co-construction of subjectivity and space in neo-liberal capitalism'. *Marketing Theory*, 13(1): 47–67.

Part IV

Social and economic transformation in East London

11 Olympics-inspired inward investment

Transforming East London?

Gavin Poynter

Introduction

London 2012 presented an important opportunity to sell the UK, particularly the city, to the world as a destination for inward investment. The day prior to the opening ceremony, the British Business Embassy hosted a Global Investment Conference in London's Lancaster House. Over 30 government ministers attended along with 200 delegates. The conference was followed by a series of meetings, one each on China and Brazil and 14 others, called industrial sector summits. The events, held at London House during Games time, were the centrepiece of the UK Trade and Industries' (UKTI) legacy strategy to raise £6 billion of inward investment in the 4 years following 2012 (DCMS, 2013:29). In the wake of the Games, Whitehall's Olympic Legacy Unit sought to ensure that government departments worked effectively together to deliver the strategy, and in subsequent months, the Prime Minister and the Mayor of London led delegations of business leaders to locations such as India and China to strengthen the UK's trade and investment ties.

For the year following the Games, the Department of Trade and Industry (DTI) recorded the raising of £2.5 billion of inward investment into the UK and the creation of 31,000 jobs, all inspired by the success of London 2012 (Her Majesty's Government/Mayor of London, 2013). Of the £2.5 billion, £1 billion was invested directly in London, bringing around 2,000 jobs via 24 projects[1] that added an estimated £535 million in Gross Value Added to the city's economy (Her Majesty's Government/Mayor of London, 2013). By the end of the second year, foreign direct investment (FDI) had risen to £4.72 billion with just over half of the projects located outside London. Two years on from the Games, the evidence suggested that the legacy strategy was on track to achieve government targets for attracting inward investment into the UK and especially London (Her Majesty's Government/Mayor of London, 2014:47). This chapter focuses upon FDI into East London and examines the trajectory of the subregion's economic development in the wake of London 2012. Distinguishing 'Olympic-inspired' investment from that which might have occurred had the Games not been held in London relies upon interpreting investor intentions and evidence drawn largely from official reports; however, some preliminary conclusions emerge.

First, London sustained its attractiveness as a destination for FDI from the pre- to post-event phases of the 2012 Games despite the onset of the global financial crisis. Indeed, the crisis assisted rather than impeded the attraction of FDI to the city since it was perceived by investors as a relatively secure location in troubled economic times. Second, and most significantly, successive governments' commitments to invest in the Games, and the infrastructure improvements they required, ensured that private enterprises could share the risk involved in investing in East London with the public sector. The state's political and financial support for the mega-event, including its continuation after the Games, provided a relatively stable setting to attract inward investment over a period of a decade or more with potential investors often securing through their dealings with delivery agencies agreements that assisted in the mitigation of risk.

Conventional interpretations refer to public sector finance being used to mobilise private sector investment, stimulating local economies through 'leverage'. Leverage is often expressed as a ratio between the additional private capital invested for every pound spent by the public purse. Here it is suggested that a more useful way of looking at the relationship between private capital and public finance in the context of the urban renewal of East London is to invert the conventional view. Private capital has benefitted considerably from the public financing of East London flagship projects through a mix of in-kind and direct transfers as well as land sales that have presented development opportunities within the Olympic park and on its borders. The state's programme of regeneration configured around the 2012 Games has given rise to transfers of value from public finances to private capital gratis.

Finally, the image-enhancing impact of the Games on East London has had implications for the types of FDI taking place, with inward investors often seeking to exploit the Olympic effect on the east side of the city to expand and diversify their property portfolios and showcase their own brand identities. Inward investment projects have provided employment and training opportunities, not least in the retail sector, but they are unlikely to contribute to the city's capacity to export high-value services or make an innovative contribution to the city's economic future. The chapter commences with a brief look at the city's economic recovery since the international financial crisis commenced in 2007–2008. The relative strength of London's performance stands in stark contrast to other cities in the UK and much of the rest of Western Europe – a performance that, by early 2014, caused some to conclude that the 'rest of the UK was being cut off from London' (Pickford, 2014).

London and FDI

FDI takes one of three forms: a foreign enterprise providing start-up capital in a UK-based branch or subsidiary (a greenfield investment), a foreign enterprise buying or selling the existing equity of a UK company (merger/acquisition) or a foreign enterprise adding to its existing investment in a UK-based company or allowing it to keep the share of the profit it makes rather than having it repatriated to the parent company. FDI is recorded in a nation's capital account as part of the balance of payments with direct investment defined as

> an investment that adds to, deducts from, or acquires a lasting interest in an enterprise operating in an economy other than that of the investor where the purpose is to have an 'effective voice' in the management of the enterprise. In FDI statistics, an 'effective voice' is measured as 10% of the share capital of a company; any investment below this is counted as 'portfolio' investment under balance of payments statistics and not included in FDI.
>
> (House of Commons Standard Note SNEP/18/28:3)

According to Kearney's 'Global Cities Outlook', London is ranked in the top four of world cities (the others being New York, Paris and Tokyo) (Kearney, 2012). The Outlook measures city performance against a cluster of indicators, including business activity, human capital, information exchange, cultural experience and political engagement. Sassen argues that the future of the world economy rests with the established 'western' cities and those expanding rapidly in the emerging economies, the networks created between them arising from their respective concentration of specialist skills and expertise in a new kind of spatial division of urban labour (Sassen, 2012:8). Rather than nation to nation, the international economy increasingly relies upon the relations between cities, organised in 'vectors' with the original being that between New York and London and one of the more recently developed and potentially significant future vectors being among Beijing, Shanghai and Hong Kong (2012:8). London's success as a global city relies, within this international division of labour, largely upon three sectors – financial services (with the city at the centre of increasingly complex circuits of international financial intermediation), business services and IT/software.

In terms of regional performance, the UK and London, in particular, have for several years been the most attractive destination for FDI in Europe (Ernst & Young, 2012). Though the financial crisis much reduced the total global inflows from the record highs achieved in 2007, the UK has retained its comparative share. By the end of 2012, the UK's share of inbound European investment projects stood at 18 per cent of the total, ahead of Germany (16 per cent) but with the latter overtaking the UK over recent years in areas of engineering, scientific equipment and manufacturing. Germany was also, according to the report, catching up with the UK in attracting inward investment in the services sector, the UK's main strength. In brief, despite increased German competition, the UK and London's comparative performance has been sustained over the period from 2007 to 2012, as Table 11.1 suggests.

There is no single and authoritative source of data for FDI into the UK or London.[2] The Ernst & Young analysis, on which Table 11.1 is based, is drawn from a database that omits merger and acquisition activity and several sectors such as 'investments in retail, hotels and leisure facilities, utility or communications fixed infrastructures and the extraction of ores, minerals and fuels' (GLA, 2005:2). The exclusion of merger and acquisition activity ensures that the data is not

Table 11.1 European FDI projects 2007 to 2012: UK market share and London's market share of UK projects

Year	Total number of UK FDI projects	Total number of FDI projects located in London	London's per cent share of UK projects	UK market share of EU FDI projects
2007	713	301	43	19
2008	686	322	47	16
2009	678	332	49	21
2010	728	289	40	19
2011	679	240	35	17
2012	697	313	45	18

Source: Ernst & Young European Attractiveness Survey and Investment Monitor (all years).

distorted by a few major acquisitions undertaken by multinational enterprises that may take place in one year, but the counting of projects often does not distinguish between additional investment in existing projects and those which are new or 'greenfield' investments (House of Commons Standard Note SNEP/18/28:3).

Some of the sectors not included in the data are of significance to London. According to a DTI report (2014) on the retail sector in the post-2012 period, for example, London is the world shopping capital, boosting more international brands than any other city and

> to capitalise on the popularity and interest in the UK and plan to expand our reach to international investors. UKTI is currently working with key international investors on over 70 separate investments, which include more than 400 new stores opening in the UK in the next two years.
>
> (DTI, 2014)

Leisure includes international tourism, a sector that government has targeted in the post-2012 setting to grow. Initial figures for 2013 provided evidence of growth in visitor numbers and spend, with London performing strongly in the wake of a boost in its popularity arising from hosting the 2012 Games:

> As a visitor destination, London is more popular than ever following the Games and, through the concerted efforts of the Mayor and his promotion organisation London & Partners, the city managed to avoid a displacement of tourists during the Olympic year and any subsequent 'hangover' effect that has been observed in some other host cities.
>
> (DCMS, 2013)

In the years prior to the financial crisis, software, IT, business services and financial services sustained a dominance as the main sources of London's FDI – contributing 32 per cent, 22 per cent and 15 per cent, respectively, of FDI jobs between 2003 and 2008 (Think London, 2009:6). Between 2009 and 2013, these sectors continued to dominate FDI flows along with a growth in FDI in infrastructure projects (spurred in particular by large-scale projects such as Crossrail). The software and IT sectors received a significant boost in 2011 as major US firms announced plans to invest in London:

> Investment in the software and IT sector in London, UK, has increased significantly during the first six months of 2011 compared with the same period in 2010 . . . From January to June 2010, $530m was invested, increasing to $3985m in 2011, more than seven times the 2010 figure. In addition, the number of projects announced for the capital has more than doubled, from 30 in 2010 to 65 in 2011.To date in 2011, Google, Intel and Cisco have announced plans to invest in London.
>
> (McLoughlin, 2011)

In 2013, 300 greenfield projects in software/IT and business services were established in London, offsetting to some extent a decline in business services and financial services (both down by 24 per cent on the previous year):

> London retained its position as the top European destination for FDI in 2013 . . . With 300 greenfield projects recorded in the year, London led the ranking, ahead of Paris with 115 projects . . . The leading sectors for investment in London in 2013 were software and IT, and business service. The largest single capital investment in the city was made by ABP China Holding Group, a China-based developer planning to transform a 140-metre-square site at Royal Albert Docks into a business district for an estimated $1.6bn.
>
> (Kaczmarsk, 2014)

In brief, despite the financial crisis and prolonged recession, London has maintained its lead in attracting FDI in Europe, even though the total volume of global and European FDI flows has been severely curtailed. It has also continued to attract significant FDI projects in specific sectors – financial and business services, IT and software and, more recently, infrastructure.

London's success compared to other cities rests upon several factors. The UK economy is 'open' to FDI, with relatively little regulatory control over overseas enterprises that seek to locate within it.[3] Second, London combines this openness with the advantage of the clustering of expertise and enterprises in specific sectors; this is reinforced by the city being the headquarters of about one-fifth of the 500 largest companies in Europe. Third, the city has, in the wake of the uncertainties generated by volatile global conditions and economic crisis in the Eurozone, provided a relatively safe haven for investors, and, finally, the city exports high value-added services which contribute to its relatively strong productivity performance compared to other cities in the UK and Europe – though cities such as Stockholm and Munich perform better on this measure because of their continued strength in advanced manufacturing (Centre for Cities, 2013; Oxford Economics, 2013).

Employment over the period 2009 to 2014 has grown by about 250,000 mainly private sector jobs, while business confidence in London's economy has been supported by state-led infrastructure and regeneration projects that have renewed parts of the inner city and improved transportation. The city's capacity to continue to attract flows of inward investment, despite the volatile trading climate that arose in the wake of the international financial crisis, created the context for the Olympic and Paralympic Games to act as a catalyst for attracting FDI into areas of East London that had been relatively untouched by such investment prior to the submission of London's bid for the Games.

The Olympics and FDI in East London

East London was presented with a unique opportunity to raise its global profile as a destination for FDI. It was chosen as the site for the Olympic park, had other brownfield areas, especially along the Lower Lea Valley, that were ripe for redevelopment and agencies, such as the London Thames Gateway Development Corporation (LTGDC), that were responsible for kick starting their regeneration. Stratford benefitted from considerable publicly funded infrastructural investment in preparation for the Games, and in the pre-event phase, the narrative of the city of London 'moving eastwards' gained considerable public attention. Its validity was underscored by the view that the Olympics was one further step in the regeneration of the east side, a process that had commenced with the construction of Canary Wharf in the 1980s and the significant infrastructure improvements that accompanied it, including the extensions of the Jubilee Line, the Docklands Light Railway and the establishment of Stratford as a major transport 'hub'.

Public agencies involved in urban regeneration, such as the LTGDC (from its inception in 2005 to its closure in 2011), city-wide government and local authorities sought in post-industrial East London to provide urban spaces that attain a competitive edge over other locations for the kinds of enterprises and industries that operate in a world economy where the barriers to the movement of resources and people have been significantly reduced. Highly mobile capital makes decisions about location based not only on traditional 'industrial' concerns about proximity to production or market but also on the quality of infrastructure, tax and regulatory policies and the potential synergies offered by the proximities to other industrial sectors in cities that project images of being knowledge-based or 'creative'. This quest for the post-industrial renewal of the urban, associated often with services and 'intangibles', generates considerable competition between cities that seek to capture inward investment (Roche, 2000:234–235; Harvey, 2001:358–359). In 2005, London as a global city certainly projected this creative 'image', but it was one that was more associated with the west of the city rather than the east. The Olympics provided an opportunity for the image to spread, to include the east. But what types of investment and development would fill the urban spaces created by the regeneration agencies in collaboration with its local public partners?

In the pre-event phase, from 2005 to 2012, FDI focused upon three main dimensions – mixed developments of housing, retail and office space, the exhibition and events industry and the creative industries, particularly the high-tech sector.[4] These developments were not all directly 'Olympics-Inspired' projects, but many investors cited proximity to the Olympic park at Stratford and the infrastructure improvements that accompanied it as reasons that contributed to their location decisions. In particular, the guarantee of continued state support for the Olympic project and the £6.5 billion associated package of infrastructure investment reduced the perceived risks facing private capital in investing in East London. The Olympic village and Westfield's shopping mall development illustrate the ways in which the Olympic project played a significant part in securing FDI, particularly in Stratford, in the pre-event phase.

The main FDI investment in the Olympic park prior to 2012 was the Olympic village constructed out of public funds when Lend Lease, a private developer, failed to raise sufficient capital to undertake the project. In summer 2011, the village was sold by the Olympic Delivery Authority (ODA) to Triathlon Homes and a commercial partnership formed by Qatari Holdings, a subsidiary of the Qatar Investment Authority, and Delancey, an international investment company. The commercial partnership paid £557 million for its share of the village site and six further plots of land located nearby. The cost of converting the athletes village into housing units with all amenities was to be met by the ODA prior to the sale. The ODA completed its work within budget despite the public funding for the construction and refitting of the village costing over £900 million. The additional plots had planning permission for the construction of a further 2,000 housing units and presented a considerable development opportunity that could be maximised over future years providing investors phased completion dates to avoid flooding the property market. Triathlon[5] took responsibility for around 1,400 homes, and Qatari Holdings owned 1,439 housing units and developed these properties for rent. Such schemes were unusual, even in London. Institutional investors (e.g. pension funds and Sovereign Wealth Funds – the huge funds built up by emerging economies such as China and Qatar) had a long history of investing in commercial rather than residential property; the move into the latter reflected the growth of the sector arising from the decline in home ownership especially in areas such as London and the opportunities presented by the scale of development that took place with the construction of the Olympic village (Bernstock, 2014:113–148; Poynter, 2013).

The main other development that secured much media attention as well as support from local public agencies was Westfield Shopping City. The Westfield Group started in Sydney and established a reputation for creating shopping centres that attracted high-profile brands. Its operations spread from Australia to the USA in the 1980s, and, subsequently, it established a strong presence in Europe. Its first London mall was located in Shepherds Bush in West London. Westfield Stratford is close to Stratford station and the entrance to the Olympic park, Though plans for developing the shopping mall were made prior to London's successful Olympic bid, the Olympic development ensured that Westfield secured the land as part of the Compulsory Purchase Order (CPO) undertaken by the London Development Agency (LDA). It also secured through this process access routes and other infrastructure to 'safeguard' its development:

the private sector investment from Westfield was around £1.43 billion for the retail elements of Phase 1 plus a further £180 million for the hotel and office elements in Phase 2. In particular, the LDA evaluation notes two explicit ways in which the investment in the 2012 Games supported this development:

1   The Compulsory Purchase Orders (CPOs) the LDA implemented as part of its acquisition process benefited Westfield Stratford City by also including land in the area which Westfield was seeking to develop. This enabled economies to be realised and also ensured that private sector investment (through Westfield) was levered in to cover some of the costs associated with the CPOs; and

2   The impact of the economic downturn on the Westfield Stratford City development was minimised 'largely because the development was so closely linked to the delivery of the Olympic Village' and as such 'it was protected by the Government under its commitments to the 2012 Games'.
(DCMS, 2013:19–20)

In November 2010, Westfield sold a 50 per cent share in its Stratford shopping centre to two pension funds – APG, a pension fund asset manager for the Dutch education, government and construction sectors, and the Canadian Pension Plan Investment Board. The sale raised about £870 million for Westfield. The shared ownership arrangement is, in turn, supported by 28 subsidiary companies that manage and develop the business. The companies are, according to United Voice, an Australian trade union, registered in Australia, the UK, Jersey, Guernsey and US, with only one of these having employees (United Voice, 2014). The complex ownership structure facilitates a 'tax-efficient' investment. In 2012, for example, Westfield Stratford's profit was £39.7 million; the subsidiaries that owned the shopping centre paid a little over £200,000 in UK tax, a rate of 0.5 per cent (United Voice, 2014:6). Westfield's investment in Stratford strengthened its image as an internationally focused shopping centre brand and enabled it to benefit from the CPO that acquired the site and considerable state investment in the infrastructure required to service it. While the state leveraged support from Westfield to meet the costs of the CPO and the mall's success since opening has stimulated local employment opportunities, it would seem that the company has been a major beneficiary of the protected environment provided by public agencies. In 2011, for example, in the wake of the sale of the 50 per cent share, Chief Executives Peter and Steven Lowy announced:

the A$2.7bn raised from joint venture deals for the Stratford shopping centre and [the] Sydney shopping centre had 'more than funded' recent agreements for major new opportunities at the World Trade Center in New York, in Milan and Brazil . . . We have been active in implementing our strategic plan of redeploying capital into high return opportunities . . . Our investment into these opportunities is more than funded by the $2.7bn of proceeds from the Stratford and Sydney joint ventures. We continue to look at attractive development and acquisition opportunities globally, and are well placed to continue to deliver sustainable earnings growth.

(Norman, 2011)

For other FDI projects in East London in the pre-event phase, the greater the physical distance from Stratford the more, perhaps, locational judgements were influenced by a wider range of perceived advantages offered by the city moving eastwards (DCMS, 2013:20). For some, however, the hosting of the Games in East London certainly influenced their development decisions. For example, ExCel London, an events and exhibition centre and eventual host of several Olympic events in 2012, announced expansion plans in 2007 that acknowledged the Games value in leveraging further business opportunities in the events industry:

> This development represents a major investment in providing event facilities of world scale in London and supports the capital's ambition to host an increasing number of high profile international shows both pre and post the 2012 Olympic Games. Building Phase 2, with the support of the industries we serve, will complete our vision for ExCeL London and provide a strong legacy for the future of the events industry in this city.
>
> (http://www.traveldailynews.com/news/article/12220/ excel-london-plans-major-capacity)

ExCel London opened in 2000 and was owned by a public company (Country Heights Holdings) whose funding was secured through a shareholding structure that was supported by a Malaysian corporate equity consortium (75 per cent holdings) and UK financial institutions (25 per cent holding). Its shares were traded on the Luxemburg Stock Exchange. The initial investment was £200 million for the first phase of the development of the centre with state aid 'providing the land, fast-track planning, business rate holidays and support for construction' (East, 2011:17). The returns for the the London Docklands Development Corporation (LDDC) would arise from taking a share in future turnover:

> Three on-site hotels with 1,000 bedrooms are planned. The LDDC is contributing to the 85 acre (34 ha) site and investing in associated infrastructure in return for a shareholding and a percentage of turnover, leaving no net cost to the public purse.
>
> (http://www.lddc-history.org.uk/royals/index.html#Excel)

ExCel London's position in the business events industry grew in the period 2000 to 2007 despite the relative geographical isolation of the Royal Docks site. The enterprise was sold by the consortium in 2008 to Abu Dhabi National Exhibitions Company with the new owners providing additional investment to create further hotel facilities and the expansion of the site to include a new International Conference Centre. It was this expanded site that was host to several indoor Olympic events in 2012.

A further addition to the events and exhibition industry arising from FDI in East London was Siemens 'Crystal' urban sustainability centre located in Newham's 'Green Enterprise District' situated at the western end of the Royal Docks. Opened in 2012, the centre's functions are twofold, as an exhibition centre for urban sustainability and an office location for Siemens Infrastructure and Cities division that has 80,000 employees worldwide and which promotes Siemens involvement in urban regeneration and development projects across the world, including supporting cities in their preparation for mega-events (Siemen, 2012:8). The Crystal's location in East London benefitted from the infrastructure developments associated with the Games and the renewal plans for the western area of the Royal Docks, including its designation as an enterprise zone in 2011. The £30 million investment provided a location for showcasing the company's expertise. The company has a long association with East London, and London 2012, as a mega-event, complemented the company's own narrative involving its expanding business in urban infrastructure construction.

As de Miranda (2012) acutely observed, such projects have few roots in their locality and contrast starkly with the embedded nature of the production plants founded over a century ago in East London. In a similarly critical fashion, architecture historian and broadcaster Long (2012) observed, following a visit to the Crystal in October 2012:

> The Crystal is a hybrid corporate HQ, deriving from the corporate landmarks commonly erected in the 2000s by German companies wanting to give their consumers the next level of intimacy with the brand. It concerns me a little that the Crystal should be the standard bearer of the new sustainable business quarter in Newham because it's a showroom more than a workplace. Yes, it represents a major investment by Siemens but there are only 150 people working here in Siemens' Cities team; many of these are travelling all over the world and not resident in London. The Crystal will create some local jobs – Siemens estimates up to 50 – but most of these seem likely to be in support roles for the visitor attraction, and in administration. Until Siemens (or indeed anyone) brings some production, and some skilled work, to Newham, I'll reserve judgment on Newham's Green Enterprise District. The Crystal is a flashy talking shop for a technology company, and one we're invited into. I urge you to go and make your own minds up about whether such companies should be allowed to plan the future of our cities.

Whether a flashy talk shop or an exemplar of environmentally sustainable construction, the Crystal, located just to the west of London ExCel, illustrates how the events industry and its focus upon business tourism and 'visitor attractions'[6] have become an important strand in East London's renewal. This was particularly evident in an agreement for the development of Silvertown Quays reached in June 2013 between Chelsfield Properties, First Base and the Greater London Authority. The Master Plan Agreement (MPA) will establish a brand park in which global enterprises will be able to showcase their products. The £1.5 billion scheme will

take a decade or more to complete. Mayer Brown (2013), the legal services company that advised the Silvertown Partnership during the creation of the MPA,
outlined the reasons for the bid's success:

> While the proposed regeneration will include housing, business space, res-
> taurants and other leisure facilities, the bid's success relied heavily on the
> concept of creating a destination for London where people can interact with a
> range of global brands, in a grand avenue of state-of-the-art 'brand pavilions'.

> Brand destinations already exist in London, Europe and across the world, for
> example, the Guinness Storehouse in Dublin, Yves St Laurent at Waterside
> Shops and Samsung at Time Warner Square. The Silvertown will be the first
> of its kind attracting people who want to experience products and brands in
> new ways and creating a leading world class centre for innovation and a true
> brand destination.

The role of FDI in the creation of mixed developments of housing, hotel and
office space in the pre-2012 phase focused largely on the opportunities presented
by the corridor of development between Canary Wharf and Stratford in the Lower
Lea Valley. Strand East, a project established in 2009 by Inter IKEA Group, for
example, promised to create up to 1,200 new homes, a 350-bed hotel, 600,000 sq
ft of commercial space including flexible work and exhibition space for creative
industries. The Group's response to interviews conducted as part of the DCMS
meta-evaluation of the Games' legacy suggests that IKEA's investment was
strongly influenced by the heritage and waterfront qualities of the site rather than
the inspiration provided by the Olympics, with the Group arguing that 'it's hard
to separate out the influence of the Games' (DCMS, 2013). While this may be
the case, Strand East's own publicity stresses the virtues of its proximity to the
Olympic park, and politicians such as London's Mayor Boris Johnson have publicly
claimed the development as part of the Olympic legacy:

> this is yet another great example of the 2012 legacy rippling out of the
> Olympic park and across east London. It will help create a vibrant quarter
> within the brand new district we are creating in London, providing much
> needed family-sized housing and new jobs. This huge investment shows the
> extraordinary confidence that exists for both this part of the capital and the
> future of the whole of London's economy.
>
> (www.designboom.com, 2012)

The IT/high-tech sector in East London reveals similar issues in determining the
role of the Olympics in catalysing location decisions of inward investors. Two
main areas have been associated with the sector – Shoreditch and the iCity development linked to the Olympic park's post-2012 use of the Press and Media
Centre. Shoreditch's 'Tech City' is a location for business start-ups that was given
extensive media attention via the publicity provided by Prime Minister David

Cameron in 2010. Over the following two years, it expanded to incorporate a growing number of microfirms, many of which identified the advertising potential of mobile telephony, developing 'apps' direct to consumers as well as innovative products of interest to large international enterprises. While larger companies have often been relatively slow to adjust their corporate communications and advertising to mobile telephony, microfirms have established niche markets for their digital products.

In this sense, a creative quarter is, perhaps, in the process of becoming a 'cluster'. The 'Tech City' concept aspires to a spatial clustering of high-tech enterprise and has drawn upon government funding to support its presentation to international venture capital and large-scale international businesses (such as Intel and Google). The potential for its expansion arises in part from the scope provided by the geographical concentration of micro- and larger scale firms in East London and the potential for its geographical reach to expand to include the area from Shoreditch to the Olympic park. Different interpretations of the potential for the development of this urban cluster have arisen from conflicting perspectives on the compatibility of existing small-scale firms sitting alongside larger scale enterprises and their capacity to join together in creative clusters. Heap argued, for example, in the *Financial Times* in 2012 that the two elements (large and small scale) will work well side by side.[7] Others, however, have doubts as reflected in discussions at a seminar held in 2011 by the FutureofLondon.org.uk (16 September 2011) on the future of Tech City[8]:

> The first of our discussion themes centred on defining Tech City, both in terms of whether it represents a genuine cluster of activity or whether it can best be understood as an inward investment branding strategy. Unsurprisingly, there was a multitude of views in the room, from those keen to emphasise the range of local activities currently going on in the Shoreditch/Old Street area and the key relationships and interactions that exist with broader creative industries, to those with a clearer focus on what is required to get major companies to locate in the area, and those neighbouring areas such as the Olympic Park and the Royal Docks. Participants recognised that this raises some difficult questions, as the needs of these two different kinds of firms (small start-ups and global mega-companies) will not necessarily align in terms of the infrastructure required to facilitate their work.

This view was broadly supported by a further report published in 2012 by Demos. The report mapped the number of microfirms located in the Shoreditch area, indicating continuing growth (over 3,000 by 2012, a near doubling since 1997) with the majority of these microbusinesses being run by young British entrepreneurs (Demos, 2012:56). The report, however, in its discussion of government policies on FDI suggested that while such government-encouraged investment had the potential to create synergies and greater shared knowledge and expertise between existing firms and incomers, it also presented a threat arising from the competition that overseas firms might pose (Demos, 2012:98). The report also suggested, following interviews with a sample of microfirms, that proximity to the Olympic park and the potential for the Shoreditch cluster to connect to it was very limited (Demos, 2012:76).

By 2014, the Shoreditch inner East London's 'cluster' of high-tech microfirms had attracted about 25 international technology companies over the period 2010–2013, but remains largely disconnected from developments within the Olympic park.[9] The Press and Media Centre, now rebadged as 'Near East', hosts BT Sport, Infinity's Stratford Data Centre and facilities for Hackney College and Loughborough University with the building run by iCity, a joint venture between Infinity, created in 2006, and Delancey, a UK private company that specialises in the real estate investment sector. iCity is seeking to develop the site further as a creative digital park, promoting it internationally as a location for FDI.

FDI's Olympic Legacy in East London

The concerted effort of government to promote London, particularly East London, as a location for FDI in the years preceding the Games, particularly since 2012, has met with some success.[10] The UK's capital has attracted several inward investment projects, mainly in the sectors that were strongly represented in the pre-2012 period.[11] Public attention, however, since 2012 has mainly focused on FDI in the property sector – prime residential property referred to as Prime Central London (PCL) and 'iconic' commercial property developments located also mainly in Central London and on the Thames river front. Fathom Consulting (2015:5) reported that

> 53% of PCL properties that sold for more than £2 million in the twelve months to March of this year went to overseas buyers. When broken down by national currency, residents of the euro area economies were at the front of the queue, and together accounted for 10% of purchases in this price bracket. Investors from the rouble bloc came in a close second, at 9%. Further up the value chain, foreign buyers become even more dominant, with the proportion of PCL properties worth more than £5 million sold to non-UK nationals close to 60%.

The consequence of such a heated property market has been a ripple effect across all property price bands. Housing costs have risen in London at levels much higher than the rest of the UK. Prime locations in inner and Central London have been especially sought after. In 2013, some 70 per cent of the higher cost new property sales went to investor purchasers, many from overseas (British Property Federation, 2013:2).

The ripple effect of this boom across East London has been variable, but three Games-'inspired' dimensions have emerged. First, some local regeneration areas such as Dalston have experienced sustained increases in house prices due in large part to the accelerated infrastructure improvements arising from the preparation for the 2012 Games. Second, some areas of the east side have become an attractive location for overseas buyers seeking new build purchases. Lastly, the enhanced image of destinations in and close to the Olympic Park and the development opportunities on its borders have attracted foreign investors to engage in innovative private rental property schemes, such as the Olympic village and large-scale mixed development schemes like Strand East.

These new developments on the east side of the city, in the post-2012 period, have been marketed to overseas buyers and not just by estate agents. The MIPIM property fair, the world's largest and most prestigious property sales event held in Cannes in March 2014, was attended by several UK local authorities, including Newham:

> public sector attendance at MIPIM has long been contentious, with budgets for local authorities' presence at the fair often stretching up to £500,000. The symbolism of council chiefs on a champagne-soaked jamboree, as swingeing cuts bite back home, has not gone unnoticed, prompting most authorities to find private-sector funding and trumpet visible results from the week of networking . . . It's not costing the public purse a penny', said Robin Wales, mayor of Newham, sitting in front of a wall declaring 'East London has arrived'.
>
> (Wainwright, 2014)

The promotion of East London to overseas investors by politicians in the wake of the afterglow of the Games has not been confined to the property market. The positive image of the Games' 'legacy' was evoked by London's Mayor Boris Johnson when he approved planning permission in 2013 for a Chinese company to develop a business port for Chinese and Asian businesses in the Royal Docks. The GLA-owned land was sold to enable the phased development of the Park with the Chinese holding company ABP promising an initial £1 billion investment that could rise to £6 billion over future years. The interim planning submission, put forward in 2011 by ABP, posed risks that were not widely publicised by the Mayor when he trumpeted the project as a great example of the post-2012 Games' effect on the renewal of East London. The risks included ABP's limited experience of overseas investment projects (mitigated in part by Stanhope, an experienced UK-based company being secured by ABP as development managers), the need for ABP to step up its marketing campaign to secure international investors for all phases of the development and the limited response specifically from Chinese companies that ABP claimed were interested in investing and moving into the business port:

> Their interim submission included 47 expressions of interest from businesses based in China, and whilst it is not possible to fully verify the extent of this interest at this stage, an initial review was conducted by London & Partners. The review provided a mixed response, which was explained by ABP to relate to the nature of their relationship with a number of the businesses and various cultural differences. However it is clear there is interest from Chinese companies wanting to work with ABP to locate in the UK, together with ABP's commitment to building 600,000 sq. ft. of first phase of development.

ABP have indicated they will commence worldwide marketing of the project once the planning application has been submitted and are keen to bring the first delegation of Banks/Funders and businesses over to London in May.

(Greater London Authority Mayor's Decisions, MD1208)

Despite these risks, the first phase of the port project was set to commence in autumn 2015. It joined a growing list of FDI projects located in East London that could be attributed, in part at least, to the 'inspiration' provided by hosting the Olympics.[12]

Conclusion

Examining the Olympic effect of FDI into East London is a complex affair. The reasons for enterprises undertaking investment in overseas locations are influenced by a number of factors, and the evidence, even from official sources, of the Games inspiring FDI decisions may be coloured by the pronouncements of political leaders at national, city-wide and local levels who seek to exploit the afterglow of a successful Games to enhance their own reputations and prove that the public investment in the mega-event was worthwhile. It is equally difficult to establish the 'true' value of FDI projects to a city's economy since the investments proposed may not fully materialise in the form that they are initially presented. Finally, it is hard to establish the relative significance to be attributed to the broader economic and the specific tangible (infrastructure) and intangible (feel good) factors, arising from London's hosting of the Games, that contribute to the city's attraction as an FDI destination.

What is clear is the active role that the state has played in sustaining London's capacity to attract inward investment, especially in East London. Public investment, direct and indirect, in the mega-event provided the context for a form of entrepreneurial urban governance to emerge in which private capital could readily share investment risks with its public sector partners. Public investment provided a relatively secure or, as a Westfield spokesperson described, 'protected' environment for FDI projects. The government and city's contractual obligations to the International Olympic Committee guaranteed an accelerated improvement of infrastructure, a favourable legal and planning framework for urban development, the creation of large-scale and integrated sites in East London and an investment opportunity shielded by the state from some of the challenges presented to private capital by the wider economic malaise afflicting the global economy. In turn, London has, perhaps, moved east into pockets of renewed urban spaces supported by FDI projects, several of whose commercial future lies, like the city's, in their capacity to engage with a world beyond their specific geographical location – whether this has taken the form of investment in property, visitor attractions, brand showcases or shopping.

Where there is evidence of the clustering of expertise and knowledge in specific sectors, FDI tends to enhance productivity and competitiveness through the transmission effects of advanced knowledge and technologies that strengthen the recipient city's integration within the international economy (OECD, 2002). The virtuous effects of FDI may, however, be negated by the 'footloose' nature of multinational enterprises, their capacity to outcompete or takeover fledgling local microfirms (as in the technology sector) or by the limited capacity (in, for example, technical expertise, infrastructure and institutions) of the host city or nation to leverage the positive effects. In London's case, concern has been expressed in the recent past about the relative strength of the 'knowledge intensity' of the city and its capacity, in the future, to compete with other more dynamic economies and financial centres arising in the world (Lucci and Harrison, 2011; Poynter, 2013). London is relatively unique in relying heavily upon a small number of key sectors such as financial services, business services and marketing. Olympic-inspired inward investment in East London has done little to modify this dependence.

The hosting of the sporting spectacle has spawned regeneration projects that contain elements of the spectacle (and speculation) – whether shopping mall, exhibition centre or avenues of brands. Such developments may affirm the ingenuity of capital in spinning off profitable and perhaps prestigious projects from state-funded urban renewal but does little to enhance the underlying productiveness of the city's economy. Through its partnership with private enterprise, public agencies secure the expertise of the private sector in development and delivery. In turn, investors gain 'fast-track' routes through planning legislation and regulatory regimes, access to assets with future development potential through land sales, improved infrastructure provision and the sharing of risk. These attributes of the 'Olympic effect' have been successful in attracting overseas investment into previously neglected areas of East London. Paradoxically, the pattern of investment the mega-event has encouraged reveals many of the underlying weaknesses and state dependence of the urban economy it is invited to energise.

Notes

1 These included inward investment projects by Dalian Wanda Group (China) and SP Setia (Malaysia) in Battersea, ABP (China) in the Royal Docks, Westfield (Australia) in Croydon and Huawei (China) in Central London and commitments from, for example, Infosys (India), Axis (India), Gensler (USA) to establish or further develop their London-based operations.
2 The main official sources of international data are UNCTAD and OECD. In the UK, the official source is the DTI.
3 The DTI described the favourable environment in the UK for FDI in the following way in its *Annual Report 2012*: 'The UK has a flexible labour market with labour regulations designed both to protect the employee and to ensure that companies can operate effectively. The UK Government is committed to creating a highly competitive tax environment, with the main rate of corporation tax being reduced to 21 per cent in 2014 and 20 per cent in 2015 – the lowest rate in the G7 and the joint lowest in the G20 . . . Innovative companies in the UK can benefit even further from additional forms of tax relief, including the "Patent Box" (which provides reduced rates of corporation tax on profits from the development and exploitation of patents), "R&D tax credits" and generous tax relief for innovative sectors'.

In addition, local enterprise partnerships and enterprise zones (replacing regional development areas) began to be established across the UK in 2011; these provide tax incentives and simplified planning rules for companies setting up in specific localities.

4 The engagement of foreign firms in the bidding process (CompeteFor) for the construction of the Olympic park and the indirect infrastructure developments taking place alongside are not included in this analysis.

5 Triathlon's purchase of homes in the village cost £278 million. The Homes and Communities Agency provided a grant of £110 million toward the cost. In effect, government transferred public money from one department to another and then to the third sector in order for the social housing consortium to buy its share of the village's housing units.

6 The Emirates Air Line cable car crossing in the Royal Docks is a further illustration.

7 Some evidence to support this positive perspective was provided by Google when it opened its East London Campus on 29 March 2012 (800 companies applied for desks on the campus). The *FT* reported: 'Courting the technology sector makes sense, given that the rather loosely defined 'internet economy' contributed £121bn to the overall UK economy in 2010, equivalent to 8.3 per cent of gross domestic product, according to a report by the Boston Consulting Group earlier this week'. But in 2012, an article in the same paper commented: 'The government rarely misses an opportunity to highlight its involvement with Tech City, although its unclear whether its cheer-leading role has, in practical terms, had much to do with the number of start-ups in the area growing from 200 in 2010 to more than 700 today. A number of companies, including Cisco, Intel and Amazon have all made pledges to do things around Tech City, but Google's building is one of the first and most concrete of those to emerge.It is harder to see what Google gets out of the Campus project, which it has characterised as a gift to the community. It is not a profit-making scheme for the internet company, and the ten-year lease and refurbishment of an office block will not have been cheap' (http://blogs.ft.com/tech-blog/2012/03/google-opens-east-london-campus/).

8 The seminar was attended by policy makers, academics and practitioners and led by, among others, The Work Foundation.

9 The companies were mainly from the USA, China, India and Europe including the American cloud storage company (Box) and a Chinese game developer (Rekoo). See http://www.londonandpartners.com/media-centre/press-releases/2013/13122013-tech-city-welcomes-major-new-international-investments-to-mark-third-anniversary

10 Over this period, the government has adopted policies designed to encourage entrepreneurs to set up in the country, for example, via the entrepreneur's visa and a tax relief scheme for the first £100,000 of investment (the Seed Enterprise Investment Scheme).

11 The sectoral and geographical distribution of this FDI in the UK is beyond the scope of this chapter. It is perhaps worth noting, however, that outside London the government records, for example, £6 billion FDI in the UK automotive sector between 2011 and 2013, mainly in the midlands and north, suggesting that some 'rebalancing' of the economy is taking place (*UK TDI Annual Report 2012*:18).

   Critics of government policy, however, suggest that the automotive industry illustrates Britain's underlying structural problems and that FDI has exacerbated such problems 'Government ministries, like BIS and DfT, do not understand the underlying structural problems about broken supply chains and the wrong ecology of ownership . . . Generally, the ecology of ownership is a serious structural constraint on export growth because it limits the capability of British firms and the ambition of foreign firms. British owned manufacturing firms on average employ 14 and will never export directly because they are trapped in a workshop sector; foreign owned firms employ 200 because the factory sector has been sold to foreign owners. But the foreign owners in automotive and other sectors generally have limited ambition because they run British branch factories as part of a global division of labour' (http://www.scribd.com/doc/122563517/The-foundational-economy-rethinking-industrial-policy-Andrew-Bowman-Julie-Froud-Sukhdev-Johal-and-Karel-Williams)

12 Lend Lease (the international quarter) – Australia; Inter IKEA (Stand East) – Sweden; Westfield (shopping centre) – Australia; Emirates (cable car) – United Arab Emirates; ExCeL Exhibition Centre – Abu Dhabi; Qatari Diar/Delancy (athletes' village) – Qatar/UK; Siemens (Crystal Sustainable Technology Centre) – German.

References

Bernstock, P. (2014) *Olympic housing*. Farnham, UK: Ashgate.

British Property Federation (2013) 'Property data report 2013', available at: http://www.bpf.org.uk/sites/default/files/resources/BPF-Property-Data-Report-2013_0.pdf (last accessed 3 June 2015).

Centre for Cities (2013) 'Cities outlook 2013', available at: http://www.centreforcities.org/wp-content/uploads/2014/08/13-01-21-Cities-Outlook-2013.pdf (last accessed 26 May 2014).

De Miranda, A. (2012) 'The real economy and the regeneration of East London', in G. Poynter, I. MacRury and A. Calcutt (Eds.), *London after recession*. Farnham, UK: Ashgate.

Demos (2012) 'A tale of tech city: the future of inner East London's digital economy', available at: http://www.demos.co.uk/files/A_Tale_of_Tech_City_web.pdf?1340965124 (last accessed 12 May 2014).

Department of Culture, Media and Sport (DCMS) (2013) 'Creating a lasting legacy from the 2012 Olympic and Paralympic Games', available at: https://www.gov.uk/government/policies/creating-a-lasting-legacy-from-the-2012-olympic-and-paralympic-games (last accessed 2 May 2014).

Department of Trade and Industry (DTI) (2014) 'UK retail industry – international action plan', available at: https://www.gov.uk/government/uploads/system/uploads/attachment_data/file/329878/UKTI_Retail_action_plan_June_2014_spreads.pdf (last accessed 9 June 2014).

Designboom.com (2012) 'Strand East: urban planning by IKEA', available at: http://www.designboom.com/design/strand-east-urban-planning-by-ikea (last accessed 3 June 2015).

East (2011) 'London's hotspot: East London issue 2', available at: http://www.slideshare.net/MarkBradbury/east1 (last accessed 20 May 2014).

Ernst & Young (2012) 'European Attractiveness Survey: 2012 performance, 2013 prospects', available at: http://www.ey.com/GL/en/Issues/Business-environment/European-attractiveness-survey—2012-performance-and-2013-prospects—FDI-scenario-in-Europe (last accessed 9 June 2014).

Fathom Consulting (2015) 'One year on and even higher', available at: http://www.developmentsecurities.co.uk/devsecplc/dlibrary/panda/PCL_Report_2013_v2.pdf (last accessed 18 May 2014).

GLA Economics and Think London (2005) *From the Ganges to the Thames: an analysis of Indian FDI into London*. London: Greater London Authority.

Harvey, D. (2001) *Spaces of capital*. Edinburgh: Edinburgh University Press.

Her Majesty's Government/Mayor of London (2013) 'Inspired by 2012: the legacy from the Olympic and Paralypmic Games', available at: https://www.gov.uk/government/uploads/system/uploads/attachment_data/file/224148/2901179_OlympicLegacy_acc.pdf (last accessed 14 May 2014).

Her Majesty's Government/Mayor of London (2014) 'Inspired by 2012: the legacy from the Olympic and Paralympic Games, second annual report, summer 2014', available at: https://www.gov.uk/government/uploads/system/uploads/attachment_data/file/335774/140723_Inspired_by_2012_-_2nd_annual_legacy_report_-_accessible.pdf (last accessed 10 August 2014).

House of Commons Standard Note SNEP/18/28 (2013) 'Foreign direct investment', available at: http://www.parliament.uk/business/publications/research/briefing-papers/SN01828/foreign-direct-investment-fdi (last accessed 20 May 2014).

Kaczmarsk, M. (2014) 'London leading European destination for FDI in 2013'. *fDiIntelligence*, available at: http://www.fdiintelligence.com/Locations/Europe/Russia/London-leading-European-destination-for-FDI-in-2013 (last accessed 3 June 2015).

Kearney, A. K. (2012) '2012 Global cities index and emerging cities outlook', available at: http://www.atkearney.co.uk/documents/10192/dfedfc4c-8a62-4162-90e5-2a3f14f0da3a (last accessed 2 May 2014).

Long, K. (2012, October 3) 'Docklands' new crystal building', *Evening Standard*, available at: http://www.standard.co.uk/arts/architecture/docklands-new-crystal-building-8195296.html (last accessed 28 May 2014).

Lucci, P. and Harrison, B. (2011) *The knowledge economy: reviewing the make-up of the knowledge economy in London*. London: Future of London. Available at: http://www.futureoflondon.org.uk/futureoflondon/wp-content/uploads/downloads/2011/10/Future-of-London-Knowledge-Economy.pdf (last accessed 14 April 2014).

McLoughlin, A. (2011) 'Investment in London's IT and software sector jumps'. *fDiIntelligence.*

Mayer Brown (2013) 'Mayer Brown advises on £1.5 billion regeneration of London's Silvertown Quays', available at: http://www.mayerbrown.com/Mayer-Brown-advises-on-15-billion-regeneration-of-Londons-Silvertown-Quays-06-11-2013 (last accessed 2 June 2014).

Norman, P. (2011, August 17) 'Westfield results buoyed by soaring UK performance', *Costar*, available at: http://www.costar.co.uk/en/assets/news/2011/August/Westfield-results-buoyed-by-soaring-UK-performance/ (last accessed 18 June 2104).

OECD (2002) *Foreign direct investment for development*. Paris: OECD.

Oxford Economics (2013) 'UK regional forecasts', available at: http://www.oxfordeconomics.com/forecasts-and-models/cities/uk-regional-forecasts/overview (last accessed 25 May 2014).

Pickford, J. (2014, January 19) 'Recovery likely to widen wealth gap between London and regions', *Financial Times.*

Poynter, G. (2013) 'Postcard from Rio', in M. Perryman (Ed.), *London 2012 how was it for us?* London: Lawrence & Wishart.

Roche, M. (2000) *Mega-events and modernity*. London: Routledge.

Sassen, S. (2012) 'Beyond state-to-state geopolitics: urban vectors dominate' in A. T. Kearney (Ed.), *2012 global cities index and emerging cities outlook*, available at: http://www.atkearney.co.uk/documents/10192/dfedfc4c-8a62-4162-90e5-2a3f14f0da3a (last accessed 2 May 2014).

Siemens (2010) *Airport Logistics*, Newsletter for Airports and Airlines, Issue 4, available at: https://www.mobility.siemens.com/mobility/global/SiteCollectionDocuments/en/news/customer-magazines-and-newsletters/airport-logistics-newsletter/airport-logistics-issue-04-10-en.pdf (last accessed 8 June 2014).

Think London (2009) 'London 2020, competing in a new FDI era', available at: http://cdn.londonandpartners.com/l-and-p/assets/media/london_2020_competing_in_a_new_fdi_era.pdf (last accessed 22 May 2014).

United Voice (2014) 'Olympic tax dodging, Westfield's corporate tax structure for tax avoidance in the UK', available at: www.unitedvoice.org.au/olympictaxdodging (last accessed 10 July 2014).

Wainwright, O. (2014, March 14) 'Anger at Cannes property fare where councils rub shoulders with oligarchs', *Guardian*.

12 The 2012 Olympics and small local business

A 5-year longitudinal study of south-east London

Peter Vlachos

Introduction

Mega-events are defined by Getz (2007:25) as those events which, due to their size or significance, can produce 'extraordinarily high levels of tourism, media coverage, prestige, or economic impact for the host community, venue or organization'. Even prior to the 2012 Games, London was already a world-renowned centre for arts, entertainment and sporting events such as London Fashion Week, London International Film Festival, several top-draw sports facilities and Notting Hill street carnival – now Europe's largest street festival with attendance of approximately 1.4 million over 2 days (Greater London Authority, 2012). London's O2 Arena is the busiest popular music venue in the world (Pollstar, 2014), and venues such as the ExCeL in East London and Kensington Olympia in West London regularly host trade exhibitions with global reach. It is against the backdrop of this dynamic and increasingly valuable emerging 'experience economy' (Pine and Gilmore, 1999; Sundbo, 2004) within the 'spectacular urban space' (Hall, 2006) that this chapter considers the impact of the world's pre-eminent mega-event – the Olympic Games – and the impact of the London 2012 Olympic Games on small local business.

Competition among cities wishing to host the Games is extremely high (Shoval, 2002). The London 2012 Games cost £8.77 billion (British Broadcasting Corporation, 2013) to deliver, a cost that was justified by politicians and advocates in large part on the basis of perceived future benefits. Hosting the Olympic Games is seen by policy makers as a way to fast-track urban economic development (Essex and Chalkley, 1998; Gold and Gold, 2008), and the Olympics are often 'sold' to the local population as a means of regenerating disadvantaged areas, begging the question of whether this leads to Olympics-led regeneration or regeneration-led Olympics (Roberts, 2000). Regime change theory (Burbank *et al.*, 2002; Andranovich *et al.*, 2001; Cook and Ward, 2010) argues that the use of mega-events as engines for economic growth represents a policy shift in which the city becomes a 'growth machine' (Molotch, 1976) whereby elected political – and unelected economic – elites dominate.

Mega-events have been criticised as harbouring 'the politics of fantastic expectations' (Eisienger, 2000:326) where projections are treated as facts. At best these growth-oriented approaches might be considered as pump-priming economic development–oriented strategies, at worst as a highly speculative (Jessop and Sum, 2000) and a 'seldom admitted gamble' (Gold and Gold, 2007) where the appeasement of privileged elites is prioritised over the needs of the local population. Cook and Ward (2010:7) suggest that mega-events such as the Manchester Commonwealth Games provided an opportunity for political elites to internalise entrepreneurialism within the governing structures and discourse. As Whitson and Macintosh (1996) have shown, the competitive and high-stake nature of Olympic Games city bids tend to downplay the potentially negative aspects. The resulting runaway urban boosterism (see Waitt, 2001 on Sydney) can derail public debate about political caution in the all-encompassing drive to win the hosting rights for the Games.

The small business perspectives

Public policy rhetoric commonly refers to small business as the 'engine' of economic growth (e.g. Crabb, 2014). The literature on enterprise and small businesses (e.g. Burns, 2011; Wickham, 2006; European Union, 2014) identifies several key characteristics of small business:

- most are very small;
- strong influence of owner-manager (and family);
- short-term horizons;
- short of cash;
- raising finance a major problem;
- local orientation;
- little influence on market;
- scope of activity limited;
- over-reliance on small number of customers.

The perspective of small local business does not fit neatly into the typical dichotomies in the contested spaces and debates, which typically pit the 'big' interests, namely, the government, the International Olympics Committee (IOC) and sponsoring multinational companies as against local interests (Cochrane *et al.*, 1996 cited in Essex and Chalkley, 1998:182).

Review of previous research on the Olympics and small business

Prior literature on the effects of the Olympics has had a tendency towards advocacy rather than critical analysis. For example, Cashman (2002:8) asserts 'it is clear that the Games can produce tangible benefits for government and business' yet offers no evidence to support his position. The core political and economic trade-off is between the upfront cost of hosting the Games (see the willingness to pay literature, e.g. Atkinson *et al.*, 2008; Heyne *et al.*, 2007; Guay, 1996) and the negative immediate impact disruption, on the one hand, and the envisioned longer term positive tourism of the Games on Olympic host cities, on the other hand. Both the costs and the benefits relating to the Games may take years to become apparent.

Negative findings from previous literature

Previous research on the economic impact of the Games on small local business has yielded mixed, and generally disappointing, results. Teigland (1999) identified a 'false' tourist postboom in which 40 per cent of full-service hotels in Lillehammer had gone bankrupt within 2 years. Local businesses are often blocked out of obtaining the benefits of the Games by big players (Hall, 2005; Hall, 2006). Only 31 per cent of small and medium enterprises, mostly Olympics suppliers, benefited from the 1988 Calgary Winter Games (Mount and Leroux, 1994). At the same time, small businesses as local entities have been found to suffer from displacement effects (Engel, 2007 in Gold and Gold, 2008).

Increased status and profile of the city does not necessarily equate with across-the-board improved business performance at individual firm level. Owen (2005) suggests that the Olympics may be more about attracting new firms rather than improving the performance of existing ones. As Chalkley and Essex (1999:367) had previously noted, such improvements may have 'major implications for the further development of the city as a business and administrative centre' in terms of upskilling general business capacity and networks, but the effects on small businesses directly are less clear.

Where economic impacts are being measured, they often contain methodological pitfalls, as Lee (2005) discovered regarding the mega-event contribution to overall tourism revenue for the 2002 FIFA World Cup in South Korea. Such impact evaluations are often based on claims made by assertion and rhetoric rather than evidence (Coalter *et al.*, 2000:51). Analyzing the World Cup held in Germany, Hall (2006) notes that, while revenue was estimated at €1.5 billion, the main beneficiaries were big-name advertisers and retail. Local business was blocked out. Local business people noted that it was Heineken and burger chains rather than German beer and sausages on the menu, using the culinary euphemism to describe the overwhelming sponsorship strength of international corporate brands. It appears, therefore, that mega-events might not be as beneficial to small business as initial claims by pro-Games advocates might suggest.

Positive findings in previous literature

The positive impacts of the Olympic Games on small business found in previous literature appear to be of a diffuse and longer term nature, the main beneficiaries potentially being policy makers and larger organisations who gain leveraging benefits. The positive effect relies on impact analysis and ripple effects (e.g. Preuss, 2002; Jones, 2001; Matheson, 2006) and legacies (e.g. Searle, 2002; Guay, 1996). Overall, the documented positive effects could be classified in five categories.

(1) Positive but short term

The Seoul Games, for instance, resulted in a short-term boost in business-related tourism a year after the Games (Kang and Perdue, 1994). Assessing the impact of the Athens 2004 Olympic Games on the Greek economy, Kasimati and Dawson (2009) noted a boost to the economy during the preparation phase and in the year of the Games with modest economic effects in the longer term. This suggests that while the Games might help to reinforce existing growth tendencies (e.g. Seoul, Beijing), the Games alone are not enough to turn around faltering cities or countries (e.g. Athens).

(2) Place-image making

Miles (2010) considers cities as urban spaces for consumption. Mega-events can contribute to the construction of a particular urban image and rhetoric, namely of the spectacular city. The alleged benefits of mega-events to business are more to image and general diffuse attractiveness of the city/region for future visitors rather than bottom-line financial gain. Hosting 'hegemonic projects' (Paul, 2004) such as the Olympic Games may contribute to urban place-image via urban trans-formation of 'the gaze' (e.g. Jansson, 2005; Lefebvre, 1974).

Positive image effects were noted in Sydney and its status as global city (Cashman and Hughes, 1999; Madden and Crowe, 1998). However, while their long-term, fuzzy, image-building effects may provide stimulus for regions or cities as a whole, as Preuss (2002) and Malfas *et al.* (2004) note, such benefits do not necessarily result in specific business impact at the individual firm level.

Ritchie and Smith (1991) noted a positive impact on the international levels of awareness of Calgary and its image as host city of the 1988 Winter Games, and at the local level, Burbank *et al.* (2002) found local citizens' pride increased. However, while Gold and Gold (2008:312) predicted that for London 2012 it was 'probable that assiduous quarrying of the Olympic brand will have some impact on the image of the five boroughs and perhaps assist local businesses', one might question such an assertion given the tightness with which the IOC controls the brand, as the IOC's 60-page guidelines (2012) for the use of the Olympics brand implies.

(3) Trigger entrepreneurship

It has been suggested (Spilling, 1996) that the Olympics might trigger invest-ment 'entrepreneurship'. In terms of enterprise and small business, for example, indirect costs and benefits might include the value to the economy of pretrad-ing support of new start-ups and the development of an entrepreneurial ethos in the mega-events city. There has been little research along these lines to explore whether this is the case in recent Games, hence one of the drivers of the present research.

(4) Event business leveraging

Several examples exist of how cities have been able to harness and develop the capacity to host future events and develop a stronger position within the live events industry, for instance, in Sydney (O'Brien, 2006). Similarly, despite the financial difficulties experienced by Montréal in the 1976 Games, the city had previously shown its capacity to deliver successfully large-scale events such as the 1967 Canadian centennial Expo, and post-1976, Montréal has developed world-class jazz, film and comedy international festivals, as well hosting car-racing events (Tourisme Montréal, 2014). South Korea has developed an ambitious active outward communications programme to build up Seoul as a destination for business and cultural travel and to promote South Korea more generally, especially in direct competition with long-time regional leaders such as Singapore and Hong Kong, by establishing a cultural centre in the heart of London (Korean Cultural Centre, 2014) and via various print and promotional initiatives.

(5) Promoting equal opportunities

Hiller (2000) notes a possible exception in Cape Town's 2004 Olympics bid whereby in South Africa the procurement process would be based on 80 per cent price and 20 per cent on addressing affirmative action policy to promote fledging black entrepreneurs. Such affirmative action could have had a positive effect on black small business and an emerging middle class. Rogerson (2009) suggested similar benefits to black-led businesses on South Africa's hosting of FIFA 2010.

Summary

The literature reviewed above suggests that the effects of the Olympics on small local businesses are at best mixed. The Games are often presented by policy makers and Olympic urban boosters as possible catalysts for business enterprise, but the actual measured effects have often been found to be diffused and short term. A number of shortcomings in prior research in relation to mega-events and small business have been identified: (a) lack of robust data set specifically on small business and mega-events, (b) weak existing quantitative data on economic impacts of events, and (c) highly politicised nature of mega-events and urban boosterism.

Given that prior research has not demonstrated benefits at the firm level, but rather a broad regional and city level, it is useful to test the experience of the Olympics as the small firm level. Did the Games encourage small businesses in the short term to take advantage of the immediate market opportunity that the Games might offer and for the longer term to invest in the development of their business? Did these small businesses experience and respond to the Olympics as an opportunity or a challenge?

Methodology and sample

The methodology followed previous research in Vancouver, using a 'living laboratory' research model (Fane, 2011) with the aim of capturing the London Olympics as a unique mass social experiment. The research consisted of three stages and used a mixed-methods, longitudinal approach. Stage 1 contained a series of six action-oriented focus group consultations – before the Games began – with small local business owners and managers (Oct/Nov 2009) in Greenwich, followed by five business coaching seminars for small business owners and managers (January–May 2010), hosted at the University of Greenwich. Semi-structured interviews with small business owners in Greenwich, Tower Hamlets and Newham were then held in November 2010, and a second street survey with 30 local businesses in Greenwich in spring 2011 captured the evolving mood of the business owners and managers and acted as pilot tests for the survey questions to be used during the next stage. Stage 2 consisted of 225 face-to-face interviews (plus nine online surveys; total n = 234) during the main Games period, plus field observations. The sample included representative small businesses from the commercial areas of six south-east (Greenwich, Woolwich, Charlton and Lewisham) and East London districts (Isle of Dogs/Canary Wharf and Newham). The districts of Greenwich, Woolwich and Newham were Olympic sites, while the other districts were within a 3-kilometre radius.

The research methodology used was based on an interpretivist, inductive, action research approach which focuses on 'gaining an understanding of the meanings humans attach to events' (Saunders *et al.*, 2009:127), the management of change, the closer collaboration between business practitioners and academic researchers (a conscious aim of the University's Olympic Challenges Fund) and the subsequent (or possibly concurrent) development of theory (Eden and Huxham, 1996:75).

Research results and discussion

Preuss (2007) has developed a useful theoretical model to describe the potential legacies of mega-events such as the Olympic Games along three dimensions: planned or unplanned, tangible or intangible and positive or negative. The present research found that all three of these dimensions were experienced by small local businesses.

Stage 1 – pre-Olympics

When we began the initial focus groups approximately 2 years before the Games, we found that the small businesses we spoke with were suffering the pressure of severe economic downturn. Thus, their orientation, as the small enterprise literature had suggested, was very much geared to meeting their short-term financial obligations. For many, just paying their rent and rates was enough to deal with. With the Games coming closer, some businesses made efforts to 'link into' the Olympics, e.g. attending Transport for London briefings, speaking with small business organisations in Vancouver, etc. As transport routes were made public, it appeared increasingly clear that businesses to the east of the park were going to be marginalised due to transport, people flow and security measures.

The findings at this stage of the research confirmed small business theory. Short-term challenges continued to be in the forefront of the minds of small local business owners/managers. Notably, the immediacy of the financial crisis ('credit crunch') overshadowed the Olympics, the latter seeming too remote both chronologically and in a business sense.

Action research impacts

There was some evidence that the Games – or perhaps more specifically this research project itself – had been of some benefit to small businesses in countering the more negative aspects of the small business 'mentality'. Participation in the research helped to mobilise small local businesses in responding to the challenges and opportunities on the London 2012 Games and thus expand their scope of influence. The research helped some business owners/managers to look beyond their day-to-day business operational issues, and it mobilised and empowered them in responding to the challenges and opportunities on the London 2012 Games.

Stage 2 – during Olympics

The choice of a UNESCO-protected world heritage site such as Maritime Greenwich for the Olympic equestrian events had been contested. Conservationists expressed concern over possible damage to the historic park. The site is regularly listed in tourist publications as a 'top ten' item, and the daily crowds streaming into the old town centre, especially during the peak summer period, attest its popularity, with the visitor economy already accounting for £1.1 billion of spending in the Royal Borough of Greenwich (Yellow Railroad, 2014).

During the equestrian day events, between 20,000 and 25,000 ticket holders travelled to Greenwich Park, mainly using public transport. Several thousand more watched from a large screen set up on the grounds of the Old Royal Naval College (ORNL). However, it appears nothing could have prepared local businesses for what transpired on the first day of the events.

Barricades had appeared overnight, blocking motor vehicle access in the town centre and controlling pedestrian footpaths. Overzealous marshalling of pedestrians prevented Games attendees from lingering at the shops along the way. Restrictions on advertising signage were actively monitored and dealt with by both uniformed police and plain-clothed council officials.

The normally busiest public transport station ('Cutty Sark for Maritime Greenwich' on the Docklands Light Railway [DLR] line) was shut for the duration of the events at Greenwich. Businesses in the town centre immediately saw a clear disruption to their regular tourist trade. The aggressive marshalling of attendees to and from the entrance gates resulted in near fisticuffs between local businesses and local authorities.

Figure 12.1 Barricades in Greenwich town centre.

Figure 12.2 Poster in pub window in Greenwich – 'LOCOG: licence to kill a town centre'.

Takings were down by 40 to 90 per cent for approximately four-fifths of the small businesses interviewed. Notwithstanding hyperboles in the heat of the moment, the negative response was clear and consistent. Businesses to the east of the park were not barricaded, but were marginalised geographically despite their close proximity, some within 200 metres of the park, and disrupted by the fact that the main road was designated as an Olympic route between Greenwich town centre and the North Greenwich arena (as the O2 Arena, formerly Millennium Dome, was named for the duration of the Games). Police guarding the alternate train station at the east end of the park (Maze Hill station) commented how quiet the area was despite the Games in progress.

Even free attractions such as the historic Painted Hall at the ORNL were bypassed as attendees rushed home to return to their hotels or dinner.

Overall, 48.6 per cent of respondents in the study said the Olympics had a negative effect on their business, 17.5 per cent judged the effects as positive and 33.7 per cent were neutral. Thus, the immediate experience of small local businesses was overwhelmingly negative or neutral (82.3 per cent) rather than positive (17.5 per cent). This is a stark contrast to the government rhetoric on the business benefits of the Games. The results from these interviews clearly suggested that the Games had not resulted in any windfall of business activity, apart from a few local winners, e.g. one local pub in Greenwich that was used as local base for the Irish equestrian team. Results in Woolwich were somewhat more positive. Here, a refurbished town centre square with a large screen for public viewing drew in locals and some adjacent shops, e.g. cafes noted increases of 10 to 20 per cent in revenue.

Figure 12.3 Streams of attendees leaving the park after an event.

Figure 12.4 Attempts by heritage site in Greenwich to entice Olympic visitors.

The small businesses interviewed showed little awareness or engagement with the CompeteFor procurement web portal. Nor were they prepared to restructure or invest in staff or capital improvements simply for the sake of the Games. There was very little appetite for investment or growth. The Olympics did not encourage small business owners to make any long-term (and very little short term) investment in their businesses, for example, there were very few who had added new staff, expanded their premises, added a new location or invested in plant or machinery.

The results showed some variation between the two Olympic districts in southeast London. Already a world heritage site, businesses at the Greenwich old town centre suffered disruption to an otherwise well-established visitor, tourist and local trade. The results in Woolwich, on the other hand, suggested some level of synergy with the 'up and coming' trends supported by new and ongoing improvements in public transport in infrastructure, city centre retail development and a residential property development boom.

The bad experience galvanised small business anger leading to threats to sue the local authorities for compensation (Binns, 2012). Surprisingly, despite these clear misgivings from small businesses, the Federation of Small Business (2013) still painted a positive picture of the Games in their report. It could be said that the less the small businesses invested, in many cases, the better off they were.

A feel-good factor enabled modest gains for some small businesses. A cycle shop in Greenwich (SE10), for instance, enjoyed an increase of 12.5 per cent also noting the feel-good factor: 'business is up, also we are winning events, everyone is in a good mood'. Compare, however, a pharmacy in the same street which was down 20 per cent in its trade: 'Very quiet, all the roads are blocked off'. A nearby restaurant showed exasperation: 'It's unbelievable, you wouldn't think an event was going on. Even the locals appear to have gone [away]'.

There was evidence of limited entrepreneurial thinking. A property agent in Woolwich (SE18) found the Games irrelevant: 'we do not deal with short-term lets'. This suggests, on the one hand, a focus on core business objectives and not being swayed by the short-term opportunities of the Games. On the other hand, it also suggests an unwillingness to explore the one-off, and possible longer term, opportunities the Olympics might offer. Organisational stretch and entrepreneurial risk were not embraced. As we see in other examples illustrated in the research, however, often those who did engage in such risk suffered as a consequence. The Greenwich lucrative–established tourist and visitor trade was disrupted. Many businesses in Greenwich town centre noted, at times with notable anger, the disruption caused by blocked roads, footpaths and access to public transport. Businesses near the closed DLR train station at Cutty Sark in the historic centre, accustomed to regular and lucrative tourist trade, saw a sharp decline as a result: 'People are diverted to different roads and they're not coming into our shop' (sandwich shop, SE10).

Some of the beneficiaries of such diversions, however, enjoyed a windfall effect with a substantial, if short term, jump in sales. Meanwhile, the displacement of local regular customers by Olympic tourists and visitors hurt some businesses (beauty shop, SE10) but benefited others (restaurant, also Greenwich). However, businesses in normally high footfall areas such as the road leading to the main gate to Greenwich Park suffered as a result of the closure of that gate during the Games. Several businesses along this route noted a decline in trade of 80 per cent or more (pub restaurant, SE10). Even taking into account hyperbolic tendencies in the responses, the detrimental effect is clear. Yet, literally just around the corner, the rerouting of pedestrian traffic saw another restaurant reporting a growth spike of 150 per cent. Meanwhile, over in Woolwich, proximity to the big screen in the town centre benefited, perhaps predictably, the burger restaurant at the edge of the square.

Small business managers felt that the Olympics benefited big business, not small business. At Greenwich market, the mood of small traders was mixed. One trader noted: 'All the big corporations are raking in all the money. And small business are left to what's left. [The] main sponsors are running the show' (market trader, SE10). However, those businesses which took a more market-oriented approach were more likely to enjoy some success. Rather than aiming to sell more of the same product to a captive visitor base, one retailer said that with 'luck and a bit of planning' adjusting their product lines resulted in a more positive experience. Several business owners who suffered during the Games expressed anger: 'I don't want anything to do with the Olympics, it's put me out of business, it's destroyed this town, it's shit' (antique dealer, SE10). Another one complained: 'Customers driven away, worse than the recession. I wish the Olympics had never happened' (jewellery shop, Greenwich market, SE10). The promise of the opportunities of the

Olympics was not fulfilled for many businesses, and the feeling of being oversold the benefits of the Games arose again and again. 'We expected more' (clothing shop, Canary Wharf, E14). Meanwhile, the new shopping centre directly adjacent to the Olympic park in Stratford was enjoying a boon (Prynn *et al.*, 2012).

Further cases revealed that small businesses who did take on entrepreneurial risk suffered as a result. Widely reported were food stalls which lay barren due to the lack of projected footfall (BBC, 2012; Binns, 2012). An attempt to run a late-night 'rave'-type London Pleasure Gardens in E16 went bankrupt (Firth, 2012; Deloitte, 2013) and shut within days. Even larger businesses like the busy O2 arena and ExCeL exhibition centre (both used as Olympic venues) had to be cautious in dealing with the potential disruption of the Games on their usual activity cycles. It could be said that the Olympics were negotiated, rather than embraced.

Summary of findings of stage 2

The findings of research during the Games period found the effects, both positive and negative, to be extremely localised. Being closer to the Olympics site meant more disruption; being further away had positive or neutral effects. A marked disruption occurred to an otherwise robust 'top ten' tourism site. Many local businesses and residents thought Greenwich was already iconic and did not need any image improvement via the Olympics. Longer term alleged benefits were of little compensation to short-term–oriented small businesses. Those who did benefit did so by focusing on adjusting their product service offer to a new customer base, rather than trying to sell existing product lines. Investing in more staff did not appear to be a good strategy. The contingency message got through, but businesses were still resentful of the disruption. In Canary Wharf, high-end knowledge/service workers and firms were able to adapt, i.e. working electronically from home, whereas small local businesses, often retail but also services, did not have such option. There was some evidence of small businesses uniting to raise their voices (Baracaia, 2012).

Stage 3 – post-Olympics

In the immediate aftermath to the 2012 London Games, ongoing troubles in the British 'high street' were prominent in the media. The Games had not had the ability to turn around the fortunes of suffering small businesses even in Olympic neighbourhoods like Greenwich town centre (Kirca, 2013).

Two years later, however, by 2014, there is evidence of institutional learning as previously suggested by research on Montréal, Sydney and Barcelona. The success of the 'Tall Ships' festival centred in Greenwich and Woolwich in September 2014 was more widely embraced by the local business community, assisted by the fact that bunting and posters were widely encouraged and available, in distinct contrast to the rigorous restrictions on use of the Olympic 'brand' in 2012. A more relaxed and festive atmosphere ensued and small local businesses responded well.

Figure 12.5 Tall Ships festival, Greenwich, September 2014.

In Woolwich, already ongoing regeneration has been driven more by transport infrastructure and residential demand than the Olympics.

The launch of a new destination management company called 'VisitGreenwich' on 22 October 2014, which aims to consolidate gains and boost visitor yield, suggests greater cooperation, though again primarily driven by larger business players and aimed more at consolidating ascendant areas such as the north Greenwich peninsula than turning around the fortunes of faltering small businesses. A general buzz continues around the regeneration of the East London Docklands area on both sides of the river. Further research would be required in the future, first, to test the findings of this study and to see if they are replicated in other mega-event cities, past and future and, second, to drill down further in terms of business type and size, proximity, demographics of owner-managers especially as there is some evidence of ethnicity as a factor.

Conclusions

The implications in practice of the study and the research results are that host cities need to be cautious in how they present the Olympics opportunities to small businesses so as not to raise false expectations and that small business owners and managers need to tread very carefully in their planning for mega-events. In a more general sense, the findings suggest that the 'local' in 'small local business' is a greater driving force than the 'business' aspect. That is to say, small local businesses are less likely to align themselves with larger businesses in trying to capture a slice of the Olympic pie, and more likely to align themselves with local residents in viewing the Olympics mainly as a hindrance to their everyday activities. The results suggest an unresolved tension or discontinuity between government policy intended to support small business as a 'catalyst of economic growth' and the Olympic imperative which appears to favour large, national and transnational interests at the expense of small local business interests and growth.

References

Andranovich, G., Burbank, M. and Heying, C. H. (2001) *Olympic dreams: the impact of mega-events on local politics*. Boulder, CO: Lynne Rienner.

Atkinson, G., Mourato, S., Szymanski, S. and Ozdemiroglu, E (2008) 'Are we willing to pay enough to back the bid? Valuing the intangible impacts of London's bid to host the 2012 Summer Olympic Games'. *Urban Studies*, 45(2): 419–444.

Baracaia, A. (2012, August 1) 'Greenwich traders win concession over their great barrier grief', *Evening Standard*, p. 20.

Binns, D. (2012) 'Gary Ince has resigned as the chief executive of North London Business after the "apparent failure" of an Olympic Games food market', *East London and West Essex Guardian*, available at: http://www.guardian-series.co.uk/news/wfnews/9865492. LEYTON__Co_organiser_of__disastrous__Olympics_market_resigns/ (last accessed 25 October 2014).

British Broadcasting Corporation (BBC) (2013) 'London 2012: Olympics and Paralympics £528m under budget', available at: http://www.bbc.co.uk/sport/0/olympics/20041426 (last accessed 24 October 2014).

Burbank, M. J., Andranovich, A. and Heying, C. H. (2002) 'Mega-events, urban development, and public policy'. *The Review of Policy Research*, 19(3): 179–202.

Burns, P. (2011) *Entrepreneurship and small business* (3rd ed.). Basingstoke: Palgrave Macmillan.

Cashman, R. (2002) *Impact of the Games on Olympic host cities*. Barcelona: Centre d'Estudis Olímpics, Universitat Autònoma de Barcelona. Available at: http://olympic studies.uab.es/lectures/web/pdf/cashman.pdf (last accessed 24 October 2014).

Cashman, R. and Hughes, A. (1999) *Staging the Olympics: the event and its impact*. Sydney: UNSW Press.

Chalkley, B. and Essex, S. (1999) 'Urban development through hosting international events: a history of the Olympic Games'. *Planning Perspectives*, 14(4): 369–394.

Coalter, F., Allison, M. and Taylor, J. (2000) *The role of sport in regenerating deprived urban areas*. Edinburgh: Centre for Leisure Research, University of Edinburgh, The Scottish Executive Central Research Unit.

Cochrane, A., Peck, J. and Tickell, A. (1996) 'Manchester plays games: exploring the local politics of globalization'. *Urban Studies*, 33(8): 1319–1336.

Cook, I. R. and Ward, K. (2010) 'Trans-urban networks of learning, mega-events and policy tourism: the case of Manchester's Commonwealth and Olympic Games projects'. *Imagining Urban Futures*, Working Paper 8, available at: http://www.sed.manchester.ac.uk/geography/ research/publications/wp/iufp/documents/iufp_wp8.pdf (last accessed 24 October 2014).

Crabb, S. (2014) 'Small business is at the heart of economic recovery in rural Wales', available at: https://www.gov.uk/government/news/stephen-crabb-mp-small-business-is-at-the-heart-of-economic-recovery-in-rural-wales (last accessed 24 October 2014).

Cunningham, J. B. (1995) 'Strategic considerations in using action research for improving personnel practices'. *Public Personnel Management*, 24(2): 515–529.

Deloitee (2013) 'London Pleasure Gardens limited (in administration)', available at: http://www.deloitte.com/view/en_GB/uk/services/corporate-finance/restructuring-services/updates-for-insolvencies/london-pleasure-gardens/index.htm (last accessed 24 October 2014).

Eden, C. and Huxham, C. (1996) 'Action research for management research'. *British Journal of Management*, 7(1): 75–86.

Eisinger, P. (2000) 'The politics of bread and circuses: building the city for the visitor class'. *Urban Affairs Review*, 35(3): 316–333.

Engel, M. (2007, July 14–15) 'Olympic losers', *Financial Times Magazine*, p. 8.

Essex, S. and Chalkley, B. (1998) 'Olympic Games: catalyst of urban change'. *Leisure Studies*, 17(3): 187–206.

European Union (2014) 'What is an SME?', available at: http://ec.europa.eu/enterprise/policies/sme/facts-figures-analysis/sme-definition/index_en.htm (last accessed 24 October 2014).

Fane, G. (2011, June 2) 'The Vancouver 2010 Olympics: a living laboratory'. Games and the city: impacts and legacies conference, University of Greenwich, London.

Federation of Small Business. (2013) *Passing the baton: How small businesses have been affected by the London 2012 Games*. London: Federation of Small Business. Available at: http://www.fsb.org.uk/policy/rpu/london/assets/passingthebaton_fsb_final.pdf (last accessed 25 October 2014).

Frith, M. (2012, August 5) 'London Pleasure Gardens go into administration', *Evening Standard*, available at: http://www.standard.co.uk/news/london/london-pleasure-gardens-go-into-administration-8008746.html (last accessed 24 October 2014).

Getz, D. (2007) *Event studies: theory, research and policy for planned events*. Oxford: Butterworth-Heinemann.

Gold, J. R. and Gold, M. M. (Eds.) (2007) *Olympic cities: city agendas, planning, and the world's Games, 1896–2012*. London: Routledge.

Gold, J. R. and Gold, M. M. (2008) 'Olympic cities: regeneration, city rebranding and changing urban agendas'. *Geography Compass*, 2(1): 300–318.

Greater London Authority (2012) 'Request for mayoral decision – MD1026: Notting Hill Carnival 2012', available at: http://www.london.gov.uk/sites/default/files/MD1026%20Notting%20Hill%20Carnival%202012%20PDF.pdf (last accessed 26 October 2014).

Guay, M. (1996, April 27) 'Legacy of the Olympic Games in Montreal – an introduction'. 3ème Congrès Olympique Canadien, Association Olympique Canadienne, Montréal, available at: http://montrealolympics.com/mg_legacy.php (last accessed 26 October 2014).

Hall, A. (2005, February 8) 'Small beer for World Cup Germans', *The Age*, available at: http://www.theage.com.au/news/Business/Small-beer-for-World-Cup-Germans/2005/02/07/1107625132417.html (last accessed 31 October 2014).

Hall, C. M. (2006) 'Urban entrepreneurship, corporate interests and sports mega-events: the thin policies of competitiveness within the hard outcomes of neoliberalism'. *The Sociological Review*, 54(2): 59–70.

Heyne, M., Maennig, W. and Süssmuth, B. (2007) 'Mega-sporting events as experience goods'. *Hamburg Contemporary Economic Discussions, No. 5*, available at: http://www.econstor.eu/bitstream/10419/25351/1/56034225X.PDF (last accessed 25 October 2014).

Hiller, H. H. (2000) 'Mega-events, urban boosterism and growth strategies: an analysis of the objectives and legitimations of the Cape Town 2004 Olympic bid'. *International Journal of Urban and Regional Research*, 24(2): 439–458.

International Olympic Committee (2012) 'IOC marketing: media guide London 2012', available at: http://www.olympic.org/Documents/IOC_Marketing/London_2012/IOC_Marketing_Media_Guide_2012.pdf (last accessed 25 October 2014).

Jansson, A. (2005) 'Re-encoding the spectacle: urban fatefulness and mediated stigmatisation in the "City of Tomorrow"'. *Urban Studies*, 42(10): 1671–1691.

Jessop, B. and Sum, N. (2000) 'An entrepreneurial city in action: Hong Kong's emerging strategies in and for (inter)urban competition'. *Urban Studies*, 37(12): 2287–2313, available at: http://www.lancaster.ac.uk/sociology/research/publications/papers/jessop-sum-USE-2000a.pdf (last accessed 31 October 2014).

Jones, C. (2001) 'Mega-events and host-region impacts: determining the true worth of the 1999 Rugby World Cup'. *International Journal of Tourism Research*, 3(3): 241–251.

Kang, Y. and Perdue, R. (1994) 'Long-term impact of a mega-event on international tourism to the host country: a conceptual model and the case of the 1988 Seoul Olympics'. *Journal of International Consumer Marketing*, 6(3–4): 205–225.

Kasimati, E. and Dawson, P. (2009) 'Assessing the impact of the 2004 Olympic Games on the Greek economy: a small macroeconometric model'. *Economic Modelling*, 26(1): 139–146.

Kirca, D. (2013, March 8) 'A nation of shopkeepers? UK seeks to keep its soul', *Associated Press*, available at: http://bigstory.ap.org/article/nation-shopkeepers-uk-seeks-keep-its-soul (last accessed 26 October 2014).

Korean Cultural Centre (2014) 'Welcome to the KCC', available at: http://london.korean-culture.org/navigator.do?siteCode=null&langCode=null&menuCode=200710260001&promImg=1198673942174.gif&menuType=CH&subImg=1198673942174.gif (last accessed 25 October 2014).

Lee, C.-K. (2005) 'Critical reflections on the economic impact assessment of a mega-event: the case of 2002 FIFA World Cup'. *Tourism Management*, 26(4): 595–603.

Lefebvre, H. (1974/1991) *The production of space*. Hoboken: Wiley-Blackwell.

Madden, J. R. and Crowe, M. (1998) 'Estimating the economic impact of the Sydney Olympic Games'. 38th Congress of the European Regional Science Association, available at: http://www-sre.wu.ac.at/ersa/ersaconfs/ersa98/papers/498.pdf (last accessed 26 October 2014).

Malfas, M., Theodoraki, W. and Houlihan, B. (2004) 'Impacts of the Olympic Games as mega-events'. *Municipal Engineer*, 157(ME3): 209–220, available at: https://opus.lib.uts.edu.au/research/bitstream/handle/10453/19761/muen.157.3.209.49461.pdf?sequence=1 (last accessed 31 October 2014).

Matheson, V. (2006) 'Major-events: the effect of the world's biggest sporting events on local, regional, and national economies'. College of the Holy Cross, Department of Economics Faculty Research Series, Paper no. 06–10, available at: http://college.holy-cross.edu/RePEc/hcx/Matheson_MegaEvents.pdf (last accessed 31 October 2014).

Miles, S. (2010) *Spaces for consumption*. London: Sage.

Molotch, H. (1976) 'The city as a growth machine: toward a political economy of place'. *American Journal of Sociology*, 82(2): 309–332.

Mount, J. and Leroux, C. (1994) *Assessing the effects of a landmark event: a retrospective study of the impact of the Olympic Games on the Calgary business sector*. Sudbury, Ontario: Laurentian University.

O'Brien, D. (2006) 'Event business leveraging the Sydney 2000 Olympic Games'. *Annals of Tourism Research*, 33(1): 240–261.

Owen, J. G. (2005) 'Estimating the cost and benefit of hosting Olympic Games: what can Beijing expect from its 2008 Games?' *The Industrial Geographer*, 3(1): 1–18, available at: http://igeographer.lib.indstate.edu/owen.pdf (last accessed 31 October 2014).

Paul, D. E. (2004) 'World cities as hegemonic projects: the politics of global imagineering in Montreal'. *Political Geography*, 23(5): 571–596.

Pine, J. and Gilmore, J. (1999) *The experience economy*. Boston: Harvard Business School Press.

Pollstar (2014) '2014 mid year worldwide ticket sales top 100 arena venues', available at: http://sprint_center.s3.amazonaws.com/doc/2014MidYearWorldwideTicketSalesTop10 0ArenaVenues.pdf (last accessed 25 October 2014).

Preuss, H. (2002) *Economic dimension of the Olympic Games*. Barcelona: Centre d'Estudis Olímpics, Universitat Autònoma de Barcelona. Available at: http://olympic-studies.uab.es/lectures/web/pdf/preuss.pdf (last accessed 24 October 2014).

Preuss, H. (2007) 'The conceptualisation and measurement of mega sport event legacies'. *Journal of Sport & Tourism*, 12(3–4): 207–227.

Prynn, J., Beard, M. and Freeman, S. (2012, July 31) 'Westfield's Games boom brings west end gloom', *Evening Standard*, p. 4.

Ritchie, J. B. R. and Smith, B. H. (1991) 'The impact of a mega-event on host region awareness: a longitudinal study'. *Journal of Travel Research*, 30(1): 3–10.

Roberts, P. (2000) 'The evolution, definition and purpose of urban regeneration' in P. Roberts and H. Sykes (Eds.), *Urban regeneration: a handbook*. London: Sage.

Rogerson, C. (2009) 'Mega-events and small enterprise development: the 2010 FIFA World Cup opportunities and challenges'. *Development Southern Africa*, 26(3): 337–352.

Saunders, M., Lewis, P. and Thornhill, A. (2009) *Research methods for business students*, (5th ed.). Harlow: Pearson Education. Available at: http://doha.ac.mu/ebooks/Research%20Methods/ResearchMethodsForBusinessStudents_Saunders.pdf (last accessed 3 June 2015).

Searle, G. (2002) 'Uncertain legacy: Sydney's Olympic stadiums'. *European Planning Studies*, 10(7): 845–860.

Shoval, N. (2002) 'A new phase in the competition for the Olympic gold: the London and New York bids for the 2012 Games'. *Journal of Urban Affairs*, 24(5): 583–599.

Spilling, O. R. (1996) 'Mega event as strategy for regional development: the case of the 1994 Lillehammer Winter Olympics'. *Entrepreneurship and Regional Development*, 8(4): 321–344.

Sundbo, J. (2004) 'The management of rock festivals as a basis for business dynamics: an example of the growing experience economy'. *International Journal of Entrepreneurship and Innovation Management*, 4(6): 587–612.

Teigland, J. (1999) 'Mega-events and impacts on tourism: the predictions and realities of the Lillehammer Olympics'. *Impact Assessment and Project Appraisal*, 17(4): 305–317.

Tourisme Montréal (2014) 'Events', available at: http://www.tourisme-montreal.org/What-To-Do/Events (last accessed 25 October 2014).

Waitt, G. (2001) 'The Olympic spirit and civic boosterism: the Sydney 2000 Olympics'. *Tourism Geographies: An International Journal of Tourism Space, Place and Environment*, 3(3): 249–278.

Whitson, D. and Macintosh, D. (1996) 'The global circus: international sport, tourism, and the marketing of cities'. *Journal of Sport & Social Issues*, 20(3): 278–295.

Wickham, P. A. (2006) *Strategic entrepreneurship* (4th ed.). Harlow: Pearson.

Yellow Railroad. (2014) *Destination management plan 2014–2018 prepared for Visit Greenwich*. Edinburgh: Yellow Railroad.

13 What do we mean by Paralympic legacy?

Shane Kerr and P. David Howe

Introduction

'Legacy talk is now all around the IOC [*and the IPC*] and the apparent simplicity of the concept. . . is the first thing to note in accounting for its attraction and ready diffusion among Olympic neophytes' (MacAloon, 2008:2065; italics indicate authors' insertion). Despite such assertions, questions like 'what is legacy?' and 'what is Paralympic legacy?' continue to be a source of bemusement within the field of sport studies since it was inserted into the Olympic Charter over a decade ago. Such is the problematic nature of legacy that Tim Hollingsworth (2012), the Chief Executive of the British Paralympic Association, tabooed referencing it in preference of the terms 'momentum' and 'change'. Our aims in this chapter are to examine legacy's problematic and nebulous nature and to address the academic sidelining of Paralympic and disability legacy.

The first part of this chapter problematises the linguistic and philosophical bases of legacy by drawing upon the work of Wittgenstein (1969). Here we also note the epistemic struggles engendered by attempts to evaluate legacy and deliberate upon the assumed efficacy of sporting spectacles to 'leave a legacy'. This deconstruction of legacy is followed by an attempt to reconstruct it through analyses of disability legacy prospectively and retrospectively. The prospective analysis examines disability legacy in the Olympic and Paralympic bid documents. While the retrospective analysis may be expressed through the following question: how did London 2012 change the social, cultural and economic position of disability?

Wittgenstein

Bourdieu *et al.* (1991) and McFee (2002) were key proponents of a reading of Wittgenstein (1969) to problematise the very basis of social inquiries of legacy. Fundamentally, Wittgenstein (1969) considered many philosophical problems to be linguistically not philosophically based. As such, we proceed from the following question: 'To what extent are the problems of legacy linguistically not philosophically based?'

To begin with, a preliminary linguistic observation relates to legacy's semantic opaqueness, in that a recurring predicament is the difficulty found in defining it. This difficulty lies at the heart of many discussions of legacy and was a problem explicitly stated in the report that came out of the International Olympic Committee's (IOC) International Olympic Symposium, titled 'The Legacy of the Olympic Games 1984–2000', held in Lausanne in 2002. This conference took place a year prior to the insertion of legacy into the Olympic Charter, yet legacy's semantic opaqueness still remains. If its contemporary persistence is doubted, Lord Harris of Haringey, the Chairman of the House of Lords Olympic and Paralympic Legacy Select Committee,[1] positing 'What does legacy actually mean?'[2] as his opening question to the second oral evidence session provides at least some, if anecdotal, evidence. This question was asked nearly a year after London 2012, a Games commented to have used the 'L word' more than any predecessor (Chappelet, 2012) and as representing a shift in legacy strategy from a post- to a pre-Games paradigm (Leopkey and Parent, 2012). Employing Wittgenstein (1969:25) – 'We are unable clearly to circumscribe the concepts we use; not because we don't know their real definition, but because there is no real *definition* to them' – we are back to square one.

The problem of understanding exactly what legacy is in the field of sports is paralleled in the academic literature. Preuss' (2007) subheading 'Towards a Definition of Legacy' or Chappelet's (2012) description of his legacy definition as a 'working definition' offer evidence of the difficulty of producing a *definitive* definition of legacy. Legacy shares this problem with other related words. For example, Alison (1986) concluded that the diversity of 'family resemblances' preclude a definitive definition of 'sport'. Disability could also be added to this list. Here Wittgenstein (1969) might have added that we can ask, *or be asked*, questions which do not necessarily have or require an answer. As such, we posit that questions like 'what is legacy?' or 'what is Paralympic legacy?' compel the production of answers and definitions that may never be completely satisfactory.

The major implications of this argument is a call for a heightened critique of the possibility of providing, or the 'need' for, a 'definitive' definition of legacy and of the adequacy of definitions of legacy found in dictionaries[3] which have often informed academic debate (Gilbert and Legg, 2011). What's more, we can begin to understand the *defining* of legacy as a contest in itself, insofar as to define legacy here would be to become embroiled in the very thing that is in contest. It is apposite that Bourdieu (1975:24) wrote, 'it is precisely because the definition of what is at stake in the struggle is itself an issue at stake in the struggle'. For this reason any definition of legacy is self-constituting (MacRury, 2008). Therefore, rather than attempt to define legacy in relation to the event, our conceptualisation turns on the institutions and actors that propose and impose definitions of legacy. Combine this with an analysis of their position and the study of legacy becomes inverted from the event to the institutions. It is in this sense that we fulfil Wittgenstein's (1969:66) empirical directive: 'Don't think, but look!'.

Another interrelated linguistic point is that legacy is afflicted with a problem of language, described by Wittgenstein (1969:17–18) as a 'craving for generality'. This point is especially apparent in exoteric discussions where legacy is used nondescriptly, or where a simple answer is assumed to be not only possible but also expected when the question 'what is the legacy?' is asked. This problem of a 'craving for generality' goes hand in hand with the polysemy of 'legacy' (Leopkey and Parent, 2012). As such, the nondescript use of legacy – that is, without reference to a specific relation, such as to sport, disability, economics or tourism, for example – compounds its capacity to confound. Clarity in reference to legacy with a specific relation is imperative.

These 'cravings to generalise' legacy are attempts to overcome its *relatable* neutrality. This is simply to identify the ease of which legacy can be related to any dimension of the Olympic or Paralympic Games. It is in this way that legacy is conceived as a plural or multifaceted concept (Chappelet, 2012; Agha *et al.*, 2012; Malfas *et al.*, 2004). More noteworthy is how *the* legacy of any Games is a symbolic amalgamation of these different legacies, although a particular legacy usually comes to predominate. For example, Los Angeles 1984's legacy is dominated by its commercialisation of the Modern Olympic Games despite there being many other considerable legacies.

It is also important to note the contingency of legacy's efficacy on its *temporal* neutrality, enabling it to be used in both a prospective and a retrospective sense. Table 13.1 illustrates in pedantic fashion the structuring by time of the questions of legacy that may be 'logically' asked.

As a simplistic language game, Table 13.1 relates legacy to the timing of the spectacle of the Olympic and Paralympic Games; however, it gives a false sense of mutual exclusivity between the different possible tenses when, in fact, they are never so easily delineated in practice. In identifying the fuzziness of these boundaries, the following question needs to be asked: when does the shift from the future and present tenses to the past tense occur? Or, when do the London 2012 Olympic and Paralympic Games become an anachronism? Such tensions are related to the struggle between those prioritising legacy's prospective conceptualisation (Girginov, 2012; Bloyce and Lovett, 2012) and those arguing that 'To grasp the power of legacies in the contemporary Olympic universe requires a retreat to the past' (Dyreson, 2008:2118), that is, in its retrospective form.

The argument presented here would seem to advocate a linguistic analysis of legacy. What is problematic about such analyses is Wittgenstein's (1969:25) identification of a basic contradiction between our habitual use of language and the formal study of it: 'we don't use language according to strict rules – it hasn't been taught to us by means of strict rules, either. *We*, in our discussions on the other hand, constantly compare language with a calculus proceeding according to exact rules'. In a similar vein, MacAloon (2008:2016) observed in his essay on legacy as brand rhetoric that 'even a properly semiotic analysis, can never get at the full range of meanings apparent only in the social contexts of speaking'.

Table 13.1 Tense language game of 'legacy'

	During-spectacle	Post-spectacle
What will be *the* legacy of *the* Games?	What is *the* legacy of *the* Games?	What was *the* legacy of *the* Games?

Source: authors' own work.

As a closing philosophical point, we would like to distinguish between the Games as an end in itself and as a means to an end. An essentialist remark is that legacy is fundamentally constituted by the Olympic and Paralympic Games. Conceptualised, then, as 'that which is left behind' is akin to the Games being formalised as a means to an end (or to *many* ends as is the case). This stands in opposition to the production and consumption of the Games as an end in itself. As a contemporary phenomenon, then, legacy has come to engender the struggles of 'what ends', 'the means' to these ends and the interpretations and evaluations of these means and ends.

This philosophical distinction between the Games as an end in itself and as a means to many ends is never fully realised in practice but rather forms a dialectical relationship that is played out in the production, consumption and historical relations of each Olympic and Paralympic Games. Both poles of this false division confer legitimacy to the spectacle, neither being self-sufficient. Recognising this reveals the domination of the producers and investors to the simultaneous production of the most spectacular Games ever, to be enjoyed in and of itself, *and* to the production of 'positive', legitimate legacies. As an anecdotal counterpoint, 'disinterestedness' within the sports field of the quandaries of legacy can be seen to be a position struggling for sport's autonomy, that is, as simply an end in itself.

Epistemic struggles

The evaluation of a Games' legacy is a difficult epistemological task for no greater reason than that it is central to their legitimacy or illegitimacy. As such, the evaluative process engenders the broader epistemic struggles of the social world and poses specific epistemic struggles for each of the fields involved or affected by the Olympic and Paralympic Games. A principle epistemological problem is the reconciliation of different epistemologies, the demand and problem of which is inculcated and felt most strongly in the political fields.

London 2012's meta-evaluation, commissioned and declared to be 'independent' by the UK government, is a recent example that illuminates the epistemic difficulties of evaluating legacy. The meta-evaluation had specific difficulties in combining what it described as its up-down and bottom-up approaches; these approaches are defined by their macro-micro approach to the problem. There was also the problem of accounting for, what Essex and Chalkley (1998:203) called the 'classic counter-factual problem'. This problem essentially relates to the 'what if', that is 'what if London had not hosted the Olympic and Paralympic Games?'.

Within the Olympic and Paralympic fields, the epistemic struggle to measure legacy is located in the Olympic Games Impact (OGI) Study. The OGI has been criticised for being an 'input-output' evaluation unable to examine the process-based construction of legacy (Girginov and Hills, 2008). It has also been argued that 'The main problem . . . with the OGGI project is that it ends 2 years after the event, which is much too soon to measure the legacy of the event' (Gratton and Preuss, 2008:1923).

With all of these problems, evaluating legacy can be related to Pascal's (1958:105) philosophical conundrum in judging morals; he wrote, 'We must have a fixed point in order to judge. The harbour decides for those who are in a ship; but where shall we find a harbour for morality?'. From this anecdote, we might ask: where shall we find a harbour for legacy? The presuppositions of sport's intrinsic value in policy (Girginov and Hills, 2009) by the IOC and organising committees, and the emphasis of positive, planned and tangible legacies in Olympic bids (Gratton and Preuss, 2008), heighten the difficulty of finding a harbour for legacy. It is also why the IOC adopts a 'pragmatic' position accepting that there is no definitive methodology to evaluate legacy (Andranovich and Burbank, 2011).

Efficacy of mega-sports events to 'leave a legacy'

Just like evaluating legacy, deliberating upon the efficacy of the Olympic and Paralympic Games to 'leave a legacy' questions their very legitimacy or, at the very least, their current organisation. In sports academia, what Bourdieu (1975:39) calls the 'objective relationship between opposing accomplices' can be seen in the debate between those who critique and those who romanticise the efficacy of the Olympic and Paralympic Games to 'leave a legacy', along with those balancing these polemical positions. These 'opposing accomplices' are equally evident throughout the bidding and hosting of the Games in broader society. Ultimately, the struggle between these positions has led and will lead to a greater formalisation of legacy.

The formalisation of legacy, first evidenced in its insertion into the Olympic Charter, is interconnected with issues such as the environmental and economic sustainability of the Games, governance and sports development (Chappelet, 2008; Leopkey and Parent, 2013; Girginov and Hills, 2008). Thus, the integration and formalisation of 'legacy' can be seen to be a converging strategy of conservation to dissipate internal and external challenges to the legitimacy of the Games and to make the impossible possible, that is, to extend the 'existence' of an 'event' beyond its immediate occurrence and its immediate social space. What's more, the formalisation of legacy throughout the production and evaluation of the Olympic and Paralympic Games must be related to the broader market of cultural spectacles. In this sense, legacy is concomitant to the conservation of the distinction of the Games and maintenance of their dominant position in the market of cultural spectacles, a position that yields maximum 'profits' for the Olympic and Paralympic Games. In addition to this, the formalisation has heightened the importance of legacy to other such temporary franchise modelled, publicly funded spectacles. This creates the possibility of comparing the legacy *capital* of different cultural spectacles, ultimately preluding the hierarchisation of this space.

A prospective sense of disability legacy

To examine disability legacy in its prospective form, we analysed Olympic and Paralympic bid documents from the last decade. The aim is to add to Misener *et al.*'s (2013) preliminary attempts to objectify the space of disability legacy. As a source, there is much scepticism and cynicism of these documents (Gold and Gold, 2008; Andranovich and Burbank, 2011; Bloyce and Lovett, 2012; Leopkey and Parent, 2012; Gratton and Preuss, 2008), and some of the stipulations have and will be further critiqued by the Paralympic literature. Despite these concerns, we continue on the basis of the expressed importance of legacy in the bid process by the IOC (2011).

The analysis found three interrelated themes: visions of disability legacy, benefits to the host city and the Paralympic movement and methods through which these visions and benefits could be achieved. In their visions of disability legacy, bid cities emphasised the promotion of the Paralympic movement, equality of experience between the Olympics and Paralympics and the celebration of both Olympic and Paralympic ideals. 'Change' came through as a common theme, often being correlated to the International Paralympic Committee's (IPC) values. The change they envisioned related to changing perceptions, attitudes and behaviour towards disability; the improvement of social awareness, understanding and sensitisation of disability; the creation of equal opportunities and fostering of social inclusion, independence and self-determination; and becoming a model for other cities, regions and countries. From a materialistic position, cities sought to promote barrier-free living.

The second theme related to the benefits for the Paralympic movement and the host city. A range of benefits was proposed from the improvement of environmental access and universal design, the passing of legislation, compliance and adoption policies, increasing accessible transport and infrastructure, improved image, awareness and understanding of disability, and equal job opportunities. Symbolic benefits for the Paralympic movement included commitment to Paralympic sport, reaching new audiences, increased awareness of Paralympic values, raised awareness of Paralympic sports, Paralympians promoted as role models, building respect for the achievements of Paralympians and providing the same world-class environment for the Paralympics. Prior hosts of Paralympic or disability sport events highlighted their historical legacies and allegiance to the Paralympic cause, while would-be hosts without a Paralympic history expressed their wish to begin one. Broader benefits for Paralympic and disability sport included the improvement of sporting opportunities, increased performance and participation, the promotion of accessible sporting activities for all and the training of coaches. Also emphasised were the benefits of inspiring athletes to new achievements, motivating 'disabled' and non-disabled to be involved in sport, and to aspire to elite performance.

The third theme related to the possible methods to achieve the above visions and benefits of disability legacy. A prime method was the shared experience of the Paralympic Games with the use of media and marketing resources to build excitement and develop awareness. The marketing campaigns would tell 'the heroic and inspiring performances' of the Paralympians (Moscow 2012 bid) and highlight the powerful stories of Paralympians (New York 2012 bid). Methods extending beyond the Games themselves included the inclusion of the Paralympics in school curriculum, the organisation of Paralympic youth camps, the organisation of Paralympic classification workshops/seminars and the establishment of new national Paralympic headquarters. The development of partnerships with governments and NGOs, the funding of relevant programmes and initiatives, the development of information technology systems and the funding of research to develop specialised materials and new technologies were also proposed. A last set of methods included integration initiatives with the corporate sector, the incentivisation of sponsors to diversify their workforce, enhancing public policies and planning, certification of disability-friendly tourism and the creation of new and renovation of pre-existing infrastructure.

A retrospective discussion of London 2012's disability legacy

There is a clear inadequacy of managerial legacy evaluations and their taxonomies to grasp the deeper complexities of the debate of London 2012's disability legacy. To redress this inadequacy and to structure our discussion, we present a basic framework that considers an overview of social, cultural and economic elements. The lynchpin question is how did London 2012 change the social, cultural and economic position of disability? Ultimately the element, positive or negative, that receives most recognition will come to be regarded as the defining disability legacy of London 2012.

The social element of London 2012's disability legacy to change social relations received much recognition. During London 2012, Sir Phillip Craven stated, 'I don't even hope, because I know (it will change perceptions)'.[4] Post-Games research and opinion polls from Channel 4 (2012a), the English Federation of Disability Sport's (EFDS) (Spring, 2012), United Response (2012) and Ipsos Mori (2012) all affirm the positive social impact of the Paralympic Games. This social impact was also paralleled by corporate sponsors such as Sainsbury's, BT and P&G,[5] professing the power of the Paralympic narrative and the impact of their engagement with the Paralympics on their employees. Equally there is the 'early socialisation' legacy of the educational and reverse integration programs such as those run by Sainsbury's.

A number of caveats challenge this rosy picture. One acknowledged by the House of Lords' (2013) *Keeping the Flame Alive* report was scepticism of the translation of this social positivity beyond disability sport and Paralympians. There are also a number of problems of such opinion poll-based research. First, they seem to have an inherently positive bias, perhaps for no greater reason than to say the Paralympics did not change your perceptions of disability is socially unacceptable. Although this is more complicated for those who said that the Paralympics did not change their perceptions but simply developed their knowledge of Paralympic sport. Clearly there is a more complex debate here than that currently predominated by 'perceptions'. Second, the timing of these polls is hugely influential. Directly after the Games, people have images clear in their mind; however, what will the perceived legacy be at the time of the publication of this chapter or in a decade's time? In other words, it is also important to recognise the superficiality of opinion polls with it often being more fruitful to ask why they were initiated at all.[6] Echoing MacAloon (2008:2062), we believe, 'A second typical response to criticism is to commission marketing studies, the drama of whose ostensible findings conceals the fact that the real action is in how the study problem is defined in the first place'.

Regardless of these caveats, London 2012's aim was to convert this positive social energy into cultural sporting habits. This goal had an obvious resonance with the whole of the UK's sports development field. Prior to London 2012, Weed and Dowse (2011) questioned the lack of any indication of direction towards inclusive practices, labelling the Games as a possible 'missed opportunity'. In the shadow of London 2012, Sport England's (2014) promotion of the increased number of National Governing Bodies committed to inclusive targets is perhaps some contrary evidence to Weed and Dowse's prophesy. Despite these clear institutional improvements, claims of a sports participation legacy appear unclear and misleading. For example, take the EFDS's (2013) reaction to a critical report by the Sport and Recreation Alliance (SRA) (2013) which claimed that clubs had seen no increase in disability sports participation since the Games. Their reaction resonates with a Wittgenstein-style language game. The EFDS (2013) attempted to contradict the SRA's claims arguing that 'intentions' to do sport had increased, as well as noting increased web traffic to Parasport.org.uk and a recently well-attended Paralympic sports festival. The EFDS is, of course, defending the landscape upon which it is seen as an authority. Right or wrong, what should be noted here is the difficulty of translating social energy into cultural habits and the heightened political demand for the latter as *the* real cultural legacy.

An often overlooked cultural legacy is the consumption of disability sport as a spectacle. The record Paralympic ticket sales in London 2012 (IPC, 2012) and the sold-out 2013 Paralympic Anniversary Games (Channel 4, 2013) offer substantive evidence of a cultural legacy. Complicating the picture are the many poorly attended events, for example, the Sainsbury's 2013 Grand Prix event held in Birmingham. However, it is recognised that such issues of demand are not limited to the Paralympic sports market. Another significant cultural legacy of London 2012 is the production of Paralympic sport as a media product which Channel 4 (2012b) described as 'revolutionary'. Channel 4's changes to production practices also set a benchmark for future Games. Significantly Channel 4's coverage also embarrassed the Olympic host broadcaster NBC into finally providing live coverage of the Paralympic Games from 2014 (Davies, 2013). Another factor that has been overlooked is the economic contribution of the Paralympics to a host city. No longer can it be seen as an act of charity. London 2012 expanded the commercialisation and distancing of the Paralympics movement from the shackles of being viewed as a charity in a number of ways. First, there was increased engagement by corporate sponsors who used the Paralympics to double the length of time they had to run marketing activation programs, although this did not occur evenly across all sponsors. There was also the settling of the financing of the Paralympics between the British Olympic Association and the British Paralympic Association. The former presupposed that the Paralympics would make a loss and did not want to foot the bill (Purdue, 2013). The successful commercialisation of the London 2012 Paralympics, namely through the sale of media, sponsorship and tickets, paves the way for future commercial expansion.

Also significant, at least for ParalympicsGB, is the increased funding of Paralympic sport from £49 million for London 2012 to £71 million for Rio 2016. Of course, the real value of a pound sterling decreases year on year and the funding removed from poorly performing sports must be noted. On the whole, the increased funding to the Paralympics is representative of the increased and relatively cheaper opportunity they offer for national recognition.

These examples of Paralympic legacy highlighted above are gladly claimed and legitimised by the sports field. They contrast to the broader economic legacy of the recent UK welfare cuts that were being legislated during London 2012. Sport's claims of autonomy will undoubtedly deny and distance itself from such legacies. Protests during London 2012 targeted the offices of Atos because of its position as a corporate sponsor of London 2012 and as contractor to perform government 'work capability assessments'. They also targeted the offices of the Department of Work and Pensions, of which the Office for Disability Issues is part of, because of their obvious legislative roles. These manifestations are symbolic of much larger societal tensions and the political discussion of which is a veritable hornets' nest. Not seeking to enter this debate in this chapter, we simply conject that future Paralympic Games will be leveraged by similar disability protest groups to highlight the economic inequality and insecurity of disability.

Conclusion

In conclusion we argue that as a contemporary phenomenon, legacy has come to engender the struggle between the Paralympic Games being produced as something to be enjoyed in and of itself and as a means to many ends, a philosophical struggle with many parallels to amateurism and professionalism. In this sense, legacy is considered as central to the legitimacy and illegitimacy of the Games going forward. This centrality means that legacy often assumes a euphemistic role for the strategies of the institutions involved.

Our presentation of disability legacy from the bid documents, although uncritical, further maps out this developing space. Somewhat more critical, our analysis of the social, cultural and economic elements of London 2012's disability legacy presents a framework to better comprehend this debate while realising that we are only scratching the surface of a fascinating and critical debate for the future.

Notes

1 The Olympic and Paralympic Legacy Select Committee was established in May 2013 and published its report in November 2013.
2 Uncorrected evidence available online: http://www.parliament.uk/business/committees/committees-a-z/lords-select/olympic-paralympic-legacy/publications/
3 For Bourdieu (1991), the process of normalisation and codification of language is exemplified by dictionaries.

4 Sir Phillip Craven stated these words in the Main Press Centre, Queen Elizabeth Olympic Park on Sunday, 26 August 2012.
5 Personal communication.
6 MacAloon (2008) raised this same concern, but in relation to Olympic marketing studies.

References

Agha, N., Fairley, S. and Gibson, H. (2012) 'Considering legacy as a multi-dimensional construct: the legacy of the Olympic Games'. *Sport Management Review*, 15(1): 125–139.
Alison, L. (1986) 'Politics and sport' in L. Alison (Ed.), *The politics of sport*. Manchester: Manchester University Press.
Andranovich, G. and Burbank, M. J. (2011) 'Contextualizing Olympic legacies'. *Urban Geography*, 32(6): 823–844.
Bloyce, D. and Lovett, E. (2012) 'Planning for the London 2012 Olympic and Paralympic legacy: a figurational analysis'. *International Journal of Sport Policy and Politics*, 4(3): 361–377.
Bourdieu, P. (1975) 'The specificity of the scientific field and the social conditions of the progress of reason'. *Social Science Information*, 14(6): 19–47.
Bourdieu, P. (1991) *Symbolic power and language*. Cambridge: Polity Press.
Bourdieu, P., Chamboredon, J.-C. and Passeron, J.-C. (1991) *The craft of sociology: epistemological preliminaries*. Berlin: de Gruyter. French original printed in 1968.
Channel 4 (2012a) 'Research: paralympics coverage helped change attitudes to disability', available at: http://www.channel4.com/info/press/news/research-paralympics-coverage-helped-change-attitudes-to-disability (last accessed 5 April 2014).
Channel 4 (2012b) 'Report and financial statements 2012', available at: http://annual-report.channel4.com/ (last accessed 5 April 2014).
Channel 4 (2013) 'The Sainsbury's anniversary games', available at: http://paralympics.channel4.com/competitions/london-anniversary-games/ (last accessed 4 May 2014).
Chappelet, J. L. (2008) 'Olympic environmental concerns as a legacy of the Winter Games'. *The International Journal of the History of Sport*, 25(14): 1884–1902.
Chappelet, J. L. (2012) 'Mega sporting event legacies: a multifaceted concept'. *Papeles de Europa*, 25: 76–86.
Davies, G. (2013, September 24) 'Paralympic movement given huge boost as American channels NBC and NBCSN will cover next two Games', *The Telegraph*, available at: http://www.telegraph.co.uk/sport/olympics/paralympic-sport/10330949/Paralympic-Movement-given-huge-boost-as-American-channels-NBC-and-NBCSN-will-cover-next-two-Games.html
Dyreson, M. (2008) 'Epilogue: athletic clashes of civilizations or bridges over cultural divisions? The Olympic Games as legacies and the legacies of the Olympic Games'. *The International Journal of the History of Sport*, 25(14): 2117–2129.
EFDS (2013) 'EFDS responds to sport and recreation alliance report', available at: http://www.efds.co.uk/news/1342_efds_responds_to_sport_and_recreation_alliance_report (last accessed 5 April 2014).
Essex, S. and Chalkley, B. (1998) 'Olympic Games: catalyst of urban change'. *Leisure Studies*, 17(3): 187–206.
Gilbert, K. and Legg, D. (2011) 'Conceptualising legacy' in D. Legg and K. Gilbert (Eds.), *Paralympic legacies*. Champaign, IL: Common Ground Publishing.
Girginov, V. and Hills, L. (2008) 'A sustainable sports legacy: creating a link between the London Olympics and sports participation'. *The International Journal of the History of Sport*, 25(14): 2091–2116.

Girginov, V. and Hills, L. (2009) 'The political process of constructing a sustainable London Olympics sports development legacy'. *International Journal of Sport Policy and Politics*, 1(2): 161–181.

Girginov, V. (2012) 'Governance of London 2012 Olympic Games legacy'. *International Review for the Sociology of Sport*, 1–16.

Gold, J. R. and Gold, M. M. (2008) 'Olympic cities: regeneration, city rebranding and changing urban agendas'. *Geography Compass*, 2(1): 300–318.

Gratton, C. and Preuss, H. (2008) 'Maximizing Olympic impacts by building up legacies'. *The International Journal of the History of Sport*, 25(14): 1922–1938.

Hollingsworth, T. (2012) 'Tim Hollingsworth: momentum and change, not legacy, are the real watchwords of London 2012', available at: http://www.insidethegames.biz/ paralympics-blogs/1010496 (last accessed 3 February 2014).

House of Lords (2013) *Keeping the flame alive: the Olympic and Paralympic legacy.* London: House of Lords.

IOC (2011) *2020 candidature acceptance procedure games of the XXXII Olympiad.* Lausanne: IOC.

IPC (2012) 'Record Paralympic Games ticket sales', available at: http://www.paralympic. org/news/record-paralympic-games-ticket-sales (last accessed 5 April 2014).

Ipsos Mori (2012) 'Ipsos MORI Paralympics poll', available at: http://www.ipsos-mori. com/Assets/Docs/Polls/Paralympics%20topline.pdf (last accessed 5 April 2014).

Leopkey, B. and Parent M. M. (2012) 'Olympic Games legacy: from general benefits to sustainable long-term legacy'. *The International Journal of the History of Sport*, 29(6): 924–943.

Leopkey, B. and Parent, M. M. (2013) 'The (neo) institutionalization of legacy and its sustainable governance within the Olympic Movement'. *European Sport Management Quarterly*, 12(5): 437–455.

MacAloon, J. (2008) '"Legacy" as managerial/magical discourse in contemporary Olympic affairs'. *The International Journal of the History of Sport*, 24(14): 2060–2071.

McFee, G. (2002) '"It's not just a game": the place of philosophy in a study of sport' in J. Sugden and A. Tomlinson (Eds.), *Power games.* London: Routledge.

MacRury, I. (2008) 'Re-thinking the legacy 2012: the Olympics as commodity and gift'. *Twenty-First Century Society: Journal of the Academy of Social Sciences*, 3(3): 297–312.

Malfas, M., Theodoraki, E. and Houlihan, B. (2004) 'Impacts of the Olympic Games as mega-events'. *Municipal Engineer*, 157(ME3): 209–220.

Misener, L., Darcy, S., Legg, D. and Gilbert, K. (2013) 'Beyond Olympic legacy: understanding Paralympic legacy through a thematic analysis'. *Journal of Sport Management*, 27: 329–341.

Pascal, B. (1958) *Pensées*. New York: E.P. Dutton.

Preuss, H. (2007) 'The conceptualisation and measurement of mega sport event legacies'. *Journal of Sport & Tourism*, 12(3–4): 207–227.

Purdue, D. (2013) 'An (in)convenient truce? Paralympic stakeholders' reflections on the Olympic–Paralympic relationship'. *Journal of Sport and Social Issues*, 37(4): 384–402.

Sport and Recreation Alliance (2013) 'Olympic and Paralympic Games – legacy survey', available at: http://www.sportandrecreation.org.uk/policy/research/olympic- and-paralympic-legacy-survey (last accessed 5 April 2014).

Sport England (2014) 'Disability', available at: http://www.sportengland.org/our-work/ disability/ (last accessed 5 April 2014).

Spring, E. (2012) 'EFDS legacy questionnaire report October 2012 – measuring the impact of the Olympic and Paralympic Games on disabled and non-disabled people', available at:

http://www.efds.co.uk/assets/0000/5208/Legacy_Questionnaire_Report_20121031 FINAL.pdf (last accessed 5 April 2014).

United Response (2012) 'Did the Paralympics affect public perceptions of disability?', available at: http://www.unitedresponse.org.uk/resources/our-infographics/did-the-paralympics-affect-public-perceptions-of-disability/ (last accessed 5 April 2014).

Weed, M. and Dowse, S. (2011) 'A missed opportunity waiting to happen? The social legacy potential of the London 2012 Paralympic Games'. *Journal of Policy Research in Tourism, Leisure and Events*, 1(2): 170–174.

Wittgenstein, L. (1969) *The blue and brown books* (2nd ed.). Oxford: Basil Blackwell.

14 Localism and a sustainable Olympic legacy

Andrew Hoolachan

Introduction

The day after news of the London winning the Olympic and Paralympic 2012 bid, four passengers blew themselves up on 7 July 2005 in an act of terror on the infrastructure of London's public transport. The four separate blasts at different places across London killed 52 people of multifaith, multiethnic and multinational profiles. In the following days, two reflections upon the events were notable in what the attacks 'meant' for British identity. Prime Minister Tony Blair at the time described the event as symbolising the strength of Britishness – that our cosmo-politan victims and our determinism against extremism show British values of inclusion and freedom. At the same time, a counternarrative from the Mayor of London, Ken Livingston, was somewhat dismissive of nationalism in favour of London as a cosmopolis, which was more connected to the rest of the world than to the rest of Britain (Graham, 2011).

In hosting international mega-events such as London 2012, cities and nations often have to share the role as hosts, often with overlapping and contradictory consequences. This tension became obvious, for instance, when Britain was objected to an act of terror while being in the Olympic spotlight. The host nation and the host city represented the attack in differing ways – one patriotic to the nation, the other celebrating the diversity of the city. Therefore, the cities in which mega-events take place are never just about the city alone, but may trig-ger local, regional, national and even international concerns, as we have seen with lesbian, gay, bisexual and transgender rights at the Sochi Winter Olympics in 2014, wherein a global community of activists was involved in speaking out against Putin's repression of sexual minorities. Despite these multiscalar concerns of Olympic events, organisational and institutional processes seek to represent the placing of the Games as a uniform space.

Representations of London had to present the host city in a very particular way, which may have been removed from the realities of life in London or indeed the UK. More significantly, however, are the complex multiscalar governance arrangements associated with hosting Olympic events, which provide catalysts for post-Games planning and development (Gold and Gold, 2010; Poynter and MacRury, 2009). In the case of London 2012, a very different set of government arrangements has been created, which were unforeseen during their planning and execution. The Localism Act 2010 is a radical overhaul of urban planning in the UK, and it is the potential future impacts of this act on the London legacy that this chapter wishes to investigate with particular emphasis on the promise of delivering a 'sustainable' legacy. This is important as it allows us to question the scalar contradictions of how a city can handle extremely rapid and intense urban change in a concentrated area while simultaneously emphasising the role of neighbourhoods and local communities as the primary agents in planning for sustainability. How can sustainable Olympic legacies be achieved in a multiscalar governance landscape which emphasises 'the local'?

London 2012: representation and emplacement

First, we need to understand how scales of governance are practiced. There is always tension between the role of the nation, the host city and, as will be shown, the site within the city. These three levels or scales usually have corresponding governance arrangements, with national, metropolitan and local governments playing varying roles, either complimentary or contradictory. The tension between the UK on the one hand and London on the other are tensions that appear repeatedly in discourse surrounding the 2012 Games and their legacy. But this is also very much a scalar politics initiated by the locating of the Games in a very specific part of London. The politics of scale has been written about extensively and in contradictory ways: from understanding geographic scales as measurable entities to seeing them merely as discursive formations (Herod, 2011; Smith, 1984; Massey, 1993). This understands scale as both a physical entity – for example, the vastness of London as a metropolis – and also as a discursive act initiated by planners and policy makers (Marston *et al.*, 2005). Indeed Localism is in itself an act of Scale-*ing*, bringing into existence an ideal level of political engagement which may not exist in reality. Thus, what follows is a discussion of the competing scales at which London 2012 was represented.

As outlined above, the major narratives were either that London 2012 was a UK Games or that it was a London Games. However, at a lower scale, we also have the neighbourhoods within East London, and Stratford is regarded as the main neighbourhood where the Games took place (GLA, 2011). But as a transport hub of pre-existing set of connections named 'Stratford' (e.g. Tube lines, overground and international rail), it could be said that the town derives more of its meaning from this massive interchange than from the town itself, the town having been heavily subject to the car-based planning of the 1960s. The original centre was destroyed and replaced by a public shopping centre, around which a very busy road cuts the centre off. On the southern side of Stratford High Street begins the Victorian urban grain of terraced housing, which has largely been left in tact, interspersed with some modernist council estates, public buildings and parks.

But can we say that the Games were really for Stratford? First, the legacy is about both transforming East London through the Olympic, now Growth, boroughs and also, therefore, the image of Greater London as a city that has eradicated subregional inequality (Mayor of London, 2014). But at the neighbourhood level, how much of 'Stratford' was actually in the Games? Although Stratford was being used as the staging of the Games, the town itself was not really part of the Games at all when we consider the geography, scale and infrastructural development. The Queen Elizabeth II Olympic Park covers an area at least twice the size of the existing town of Stratford as it was built on a large site of continuous derelict land to the north. This is different to some events such as Barcelona 1992, where Olympic venues were distributed throughout the city (Gold and Gold, 2010). The idea then that the Games were taking place 'in' Stratford should really be thought about as taking place 'at' Stratford; the construction of an entirely new city on the border of the existing town cannot constitute the claim to be part of Stratford. Even if connections were made to subtly integrate broader elements of the Games and the legacy into the dense fabric of Stratford town, there remain immense physical barriers to the notion that the Queen Elizabeth Olympic Park and athletes village are connected to Stratford town. Thus, we must remember that while official discourse about London 2012 and their legacy was often between national and London interests, the physical space of Stratford was somehow lost or misrepresented in favour of the massive regeneration of the London Legacy Development Corporation (LLDC) area and the broader socio-economic transformation (convergence) of East London.

Like any Olympic bid, the host city must naturally be represented as a coherent whole due to institutional arrangements. But in each case, the coherence of the city never really exists; all cities have uneven geographies of development, and increasingly mega-events are used to regenerate the poorest parts of these cities (Gold and Gold, 2008). In other words, the 'London' that exists for the Olympic bid must naturally ignore the uneven spatial complexities within London, not just between the varying neighbourhoods surrounding the Queen Elizabeth Olympic Park. The London which was presented for the bid was that of a coherent city with a broadly uniform poor east, which needed a mega-event to create lasting prosperity and growth for this part of the city (MacRury and Poynter, 2009). However, this is a long-standing imaginative trope about London's linear geography of social inequality as noted by Paul Newland in *The Cultural Construction of London's East End*. This imaginative idea of a lacklustre east which has always been the poor relation of West London has ambiguous territory and probably exists as powerfully as an imagined space, as much as a physical one (Newland, 2008). Indeed, the policy narrative surrounding legacy has been all about changing the *lifestyles* of the east of London, in effect making them more akin to the west (LLDC, 2012).

Therefore, the idea that this is merely a London Games is not the full picture when we consider policy narratives and urban geographies within East London; socio-economic 'convergence' operates at a very wide scale and the intensely focused regeneration project 'at' Stratford covers an island of development with a distinct planning regime run by the LLDC. How can a unified sustainable legacy be achieved if *at least* two separate scales – 'Stratford' and 'East London' (also Lea Valley, Thames Gateway, Cambridge–London growth corridor etc.) – are being governed and planned in entirely different ways?

Considering a sustainable Olympic legacy

Of course, the situation outlined above does not consider the possible futures outlined by the LLDC and physical changes that will be implemented. 'Legacy' has been defined in varying ways and has changed since the initial five legacy promises. The clearest current meaning of 'legacy' can be ascertained from a report from 2013 – *Inspired by 2012: The Legacy of the London 2012 and Paralympic Games* (HM Government and Mayor of London, 2013). Interestingly, this is a joint report by the UK government and the Mayor of London, highlighting the twin role of the city and the nation. The report breaks legacy down into five chapters: Sport and Healthy Living, Regeneration of East London, Economic Growth, Bringing Communities Together and the Legacy from the Paralympics. Under this broad banner are included physical regeneration and policy drivers. There are, however, significant differences in the report from the initial stated aims of legacy, which focused on a very broad definition of sustainability, with an auditable target of 'convergence' (see, e.g., change from *Five Legacy Commitments* [Mayor of London, 2008] and *Convergence Action Plan Framework* [Mayor of London, 2011]). Convergence theory has existed in many other sciences such as epidemiology and, when applied to urban governance, aims to literally converge statistics on multiple deprivation, so that people living in the five growth boroughs have the same life chances as the London average within 20 years of the Games. Given the range of time frames, policy names and policy aims, a recent report from the House of Lords Select Committee on Olympic and Paralympic Legacy noted several risks to the legacy that are emerging and that '[t]here is confusion on the timeframes and targets involved in delivery and a lack of clear ownership of legacy as a whole' (House of Lords, 2013).

One of the reasons for the lack of clarity on 'legacy' could arise from it being underpinned by a vague definition of sustainability. Meaning 'everything and nothing at the same time' and being a 'floating signifier', Swyngedouw (2009) has argued that sustainability in policy has become almost meaningless. Sustainability in policy has been defined in a variety of ways, and there exists no single definition of what it entails despite the definitions sharing common features. To understand their similarities and differences however, we can look to three different models of sustainable development (Lombardi *et al.*, 2010). Most policy exists as part of a 'power-geometry' as Massey (1993) would say, and as such, there can be no objective sense of rationality despite this claim being utilised.

The first model posits that to have sustainable development we must have an equal balance between social, economic and environmental realms (Campbell, 2007; Lombardi *et al.*, 2010; Rydin, 2010). When we balance these three perfectly, we achieve sustainable development. The second model posits that the environmental realm constrains the economic realm. Within the economic realm lies the social realm. This containment idea proposed that society, economy and environment are not equal. The third model is similar to the second in that sustainability development is constrained absolutely by the environment. But instead of economy and society belonging to separate realms, they are treated as 'socio-economy', highlighting that society and economy are interrelated processes which cannot be so easily prescribed (see Lombardi *et. al.*, 2010).

There are, of course, underlying assumptions to these models. First, the idea of the 'model' itself is highly problematic as it assumes we can somehow reflect the entirety of human–environment relations. Further, they decontextualise such relations and networks, disregarding space, power and institutional arrangements. But most importantly for this chapter, they are nonscalar. At what scale do these models function? Clearly the latter two achieve some form of consideration that there is a maximum scale, which are global environmental limits. However, when nations, regions, communes, localities and homes implement sustainable develop-ment, can and should each of these scales plan equality for each realm? Do some scalar arrangements such as the city-state achieve more, for instance, regarding economic growth than, for example, nation-states? And who may do more for environmental protection? Thus, in such models, there is no real-world considera-tion of institutional capacities.

Another broader problem with such models is that they are removed from politics. We may ask, if their aim is to achieve sustainable development, then what exactly are we sustaining? The continuation of environmental disadvantage and unequal access to opportunities in our cities (Harvey, 1997)? The continuation of mass global poverty and slum settlements in the global South (Mohan and Stokke, 2010)? There are, therefore, other models which also try to understand how far sustainability goes, from completely replacing capitalism to transitioning slowly out of oil dependency or more incremental changes (Lombardi *et al.*, 2010). The problem with sustainability is that politicians from a variety of spectrums could be speaking the same language but actually mean very different things (Carter, 2007). For example, the word conservation to some might sound like a valid pillar of green politics. But is it not also a conservative idea of preserving existing struc-tures, landscapes or buildings? Thus if sustainability is a political notion, which has very real effects in different places, how can we interrogate the London legacy with its emphasis on sustainability and the Localism Act, with its notion that the scale of sustainability is the responsibility of communities and individuals?

Localism and sustainability in London: at odds?

Localism is a popular idea which has circulated for a long time in respect to the organisation of socio-economic systems (Haughton and Allmendinger, 2013). Although various historical, cultural and institutional circumstances alter the applied result of any Localism, at its simple basis they are uniformly similar; that social, political, economic or environmental systems should operate at a smaller scale than they are currently exercised over. It is an articulation of transition, away from regional, national and global scales, to bringing people, goods, services and manufactures back to a more 'natural' scale (Schumacher, 1993).

Yet, there are varying political impulses within Localist discourse, which seem to use the same language. The first, and most relevant today, is that Localism should be used to bring power back to 'the people' and conjures up a simpler time when democracy was accountable to local people and places (Clarke and Cochrane, 2013). This argument is used on the political Right as undermining big government, as redefining local culture in the face of globalisation and immigration and implying that local decision making is the most rational and efficient way of creating socially just economic growth and resource allocation. The Left have also used Localism as a way of supporting communities against corporations, to support independent small businesses, to establish radical communes which challenge mainstream societal norms and in the first fights for democratic representation.

Throughout the twentieth century, Localist policies ebbed and flowed even when they were not explicitly Localist. For example, the first garden cities were planned around an ideal form of what a locality ought to be and so were many neighbourhoods and suburbs during the period of mass social housing (Hall, 2006; Wilson, 1991). The neighbourhood unit had an implicit reflection of what societal norms were at the time about an 'ideal' neighbourhood, with shops, schools and parks distributed evenly between each neighbourhood unit.

Localism as a less functional and more abstract idea, focusing on sense of place, developed more strongly in the late twentieth century. Many had critiqued the notions that social life in cities was so simple, and writers like Jacobs and Alexander confirmed that cities had fields of overlapping needs, contradictions and complexities that earlier planners had not considered (Jacobs, 1961). Thus, in the cultural regeneration of cities from the 1980s, we see an adoption of these ideas, with localities comprising fluid and ambiguous quarters with permeable edges which can be subject to change and interpretation (Carmona *et al.*, 2003; Gehl, 2011). However, Allmendinger and Haughton (2013) argue that Localism in some form has been promoted by governments of the Left and Right since the shift to neoliberalism in the late 1970s. Localist policies have justified a retreat of the broad structures of the state on the one hand while promoting the enabling probusiness urban regimes on the other, as cities became 'entrepreneurial' and responsible for their own successes. The current invocation of Localism is nothing really new, but rather a continuation and intensification of this process of removing state responsibility under the veneer of 'local empowerment'.

The Localism Act 2011 seeks not to plan in a functional or cultural way as above but to enable the new vision of cities through governance. This rests on the view of planning which the coalition shared prior to coming to power in 2010. Their view was that the Labour administration (1997–2010) had presided over an enormous growth in the state apparatus. At the same time, many of the social problems which they had originally campaigned against had not improved, and this was allegedly because decisions are best made not by inefficient governments but by individuals (DCLG, 2011). The image of 'the people', which has been so strongly evoked under the Localism Act, will be the driving force of new urban planning and will challenge the bureaucrats and decision makers who are no longer experts or to be trusted with decision making.

The populist tone of this new policy direction is already evident in the naming of their public disseminations. *A Plain English Guide to the Localism Act* (2011) claims to present the basic facts of the Localism Act to a 'common sense' public who undoubtedly all speak English as their first language.

> For too long, central government has hoarded and concentrated power. Trying to improve people's lives by imposing decisions, setting targets and demand-ing inspections from Whitehall simply doesn't work. It creates bureaucracy. It leaves no room for adaptation to reflect local circumstances or innovation to deliver services more effectively and at lower cost. And it leaves people feeling 'done to' and imposed upon – the very opposite of the sense of partici-pation and involvement on which a healthy democracy thrives.
>
> (DCLG, 2011:1)

This is the opening text from the *Plain English Guide* by Greg Clarke, M.P. We can clearly see the antistate impulse and the almost victim-like language used in referring what is 'done to' people. The clauses of the Localism Act give a vast set of new powers to councils, but also put their plan making at risk. The Localism Act gives local authorities the power of general competence, meaning they have the same powers as individuals under the law. This gives them a great amount of freedom – to work with neighbouring councils, to raise money and to procure services in different ways. But the Act also allows community groups to submit their own neighbourhood plans to challenge that of their local authorities, and communities are given powers to prevent local authorities from implementing their own plans. The Act has abolished regional planning agencies such as the London Development Agency (LDA) and abolished what were perceived as top-down targets for housing (DCLG, 2011).

There are, of course, many arguments against placing emphasis on simply one tier of planning (Cox and Mairtt, 1989; Deas, 2013; Parvin, 2011; Pratchett, 2004). Part of the problem is where sustainability and Localism overlap theo-retically, namely the notion of 'holism'. This is the idea that communities can be planned in optimal sizes, just like the idea that cities have a 'natural' limit to environmental resources (Carter, 2007; Swyngedouw, 2009). This powerful and attractive idea has given us garden cities, eco-towns, green belts and Localism (Hall, 2006; Welter, 2002). But it is an idea that we need to treat with caution. In terms of economics, local businesses are surely valuable and popular. They create diverse economies and are more accountable to their local impacts. But to have an economic model based purely on the locale alone can often induce problems. Can any thriving centre really exist without some degree of interac-tion with regional, national and global supply chains, consumers, currencies and regulatory frameworks? It does not take much explanation to see that purely localised economies could fail if there is not some degree of outside interaction (Carter, 2007). In terms of society, does having a purely local democracy which is more powerful than higher scales or discourages interaction and integration in places where people from far away can come together provide better oppor-tunities? It has been argued that a purely local mindset can lead to xenophobia or racism, but also lack in talented individuals and a diverse knowledge base

(Young and Allen, 2011). In terms of the environment, do the flows and processes of nature, from water, waste, carbon and pollution, really have a political boundary? Should we only view environmental issues as a local problem,
hoping that the sum of our collective local efforts could be felt at the global
scale? Often there are regional, national and global frameworks that must work
with local practises in order to create effective strategies (Birkenholtz, 2012;
Bulkeley and Kern, 2006). Following the staging of the Games, the organisations responsible for the Games' execution were incorporated into a single
development authority which has responsibilities over planning, development
and design from within its borders. This contrasts with neighbouring authorities
such as Newham Borough Council whose ability to plan has been substantially
weakened under cuts and new clauses initiated by the Localism Act. This has
achieved exactly what the Act wishes to enable; it *localises* decision making
to smaller urban areas with two effects: it has potential to give neighbouring
boroughs widely contrasting planning tools and strategies and, secondly, may
exacerbate differences between and within boroughs.

The future development of the sustainable legacy has come to mean both the
socio-economic 'convergence' that will take place in the growth boroughs and the
intense physical transformation of the LLDC area into an exemplar low-carbon
community. From a purely physical position, the LLDC plan is commendable
for its total adoption of a radical low-carbon community, combining the years of
best practice in planning theory and Rogers' compact city ideas (Rogers, 1997)
that were advanced during the 'urban renaissance' of the Labour government
(Colomb, 2007). But this leads to a tension between, on the one hand, an island
of high-quality urban design centred on carbon neutrality and, on the other, a
fragmented and disjointed vision for the surrounding areas of East London, only
focused on the socio-economic understanding of sustainability, i.e. convergence.
As one of the original aims of the Olympic legacy was to literally transform East
London with sustainability at the core, the current situation of fragmented governance and vague definitions is likely to lead to failure. The Localism Act is
partially responsible for the fragmentation and is unlikely to make a broad vision
of sustainability any easier. It seems that the LLDC area, with its focus on sustainability, has led to holism, the idea that the environment can be governed and
planned for with 'natural' limits. Beyond the LLDC area, however, environmental
considerations are expressed in drastically differing ways, owing to how localist
policies have affected planning in London.

The case of the Jubilee Greenway: fragmented governance

Running northwest–southeast almost continually from Victoria Park to Beckton
is the Northern Outfall sewer, which in the 1980s was upgraded slightly to
enable walking and cycling on top of it. It is one of the longest uninterrupted
pedestrian routes in East London and is used mainly by cyclists and walkers and
is part of the London Jubilee Greenway (now known as the 'Greenway'). It is
raised from Victoria Park to Plaistow, about 3 metres above the natural elevation

of the ground, eventually coming back down to be submerged under the ground so that the pathway is at ground level. Access to the Greenway is poor; it is owned by Thames Water and is fenced on both sides, meaning that access takes the form of gates or ramps at specific intervals. However, these access points must be known and found in the characteristic disorienting urban morphology which surrounds it.

There have been many attempts prior to the abolition of the LDA to link up the surrounding parts of the LLDC area, most notably in the document *Stitching the Fringe*, by Design for London (2012) which was also abolished, although some key staff members later joined the LLDC. The Greenway had also been considered in 2010 as a key piece of infrastructure which could be integrated into the legacy, and the LDA commissioned a 'Wider Strategy' which was an extremely detailed proposition of the Greenway's potential, including a break-down of costs and time scales (Adams and Sutherland, 2010). However, as an architect who worked on the strategy said, with the abolition of the LDA as part of the Localism Act, the direct funding streams in place to undertake this project are no longer there.

This represents a lost opportunity. A fully integrated walking–cycling route which can go from a quiet, hidden space that no one uses to a busy public thoroughfare seems to be directly helping to achieve elements of a vaguely defined 'sustainability' and convergence. A busy walking–cycling route which encourages physical mobility and the associated health benefits, access to 'greenspace', opportunities for community meeting and collaboration, all meet certain criteria of a sustainable urbanism. In addition, the scale of the Greenway, in linking up the fragmented neighbourhoods across Newham, many of which suffer social exclusion, could enable the broader convergence idea focused on reducing socio-economic disadvantage on the scale of East London.

The Greenway example shows the potential negative impacts Localism poses, when we are trying to achieve a broad-based sustainable legacy. This is an issue not just for London but the UK as a whole. No sustainability plan can exist at a romanticised scale of 'the Local'. Sustainable urban planning needs regional coordination and strong institutions at local, regional and national tiers of planning, with defined outcomes. Localism merely undermines local authorities who have suffered large funding cuts and may exacerbate unequal access to planning processes between wealthy educated established boroughs and transient, poor and less educated ones. The context of this happening in spite of the glorious aims of the London 2012 Games implies a disconnect in policy: between relying on a monumental mega-event to 'transform' a deprived part of East London, and a valorisation of the power of local communities to empower change. It is no surprise, therefore, that in Newham – a borough where, according to a local planner, an estimated 30 per cent of population turn over each year – not a single community plan as allowed under the Localism Act has been submitted. This leaves only an extremely well-equipped LLDC to plan almost an uncontested model of a sustainable community, alongside a poorly equipped ring of boroughs. Will this governance landscape provide a 'sustainable legacy' for East London?

Tensions between some of the host boroughs and the LLDC are a cause for concern. In setting out planning policy, making planning decisions and negotiating Section 106 agreements, the LLDC needs to ensure that it is working closely with the relevant local authority for the area concerned. The LLDC should examine its working practices and decision making structures in this regard, taking on board concerns raised by the host Boroughs. Strong joint working will be essential to developing and delivering a clear vision for the future of East London.

(House of Lords, 2013:93)

Conclusion

Gold and Gold (2010) have argued that mega-event delivery has gone through a range of paradigms and that in the late twentieth century, and since Los Angeles, we are in a neoliberal paradigm of Games delivery. This would match the view that 1979 onward has been generally the age of the expansion of neoliberalism across the world (albeit with enormous resistance). What are we to make of London 2012 then and its execution of a sustainable legacy under a Localist agenda? There was a time before the bid when the emergence of a 'sustainable' paradigm could have been cited, but this has now fallen by the wayside. In fact, sustainability as a policy driver has merely become another tool of the neoliberal agenda. It is used to facilitate fundamentally the same processes of land acquisition and intense regeneration as previous Games. The way in which anything can be labelled 'sustainable', because of the sheer scope of the policy area and overlapping definitions by multiple agencies, allows a very broad range of plans to develop. It is no surprise, therefore, that three separate scales of planning – the Localism Act, the convergence plan for East London and the national government – consider themselves to be pursuing the 'sustainable' yet fail to provide some of the most obvious urban upgrades and interventions on the ground, creating more of the same forms of rapid urban regeneration that epitomises the neoliberal paradigm.

References

Adams and Sutherland. (2010) 'Wider greenway vision study', available at: http://www. adams-sutherland.co.uk/170-wgw-1.htm

Birkenholtz, T. (2012) 'Progress in human geography network political ecology: adaptation research'. *Progress in Human Geography*, 36(3): 295–315.

Bulkeley, H. and Kern, K. (2006) 'Local government and the governing of climate change in Germany and the UK'. *Urban Studies*, 43(12): 2237–2259.

Campbell, S. (2007) 'Green cities, growing cities'. *Journal of the American Planning Association*, 62(3): 296–312.

Carmona, M., Heath, T., Oc, T. and Tiesdell, S. (2003) *Public places–urban spaces: a guide to urban design*. Boston: Architectural Press.

Carter, N. (2007) *The politics of the environment: ideas, activism, policy* (2nd ed.). Cambridge: Cambridge University Press.

Clarke, N. and Cochrane, A. (2013) 'Geographies and politics of localism: the localism of the United Kingdom's coalition government'. *Political Geography*, 34: 10–23.

Colomb, C. (2007) 'Unpacking new labour's "urban renaissance" agenda: towards a socially sustainable reurbanization of British cities?' *Planning Practice and Research*, 22(1): 1–24.

Cox, K. and Mairtt, A. (1989) 'Levels of abstraction in locality studies'. *Antipode*, 21(2): 121–132.

DCLG (2011) *The plain English guide to the localism act.* London: DCLG.

Deas, I. (2013) 'Towards post-political consensus in urban policy? Localism and the emerging agenda for regeneration under the Cameron government'. *Planning Practice and Research*, 28: 65–82.

Design for London. (2012) *Stitching the fringe: working around the Olympic park.*

Gehl, J. (2011) *Life between buildings: using public space* (6th ed.). Washington, DC: Island Press.

GLA (2011) *The London Plan.* London: GLA.

Gold, J. and Gold, M. M. (2008) Olympic cities: regeneration, city rebranding and changing urban agendas. *Geography Compass*, 2(1): 300–318.

Gold, J. and Gold, M. (2010) *Olympic cities: city agendas, planning, and the World's Games, 1896–2016.* London: Taylor & Francis.

Graham, S. (2011) *Cities under siege: the new military urbanism.* London: Verso.

Hall, P. G. (2006) *Cities of tomorrow: an intellectual history of urban planning and design in the twentieth century.* Malden: Blackwell.

Harvey, D. (1997) *Justice, nature and the geography of difference.* Oxford: Wiley-Blackwell.

Haughton, G. and Allmendinger, P. (2013) 'Spatial planning and the new localism'. *Planning Practice and Research*, 28: 1–5.

Herod, A. (2011) *Scale.* Abingdon, UK: Routledge.

HM Government and Mayor of London (2013) 'Inspired by 2012: the legacy from the London 2012 Olympic and Paralympic Games', available at: https://www.gov.uk/government/uploads/system/uploads/attachment_data/file/224148/2901179_OlympicLegacy_acc.pdf

House of Lords (2013) 'Keeping the flame alive: the Olympic and Paralympic legacy', available at: http://www.publications.parliament.uk/pa/ld201314/ldselect/ldolympic/78/78.pdf

Jacobs, J. (1961) *The death and life of great american cities.* New York: Vintage Books.

LLDC (2012) *Your sustainability guide to Queen Elizabeth Park 2030.* London: LLDC.

Lombardi, R. D., Porter, L., Barber, A. and Rogers, C. (2010) 'Conceptualising sustainability in UK urban regeneration: a discursive formation'. *Urban Studies*, 48(2): 273–296.

MacRury, I. and Poynter, G. (2009) *London's Olympic Legacy.* London: University of East London.

Marston, S.A., Jones III, J. P. and Woodward, K. (2005) Human geography without scale. *Transactions of the Institute of British Geographers*, 30: 416–432.

Massey, D. (1993) 'Power-geometry and a progressive sense of place' in J. Bird, B. Curtis, T. Putnam and L. Tickner (Eds.), *Mapping the futures: local cultures, global change.* London: Routledge.

Mayor of London. (2008) *Five legacy commitments.* London: Mayor of London.

Mayor of London. (2011) *Convergence framework and action plan 2011–2015.* London: Mayor of London.

Mayor of London. (2014) *Draft further alterations to the London plan.* London: Mayor of London.

Mohan, G. and Stokke, K. (2010) 'Participatory development and empowerment: the dangers of localism'. *Third World Quarterly*, 21(2): 247–268.

Newland, P. (2008) *The cultural construction of London's east end urban iconography, modernity and the spatialisation of englishness*. Amsterdam and New York: Rodopi.

Parvin, P. (2011) 'Localism and the left: the need for strong central government'. *Renewal*, 19(2): 37–49.

Poynter, G. and MacRury, I. (2009) *Olympic cities: 2012 and the remaking of London*. Farnham, UK: Ashgate.

Pratchett, L. (2004) 'Local autonomy, local democracy and the "new localism"'. *Political Studies*, 52: 358–375.

Rogers, L. R. (1997) *Cities for a small planet: Reith lectures*. London: Faber & Faber.

Rydin, Y. (2010) *Governing for sustainable urban development* (1st ed.). London: Routledge.

Schumacher, E. F. (1993) *Small is beautiful: a study of economics as if people mattered*. London: Vintage.

Smith, N. (1984) *Uneven development: nature, capital and the production of space*. Oxford: Blackwell.

Swyngedouw, E. (2009) The trouble with nature: ecology as the new opium for the masses. New York: Pace University.

Welter, V. (2002) *Biopolis: Patrick Geddes and the city of life*. Cambridge: MIT Press.

Wilson, E. (1991) *The sphinx in the city*. London: Virago Press.

Young, I. M. and Allen, D. S. (2011) *Justice and the politics of difference*. Princeton, NJ: Princeton University Press.

15 Edgelands and London 2012

The case of the Lower Lea Valley

Oliver Pohlisch

Introduction

'Inevitable and, while perhaps unfortunate, just a "natural" part of the cycle of urban development' is a view shared by many policy makers and planning practitioners on displacement triggered by mega-events (Porter, 2009:395). Indeed, over the last decades, mega-events have been increasingly used as an opportunity to push through urban regeneration plans and forced evictions, e.g. of almost 1.5 million people in preparation for Beijing 2008 and an estimated 30,000 who will have to be removed by the time the Olympic Games start in Rio de Janeiro in 2016 (Halais, 2013). These developments are seen highly critically by UN agencies (UN-Habitat, 2011) and NGOs (COHRE, 2007). Displacements due to mega-events are not only a problem in the Global South. UN-Habitat (2011) also criticised the eviction processes in East London's Lower Lea Valley in the run up to the 2012 Olympics. Yet, this issue is rarely acknowledged in post-Games evaluations of London's Olympic experiences. This is a typical feature of mega-event–induced relocations: once they have taken place, the focus of attention moves on to what is then created on the 'prepared' sites (Raco and Tunney, 2010:18).

In this chapter, I trace various former occupants of London's Lower Lea Valley, which was cleared in preparation for the 2012 Summer Games, to illuminate the contradictions of that particular eviction process. After outlining *edgeland* as a distinctive type of space, which over the last decades increasingly became a 'testing ground' for urban redevelopment by means of festivalisation, I will focus on the edgelands of the Lower Lea Valley, before it was transformed into the main stage for the Olympics. I then briefly discuss the legal framework of land acquisition in the UK and describe a few examples of occupants being evicted from the Olympic area in the Lower Lea Valley. The question this chapter addresses is whether a complete clearance in order to create landmark regeneration projects is an appropriate way to handle edgelands.

Edgelands and planning

Urban areas that are considered 'run down' and unattractive will often be designated as future sites of Olympic venues and infrastructure (COHRE, 2007).

These areas can be broadly classified as peripheral. Abdou Maliq Simone (2007) uses the term periphery in a sense that goes beyond a fixed geographical entity. In a political sense, it is a means of altering the relevance of a specific space through the shifting terms of association with other spaces. Remnants of old projects and those of the new, in various stages of completion, intersect in the periphery. What Simone's terminology lacks, however, is a thorough consideration of the materiality of space, which would allow a finer distinction between various kinds of peripheries. Shoard (2002:1) characterises edgelands as 'an apparently unplanned, certainly uncelebrated and largely incomprehensible territory where town and country meet', while Farley and Symmons Roberts (2012:4–5) claim that using the term edgeland to signify city fringes, where 'overspill housing estates break into scrubland, wasteland', may help to bring these areas back into the collective consciousness.

Edgelands are, however, not exclusively found on the present-day border between the urban and the rural; they also survive in built-up areas. This correlates with what Simone (2007:465) describes as 'near-peripheries' that were 'leapfrogged' by development and thus became problematic interstices between differentiated growth poles. Wood (2004) considers the emergence of wasteland in British cities as a symptom of urban decay that had already started before the Second World War, but was covered by the extensive reconstruction activities in the postwar era. Since the 1960s, British industry was hit hard by rationalisation processes, plant closures and the outsourcing of manufacturing to low-wage countries, all of which caused a collapse in demand for urban land (Wood, 2004). Relocating enterprises left behind vacant land ('brownfield sites'), growing unemployment and deprivation.

In Britain, challenges provided by edgelands, particularly those impacted by deindustrialisation, have been addressed by installing powerful quango agencies to accelerate major property-led projects and ensure that they are realised with a minimum of local opposition and participation (Raco and Tunney, 2010). The London Docklands Development Corporation (LDDC), established in 1981 in order to incorporate the capital's former port area into London's Global City economy (Colenutt, 1994), has since served as a model for other planning bodies. The LDDC's resources and development visions came directly from central government, who conceived of spatial interstices as blank spaces ready for transformation into highly visible regeneration landscapes. During the heydays of this approach, in the 1980s and 1990s (Raco and Tunney, 2010), many derelict sites were regenerated, either by erasing them entirely or by converting former industrial buildings into homes, offices and retail outlets as part of the promotion of a new industrial aesthetics (Edensor *et al.*, 2012; Muller and Carr, 2009).

But there are alternative views on edgelands, arguing that these spaces need to be protected and saved from redevelopment since their scruffier parts serve as valuable refuge for urban wildlife (Shoard, 2002; Edensor *et al.*, 2012). Moreover, edgelands provide space in which numerous unauthorised and improvisational human activities may occur, e.g. living in temporary shelter, growing vegetables, fly tipping, car parking, dog walking and collecting building materials

Figure 15.1 Open green spaces in the pre-2007 Lower Lea Valley before edgeland
        clearance.

or firewood. The absence of direct regulation in such territories also facilitates
hedonistic pursuits like raving, drinking, sex and drug use, whereby the lines
between pleasure, work and addiction get blurred. The peculiar surfaces of
edgelands offer potential for a range of physical engagements like climbing,
parcouring, skating, skateboarding or mountain biking (Edensor *et al.*, 2012).
Not least, edgelands may provide a sanctuary for informal gatherings of teenagers
(Ward Thompson, 2012).

Edgelands also inspire artists. They provide material for artefacts, canvas for
graffiti (Edsenor *et al.*, 2012) and scenes for photo shoots (Woodward, 2012).
Particularly in the mid-1990s, photographers were attracted to the 'evocative
potential of the city's terrain vagues', which stemmed from 'the relationship
between the absence of use, of activity, and the sense of freedom, of expectancy'
(Solà-Morales Rubió, 1995:119–120). Edensor *et al.* (2012) describe how the
initial attraction of industrial ruins as a realm outside of official artspace has led
to more organised attempts to utilise them as sites of exhibition. Nowadays, stu-
dios and galleries are familiar features of converted manufacturing premises in
edgelands, because commercial rents in other places have become unaffordable
for many in the 'creative industries'.

Edgelands function as archaeological sites revealing different layers of urban
development (Shoard, 2002; Jorgensen, 2012) and as 'literal archive' (Simone,
2007:466) where something is continuously added, subtracted and destroyed. But
edgelands are not only a museum of the industrial past; they also accommodate

vital infrastructures, like rubbish tips, electricity substations, sewage works, gas-holders or motorway interchanges (Shoard, 2002). They offer cheap and flexible premises for small and medium-sized enterprises (Raco and Tunney, 2010). Simone (2007) concludes that the periphery is a site for economic and social operations that cannot be absorbed by the city itself, but which are still necessary, e.g. for attracting investment.

The Lower Lea Valley

The Lower Lea Valley, where much of the 2012 London Games took place, is an area of edgeland in East London located in the London boroughs of Tower Hamlets, Hackney, Newham and Waltham Forest. The settlement around the Lea remained of rural character until the mid-eighteenth century, when the availability of energy and the good transport connections promoted the early industrialisation of the valley. Around 1900, the area constituted Britain's second largest continuous industrial zone after Birmingham (Yarham and Archer, 1991). Its rise was accompanied by the construction of canals which served to transport coal and building material for the rapidly growing metropolis, but lost its economic importance as soon as East London was connected to the railway network (Game and Whitfield, 1996). Stratford Railway Works, where engines were constructed and maintained, became one of the region's major employers at the beginning of the twentieth century (Yarham and Archer, 1991).

Yet, soon deindustrialisation processes began affecting East London, combined with the relocation to southeast Essex of those factories that needed space to expand. Fuelled by the interwar housing boom, the Lower Lea Valley was briefly transformed into a new centre of furniture production (Poynter, 1996). During the Second World War, the area was heavily bombed. Reconstruction in the postwar period was characterised by further expanding the motorised individual transport infrastructure in the Lower Lea Valley, consolidating its function as a transit zone between Inner London and the new commuter towns in Essex (Yarham and Archer, 1991). The Stratford Railway Works closed in the 1960s and the furniture industry had largely disappeared by the mid-1980s (Poynter, 1996). Despite this, the area was still a place of diverse economic activities at the beginning of the twenty-first century. Industrial production remained significant, amounting to more than a third of all businesses (Mann, 2006). The Lower Lea Valley's proximity to Central London combined with relatively cheap property and land prices attracted small and medium enterprises, but also artists. Its affordability resulted from the fact that it was 'undesirable' for other uses (Raco and Tunney, 2010:10). One activity that thrived particularly in the open spaces of the Lower Lea Valley was gardening. In the 1920s, banker and philanthropist Major Arthur Villers created allotments for local workers on a former landfill site. As a believer in the social reform movement, Villers had previously purchased abandoned gravel-pits in order to turn them into playing fields for Eton Manor Sports Club. While the club dissolved in 1967 and its facilities closed in 2001 (Davis, 2008), the football pitches at the Hackney Marshes northwest of Eton Manor continued to be frequented by the players of a local amateur league.

In 1975, Eastway Cycle Circuit, a race track for amateurs, was realised as the only part of an ambitious postwar plan to transform the Lower Lea Valley into a modern leisure and recreation park for all Londoners, with a futuristic 'Fun Palace' at its heart. Responsibility for implementation was the Lower Lea Regional Park Authority founded in 1964 by a consortium of the Greater London Council, all London boroughs and several local authorities of towns and counties outside the capital. They sought to organise a coherent development of an area of about 4,000 hectares of land and water stretching from the mouth of the River Lea into Hertfordshire (Elks, 2008).

While, in the mid-1980s, environmental protection clearly had become part of the Park's agenda and the Greater London Council (1986:5–12) before its abolition had made determined efforts to preserve the wastelands that had evolved in the lower section of the Lea Valley, the public discourse changed significantly during the 1990s. The valley started to be described as an area covered in derelict buildings, large vacant sites and obsolete infrastructure. It became a focal point of development, incorporated in the East Thames Corridor, later the Thames Gateway, which was intended to accommodate southeast England's growing population and the booming Global City economy (LDA, 2006). London and Continental Railway, a UK government-owned company responsible for building the rail link between Central London and the Channel tunnel, purchased the former Stratford Railway Works land in the mid-1990s as future site for a station on the new high-speed line. They also signed a deal with property developers to build a shopping complex on the abandoned railway yard (Minton, 2012). The Greater London Authority (GLA), newly established in 2000, further encouraged this trend (GLA, 2004), by identifying the Lower Lea Valley in its spatial development strategy as an opportunity area that could provide new jobs and housing and might be used to stage Olympic Games if London decided to submit a bit.

Mann (2006) argues that, due to London's structural housing shortage and the continuing property boom, the Lower Lea Valley developed into a conflictual terrain, where the need for open space and the expansion of industrial capacities collided with the demand for more residential space. Residential buildings in the sparsely populated Lower Lea Valley were concentrated in Hackney Wick and along Stratford High Street. Somewhat set apart from other built-up areas lay the Clays Lane Estate, which had been completed in 1978 as cooperative housing, providing cheap accommodation for single persons on low income. The area also featured a University of East London (UEL) student village, two authorised traveller sites, some informal traveller pitches and provided temporary or permanent shelter for homeless people.

Presenting the Lower Lea Valley as an area being in urgent need of regeneration, which would only gain momentum with the help of a mega-event, was a rhetoric constantly used by planners and politicians for justifying London's Olympic bid (Raco and Tunney, 2010). The key arguments for regeneration were that local communities were among the most deprived in Britain; the land was heavily contaminated; and the area was generally derelict, difficult to access, underused and abandoned (Davis, 2011). The suggested solution was a large-scale intervention rather than regeneration in parts or increments. The Olympic Games provided the necessary justification for assembling land by the state – with the instrument of compulsory purchase orders (CPOs) as a last resort.

Compulsory purchase order

From the late nineteenth century to the 1970s, British local authorities predominantly used compulsory purchases to replace slums with new social housing, thus reflecting the ideals of the welfare state (Christophers, 2010; Kearney, 2014). More recent cases of CPO-led regeneration, however, demonstrate a profound change in how these coercive powers are used. Although authorities serving CPOs continue to express their commitment to public interest and the well-being of the area concerned, their planning policy is, at the same time, centred on enhancing private sector capital accumulation (Christophers, 2010).

The camouflaging of what is increasingly referred to in the legal literature as 'public-private taking' (Christophers, 2010:866) was set by recent amendments in legislation such as the Planning and Compulsory Purchase Act of 2004, which was intended to speed up the CPO process in order to facilitate the land acquisition for redevelopment and regeneration (Raco and Tunney, 2010; Christophers, 2010). It has been criticised for placing far greater importance on the economic impact of new developments than on the negative effects on existing occupants of the land (Minton, 2012). As the biggest ever Compulsory Purchase Order programme in England, the London Olympics presented an important test for the then new legislation (Raco and Tunney, 2010). In tune with the urban policy of New Labour, with its focus on creating 'partnerships between government and civil society' (Imrie and Raco, 2003:7), the London Development Agency (LDA) started consultations with property owners, lease holders and tenants in the Lower Lea Valley long before London's Olympic bid was successful.

The fact is that almost all previous Olympic Games have had as one of their key features the limited degree of consultation conducted with individuals and groups that were affected by the planning of the mega-event (COHRE, 2007). Unlike more open-ended projects, the preparation of the Olympics has a fixed time frame by which projects have to be completed, no matter what problems and obstacles have to be overcome. Moreover, the involvement of business and political elites in the infrastructural and other development aspects of hosting the Olympics implies that their interests are prioritised over those of occupants or residents who usually belong to the most marginalised and vulnerable sectors of society (COHRE, 2007). On the other hand, the high visibility of the Games may enable a broad spectrum of local interests to draw public attention to the impacts of the planning, making the mega-event particularly vulnerable to protest campaigns (Raco and Tunney, 2010).

Negotiations and confrontations

The LDA's Compulsory Purchase Order Lands 2005 document lists 792 separate parcels of land under different ownerships (Davis, 2008:11), situated between the Hackney Marshes in the north and Stratford High Street in the south. The 'emptying' of the area in preparation for the London 2012 Olympic and Paralympic Games affected a wide range of stakeholders, some using the space (a) for work, including artists and small and medium-sized businesses owning or renting commercial properties, (b) for housing, e.g. tenants of the Clays Lane Estate, travellers, students in the UEL student village and (c) for recreation, e.g. people enjoying the open spaces, but also the Eastway Cycle Circuit, Hackney Marshes and Manor Garden allotments. I discuss here three case studies of affected user groups: the Marshgate Lane Business Group (MLBG), the Clays Lane Estate tenants and the gardeners of the Manor Garden Society.

Marshgate Lane Business Group

The vast majority of private land owners in the Lower Lea Valley were either businesses that also operated from their premises in the Lower Lea Valley or tenants of commercially used properties. Particularly the former, mostly located in the Marshgate Lane area, started to oppose the Olympic project soon after being approached by the LDA. The MLBG quickly became a vehicle of campaigning against the proposals of the LDA. The MLBG attempted to contest the dominant characterisation of the Lower Lea Valley as 'derelict' and turned directly to the International Olympic Committee, expressing its rejection of London's bid as it stood because of the negative effects a regeneration driven by Olympics would have on local businesses and residents (Raco and Tunney, 2010). Yet, the businesses did not speak with one voice. Those companies who were lessees of

Figure 15.2 Business in the Marshgate area before clearance of the Olympic site.

premises rather backed London's bid for the 2012 Olympics, even if this had negative effects on their performance (Raco and Tunney, 2010). The bid's success in July 2005 undermined much of the collective sense the businesses in the Lower Lea Valley had developed. The MLBG meetings stopped and most companies focused on individual negotiations (Raco and Tunney, 2010). The majority of businesses reached agreements with the LDA before the CPO was issued (COHRE, 2007), and it turned out that particularly those enterprises whose owners were the most prominent critics of the LDA received an expeditious handling of their cases (Raco and Tunney, 2010).

Allotment gardens

The actions of occupants of land that was owned by public bodies or publicly funded organisations ranged from abandoning any protest against the Olympic plans in order to secure an acceptable alternative facility elsewhere, to sustaining as long as possible the claim to remain at the location notwithstanding the preparation and staging of the Games in the immediate proximity. While, for instance, the organised users of the Eastway Cycle Circuit downplayed the importance of their sport venue's location and fully concentrated on negotiating a replacement facility of high quality elsewhere (Davis, 2011), the site and location in the Lower Lea Valley was pivotal to the allotment holders of the Manor Gardening Society (MGS). They regarded their community as so strongly linked to their site that the loss of the one would compromise the survival of the other (LDA, 2006).

Figure 15.3 Manor garden allotment site before the London 2012 Olympics.

The LDA initially ignored the communal character of the allotment gardens and attempted to persuade gardeners to relocate individually to other allotments in East London (Davis, 2011). Later on in the consultation process, the LDA offered the MGS, representing the allotment holders, a group move to a new site at Marsh Lane half a mile north of the original site. At the legally required public inquiry hearing in summer 2006, the plot holders appealed against their relocation to what they considered an unsuitable site. They submitted an alternative proposal that integrated the existing allotments into the Olympic project (LDA, 2006). Although their displacement was confirmed by the Secretary of Trade and Industry, the gardeners continued to campaign for their right to stay, accompanied by widespread media coverage that mostly supported their concerns. The judicial dispute ended, nevertheless, with the gardeners accepting a group relocation to Marsh Lane, albeit only after the harvest season.

Clays Lane Estate

The Clays Lane Estate tenants' reactions to the plans to demolish their homes for the construction of Olympic facilities were in part a response to the fact that the LDA, in ways similar to its initial treatment of the allotment holders, denied the tenants recognition as a community. Referring to the failure of the cooperative self-government that had resulted in the take-over of the estate by Peabody Trust in 2005, the LDA (2006) argued that there was no public interest in maintaining this project of communal living. Knowing that the tenants were indeed divided into various interest groups, the LDA soon started the individual allocation of self-contained apartments that were spread over East London and beyond.[1]

Figure 15.4 The Clays Lane Estate before the clearance of the Olympics site.

However, a significant proportion of tenants objected to their displacement. At the public inquiry, they questioned the necessity of using the land on which the Clays Lane Estate was located for the construction of the athletes' village (Cheyne, 2009:407). They deplored the way the LDA officials handled their case, blaming them for the poor quality of information given, providing a flawed advice service, replacing an exhaustive survey on the tenants' needs with a more restricted one, changing or ignoring commitments and delaying a solution for group moves (LDA, 2006). Clays Lane Estate residents submitted affidavits in which they, for instance, argued that the relocation proposals made by the LDA did not take into account the comparatively low rent, the security of tenure, the high standard of design, the secluded location and the access to lots of green open spaces that they enjoyed (LDA, 2006).

The inspector appointed to review the evidence submitted by objectors at the public inquiry fully supported the arguments of the LDA and recommended to keep the Clays Lane Estate in the CPO area (LDA, 2006). Accordingly, the Secretary of State for Trade and Industry gave green signal to its demolition. The tenants then went to the High Court, but failed to convince the judge with their claim that the LDA lacked a proper relocation strategy (Cheyne, 2009). The last months before leaving the estate became very uncomfortable for the remaining tenants. The windows of abandoned apartments were barricaded; demolition and excavation work started around the estate and some people, without any prospects for an alternative accommodation up to the last moment, were threatened with loss of compensation and a forced eviction leading to homelessness (Cheyne, 2008).

Summary of eviction struggles

The consultations between the authority responsible for land acquisition and the occupants of the area failed to prevent resistance by those facing eviction. Although the occupants were able to express their concerns and wishes during the public consultation process, the decision making remained fully in the hands of officials and planners, with the indispensable and nonnegotiable objective of clearing the land needed for staging the Games.

User groups who challenged the LDA's relocation policy or insisted on staying put were confronted with a CPO process whose outcome was all too predictable. Their objections against the CPO resulted in a public inquiry run by an inspector who would advise the Secretary of State for Trade and Industry. The latter, being a member of the government that supported and funded the Olympic project, would then decide whether to grant the CPO. It was unlikely that he would have taken decisions that might have led to the time frame of Olympic planning to be challenged.

The CPO process in the Lower Lea Valley hence continues the history of highly questionable land acquisitions in Olympic host cities. The process was institutionally flawed and the counterparties involved were provided with unequal financial and personal resources. Staff at the LDA had the necessary expertise and financial means for the task of clearing the CPO area, whereas most occupants facing displacement had to deal with this massive intervention into their lives in addition to their regular responsibilities (Raco and Tunney, 2010). Yet, some occupants, usually those who became spokespersons of the different user groups, gathered a profound knowledge of planning laws and regulations during the proceedings. A defining feature of the spokespersons' strategies was to emphasise the communal character of their groups. However, most groups experienced internal disputes about the extent to which they should oppose relocation, and members found themselves in the unsettling situation weighing up their own interests against their loyalty to the group (Davis, 2011).

The occupants in the Lower Lea Valley also made efforts to gain the support of the media and of politicians and NGOs. Although the high visibility of the Olympic project helped to turn the spotlight on the area, the campaigners did not manage to gather widespread public backing. Their previous socio-economic peripherality had prevented most of them from developing efficient campaigning skills, but even more crucial was the strength of the London-wide euphoria over the Olympics that made it difficult for critical voices to be heard (Raco and Tunney, 2010:15). A notable exception was the allotment holders association who linked their resistance against eviction to the demand of being incorporated into the Games. Through their extensive PR work, they gained the sympathy of a middle-class public that was just discovering allotments as the new urban idyll.

There was practically no collaboration between the different campaign groups. Instead of focusing on their (shared) unique environment that, if lost, would unlikely to be found anywhere else, they stressed their importance as a community that should survive relocation. Some groups even feared that an alliance with others would endanger their own struggle.[2] The fact that the occupants of the Lower Lea Valley perceived of themselves as too heterogeneous to find common ground further reproduced the dominant discourse of the area as degraded, fragmented and splintered, and it made it easy for the LDA to atomise the users' interests. With one publicly known exception,[3] there was no need for the LDA to enforce eviction by police measures. Demolition even started while the last residents were still on site. A *tabula rasa* was produced from which all traces of former life and occupation had been removed and that was enclosed by an 11-mile long, 10-foot high fence of blue-painted plywood in the years before the Olympics took place (Davis, 2008, 2011).

Replacement and compensation

A good part of the evicted businesses survived the relocation. While the largest companies managed to move to replacement facilities that even advanced their competitiveness (Davis, 2011), the experience of the CPO process had a more negative impact on smaller businesses, with liquidation being the most serious threat (Raco and Tunney, 2010).[4] By law, recipients of CPO compensation shall not benefit financially or profit from the inflation in property values that follows. Many of the businesses complained that this principle led to major underestimates of the true costs of relocation, since the LDA made the valuation of their land before news of the bid ensured a rise in real estate prices in East London (Raco and Tunney, 2010; COHRE, 2007; Beard, 2005). There was also some evidence of land owners profiteering from the fact that over 200 firms were forced to simultaneously look for new premises within a strictly defined time scale. Fifty-five per cent of the participants of a survey conducted among relocated businesses reported that they moved to sites that were 'significantly more expensive', 15 per cent stated that their new property was 'slightly more expensive' than their old one (Raco and Tunney, 2010:12). And quite a few business owners described their new site as inferior to what they had before with regard to the proximity of suppliers and customers as well as the journey to work for the employees (Raco and Tunney, 2010).

The net differences in land values played a key part in the government's funding plans for the Olympics, since it had calculated a total of £800 million as revenue from property sales after the Games. The land acquisition in the Lower Lea Valley was consistent with the 'public-private-taking' that dominates CPO processes in contemporary Britain, whereby a transfer takes place of assets and profits from small and medium businesses in the pre-2007 valley to the development agencies and real estate companies that inherited the post-Games premiums (Raco and Tunney, 2010:11).

The Clays Lane Estate tenants with claims to compensation received £8,500 for the loss of their homes and for relocation expenses (COHRE, 2007:185). Beside this, the LDA failed to deliver on its initial promise that all tenants would be able to choose their new residence. Many found it impossible to get flats in their preference areas (Cheyne, 2008). Clays Lane Estate tenants who managed to secure their right to move to a flat owned by a housing association faced a selection procedure which allowed them to reject the first two offers, forcing them to take the third one in order not to lose their relocation rights[5] (Hatcher, 2012). In general, the relocated tenants expressed their satisfaction with their new accommodation. What they missed from Clays Lane was the estate's communal areas and facilities. They recalled a vibrant social life at Clays Lane, whereas they complained about the anonymity of their new place of residency.[6] All efforts to realise a group move fizzled out. However, the LDA denied any responsibility for the failure of establishing a housing project comparable to the Clays Lane Estate, blaming the tenants for their inability to act cohesively on this issue (Davis, 2011).

While the MGS succeeded in securing a compensation of £800 for each allotment lost, a significant number of plot holders did not take part in the collective relocation to the transitional site at Marsh Lane, either opting for allotments somewhere else in East London or simply giving up gardening as the consequence of the negative experiences of the eviction process.[7] The move of the remaining members was not very smooth. Access to the new plots was delayed due to ongoing construction work (Games Monitor, 2011), and later drainage problems caused flooding of one-third of the gardens.

Over the following years, the plot holders managed to improve the conditions at Marsh Lane but remained hopeful to be able to return to the Olympic park in 2014. Indeed, beside the users of the Eastway Cycle Circuit, the plot holders of the Manor Garden allotments were the only former occupants who had obtained assurances that they would be provided with new permanent facilities in the Olympic park after having endured a 7-year period on their transitional sites. However, the return will lead to a further split-up of the community, since the MGS had to accept a move to two separate sites, situated about a mile apart and under different land ownership. There was also some criticism about the quality of the sites, since one would be squeezed between a rail track and Stratford High Street and the other would be in the immediate proximity of the A12 Road (Beard, 2010). The latter is currently in danger since the council of Waltham Forest, assisted by the Lea Valley Regional Park Authority, refused its setting up and instead applied for planning permission to the London Legacy Development Corporation to create a meadow at this site, while it has given the allotments at Marsh Lane permanent status (Cheyne, 2014; Appleby, 2014).

Summary of the relocation processes

The relocation processes can be divided into acts of inclusion, of a renewed peripheralisation and, finally, of disappearance. The allotments were selected to be reestablished in the post-Olympic park, since their organised users were able to link group interests to the renewed popularity of their activities. Allotment gardens appealed to the urban middle classes who had developed a heightened awareness of healthy nutrition and local food production. The incorporation of the facility into the newly produced space, nevertheless, went along with their significant adaptation to a much more managed environment than the pre-2007 Lower Lea Valley.

The expectation that the gardeners should be content with the new location at the less attractive margins of the post-Olympic park reflects, however, common prejudices against allotments as semi-private spaces, which might become untidy and then 'contaminate' their more ordered surrounding. In the future, the gardeners will have to deal with more external interferences, because the Park, of which they are part, is intended to be heavily utilised, and they will adjoin denser residential neighbourhoods. Conflicts between plot holders and park visitors as well as residents could stem from differing views on accessibility and appropriate use and behaviour.

The overwhelming majority of businesses evicted from the Olympic site moved to the eastern outskirts of London, to the banks of the River Roding or along the Thames in Barking. These remaining edgelands are currently undergoing a profound alteration, with new out-of-town shopping centres and new industrial parks springing up. Moving 'dirty' (e.g. polluting, noisy) industries out of the city, usually downstream and downwind, is a classic pattern of urban development – freeing land for other uses, such as high-end residential developments or the activities of the service sector, in the last 15 years increasingly the so-called creative and leisure industries – and ensuring higher profits for land owners. It is also clear that the large-scale clearance of the Lower Lea Valley pushed informal commercial activities either to other areas in East London or, in some cases, caused them to vanish.

Although the Clays Lane Housing Cooperative had already ceased to exist two years before the demolition of the estate, the dispersion of its former residents all over London proved the end of a rare and alternative housing project. Regardless of the difficulty of establishing coherent groups for collective action among the former Clays Lane Estate tenants, the LDA could have provided a new housing complex with space for communal living for single persons on low income. Instead, the LDA openly dismissed this residential form as 'outdated'.

What former Clays Lane Estate tenants once regarded as contributing to the good quality of their old living place and what gave the Lower Lea Valley its distinct character as an edgeland has been much diminished. The wildscapes along the River Lea and its tributaries will not be replaced by open spaces of a similar kind elsewhere, since the London Olympic and Paralympic Act of 2006 dispensed the authorities from their duty to provide compensation for the green spaces that had been lost during the preparations for the Olympic Games.[8] The now opened Queen Elizabeth Olympic Park is claimed to include 'wild habitats'. But these comparatively small spots are contained in a highly managed surrounding, being themselves objects of increased surveillance in order to guarantee their purity.

Conclusion

The eviction process in the Lower Lea Valley highlights how specific urban spaces, namely edgelands, have increasingly become the terrain of a regeneration that operates with the spectacular and highly visible. Its prerequisite is a prevailing discourse that constantly dismisses edgeland as unappealing spaces that urgently need to be transformed.

Linking the regeneration of the Lower Lea Valley to the staging of the Summer Games allowed the state to compulsorily acquire land on a large scale. Looking closer at the CPO process, it becomes clear that it represented a massive intrusion into the lives of the former occupants of the valley, causing significant material loss and emotional impact. As with eviction processes arising from Olympic planning elsewhere, it mostly affected people at the lower end of the social scale. Although there were consultations, they were characterised by legal frameworks and conditions set by authorities that were much better equipped with financial and logistical resources than those trying to resist displacement.

Changes in the planning legislation during the years prior to the Olympics were of benefit for the land acquisition as it happened in the Lower Lea Valley. The CPO process can be partly regarded as an example of the increasing practice of public-private-taking, whereby the state, while claiming a legitimate public interest, provides for a redistribution of private property. Helpful in this 'land-grabbing' process was the obvious democratic deficit in the objection procedures. All of this resonates with what Simone (2007:462) describes as the state exceeding its own 'core' values and technologies in order to restrain the periphery. In addition, the heterogeneity of the responses of the Lower Lea Valley's user groups proved to be an obstacle to joint resistance. Arguably, they internalised the discourse of the area's inferiority by more or less deliberately keeping their struggles and resistance against eviction separated from each other. With their relocation, those communities that constituted the 'characteristic features' of the site pre-2007 became themselves subject to significant changes. Some of them were incorporated into more managed, central spaces, thereby undergoing a kind of domestication. Others were dispersed to locations that are now as peripheral as the Lower Lea Valley had been a decade ago.

There is too little knowledge about the role of edgelands in contemporary urban areas. Parallel to its geographical, social and political peripherality, edgelands are also too little researched by academic disciplines that deal with urban matters, since they tend to be rather preoccupied with central or more clearly defined spaces. I fully subscribe to Shoard's (2002:17–18) call for more research on edgelands, within and outside of academia. Above all, the occupants of edgelands themselves should be supported in developing a greater awareness of the environment in which they are living, working or doing recreational activities, so that they may be more able to adequately respond to planning schemes imposed upon them 'from above'.

Such moves might help change the present planning discourse on edgelands that is overwhelmingly focused on its denigration. In the case of the Lower Lea Valley, this led to an urban restructuring that caused many people to suffer. As Raco and Tunney (2010:19) have argued, in challenging the dominant discourse, planners might conceive that, instead of applying the *tabula rasa* principle, incremental change that is less obsessed with the spectacular and the high visibility of many large-scale regeneration projects may be better suited to accommodate the hidden potential of edgelands.

Notes

1 The 550 mostly foreign students who lived in the East University Park Village at Clays Lane were called upon to leave their apartments even before the International Olympic Committee awarded the 2012 Olympics to London. The LDA insisted that the students' village should be emptied by June 2005 (COHRE, 2007).
2 As the author of this chapter has learned from interviews with representatives of individual occupants groups.
3 Rob Rowen, 75, the occupant of an isolated small house nearby Old Ford Locks, once owned by the water board and with no sanitation, gas or postal deliveries, refused to leave the place where he lived for 42 years voluntarily (Leapman, 2007). His whereabouts after his eviction with police and bailiffs present is not known.
4 The LDA (2008) reported that 25 enterprises with a total of 65 employees ceased to operate as a direct result of displacement. Further 10 companies with 54 employees are unaccounted for.
5 Some of the tenants who stayed at the estate until just before its clearance had no other choice but to seek temporary accommodation in hotels or hostels or agreeing to timely limited tenancies (Cheyne, 2008).
6 According to five former Clays Lane Estate tenants interviewed in autumn 2012.
7 As reported by a member of the MGS interviewed in September 2012.
8 This dispensation was granted on the grounds that a replacement on this scale was not feasible (LDA, 2006:16).

References

Appleby, M. (2014, March 7) 'Corporation upsets locals over Olympic allotments', *Horticulture Week*, available at: www.hortweek.com/Parks_and_gardens/article/1283262/corporation-upsets-locals-olympic-allotments/ (last accessed 27 July 2014).

Beard, M. (2005, August 13) 'Business on Olympic site fight to avoid eviction', *The Independent*.

Beard, M. (2010, June 28) 'Gardeners feel "betrayed" by Olympics offer', *London Evening Standard*, available at: http://www.standard.co.uk/news/gardeners-feel-betrayed-by-olympics-offer-6485589.html (last accessed 27 July 2014).

Centre on Housing Rights and Evictions (2007) *Fair play for housing rights – mega-events, Olympic Games and housing rights*. Geneva: COHRE. Available at: http://www.ruig-gian.org/ressources/Report%20Fair%20Play%20FINAL%20FINAL%20070531.pdf (last accessed 11 April 2015).

Cheyne, J. (2008, February 3) 'London 2012 Olympic evictions: Jowell's "Parliamentary" answer and an evictee's response', *Games Monitor*, available at: http://www.gamesmonitor.org.uk/node/558 (last accessed 27 July 2014).

Cheyne, J. (2009) 'Olympian masterplanning in London'. *Planning Theory & Practice*, 10(3): 404–408.

Cheyne, J. (2014, January 12) 'Manor gardens allotments: a scandalous legacy', *Games Monitor*, available at: http://www.gamesmonitor.org.uk/node/2186 (last accessed 27 July 2014).

Christophers, B. (2010) 'Geographical knowledges and neoliberal tensions: compulsory land purchase in the context of contemporary urban redevelopment'. *Environment and Planning A*, 42: 856–873.

Colenutt, B. (1994) 'Docklands after Canary Wharf' in B.-P. Lange (Ed.), *Die neue Metropole: Los Angeles – London*. Hamburg: Argument-Verlag.

Davis, J. P. (2008) 'Inside the blue fence: an exploration', available at: http://www.lse.ac.uk/LSECities/citiesProgramme/pdf/citiesLAB/citiesLAB_davis.pdf (last accessed 27 July 2014).

Davis, J. P. (2011) 'Urbanising the event – how past processes, present politics and future plans shape London's Olympic Legacy', unpublished PhD thesis, London School of Economics and Political Science, London, available at: http://etheses.lse.ac.uk/382/1/JulietDavisPhD.pdf (last accessed 27 July 2014).

De Solà-Morales Rubió, I. (1995) 'Terrain vague' in C. Davidson (Ed.), *Anyplace*. Cambridge: MIT Press.

Edensor, T., Evans, B., Holloway, J., Millington, S. and Binnie, J. (2012) 'Playing in industrial ruins – interrogating teleological understandings of play in spaces of material alterity and low surveillance' in A. Jorgensen and R. Keenan (Eds.), *Urban wildscapes*. London: Routledge.

Elks, L. (2008) 'The Lee Valley Regional Park: a historical perspective', *Hackney History*, 14, available at: http://www.leamarsh.com/LVRPA/pix/Laurie%20Elks%20on%20History%20%20of%20LVRPA.PDF (last accessed 27 July 2014).

Farley, P. and Symmons Roberts, M. (2012) *Edgelands – journeys into England's true wilderness*. London: Vintage Books.

Game, M. and Whitfield, J. (1996) *Ecology handbook no. 27: nature conversation in Tower Hamlets*. London: London Ecology Unit.

Games Monitor (2011) 'Background paper on the London 2012 Olympics 1', *Games Monitor*, available at: http://www.gamesmonitor.org.uk/files/BriefingPaper1-Impact.pdf (last accessed 27 July 2014).

Greater London Authority (GLA) (2004) *The London plan – spatial development strategy for Greater London*. London: GLA.

Greater London Council (1986) *Ecology handbook no. 4: a nature conservation strategy for London: woodland, wasteland, the tidal Thames and two London boroughs*. London: Greater London Council Transportation and Development Department.

Halais, F. (2013) 'Rio's favela residents fight mega-event eviction', *Open security – conflict and peacebuilding*, available at: www.opendemocracy.net/opensecurity/flavie-halais/rios-favela-residents-fight-mega-event-eviction (last accessed 27 July 2014).

Hatcher, C. (2012) 'Forced evictions: legacy of dislocation on the Clays Lane Estate' in H. Powell and I. Marrero-Guillámon (Eds.), *The art of dissent – adventures in London's Olympic state*. London: Marshgate Press.

Imrie, R. and Raco, M. (2003) *Urban renaissance? New labour, community and urban policy*. Bristol: Policy.

Jorgensen, A. (2012) 'Introduction' in A. Jorgensen and R. Keenan (Eds.), *Urban wildscapes*. London: Routledge.

Kearney, H. (2014) 'A compulsory purchase for London', The contemporary city, available at: www.newleftproject.org/index.php/site/article_comments/a_compulsory_purchase_for_london (last accessed 27 July 2014).

Leapman, B. (2007, June 17) 'Veteran to be forced out for Olympic park', *The Telegraph*, available at: http://www.telegraph.co.uk/news/uknews/1554771/Veteran-to-be-forced-out-for-Olympic-park.html (last accessed 27 July 2014).

London Development Agency (LDA) (2006) 'The London Development Agency (Lower Lea Valley, Olympic and Legacy) Compulsory Purchase Order 2005'. Report to the Secretary of State for Trade and Industry. Available at: http://www.gamesmonitor.org.uk/files/Inspectors%20recommendation%20to%20Secretary%20of%20State-3875798-1.pdf (last accessed 27 July 2014).

London Development Agency (LDA) (2008) 'Response to Mr. Julian Cheyne's request for Information / Freedom of Information Act 2000', FOI 291, 30 June, available at: www.gamesmonitor.org.uk/files/business relocation FOI response.pdf (last accessed 27 July 2014).

Mann, W. (2006) 'Bastard countryside: the mixed landscape of London's Lower Lea Valley', *Rising East Online*,5.

Minton, A. (2012) *Ground control – fear and happiness in the twenty-first-century city*. London: Penguin Books.

Muller, S. and Carr, C. (2009) 'Image politics and stagnation in the Ruhr Valley' in L. Porter and K. Shaw (Eds.), *Whose urban renaissance? An international comparison of urban regeneration strategies*. London: Routledge.

Porter, L. (2009) 'Planning displacement: the real legacy of major sporting events'. *Planning Theory & Practice*, 10(3): 395–399.

Poynter (1996) 'Manufacturing in East London' in T. Butler and M. Rustin (Eds.), *Rising in the east – the regeneration of East London*. London: Lawrence & Wishart.

Raco, M. and Tunney, E. (2010) 'Visibilities and invisibilities in urban development: small business communities and the London Olympics 2012'. *Urban Studies Journal*, 47(10): 2069–2091.

Shoard, M. (2002) 'Edgelands' in J. Jenkins (Ed.), *Remaking the landscape*, London: profile books, available at: http://www.marionshoard.co.uk/Documents/Articles/Environment/Edgelands-Remaking-the-Landscape.pdf (last accessed 27 July 2014).

Simone, A. (2007) 'At the frontier of the urban periphery' in M. Narula, S. Sengupta, J. Bagchi and R. Sundaram (Eds.), *Sarai reader 07: Frontiers*. Delhi: Center for the Study of

Developing Societies. Available at: http://archive.sarai.net/files/original/e3366451a06d9b-be4187fac6a550ec91.pdf (last accessed 27 July 2014).

UN-Habitat (2011) *Forced evictions – global crisis, global solutions*. Nairobi: United Nations Human Settlements Programme. Available at: http://mirror.unhabitat.org/pmss/listItemDetails.aspx?publicationID=3187 (last accessed 27 July 2014).

Ward Thompson, C. (2012) 'Places to be wild in nature' in A. Jorgensen and R. Keenan (Eds.), *Urban wildscapes*. London: Routledge.

Wood, B. (2004) 'Western European vacant land – an overview of its history, context and policy in the twentieth century' in R. Greenstein and Y. Sungu-Eryilmaz (Eds.), *Recycling the city: the use and reuse of urban land*. Cambridge: Lincoln Institute of Land Policy.

Woodward, C. (2012) 'Learning from Detroit or "the wrong kind of ruins"' in A. Jorgensen and R. Keenan (Eds.), *Urban wildscapes*. London: Routledge.

Yarham, I. and Archer, J. (1991) *Ecology handbook no. 17: nature conservation in Newham*. London: London Ecology Unit.

16 Paralympic branding

Iain MacRury

In the shadow of its illustrious elder sibling, but casting a distinctive light of its own, the Paralympics has become the second largest multisport event in the world.[1] This chapter examines interactions between Paralympic sports[2] and the organisation of related communications and representation of the Paralympics. This conjunction has been conceived of as the production of a Paralympic *brand*, with the work of the International Paralympic Committee[3] (IPC) now central to a focused orientation encompassing delivery, development and communications about disability sports. Components in the brand strategy include stabilising alignments with partners (e.g. the International Olympic Committee [IOC] and sponsors), aestheticisation, packaging the image, intelligibility and saliency of Paralympic sport (for commercial consumption and use), and tapping Paralympic heritage to authenticate the brand.

Branding the Paralympics involves an array of activities – first, building the brand itself, asserting the meanings and value of the Paralympics to attract interest and audiences; second, building commercial sponsorship partnerships in and through Paralympic sports to raise revenue; and third, more broadly, building awareness, communicating a suitable 'vision' of Paralympic sport and of disability, aiming to address prejudice, misconceptions and various forms of exclusion. The aim is changing attitudes and social practices related to disability.

The Paralympic brand, as it has developed, has become intimately entwined with the Olympics and so too with the Olympic governing body – the IOC. The Paralympics have not, however, become either fully adopted in or subsumed by the Olympic brand. It might seem natural that such collaborations should now be in place. The Olympics and Paralympics have operated side by side for decades. However, a historical view of the relations between the two organisations shows some turbulence and difficulty in the relationships (Howe, 2008; Brittain, 2013). This has sometimes been played out at the level of brand imagery – with rivalry and prohibition enforced around Olympic intellectual property, such as the five rings logo.

The Paralympics brand is tied necessarily, too, to showcase Paralympic events, most recently the Summer Paralympic Games in London 2012 and the Winter Paralympics in Sochi 2014.[4] The host city–based organisation committees of those Games, the respective Organising Committee of the Olympic Games (OCOGs), play a fundamental role for the Paralympics. There is typically, too, a promise in host cities that the Paralympic events stand as an opportunity to revitalise the urban fabric so that fuller recognition of the needs of disabled people is incorporated in new facilities and in 'legacy' regeneration schemes – transport and housing, for instance. The Paralympics provides a focus to the host city's claim: 'This is an accessible city' so that the Paralympics makes a contribution to the city brand. Paralympic branding, alongside a relationship with the IOC and its global activities, realises some of its aims within local branding, marketing activities and partnerships through the host city, including seeking to influence soft factors, attitudes and understanding about disability in the host nation.[5]

Paralympic mega-events and institutional relationships around them have developed within a short historical period, spanning back to the founding events, initially at Stoke Mandeville Hospital in 1948 (Brittain, 2013). The 1948 Games had 16 participants in an archery demonstration (Brittain, 2013). The innovative aim, led by Ludwig Guttman, was to use the sport to contribute in the postwar rehabilitation of this small group of servicemen in the spinal injuries unit. Its date was significant. The event coincided with the opening of the 1948 London Olympics. The pace of growth since 1948 is startling. At Rio 2016, it is expected that 4,350 Paralympians from more than 160 nations will take part in the competitions.

The articulation of ideas and focused practices associated with a Paralympic *brand*, as such, has emerged, primarily only since the 1990s. Paralympic logos, symbols and various efforts to ensure some commercial return through events had been made in earlier periods, as well as campaigns to raise consciousness and understanding regarding disability sports (Brittain, 2013; Frost 2013).[6] Such efforts, in keeping with the times and aims of the Paralympic movement in those times, were not foregrounded, nor systematic.

The IOC's TOP Scheme, which began in earnest after the 1992 Games in Barcelona (Payne, 2012), has not included the Paralympics directly. A prevailing factor in the period when TOP was becoming established and when the IPC was testing the 'marketability' of its own brand rested in the perception, articulated by former IPC head Bob Steadward, that 'we know that the severity of disability can be unsettling for some people, because it's a reminder, a reality check, of how fragile the human body is. Some companies, I'm sure, fear that image' (see Cole, 1999 cited in Howe, 2008:84). This was the period when, too, the IPC (founded in 1989) began to operate more actively in the commercial realm. Since the 2000 Sydney Games, the IPC has developed closer links with the IOC – including a series of lately renewed commitments for joint host cities for the respective Games. Paralympic brand marketing activities run alongside[7] the IOC's brand management programmes, cutting across broadcasting, media and advertising, marketing and merchandising activities.

The Paralympics and the Olympics

Branding advocates typically prefer to see branding expertise as encompassing more than just the 'surface' matter of logos. Nevertheless, the story of some of the symbolic branding imagery around the Olympic and Paralympic Games traces tensions – not only the creative tensions that have seen a culture foregrounding 'inclusion' and 'co-operation' but also conflicting relations indicating unease in the partnership. The 1980s are the pivotal decade in the story of the Paralympic brand.

The Moscow Games did not include a Paralympic event at all, with little interest in or understanding of the idea or value of disability sport evident in the Moscow organising committee[8] amounting to a deliberate exclusion of the idea of the Paralympics. The 1980 Paralympic Games took place in Antwerp.

In 1984, after Los Angeles emerged as the only credible city bidding to host the Games, the private sector–driven approach to Olympic hosting (MacRury, 2009) did not extend to supporting a Paralympic component in the event, so that in 1984 two rapidly organised events took place in two locations, one at Stoke Mandeville and the other in New York. These linked Games covered complementary arrays of sports to support the developing Paralympic roster of events.[9] These Games are notable for foregrounding an ethos of participative engagement (Howe, 2008).

An important moment came with the 1988 Seoul Games. After the former period of divergences, the Olympics and Paralympics once again took place in the same city. As Howe describes,

> The Seoul Paralympics of 1988 were a watershed in the history of the Paralympic Movement. For the first time, Paralympic athletes were given the opportunity to compete using the best sporting facilities that the world had to offer. These Games started the transformation from a participation-based model of sport for the disabled to the high-performance model that exists today.
>
> (2008:28)

However, despite some operational cooperation around the substantive activity of sports, in relation to the 'brand', an argument about 'logos' revealed emergent tensions between the Olympic and Paralympic brand owners.

The logo designed for the Paralympic Games used five 'tae-guks', a traditional Korea motif evoking a wheel in motion and capturing ideas about global connection across continents (Britain, 2013). As the logo became more widely used, the IOC turned the vigilance (see, e.g., Barney *et al.*, 2002) that it had periodically applied stringently to perceived abuses of Olympic brand imagery onto the IPC. The IOC noted similarities between its five rings and the new Paralympic logo. They offered an ultimatum to the IPC: change the logo or lose the patronage and partnership of the IOC (Mason, 2002, cited in Howe, 2008:31). The IPC logo was, reluctantly, changed.

These tensions have been resolved, at least on the surface (Purdue, 2013). Incrementally, through Sydney, Athens and Beijing Games, greater levels of cooperation have been evident. Fast-forward to London 2012 and a significant difference in approach is now in place. Full cooperation has been evident in terms of organisation and branding. The Olympics and the Paralympics are now seen as 'one' activity in many ways. A deliberate policy of integration was in place throughout bid and delivery phases (2003–2012). LOCOG went further than previous organising committees. Frost gives an upbeat 'insider' account:

Besides organising both Games with the same staff and resources, it also merged the logos and branding. The Olympic branding is the most heavily protected brand imaginable . . . To use the same logo outline shape for both the Olympic rings and the Paralympic Agitos was radical. Again, to discuss the International Paralympic Committee's dilemma, it undoubtedly gave them more profile than ever before. But it also reduced their distinctiveness as apart from the Olympics.

(2014:32–33)

The integrative work extended beyond the shared logo shape. The decision to name the 2012 Olympic and Paralympic mascots 'Wenlock' and 'Mandeville' asserted the co-partnership and equivalent value of respective Olympic and Paralympic heritages[10] – with the names referencing Britain's past contributions in the foundations of the Modern Olympics and the Paralympic movements. The 2012 Olympic and Paralympic Games demonstrated an unprecedented level of alignment in terms of both brand and operations. This included work with partner brands.

The Paralympics, nevertheless, remains as a distinct 'brand' not least because it maintains a separate logo, the Agitos, and asserts its own mission – 'To Enable Paralympic Athletes to Achieve Sporting Excellence and Inspire and Excite the World'. The IPC asserts its motto 'Spirit in Motion' (IPC, 2013c). The motto certainly echoes Coubertin and the language of olympism, but it does not replicate the IOC's *Citius-Altius-Fortius*.The Paralympics has its own partnership scheme, adjacent to TOP, with sponsors operating at global and international levels, as well as some individual associations at national level, sponsoring individual athletes, teams and national Olympic organisations and activities. Some TOP partners also sponsor the Paralympics. Some choose not to do so. Table 16.1 shows the tiered membership of the sponsors and partnership schemes for the Paralympic brand.

A further category of Paralympic sponsor includes those partners who work at a national level.[11] A notable instance in this group is the partnership between Sainsbury's and the London Paralympics. The IPC is not entitled to directly use or

Table 16.1 Paralympic partners 2014 (IPC, 2014)

Sponsor	Area of commercial activity and partnership
	Worldwide partners
Atos	IT specialists, also an Olympic partner
Ottobock	Company producing rehabilitation and mobility products
Samsung	Mobile telecom partner, also an Olympic partner
Visa	Payment systems partner – also an Olympic partner
	International partners
Allianz	Insurance and financial services partner
British Petroleum	International energy company (oil/gas)
DB Schenker	Logistics, freight and other travel/transport services

to confer usage rights of the IOC's brand or intellectual property assets – notably the famous five rings. As the terminology of Paralympics implies, the organisations operate both together and apart.[12]

In its contemporary formation and scale, the Paralympics has become a considerable brand presence. This is evident in the impact and seeming effect of the Paralympic brand enterprise, summarised most especially at London 2012 in some impressive accounts of reach and exposure.

Brand performance

The London 2012 Paralympic Games have actively sought to boost its TV ratings. TV remains a major underpinning in the value and impact of a brand as asset, taking part in a broadening marketing mix and within a techno-media ecology that continues to rapidly diversify brand communications in terms of new channels and new relations between brands and consumers. TV remains a major platform for sponsored partnership. In an era of global marketing, the Paralympic broadcasters' reach into more than 115 countries and territories, coupled with its delivering the largest ever international audience for the Paralympic Games, provides an important basis for pitches to new and continuing sponsors. This will further the IPC commercial-mission aim: 'to ensure the means necessary to support future growth of the Paralympic Movement' (IPC, 2010:13).

The IPC outlines it brand's capacity to garner and focus exposure, for its mission and for the promotional missions of sponsors. The IPC commissioned research, reported in its annual report (IPC, 2013a:15) after 2012 to capture impact and reach, highlighting major growth; including a cumulative international audience of 3.4 billion watching the Paralympic Games. It is an increase of almost one billion when compared with the figure achieved for the Beijing 2008 Games. As a result of more countries showing the Games, the number of hours of broadcast outside the UK grew by 82 per cent when compared with the 2008 Beijing Paralympics.

The IPC (2013a:27–30) also notes success in new and nontraditional media channels. On top of TV growth, a further 9.9 million video views were recorded on the IPC's YouTube channel – as the brand goes 'multi-platform'. Nearly two million people visited www.paralympic.org during the Paralympic Games. In 2012, social media were established as a mainstream element in Olympic and Paralympic experience; for instance, there were 82.1 million views of the IPC's Facebook pages. In December 2012, a world-wide report by Twitter[13] indicated that #paralympics topped the table for the most trending UK sport event of 2012, with rates higher than #olympics and other sports brands. A major part of the effort to establish the power of the Paralympic brand is by highlighting press commitments. A total of 1,950 written press, photographers and non-rights holders attended the Games from 818 different media organisations[14] with a strong mix of both UK-based and international press. These figures give an alternate picture from the account given of a prior Games (Golden, 2003). This indicates a significant step change in the brand's pull – with newsworthiness a major plank in the effort to establish the Paralympic brand as a channel for use by sponsors and partners. This focused packaging of the brand-as-channel has led to increased interest and engagement with the Paralympics. *The Paralympian*, the IPC's magazine, increased its online readership in 2012 by 550 per cent during the year. The IPC identified a massive shift with 20 million recognising the logo after the Games, up from half a million (IPC, 2013a:15, 27–30). The figures partly represent a 'blip' based on the 2012 Games. However, as anthropologist David Howe (2008, 2013) observed, based on a long-standing and intimate engagement with the Paralympics, there has been a real change:

> One of the things that amazed me is how the British media has now embraced Paralympic sport. Just over 20 years ago at the 1992 Barcelona Paralympic games the BBC televised only a few live events on *Grandstand* . . . At London 2012 I expected the spotlight to be much more intense, since every passing Paralympic there has been an increased media presence – and I was not disappointed.
>
> (2013:130)

Positive accounts of the Sochi Paralympics focus on the increased interest from the US audience in the Paralympics. NBC, which does not have a strong record of broadcasting the Paralympics (while being the leading Olympic broadcaster in the crucial-to-sponsors US market), has now become more interested. Head of IPC Sir Phillip Craven picked out NBC's coverage for comment: 'Having received criticism for their lack of London 2012 coverage, NBC, NBC Sports Network, and the USOC teamed up to ensure there would be no repeat in Sochi' (IPC, 2013b). The Sochi 2014 Paralympic Winter Games were 'the most watched in history' with a global audience of over two billion people (IPC, 2013b).

There is a reciprocal relationship between, on the one hand, the growth of the media platform for Paralympic sport, the multiplication of channels, the expansion of audiences and the increasing number of 'territories' reached and, on the other, the growing power or 'equity' in the Paralympic brand. Whether or not the Paralympics is classified as a sideshow (Gilbert and Schantz, 2008), in media terms, it can now claim to represent a 'big tent' of its own, a developed platform for the brand to thrive. This is a big draw. Mega platforms for brands are sought after in the global media market for sponsors. The fragmentation and multiplication of main media (press and TV in particular) means that the ambition to reach large national and global audiences rests on a limited number of big-hit events. Sports are the major instances of what can be called 'global-water cooler media'. The Paralympics brand's capacity to play in this market is a big achievement in marketing terms.

Heritage: authenticating the brand

In August 2013, almost a year after the London 2012 Paralympics closed, the IPC announced that it would involve UK in all future Paralympic Games Torch Relays. This gesture affirms a foundational role for the UK, similar to the one that has been given to Greece by the IOC for the Summer Olympics, where a flame is lit at Olympus. Now, for the Paralympic Games, the connection between its origins and Stoke Mandeville in 1948 is affirmed, not just via the ephemeral logo 'Mandeville' but through a regular, instituted celebration.

In the UK, National Paralympic Day was staged on 7 September 2013 in Queen Elizabeth Olympic Park. There is an intention to establish this day as a permanent feature of the national sporting calendar. These moves affirm heritage; they build a story. In future, they will support production of (brand-rich) narrative, news and coverage in advance of future Paralympic Games.

In imagination, future torch relays will join up present and a past – authenticating the next iteration of the Paralympic events – and here, in the UK, an annual reminder of London 2012 and of Stoke Mandeville 1948. This will serve the 'memorial' aspect of legacy. Such activities are, in many ways, good history. But the work of authentication is primarily also excellent branding. Indeed, this story-making work is but one of many instances where the IPC is actively and assertively clarifying and articulating Paralympic assets, extending a process that has been underway in earnest for at least two decades. There remains in this a political dimension, at least in potential terms. Embedded in the heritage of Paralympian activity lies occasion to annually open debate about the history of disability, including its contemporary history – this might include aspects of a critical counternarrative – testing the Paralympic 'legacy' beyond mere commemoration.

Aestheticisation: from sports to sports brand

The IPC's brand strategy amounts to a deliberate effort at 'packaging' the Paralympics in formats conducive to the brand mission. On the sports side, this has included detailed work reviewing the complex classification systems across sports whereby athletes are placed in categories to reflect the degrees and kinds of impairments in order to produce a relatively level playing field, to ensure competitiveness and to manage the programme in terms of inclusivity. This also impacts the viability of some events. This work has had some significant impact on the substantive constitution of the Paralympic Games (see Howe, 2013, 2008; Purdue and Howe, 2013 for detailed discussion) and their ethos over the past decades. The classification system amounts to a form of packaging and encompasses the Games as a framing regulatory regime. Classification concretely impinges on the sport and underpins more superficial branding activity, notably around the aesthetics and presentation of the disabled sports, seeking to make Paralympic sport telegenic and intelligible to the casual audience.

2012 saw a parallel and extensive creative endeavour: aestheticisation. An indicative instance is represented by Richard Booth's (Booth and Beckerman, 2011) photographic anthology titled *Power and Movement: Portraits of Britain's Paralympic Athletes*. This is an impressive collection. It consists of artful photographs capturing individual sportsmen and women in moments of action and contemplation. The subject is 'sport' – Paralympic sport in particular. However, the style is not the style of sports photography. The pictures of the Paralympic athletes deploy the conventions of portraiture photography and 'commercial realism' (Goffman, 1979). The framing highlights the athleticism and high-performance nature of Paralympic sport. Motion blur and moody black-and-white photography underpin an aesthetic intervention in the creation of the Paralympian and the idea of Paralympic sport. The collection, commissioned by LOCOG, is produced in high-quality coffee-table format. It provides a specialist contribution to the formation of the Paralympic brand – a showcase of the inspiration and marketability of the Paralympian embedded in an authentic celebration of talent and commitment. It represents an heroic set of imagery.

This is in line with the notion of the Paralympian as exemplar athlete. Within the framing (Goffman, 1979), athletic power and the prowess of the athletes are accentuated. It is an invitation to look again, to reframe disability. The nature and origin of disability and the idea of disabled athletes participating or involved in any kind of rehabilitation or in need of social adjustment or accommodation is confidently sidelined in favour of compositions underlining and affirming an aesthetic that captures not only the important truth, i.e. the performative excellence of the Paralympic athletes, but which also thereby valorises a certain subjectivity – triumphant, achieving, winning.

Booth explains: 'for the camera, I decided I wanted to show every nuance of the athlete in motion. This led me to use the same equipment that I use for my advertising imagery, as it gave me the control I needed' (Booth and Beckerman, 2011:11–12). The framing text amplifies the imagery. The words echo the pictorial focus on athlete qua athlete. Evident, too, is the background language of Olympism, but melded with a motivational discourse connected to LOCOG's commitment to the idea of 'inspiration'. The images have dynamic titles: 'Queen of speed, . . . , Winning wheels, . . . , New horizons, . . ., True grit, . . . , poetry in motion, . . . keeping in balance, . . . driven to win, . . . a force for the future' (2011:11–12).

The aim to control Paralympic imagery within the frame of a specific commercial-aesthetic-vision and ethos extends to more general guidance. From the IPC's instructions to brand partners and media photographers in its brand-style guidance, it is clear that quite specific framing is required:

- In all photographs the athlete should be the central focus, not his or her impairment.
- The athlete's impairment should not be concealed but demonstrated in a self-confident and self-evident manner.
- Genders, nationalities, sports and disabilities groups etc. should always be treated equally.
- The photos we use are physical and triumphant, dynamic, and international.

(IPC, 2013c:18)

This phototrophic anthology and the aesthetic and representational style performed and instituted under the brand head successfully provide the cultural correlate of, the concrete expression of, a mission ongoing within the IPC, one described as a restructuring from a disability and medical model to sports-based competition (Legg and Steadward, 2011). This is the vision of achievement sport framed for a commercial aesthetic.

Meet the Superhumans

This aesthetic is given prominence in a highly significant further intervention. Channel 4's 90-second-long film *Meet the Superhumans* was greeted as a commercial and critical success. The film headlined Channel 4's media partnership with the Paralympics, a 'trailer' prom for the coverage of the Paralympic Games, and building on a series of interventions from the broadcaster[15] and including the Freaks of Nature marketing trail.

> The Freaks of Nature marketing trail is part of a bold campaign that portrays Paralympians as Channel 4 feels they should be seen – supremely talented athletes who, like their able bodied sporting counterparts, are set apart from the rest of us by their staggering ability, not their disability. And this reflects our ambitions for our coverage of the London 2012 Paralympic Games themselves – encouraging viewers to focus on the awe-inspiring ability on display throughout.
>
> (Davies, 2010)

Channel 4 acting for the first time as the main Paralympic broadcaster having taken this from the BBC was a major commitment that the channel needed to succeed. It did. It was a good partnership serving to reaffirm Channel 4's public service remit, while also providing an opportunity to remind audience of its commitments to creative and challenging broadcasting. The promo served a commercial purpose too. Channel 4 needed its broadcast schedule to be attractive and exciting – and it attracted record audiences. Finally, too, it served the Paralympics, offering a vehicle to state and restate an arresting new vision of Paralympic sport – and disability. The high impact and affectively rich short film in its conception and execution comes straight from the toolbox of contemporary televisual advertising. Moody imagery and a hard-hitting soundtrack underline the visceral competitiveness and commitment of Paralympic sport – interspersed with hints at the backstories that led to some of the athletes' disabilities – eschewing sentimentality in favour of affective charge. The main proposition: These athletes are 'superhuman'.

The combination of violent physicality and the affective-emotional mix hinted at in stories of loss and overcoming written into the montage narrative produces an arresting set of moments on screen. The claim that the promotional film would raise a few 'goose bumps' (Beattie 212) is not casually made. The ad-promo would garner attention and change minds. *Meet the Superhumans* was a successful and deliberate attempt to move disability sport from a discourse of sentiment (and sentimentality) to one where affective engagement was more forcefully framed: physical, visceral and challenging – as well as inspiring and uplifting. As such, the ad stands up well. It is an excellent piece of marketing and, no doubt, stood as a major contribution in and platform for both Channel 4's coverage and the broader experience of the Paralympic brand in 2012.

This film has subsequently won significant awards and is recalled as a contributing factor in the success of the Paralympics 2012, setting the tome for the reception of the event – contributing, and even driving wide appeal, to underlying audience engagement, memorability and recorded public attitude changes in the period.[16] Nevertheless, some critical analysis has questioned the broad strategy and execution of 'superhuman' or 'supercrip' discourses. As Silva and Howe (2012) set down:

> The attempt to cover the Paralympic Games in the same manner as Olympics by Channel 4, portraying athletes as 'Freaks of Nature', may ultimately undermine the intention of equal treatment because it triggers and reinforces representations of disability as freakery and Otherness.

At stake is the extent to which the assertion of the Paralympian as in some sense transcending his or her disability through high-performance sport. This is especially the case if and as the predominant coverage of disability issues takes place within the frames and times afforded by coverage foregrounding elite sport.

> Supercrip narratives can be considered to be an expression of society's low-level expectation placed upon people with disability, which ultimately perpetuates the understanding of their existence as a 'problem.'
>
> (Silva and Howe, 2012)

Furthermore,

> In presenting disability as 'nothing but' a problem, these narratives limit the possibilities of living with impairment in any other way.
>
> (Silva and Howe, 2012)

There is a risk that in relegating former paradigms (rehabilitation-sport and social-participative sports), placing sociality and disabled embodiment out of the frame, perceptions and conceptions of disability might become preoccupied with a vision of disability that places it outside the frames of ordinary human experience, as well as ordinary social planning, societal engagement, thinking and proper accommodations.

Brand partnerships: Sainsbury's and Atos

The arresting imagery of the Paralympian-in-action certainly served to engage interest. It supported significant successes for brand partners. One main aim following the establishment of the Paralympics-as-brand is to work with partner sponsors. Sainsbury's has made much of the work it has done in activating their relationship with the Paralympics. The retailer's success was partly connected to the standout nature of their relationship, specifically their decision to focus solely on the Paralympics rather than on the Olympics as a whole.

Sainsbury's talk positively about their values-based commitments but they underline that they bring sustainable commercial advantage as well as great pride. The Corporate Social Responsibility (CSR) orientation is exemplified by CEO Justin King in the annual report to shareholders.

> we aimed to be much more than a sponsor and to play our part in ensuring the success of the Games, as well as creating a lasting legacy. Our legacy programme has already contributed £2 million of funding for schools, clubs, and organisations to ensure that the next generation of Paralympic athletes get the support and coaching they need.
>
> (Sainsbury Plc, 2013:5)

One measure of brand marketing success found that Sainsbury's was ranked among the best remembered sponsors out of all the Olympic sponsors at London 2012, including TOP partners from the Olympics and also many partnerships that had spread across Olympic and Paralympic events.

> Sainsbury's finished 2012 as the third most recalled Olympic sponsor, ahead of all domestic sponsors, and ahead of 16 other brands who had sponsored the Olympics and Paralympics . . .
>
> (Marketing Society Awards, 2013:21)

It would be a mistake, however, to propose (even in purely commercial or CSR terms) that sponsoring the Paralympics has been an unmitigated success for all partners.

The superhuman paradox: a polarising discourse of disability

Atos are IT specialists and also a TOP Olympic partner. They sought to extend their TOP relationship to include the Paralympics. Controversy erupted during the Paralympic Games as it became clear that Atos were majorly involved in multimillion-pound contracts delivering 'Work Capability Assessments', controlled on behalf of the UK Department for Work and Pensions, in a period where UK government policy has been intent on cutting social benefits and support, including for people declared unable to work due to illness or disability.

Many of these Atos-run assessments directly affected disabled people. Large numbers lost benefit entitlements and were declared 'fit for work' often, as protests underlined, despite their serious, long-standing disabilities and health conditions. This led to demonstrations before, during and after the Games. It led to some dissent and debate from athletes around the opening ceremony (Taylor, 2012). Talk of boycotts and continuing critique of the association indicate the sponsorship links did not have the desired marketing effect.

When, in 2014, Atos announced early withdrawal from its government con-tract to deliver health assessments, Richard Hawkes, CEO of a disability charity Scope, said: 'I doubt there's a single disabled person who'll be sorry to hear that Atos will no longer be running the fit-for-work tests' (BBC, 2014).

The Atos story articulates a 'gap' in public conceptions of disability, between the Paralympic-branded version of disability and some of the concrete-material everyday versions and experiences of disability. As with the 'Para-' and 'super' narratives that place disability somehow 'outside or on the edge' of human experi-ence, there is a risk that discourses, perceptions and practices become bifurcated between real and ideal visions. Disablement becomes 'split', thinking becomes polarised; fixation on the ideal stands as an alibi for ignorance or negligence in relation to important realities. The Atos sponsorship situation exposed a deeply problematic instance of what happens when that bifurcation and polarisation illustrate a contradiction in the real organisation of social life.

A further critical assessment of Paralympic sponsorship taken from the point of view of the sponsored athletes highlights both the volatility of the sponsorship 'mar-ket' for individuals and also the emphasis on performance and 'medal' count in relation to government support. The paradigm of achievement looms large in marketing and promotion-driven models of sport – and in various ways jeopardises the contribution sport can make in terms of rehabilitation and participation.These discourses become secondary or occluded. Reynolds (2013) writing for marketing magazine *The Drum* notes the practical consequence of scare and achievement-oriented sponsorship:

> 2012 gave birth to so many Paralympic stars that sponsoring them all is impos-sible, so they are forced to cherry pick. BMW, for example, has continued to sponsor a handful of athletes but its sponsorship of the majority has ended, as it has been replaced by Nissan as the official car partner in the run-up to Rio.

A double blow falls for those whose achievements seem unable to attract long-term sponsorship interest and in the context of performance-based application of medal count metrics. This leads to the cutting of individual funding or sometimes funding for whole sports categories. For those outside of the star firmament, par-ticularly in those sports which suffered a big cut in UK sport funding after the Paralympics, such as sitting volleyball (£800,000 cut to zero), they will simply have to work day jobs or get family support if they want to carry on playing (Reynolds, 2013).

Critique: inclusion and occlusion

A marketing logic has become infused in the logics and values of Paralympism. This marketing logic has amplified and been amplified in the reconstruction of Paralym-pic sport as 'achievement' sport (Bale, 2004), sport that emphasises performance, winning and records (within a tight disciplinary regime) over other forms of engage-ment. This is the type of sport that seems to be most readily 'branded'. Achieve-ment (and its ritualisation) is a necessary part of sports' cultural contribution. It is an insufficient frame for thinking about sport-as-a-whole and Paralympics in particular.

Achievement-oriented sport should not become a metonymic displacement for the broader contribution that sport can and does make in human experience, as a whole, including for disabled people.

The relations between ends and means have changed for Paralympism throughout its history, often reflecting progressive thinking about disability – moving away from a medical model (focusing on the impairment not the person) or a model that risked foregrounding dependence (and so undervaluing individual agency and initiative) – the social model. These prior reframings have been realised in terms of phases that identify orientation towards, initially, Paralympic sport as a means towards rehabilitation – linked to a 'medical model' of disability originating with Guttman himself and the first 1948 Paralympics. Then, and as the Paralympics developed in scale and in global reach, in the 1960s and 1970s and as cultural shifts underlined a wider perspective on disability (outside the individual and beyond the disability), a social model of disability produced a paradigm in which the Paralympics became a means towards participation – with disability sport an important component in the wider discourse of 'sport for all', and with 'taking part' standing as a major end, an end that placed the Paralympics as a social 'good in itself'. This echoed with some of the heritage of Olympism and the notion of sport as a social good (as well as a human right), those elements of the philosophy captured in phraseology, such as this attributed to Coubertin – 'The most important thing in the Olympic Games is not winning but taking part; the essential thing in life is not conquering but fighting well'. Conversely, contemporary Paralympic sport has increasingly followed the paradigm shift affecting all sports, to become part of what Bale (2004) has called achievement sport, amplified in and amplifying a hyperpromotional tone.

Beyond achievement

The *Meet the Superhumans* campaign and the broader perception that the Paralympics risks, at times, aestheticising and euphemising experiences of disability have prompted some satirical responses, notably from performance artist Katherine Araniello whose YouTube video piece deliberately echoes the clichéd language of some media coverage of disabled sports.

> *Thank you so much*
>
> *I couldn't have done it without you*
>
> *I never knew someone like me*
>
> *Could be of such sporting excellence . . .*
>
> *Get down to your local sport centre*
>
> *And get involved with sport*
>
> *It's the only thing there is*
>
> *For people like us . . .*

(Araniello, 2012)

This satirical piece, part of a programme of performance art that challenges some of the feel-good narration that seeks to celebrate 'triumph over adversity', under-scores an observation made by Wendy Seymour (1998) who has produced some important work on disability and embodiment. While paralysed people may find inspiration in the sporting feats of other people with disabilities, the 'trickle-down' effect may be less than imagined (Hindson, Gidlow and Peebles, 1994), and few able-bodied people would aspire to being in such a position (Seymour, 1998:124).

The development of the Paralympic brand is regularly presented in a manner that is not far short of triumphant. There have been evidence-based successes in relation to some of the high-level indices selected to demonstrate shifts in percep-tion, attitudes and understanding of disability sport, and of the experiences of disabled people. The Paralympic brand's exposure invites a question. Why is it that the public contemplation of, engagement with and understanding of disability seems to need to happen more often than not within the framings that sport can afford, and within the framing of a sports brand heftily inflected by the aesthetics and values of 'achievement sport'. There is a risk that the Paralympic limelight – for all its brightness – occludes a more comprehensive vision of disability. It produces blind spots.

As Rio approaches, the movement towards a further focus on performance-based celebrity-oriented achievement sports (at the expense of other Paralympic missions) seems set to continue. Marquez *et al.* (2013:583) describe 'increasing professionalisation' and 'directions proposed by the media' as a precursor to an approach whereby 'high performance sport might be improved, showing its ability to create idols, produce pleasurable emotions and attract interest of consumers'. This is the model of a promotional brand. But it risks the production of the disabled body for others rather than body for self (Seymour, 1998), suggesting a narrative of commodification and performance that can impinge upon broader understanding, apprehension and experiences of disability and sport. These will occlude other narratives around disability, including those entailed to previous models of 'social-participative' and 'rehabilitative' sports.

The Paralympic brand has spearheaded recent strategy on the part of the IPC. Since the 1990s, the IPC has worked, increasingly deliberately to marshal the attention, the popularity and the distinctive affective power of the Paralympic event in what has amounted to a radical reformation of Paralympic sport. The aims of this reformation have been, in part at least, to better ensure that the Para-lympics 'package' more fully aligns with the demands placed on global cultural and sporting brands – brands deployed as platforms for sponsorship, marketing and for the garnering of global attention.

The development of the Paralympic brand cannot be seen in isolation from the adjacent and longer standing work of branding the Olympics, nor from the more widespread reconception of numerous organisational, marketing and communica-tions activities within the framework of brand management, a way of doing things that has come to heavily inflect or even take over as the practical default orienta-tion for both commercial and (formally and formerly) noncommercial entities.

Branded profile, performance, achievement and success are sometimes bought at the cost of other forms of connection, of complexity and meaningful social engagement in and through disability sport. The Paralympics needs to fight to preserve those aspects of its history and mission as it strives to compete in the global branding arena.

Notes

1 A record 4,237 athletes from 164 countries took part in London 2012 (IPC, 2013a).
2 Paralympic sports developed either as adaptations of an equivalent able-bodied sport or as one with no able-bodied equivalent devised to accommodate the impairment type (Webborn and Van de Vliet, 2012:65–71).
3 The IPC was founded in 1989. It operates across multiple sports and brings together the various single-disabled sports organisations.
4 The IPC has involvement in other events, notably the Commonwealth Games.
5 Considerable effort is meant to find high-level indices of this brand impact, notably, with reference to the UK in the DCMS-commissioned meta-evaluation, which includes a corpus linguistics–based assessment of positive linguistic traces of attitude change (DCMS, 2013). ONS Opinions and Lifestyle Survey has produced a series of recent assessments (ONS, 2014) as have third-sector bodies. Attitudes to disability are traced, too, in the IOC's Olympic Games Impact study produced for each Olympic and Paralympic Games.
6 Frost (2013) discusses Paralympic imagery in Tokyo 1964 in relation to establishing a social understanding of disability.
7 The 'Para-' prefix on Paralympics formerly referred to Paralplegia. It now accentuates the relationship with the Olympics: the word 'Paralympic' derives from the Greek preposition 'para' (beside or alongside) and the word 'Olympic'. Its meaning is that Paralympics are the parallel Games to the Olympics and illustrates how the two movements exist side by side (IPC, 2014).
8 Sochi hosted the Paralympics in 2014 although some further infringements of Olympic commitments to inclusion and diversity were widely reported, notably around questions of sexuality.
9 Initial arrangements for a Paralympic Games to take place at University of Illinois, Chicago, had collapsed due to financial difficulties (Brittain, 2013).
10 Butler and Bissel (2013) nevertheless find – within the intention to give prominent representation to disability – some cause for speculation about the successful execution of the film, specifically claiming that Mandeville's disability is not consistently represented positively.
11 The current national-level sponsors of the British Paralympic association are Adidas, British Petroleum, BT, Deloitte, EDF Energy, Hogan Lovells, Mondelez, Nissan and Sainsbury's.
12 The complex relations between IOC and the Paralympics frame many discussions, including in the title of a significant collection of essays which asks whether Paralympics represent empowerment for athletes or stand as a 'sideshow' (Gilbert and Schantz, 2008).
13 The report can be found at: https://2012.twitter.com/en-gb/trends.html
14 Representing a drop of 150 media on the number that attended Beijing in 2008.
15 This included the documentary series *Inside Incredible Athletes*.
16 ONS (2014) as well as the D&AD (2013) and Marketing Society Awards (2013) provide case studies or data. All signal a successful intervention in terms of high-level attitudinal change – framed in marketing terms.

250   *Iain MacRury*

References

44444

Araniello, K. (2012) 'Meet the Superhumans'(Part 2)', available at: https://www.youtube.com/watch?v=kiEF2VfR2Ok (last accessed 5 May 2014).

Bale, J. (2004) *Running cultures: racing in time and space.* New York: Frank Cass.

Barney, R. K., Wenn, S. and Martyn, S. (2002) *Selling the five rings: the International Olympic Committee and the rise of Olympic commercialism.* Salt Lake City: University of Utah Press.

BBC (2014) 'Fit-to-work tests: Atos contract to end', available at: http://www.bbc.co.uk/news/uk-26766345 (last accessed 5 April 2014).

Booth, R. and Beckerman, D. (2011) *Power and movement: portraits of Britain's Paralympic athletes.* Chichester: Wiley.

Brittain, I. (2013) *From Stoke Mandeville to Sochi: a history of the summer and winter Paralympic Games.* Champaign, IL: Common Ground.

Butler, S. and Bissell, K. (2013) 'The best I can be: framing disability through the Mascots of the 2012 Summer Olympics and Paralympics'. *Communication & Sport,* doi: 10.1177/2167479513500137

Cole, C. (1999, August 28) 'Faster, higher poorer', *National Post.*

D&AD (2013) 'Meet the Superhumans: D&AD case study', available at: http://www.dandad.org/en/meet-superhumans/ (last accessed 5 May 2014).

Davies, G. (2010, August 10) 'London 2012 Paralympics: Channel 4 makes disability sport its main event', *Telegraph,* available at: http://www.telegraph.co.uk/sport/olympics/7934650/London-2012-Paralympics-Channel-4-makes-disability-sport-its-main-event.html?mobile=basic (accessed 11 April 2015).

Department for Culture, Media & Sport (DCMS) (2013) *Report 5: post-Games evaluation: meta-evaluation of the impacts and legacy of the London 2012.* London: DCMS.

Frost, D. J. (2013) 'Sporting disability: official representations of the disabled athlete at Tokyo's 1964 Paralympics'. *Asia Pacific Journal of Sport and Social Science,* 2(3): 1–14.

Frost, S. (2014) *The inclusion imperative: how real inclusion creates better business and builds better societies.* London: Kogan Page.

Gilbert, K. P. and Schantz, O. (2008) *The Paralympic Games: empowerment or side show?* Maidenhead: Meyer & Meyer.

Goffman, E. (1979) *Gender advertisements.* New York: Harper & Row.

Golden, A.V. (2003) 'An analysis of the dissimilar coverage of the 2002 Olympics and Paralympics: frenzied pack journalism versus the empty press room'. *Disability Studies Quarterly,* 23(3/4), available at: http://www.dsq-sds.org/article/view/437/614 (last accessed 8 October 2013).

Hindson, A., Gidlow, B. and Peebles, C. (1994) 'The trickle down effect of top level sport: myth or reality? A case-study of the Olympics'. *Australian Journal of Leisure and Recreation,* 4(1): 16–24.

Howe, P. D. (2008) *The cultural politics of the paralympic movement: through an anthropological lens.* London: Routledge.

Howe, P. D. (2013) 'Supercrips, cyborgs and the unreal Paralympian' in M. Perryman (Ed.), *London 2012: how was it for us?* London: Lawrence & Wishart.

IPC (2010) 'Forword' by Sir Philip Craven, *Paralympic Administration Manual. Module 1: Paralympic movement,* p. 1.3. Available at: http://www.paralympic.org/sites/default/files/document/131125102258870_ipc-administration-manual-section1.pdf (last accessed 12 April 2015).

IPC (2013a) *International Paralympic Committee Annual Report 2012.* Bonn: IPC. Available at: http://www.paralympic.org/sites/default/files/document/130710121410906_web_ipc_13_annualreport_2012_final.pdf (last accessed 11 April 2015).

IPC (2013b) 'Paralympics watched by over two billion viewers', available at: http://www.paralympic.org/news/sochi-2014-paralympics-watched-over-two-billion-viewers (last accessed 11 April 2015).

IPC (2013c) *IPC style guide*. Bonn: IPC. Available at: http://www.paralympic.org/sites/default/files/document/130507184600562_ipc+style+guide.pdf (last accessed 11 April 2015).

Legg, D. and Steadward, R. (2011) 'The Paralympic Games and 60 years of change (1948–2008): unification and restructuring from a disability and medical model to sport-based competition'. *Sport in Society: Cultures, Commerce, Media, Politics*, 14(9): 1099–1115.

MacRury, I. (2009) 'Branding the Games: commercialism and the Olympic city' in G. Poynter and I. MacRury (Eds.), *Olympic cities: 2012 and the remaking of London*. London: Ashgate.

Marques, R. F. R., Gutierrez, G. L. Almeida, M. A. B. D. and Menezes, R. P. (2013) 'Media and Brazilian Paralympic movement: relationships under Brazilian Paralympic Committee manager's perception'. *Revista Brasileira de Educação Física e Esporte*, 27(4): 583–596.

Mason, F. (2002) 'Creating image and gaining control: the development of the cooperation agreements between the International Olympic Committee and the International Paralympic Committee' in K. B. Wamsley, R. K. Barney and S. G. Martyn (Eds.), *The global nexus engaged: past, present, future interdisciplinary Olympic studies: Sixth International Symposium for Olympic Research*. London: International Centre for Olympic Studies, University of Western Ontario.

ONS (2014) 'Paralympic data from the ONS Opinions and Lifestyle Survey'. Department for Work and Pensions, available at: https://www.gov.uk/government/uploads/system/uploads/attachment_data/file/326220/opinions-survey-ad-hoc-paralympic-statistics-release-july-2014.pdf

Payne, M. (2012) *Olympic turn around*. Oxford: Infinite Ideas.

Purdue, D. E. (2013) 'An (in)convenient truce? Paralympic stakeholders' reflections on the Olympic–Paralympic relationship'. *Journal of Sport & Social Issues*, 37(4): 384–402.

Purdue, D. E. and Howe, P. D. (2013) 'Who's in and who is out? Legitimate bodies within the Paralympic Games'. *Sociology of Sport Journal*, 30(1): 24–40.

Reynolds, J. (2013) 'Where did the sponsors go? For some Paralympians, it seems London 2012 never happened, the drum', available at: http://www.thedrum.com/opinion/2013/09/20/where-did-sponsors-go-some-paralympians-it-seems-london-2012-never-happened (last accessed 5 January 2014).

Sainsburys Plc. (2013) 'Annual report and financial statements 2013'.

Seymour, W. (Ed.) (1998) *Remaking the body: rehabilitation and change*. Sydney: Allen & Unwin.

Silva, C. F. and Howe, P. D. (2012) 'The (in)validity of supercrip representation of Paralympian athletes'. *Journal of Sport & Social Issues*, 36: 174–194.

Taylor, J. (2012) 'Hundreds protest against Paralympics sponsor Atos as anger about its role in slashing benefits bill intensifies', available at: http://www.independent.co.uk/news/uk/home-news/hundreds-protest-against-paralympics-sponsor-atos-as-anger-about-its-role-in-slashing-benefits-bill-intensifies-8092512.html (last accessed 5 May 2014).

Webborn, N. and Van de Vliet, P. (2012) 'Paralympic medicine'. *The Lancet*, 380(9836): 65–71.

Part V

Cultural legacies of London 2012

17 Placing culture at the heart of the Games

Achievements and challenges within the London 2012 Cultural Olympiad

Beatriz Garcia

Introduction

Putting 'culture at the heart of the Games' was one of the central promises of the cultural chapter within London 2012's Olympic Candidature Files and remained a distinct aspiration of the Games' official cultural programme, including the 4-year Cultural Olympiad (CO) culminating in a 12-week London 2012 Festival in 2012. In London, 'placing culture at the heart' signified placing *the arts and creative industries* at the centre of the Games-hosting process, and thus, throughout this chapter, the reference to 'culture' is meant in that sense.

While many other host cities have aspired to achieve a synergies between culture, sport and education, success in this area has eluded most Games editions (Garcia, 2012a). Ongoing challenges with branding and marketing regulations, budget limitations and the publicity priorities of core Games stakeholders all frustrate achievement in this aspect of the hosting process, making culture – understood as arts and creative practices – one of the most difficult things to get right within an Olympic and Paralympic programme. This chapter explores London's claim to have fulfilled this vision while also indicating the challenges the host city's stakeholders faced to make it a reality. The chapter focuses on three main questions:

1 How was the aspiration to place culture at the heart of the games defined?
2 How was it delivered?
3 Did the UK cultural sector value the existence of a Games cultural programme?

The findings presented are informed by over a decade of research into the cultural policy dimensions of the Olympic Movement (see Garcia, 2008, 2011, 2012a, 2012b, 2014) as well as the first nation-wide evaluation of an Olympic cultural programme commissioned by an Olympic Organising Committee for the Games – the 2-year *London 2012 Cultural Olympiad Evaluation* (Garcia, 2013a). Findings derive from the analysis of official documentation produced by the London 2012 Culture Team; final summaries and recommendations presented by the London Organising Committee for the Olympic and Paralympic Games (LOCOG) as part of its Olympic Transfer of Knowledge programme (LOCOG, 2012a, 2012b) and the London 2012 debrief to the International Olympic Committee (IOC) and future Games hosts (IOC, 2012a). Finally, they build on the analysis of key stakeholder interviews, public and audience surveys produced for LOCOG, a survey of all CO projects conducted by the Institute of Cultural Capital (ICC) and DHA and 16 case studies (Garcia, 2013b).

Definition: original vision and core values

Opinions vary over the most effective approach to position arts activity more centrally within the Games-hosting process. The London 2012 CO explored multiple angles simultaneously by firstly developing a 4-year lead-up programme using an 'open source' approach to programming which involved many grassroots organisations beyond the arts world and, secondly, crowning the Olympiad with a 12-week London 2012 Festival focused on artistic excellence and 'world-class' acts (LOCOG, 2012a). The former was aimed at empowering communities, broadening the opportunities for direct involvement and a sense of shared ownership over the programme; the latter focused on creating distinct messages attractive to arts peers, the national and international media and audiences beyond immediate communities of interest.

In order to facilitate a thematic coherence between a broad CO involving multiple ownership of programming and a single curated London 2012 Festival, the LOCOG culture team committed to a series of core narrative angles or values. These evolved from the London 2012 Candidature File culture chapter (London 2012, 2004) into the original CO vision (LOCOG, 2007) and the final main objectives of the London 2012 Festival (LOCOG, 2012a). These narrative angles emphasised:

- engaging young people as artists, producers and audiences;
- raising the profile of Deaf and disabled artists and providing more opportunities to showcase their work;
- inspiring and involving the widest and most inclusive range of UK communities, reaching every region in the UK;
- showcasing the UK as world leading hub of creativity and creative industries, helping to develop cultural tourism;
- celebrating London and the whole of the UK welcoming the world – its unique internationalism, cultural diversity, sharing and understanding;
- creating opportunities for large-scale and active participation.

According to the LOCOG communications team, the emphasis on inclusion and diversity made these angles not just valuable cultural objectives but also important assets for the London 2012 communication strategy at large. As a result, the CO featured prominently within two of LOCOG's main communication strands: the 'engage audiences' and 'create atmosphere' strands (LOCOG, 2011; pers. comm., 3 September 2012).

The fact that CO activities could play a dual role (as both a cultural and a communication asset) has been rare in previous Games editions and explains its traditional isolation from mainstream Games narratives (see Garcia, 2012a). In the case of London, although the CO received low levels of coverage and some negative press in 2009 and 2010, by the end of 2012 and early 2013, references to the CO and London 2012 Festival were common within the national UK media as well as within public statements and reporting by Games (as opposed to specifically arts) stakeholders such as VisitBritain, the British Council and the Department for Culture, Media and Sport. References to the CO were also widely profiled within the final London 2012 debrief to the IOC and future Games hosts in Rio de Janeiro (IOC, 2012a) and infiltrated the final narrative of other Games programmes. This was done via the usage of CO imagery as evidence of Games engagement and atmosphere, thus overcoming the traditional perception that culture only operates within its own niche and is disconnected from other Games dimensions.

Analysis of London 2012 website pages as well as their end-of-project documents[1] shows that images from iconic London 2012 Festival events were used across LOCOG team debrief presentations beyond those specific to the culture team. These included:

- *Communication and Engagement debrief*, which referred to CO audience numbers as exemplary of Games engagement and noted how the CO was a key asset within LOCOG's 'Join In' programme and included the Games-dedicated mobile app (IOC, 2012b).
- *Spectator Experience debrief*, which included reference about London 2012 Festival activity taking place within the Mayor of London programme (IOC, 2012c).
- *Brand and Look of the Games debrief*, which referred to the CO and *Inspire* programme as key contributors to 'Telling the Story' of the Games and encouraging people to 'Join the Journey' as well as exemplifying the 'One Logo' approach (IOC, 2012d) (see section 'Delivery').

Despite these achievements, some important narrative challenges remained. Representatives from the IOC and the International Paralympic Committee (IPC) as well as early CO stakeholders noted the difficulty of sustaining an emphasis on issues 'unique to the Olympic and Paralympic Movements' (pers. comm., 8 August 2012). For the IOC and IPC, 'engagement and atmosphere' are clear priorities of the Olympic cultural programme, and while the programme is also expected to be a platform to 'showcase the culture of the host nation', this should be complemented by an exploration of specific Olympic and Paralympic values and heritage (pers. comm., 8 August 2012, 9 September 2012).

The analysis of points of view on these issues across the IOC, IPC and UK-based cultural stakeholders suggests that there are wide variations in how the notions of Games-related 'values' are interpreted resulting, at times, in opposing agendas regarding what is felt to be the right value to pursue. This is evident when looking into the articulation of the main CO themes, particularly those presented as inspired by the Olympic and Paralympic Games, as discussed below.

Reflecting Olympic and Paralympic-inspired themes

The original London 2012 cultural vision emphasised Olympic and Paralympic values and themes. There were proposals to construct a '*Friend-ship*' which would travel from the Beijing 2008 Games to London. Also, there was a plan for a *World Cultural Fair* bringing representatives from every nation competing at the Olympics, an international Torch Relay visiting the nations of Nobel Peace Prize laureates in acknowledgement of Olympic Truce aspirations and a commitment to placing young people at the programme's centre (Garcia, 2012b:201–203). The spirit of these aspirations influenced final programming priorities, which was visible in the large-scale international approach of a number of flagship projects, the exploration of 'peace' as an inspiration for artistic expression and the clear dominance of projects dedicated to young people. However, while at the bid stage, these angles were clearly framed by narratives specific to the Olympic Movement, and partly inspired by its founder Pierre de Coubertin, by the time of their delivery most of that original context and explicit linkages had been lost.

CO delivery partners were asked to indicate whether their organisation's experience with their projects led to greater involvement in pursuing values as defined in the CO programme's original vision; 409 projects out of 551 (74 per cent) addressed this question and ticked against multiple options. The response split is presented in Table 17.1.

It is apparent that the values of internationalism or 'international understanding' dominated the highest number of projects (43 per cent), with many projects involving artists from every competing nation or all continents and a significant proportion emphasising their links with past or future Games hosts. Among the first, at least four flagship projects involved artists from all 204 competing nations.[2] Many more projects committed to including artists from all continents, such as the *World Shakespeare Festival* (which included *Globe to Globe*, dedicated to presenting the 37 plays by Shakespeare in 37 different languages by production companies from 35 different nations).[3] Regarding the links with past or upcoming Olympic host nations, Brazil was one of the countries bringing the largest contingent of artists,[4] while China brought 70 artists.

Table 17.1 Delivery partners' response: involvement in pursuing CO values

Cultural Olympiad values		
Achieving international understanding	177	43%
Bringing together culture and sport	118	29%
Breaking boundaries between ability and disability	101	25%
Raising awareness of health and well-being	99	24%
Using culture and sport to advance peace	55	15%
Raising awareness of environmental sustainability	60	13%
None	81	20%

Source: *ICC/DHA Project Survey 2012* (Garcia, 2013b) (N = 409).

The relationships with these two nations also stand out in terms of confirmed international exports: both China and Brazil agreed to take over a range of 2012 CO activities, which represents a notable Games legacy in terms of cultural exchange.

The second highest scoring of CO values was '*Bringing together culture and sport*' (29 per cent of respondents). This link was emphasised by a significant number of regional programmes funded by the newly created Legacy Trust UK (LTUK) fund (see Garcia, 2012c) and resulted in 143 new partnerships between art and sports organisations. Several UK regions did in fact dedicate their full programme to exploring this connection, as evidenced by *imove* in Yorkshire, *Moving Together* in the West Midlands and *Relays* in the South West. During Games time, one of the most high-profile projects that brought together culture and sport was the *Art in the Park* public art programme at the Olympic Park, including Anish Kapoor's *Orbit* towering over the main stadium. Other projects included an artwork on the road coinciding with the Olympic cycling road race by artist Richard Long, and foil blankets conceived by artist Jeremy Deller being handed out to marathon runners.

Similar levels of response emerged for '*Raising awareness of health and wellbeing*' and '*Breaking the boundaries between ability and disability*' (25 per cent of respondents). This resulted in the creation of the *Unlimited* programme, involving 29 new commissions by Deaf and disabled artists which were developed throughout the Olympiad period across the UK and culminated in London during the Paralympic Games.[5]

Further, the number of projects indicating that their work had used '*culture and sport to advance peace*' (55) was also significant, especially since this is not a common focus for arts programming in the UK and can be seen as clearly responding to the Games. High-profile examples included the multiregion visual and sound (poetry) installation *Peace Camp*, two pop-music concerts under the banner of the *Peace One Day* organisation in Derry-Londonderry and London, and the performance by conductor Daniel Barenboim and his West-East Divan Orchestra of Israeli and Arab musicians. Interestingly, the peace narrative was also taken up by major cultural stakeholders delivering work beyond the remit of the CO. This was the case for the Edinburgh International Festival, which referred to the Olympic Truce principle explicitly within the introduction to its 2012 programme.

Despite these achievements, which, both in the case of the art and disability- and peace-inspired projects, were widely noticed within the UK and international arts worlds, their immediate impact on the Olympic and Paralympic Movements was limited, as evidenced in the level of involvement and awareness about them by members of the Olympic and Paralympic Families.[6] The most likely explanation for this is that the themes were mainly used to highlight the contribution the arts world can make to either topic, without necessarily engaging in full with the specific history and institutions championed by the IOC and the IPC, such as the Olympic Truce Foundation in the case of the peace agenda.

Delivery: branding and team placement within Games operations

Branding approach: one-logo family

A distinct achievement of the London 2012 communications approach that was highlighted in all documentation handed over to the IOC as part of the final debrief and Transfer of Knowledge programme was the commitment to create and maintain a 'One Logo Family' across all channels (LOCOG, 2012b). This was the first time in a Games edition that the CO visual identity was exclusively a variation on the main Games logo rather than a different pictogram. The concept of culture at the heart of the Games was, therefore, reinforced through integrated and highly visible branding.

The most significant distinction within two of these CO marks was the elimination of the 'Olympic rings': the *Inspire* programme and the London 2012 Festival. This design represents an Olympic branding innovation and was led from its inception by the culture team. The proposal to create versions of the London 2012 logo without the rings started with the conception of the *Inspire Mark* back in 2007. Since then, the *Inspire Mark* had been highlighted by IOC representatives as a key innovation and a step forward to provide an anchorage for locally owned initiatives, providing a more inclusive Games-related mark while avoiding ambush marketing. As one LOCOG source put it,

> [*Inspire* was a] mechanism for all sorts of people to share the limelight or the 'magic dust'. Expectations seem to have been high that we would only work with the usual suspects [in the arts world] [but *Inspire* is admirable] for its democracy. [The result has been the possibility] to populate the Cultural Olympiad with projects . . . from the sorts of organisation that aren't (or weren't) even officially constituted but wanted to do something for the Games and be treated with equal respect and enthusiasm alongside what they saw as well-resourced organisations already on the radar of the funding bodies and media.
>
> (pers. comm., January 2012)

The 'no rings' but 'one logo' approach had two main positive effects in terms of placing culture at the heart of the Games. First, it made it easier for a wide diversity of culture stakeholders, including businesses, to find ways of creating an association with the Games that did not conflict with the commercial interests

Figure 17.1 CO visual identity.

Source: reproduced with kind permission from London 2012.

of IOC global sponsors. Second, it provided a milestone towards uniting Olympic and Paralympic messages, as the CO made no differentiation between the two Games and presented a single programme rather than two separate ones.[7]

Despite these achievements, the brand's application encountered some challenges, which explain the difficulty of securing public awareness about the CO in the early stages. These were ongoing barriers to the proposed brand licensing implementation and limited brand visibility. The first issue is best exemplified by the *Inspire Mark*, which was created early in the programme and required a testing period. In the early stages it was unclear whether access to this mark granted permission to include explicit CO references within the promotional literature. Once the London 2012 Festival mark was created, the value of the *Inspire Mark* was put into question within some circles – particularly well-established cultural organisations. This explains the mixed reactions of delivery partners when asked about the benefits of their association with the CO and Festival. As a result, some organisations who were granted the licence decided not to use it (e.g. Edinburgh Festival Fringe). This resulted in a distancing of their project from the Games narrative.

Regarding brand visibility issues, the CO was composed of a plethora of strands and event umbrellas, some of which gained greater visibility and buy-in from contributing partners and sector peers than others. These range from early flagship proposals such as the *World Shakespeare Festival* to regional programme brands and subbrands such as *We Play* in the North West composed, in turn, of subprogramming strands with a strong identity (e.g. *Abandon Normal Devices*, *Lakes Alive*, *Blaze*). Audiences and the media tended to recognise these specific umbrellas rather than the wider CO association.

Team positioning within LOCOG: move into the brand and marketing division

Beyond the branding approach, another key decision from a positioning point of view was the transfer of the culture team from its original location within the culture, ceremonies and education division into LOCOG's brand and marketing division. LOCOG representatives indicate that such transfer accelerated some of the brand-related developments just mentioned as well as facilitating other positioning achievements. The latter could be described as key infiltrations within mainstream Games operations, which assisted ensuring visibility and linkage across LOCOG teams. They included:

- full integration of the CO within the *Look of the Games* programme, which involved a coherent approach to dressing the host city during Games time, including a 'pink ribbon' in a widely recognisable London 2012 colour pattern for London 2012 Festival venues;
- location of the CO press officer within the main LOCOG press and media team, enabling daily briefings on culture to the rest of the Games communication and engagement division and leading to some presence within

the London 2012 Main Press Centre (e.g. press briefing on the *Unlimited* programme to IOC- and IPC-accredited Games journalists)[8];
- pervasive presence of references to the CO and Festival within brand and marketing presentations to the Olympic and Paralympic Families in the build-up to the Games as well as within the final debrief.

On the flip side, some of the interviewed stakeholders felt that the relationship of the CO with other cultural programmes weakened over time. This is reflected, in varying degrees, across the Live Sites programme, the Torch Relay, the Ceremonies programme and the Volunteering programme, none of which achieved the kind of relationship proposed within the bid documents (see London 2012, 2004). Further, the relationship between the CO and the Education programme, *Get Set*, was practically nonexistent (see Garcia, 2012b).

Stakeholder impact: relevance to artists and delivery partners

A final area worth interrogating is how valuable it was for artists and delivery partners to be presenting their work in the context of the Games. A traditional challenge to make culture central to the Games experience has been the perception that the cultural sector cannot benefit from this association as they must fight for resources against sport stakeholders and the media attention moves away from their work. Challenging such preconceptions, British Council representatives indicate that the Olympic connection and sport in general provided a space for many organisations to come together that would have not otherwise, and this increased the ambition and outcome of a wide range of initiatives. In their view, the 'Olympic Games provided a safe environment to deal with some issues that would have been difficult to touch on otherwise' (pers. comm., June 2012).

Key benefits

When asked what were the main benefits of being part of the CO, delivery partners highlighted in particular the opportunity to raise their national profile as well as being part of a 'bigger national celebration' and attracting different participants or audiences (*ICC/DHA Project Survey 2012*). Table 17.2 shows the percentage of responses against all projects who responded to this question (446 out of 551).

Those projects indicating that they saw no actual benefit being part of the CO were asked to explain why. The main issues raised were that they were not allowed to credit the CO at the time of the project (in some cases, despite having an *Inspire Mark*). In others, this is because they felt they would have achieved the same profile or presence without the association.

> Our project was already on a large scale and would have been delivered in the same way without being part of the Cultural Olympiad. We are not aware of having gained particular new audiences or recognition as a direct result

of involvement with the Cultural Olympiad, to which the project was added quite late in the day.

(ICC/DHA Project Survey 2012)

An important aspect emphasised by delivery partners was that without the CO their project would not have existed, that is, the CO 'created the opportunity' for their project to happen in the first place (*ICC/DHA Project Survey 2012*). A range of projects also emphasised how being part of the CO added to their sense of 'pride' and 'confidence' (civic pride for their community, pride as artists having a 'life-changing experience'); how being endorsed by the CO 'enhanced their marketing profile' and contributed to increasing international media attention (particularly for projects showcasing the work of Deaf and disabled artists, for which the CO connection brought a 'new context' or 'new platform'); how it provided access to highly specialised teams which, in turn, raised the quality thresholds for producers and artists (in particular, for work in an international setting)[9]; and how it encouraged different kinds of partnership and collaborations, largely thanks to the added confidence that having 'early Cultural Olympiad endorsement' – and thus being part of a broad national celebration – brought to otherwise reluctant local or regional stakeholders. Many projects highlighted the value of being part of a broader umbrella programme to profile aspects that may otherwise have operated in isolation. As an example, this was noted with regard to the Deaf and disability angle as promoted by the *Unlimited* programme and *Accentuate* in the South East, as well as the international angle brought by the *World Shakespeare Festival* and the young people emphasis brought by dedicated regional or national programmes such as *NE-Generation* or *somewhereto_*.

This returns focus to the importance of having chosen a series of core values or narrative angles as key anchors to the CO and having developed them with a

Table 17.2 Main benefits of being part of the CO

Cultural Olympiad benefits	
Gained greater national profile	67.0%
We feel part of a bigger national celebration	65.7%
Attracted different participants/audiences	59.4%
Increased the ambition/scope of our project	50.7%
Worked with partners we would not normally work with	49.6%
Attracted participants/audiences new to the arts	40.0%
Engaged more local participants/audiences	39.7%
Gained greater international profile	32.0%
Explored different areas/established new synergies	23.3%
More UK visitors from outside our area	18.0%
More international visitors	12.3%
Other	8.5%
None	3.6%

Source: *ICC/DHA Project Survey 2012* (Garcia, 2013b) (N = 446 projects).

degree of consistency from the bid stage onwards, as described above (see section 'Definition' above). Although it is unclear from survey results whether the Games connection was consistently seen as an added point of distinction or value,[10] the emphasis on Olympic or Paralympic Games inspired themes such as young people and internationalism, and breaking the perceived barriers of disability is noted as an important step forward to revitalise work in these areas, bring new kinds of artists to the limelight, create new types of collaborations and attract different kinds of audiences.

Challenges

As part of the broader *Cultural Olympiad Evaluation* exercise, to gain some closer qualitative insight into the experiences of artists, participants and event organisers, research was conducted on a series of case studies across projects with a particular emphasis on young people's engagement (11 case studies), profiling of artists with disabilities (nine case studies) and tourism promotion (three case studies, of which two are also exemplars of digital innovation) (Garcia, 2013b:13). While the range of benefits highlighted by delivery partners broadly coincide with the point noted above, they also noted ongoing challenges that limited the value of being part of the CO and being associated with the Games. These were mainly related to management and branding issues.

From a management point of view, as has been discussed extensively about previous Games editions (see Garcia, 2012a), there were some complex challenges for cultural organisations and artists to operate within the CO. Project managers of youth-oriented projects did not find it easy to think and plan strategically because of the complex funding and partnership arrangements set up to deliver their projects and the ongoing restructuring and funding cuts happening in many partner organisations. The need to report different information to multiple funders and the negotiations around how partners should be credited and acknowledged given the strict (and changing) branding requirements associated with the CO were felt to be time-consuming and stressful. In the context of *Unlimited*, artists valued the support they had received from LOCOG and related agencies to develop and manage their commissions, but some felt that more could have been done to broker opportunities to show their work. While some found the reporting requirements to be an unnecessary burden, others felt that they helped them to keep on track. Many of the artists acknowledged the support and encouragement received from the main funder, Arts Council England, who championed and facilitated their projects from the start of their application process through to their completion. But they found it difficult to respond to opportunities because of LOCOG 'wanting to retain control', particularly over the timing of previews, which can be seen as an unavoidable consequence of creating a joint programme and wanting to ensure appropriate timing coordination with the hosting of the Paralympic Games.

Also in common with previous Games editions, despite the many advances made with the approach to branding by London 2012, artists and producers across many projects still reported a series of difficulties in meeting LOCOG's branding requirements, particularly in the early stages. The process of getting approval for marketing material was complex and time-consuming and in some cases created problems when artists or organisations missed venues' print deadlines. In the case of *Unlimited*, there was no central website which brought together information about the commissions, and some artists felt that the programme had become lost in the wider CO and might have benefited from additional strategic support.

The final point raised by many delivery partners, beyond the case study interviewees, relates to the difficulty in either fully understanding or explaining to others what the CO was about. This was particularly noted for projects that did not become part of the London 2012 Festival, which provided greater focus and national media visibility in 2012. For instance, one project notes how, despite achieving their own core objectives (e.g. supporting creative innovation), they had some difficulty regarding the location of this project within the wider regional CO programme and with the visibility of the Olympiad more generally:

> One key concern highlighted by many stakeholders relates to the lack of understanding of the Cultural Olympiad amongst stakeholders outside of the programme, the audiences and communities it serves to benefit, and also the media. This is not isolated to the East Midlands and is felt amongst stakeholder to be very much a national issue and therefore the responsibility of LOCOG to address.
>
> (Focus, 2010)

In the case of projects focused on young people, many case study interviewees did not report the CO being a significant motivating factor for participants after the initial connection had been made and described the positive and negative aspects of being associated with the CO as finely balanced.

> The Cultural Olympiad was a benefit because it was timed. It was a hook for the young people to be part of something big. But you had to start by explaining to young people what the Cultural Olympiad was – they [LOCOG] needed to be a bit more savvy about branding it. It was hard for young people to understand why if they were such an important part of the Cultural Olympiad, they couldn't get involved in other things such as the Torch Relay, difficult to manage their expectations.
>
> (pers. comm., December 2012)

It is worth noting, however, that these challenges were consistently raised as a frustration in the early years and that most issues had been addressed by the end of the Olympiad. The expectation from many was that, given the emphasis on evaluation and knowledge transfer, the lessons learnt in London should be passed on to future hosts more easily than has been previously the case so that positive templates, such as a more flexible approach to branding via the *Inspire Mark*, can be implemented earlier in the hosting process.

Overall, what comes across most clearly around the 2012 CO is that the achievements were shared by the sector, not just enjoyed by the organisers, with individual regions and nations breeding their own successes. Further, the London 2012 Festival brought a distinct aspirational focus to an otherwise dispersed programme and fulfilled a crucial Games-time objective to bring the nation together in a common endeavour. Yet the broader CO allowed this common cultural endeavour to be marked by the diversity of curatorial visions, varied ideals and even controversial ideas about the role culture should play within the Olympic programme. As an agitator and aggregator for an aspirational series of programmes, the London 2012 culture team can claim to have placed culture at the heart of the Games in one important respect – by engaging in discussion and considering angles that touched (even if, at times, failed to fully deliver) on the interests of all Games stakeholders.

Conclusions: immediate legacies for the Olympic and Paralympic Movements

By 2014, the first London 2012 CO legacies are apparent and range from benefits for future Games hosts to benefits for cultural stakeholders across the UK's nations and regions. The CO's operational and programming framework has informed the planning and delivery of Olympic and Paralympic cultural programmes in Sochi 2014 and Rio 2016. In particular, the CO's extensive collaborations with artists from Rio and Brazil have foregrounded important cultural dimensions of the 'To Rio 2016' programme, while London 2012 Festival partners built bridges with other UK-based major events' cultural programmes, such as Derry/Londonderry 2013 UK City of Culture and the Glasgow 2014 Commonwealth Games. This concluding section focuses on a reflection about the strongest cultural legacies for future Games hosts, as this is the area that has been most consistently overlooked in previous Games editions.

The London 2012 CO tested and delivered a range of innovative practices which serve as a template for future Games. Key aspects of this were a more flexible branding framework for cultural partners and comprehensive nation-wide funding and delivery mechanisms. On the first point, the creation of the *Inspire Mark* enabled a wide range of organisations to associate with London 2012 without creating conflict with the interests of the Games' commercial partners, and this expanded considerably the opportunities for inclusion of diverse activities, particularly at grassroots level.

Olympic Movement stakeholders have also highlighted the added value of key programming decisions that had no precedent in previous Games. In particular, the *Unlimited* programme acted as a multiyear cultural bridge between the Olympic and Paralympic Games. This programme culminated during the Paralympic Games in London, but had been promoted as a CO Major Project since 2008 and took place in diverse parts of the UK in the years preceding 2012. Informants at the IOC indicate that they would support a similar approach in future Games, thus encouraging a joint cultural programme rather than a division between Olympic and Paralympic cultural activities. This London 2012 legacy is already materialising in the lead up to Rio 2016, and it is one of the key learning points highlighted by Rio de Janeiro's cultural authorities.

Finally, the approach to partnership and, in particular, the explicit emphasis on handover activity, resulting in significant collaborations with the hosts of future one-off UK events as well as future Olympic and Paralympic Games hosts, can be seen as the source of additional legacies for both Movements and as evidence that the CO can influence the framing of other major events. For the Olympic and Paralympic Movements, to observe such extensive collaboration across Games hosts is another indication of the significant ways in which the cultural programme can promote international understanding, and this is an additional Games legacy.

The evidence presented in this chapter and the extensive range of dedicated evaluations, from the broad CO framework to countless national and regional projects across the UK, is proof of the dedication to fully document this experience so as to extract key lessons and facilitate knowledge transfer. This is the first time that the official Games cultural programme is examined in such detail. This exercise has provided previously unavailable insights into how a CO can make a difference, not only to the Games but also to the host city and nation's approach to delivering and experiencing culture and the arts. These pages provide evidence of the scale and breath of London 2012's cultural achievements as well as the reasons for ongoing challenges and should be seen as a useful point of reference for major cultural programming within large sporting events for years to come.

Acknowledgements

The author wishes to thank the IOC for granting access to the Olympic Transfer of Knowledge extranet and allowing reference to selected documentation about the London 2012 cultural programme. The research informing this chapter was developed with support from Tamsin Cox, DHA Head of Policy, who led the *ICC/DHA Projects Survey*, and Kate Rodenhurst, who led the Case Studies Research. The full *London 2012 Cultural Olympiad Evaluation* report and related appendices are accessible at www.beatrizgarcia.net

Notes

1   Documents accessed via the Olympic Games Knowledge Management extranet with kind permission from the IOC.
2   The most notable attempts were *BT River of Music*, a weekend of free contemporary music acts involving 202 nations, and *Poetry Parnassus*, a gathering of poets representing 204 nations. Other projects emphasised the connections between the UK and the 204 Olympic nations. These included *The World in London*, which represented almost every Olympic nation via photographs of London-based people from around the world, or *Discovering Places: Walk the World*, which explored how 'these countries and their people have shaped our [natural] surroundings' (*ICC/DHA Project Survey 2012*).
3   In the aftermath of its world-renowned Festival, Edinburgh also used the Games as a springboard to launch the first *International Culture Summit*, asking culture ministers

from across the world coinciding in London for the Games to travel up to Edinburgh on the day after the Olympic closing ceremony.

4   The *ICC/DHA Project Survey* indicates there have been 270 artists from Brazil, the sixth largest overseas contingent after Germany, Venezuela, the US, France and Ireland.

5   A full report on London 2012 projects dedicated to showcase the work of Deaf and disabled artists across the Olympic and Paralympic periods is available as a case study at
    http://www.beatrizgarcia.net/?portfolio=london-2012-cultural-olympiad-2

6   This has been noted in a number of stakeholder interviews with representatives of both the IOC and the IPC. In the case of the IPC, while the contribution of Deaf and disabled artists to the Paralympic opening ceremony was extensively praised and the ceremony was viewed as the best in Paralympic history, understanding of the merit of *Unlimited* to advance the Paralympic cause was less forthcoming. Views on this differ between IOC and IPC representatives: while the IOC refers to *Unlimited* as one of the most distinctive aspects of CO programming and praise the fact that it developed across both Games thus providing a valuable bridge, IPC representatives claim not to have been sufficiently involved and did not see it as directly relevant to their immediate stakeholders. This speaks to the need to keep advancing this valuable but complex area of Games cultural programming and finding more bridges and a common language, not just across both Games but between the arts world and representatives of both Movements.

7   The *Unlimited* programme was the main umbrella under which the CO presented work by Deaf and disabled artists, and its finale was presented in London during the Paralympic Games. However, build-up activity had developed throughout the preceding years and took place in other parts of the UK, and other CO strands also made an emphasis on showcasing the work of disabled artists since 2009, in particular, the LTUK-funded *Accentuate* programme in the South East. This can be seen as evidence that activity inspired by the Paralympics was fully integrated within the main CO narrative rather than being a separate programme only relevant in the context of the Paralympic Games.

8   Despite these achievements, the presence of the CO within mainstream Games media environments was limited. Observations throughout the Games period show that information about the CO had a very low presence within the Main Press Centre, International Broadcasting Centre and the media centre dedicated to nonaccredited journalists (London Media Centre). As was the case in previous Games editions, the most effective asset for the CO to engage the media was to establish its own dedicated Festival Press Centre. But while the latter ensured a good flow of communications with the press culture critics (and clearly resulted in significant volume of coverage), it was not necessarily conducive to positioning the programme as central to the Games.

9   Some groups noted the value of having 'specialist support from the London 2012 Festival team when the Visas for all the [project] artists were refused [entry] and direct contact was made between LOCOG and [the relevant] Consulate Office' (*ICC/DHA Project Survey*).

10 For example, one delivery partner noted: 'The outcomes and benefits highlighted . . . are considered to be a result of the inclusive and accessible nature of the making of [the project] rather than solely related to affiliation with the Cultural Olympiad' (*ICC/DHA Project Survey*).

References

Focus (2010) *Igniting ambition draft report*. Nottingham: Arts Council England.

Garcia, B. (2008) 'One hundred years of cultural programming within the Olympic Games. (1912–2012): origins, evolution and projections'. *International Journal of Cultural Policy*, 14(4): 361–376.

Garcia, B. (2011) 'The cultural dimension of Olympic Games: ceremonies and Cultural Olympiads as platforms for sustainable cultural policy' in E. Fernández Peña, B. Cerezuela, M. Gómez Benosa, C. Kennett and M. de Moragas Spà (Eds.), *An Olympic mosaic: multidisciplinary research and dissemination of Olympic studies: CEO-UAB, 20 years*. Barcelona: Centre d'Estudis Olímpics, Universitat Autònoma de Barcelona.

Garcia, B. (2012a) *The Olympic Games and cultural policy*. New York: Routledge.

Garcia, B. (2012b) 'The Cultural Olympiad' in V. Girginov (Ed.), *Bidding, delivering and engaging with the Olympics*. London: Routledge.

Garcia, B. (2012c) *The London 2012 Cultural Olympiad: a new model for nation-wide Olympic cultural legacy*. Lausanne: IOC–Olympic Studies Centre.

Garcia, B. (2013a) *London 2012 Cultural Olympiad evaluation: final report*. London: Arts Council England.

Garcia, B. (2013b) *London 2012 Cultural Olympiad evaluation: appendix 1. technical appendices*. London: Institute of Cultural Capital and Arts Council England.

Garcia, B. (2014) 'Editorial'. *Cultural Trends*, 23: 1–6.

IOC (2012a, November 18) *London 2012 debrief presentations*, Rio de Janeiro.

IOC (2012b, November 18) 'Communication and engagement'. *London 2012 debrief presentations*, Rio de Janeiro.

IOC (2012c, November 18) 'Spectator experience'. *London 2012 debrief presentations*, Rio de Janeiro.

IOC (2012d, November 18) 'Brand and look of the Games'. *London 2012 debrief presentation*, Rio de Janeiro.

LOCOG (2007, December) 'Values and themes for the Cultural Olympiad' (LOCOG documentation).

LOCOG (2012a) *London 2012 Festival objectives*. Submitted by LOCOG to the IOC as part of its Olympic Games Knowledge Management.

LOCOG (2012b) *Culture knowledge report*. Submitted by LOCOG to the IOC as part of its Olympic Games Knowledge Management.

London 2012 (2004) 'Theme 17: Olympism and culture'. *Candidature file for the Games of the XXX Olympiad*, Vol. 3. London: London 2012 Candidate City.

18 A 'big' legacy?

Evaluating volunteers' experiences of London 2012 and beyond

Linda Wilks

Introduction

This chapter focuses on the relationship between Olympic volunteering and subsequent community engagement in order to throw light on this aspect of the socio-cultural impacts and legacies of the London 2012 Olympic and Paralympic Games. The experiences of 20 London 2012 Olympic and Paralympic volunteers are explored against a community engagement–related policy backdrop. The theoretical framework of Van Gennep's (1960/1908) three-stage rites of passage is used to structure the findings.

The inspiration for this study is a London 2012 legacy commitment – that the volunteers would be stimulated to use their newly formed skills and expertise to benefit their local communities after the Games (Department for Culture, Media and Sport, 2010). The Department of Culture, Media and Sport links this commitment to the government's aim of promoting a 'Big Society', which puts an emphasis on community self-help.

The political context

The importance of legacy was a cornerstone of the British government's rhetoric relating to the Games, including regeneration of the East End of London and stimulation of interest in sport. Volunteering was also included in the legacy plans, as this quote from Deputy Prime Minister Nick Clegg illustrates: 'The Games has long depended on the dedication of volunteers. At London 2012, we're looking not only to celebrate this Olympic spirit, but use it to get more people volunteering in future' (Department for Culture, Media and Sport, 2012:51).

The contribution of the volunteers to the London 2012 Games was stressed continually during the Games, with government and Olympic officials expressing appreciation in their speeches. Standing ovations for the 'Games Makers', or volunteers, in the Olympic stadium during the Olympic and Paralympic closing ceremonies broadcasted across the world also highlighted the appreciation of their role. Shortly after the Games, the Prime Minister awarded a 'Big Society Award', the fiftieth of its kind, to the London 2012 volunteers in recognition of their contribution. The presentation of the award at Number 10 Downing Street also provided an opportunity to make explicit the link, with the Prime Minister announcing: 'I've spent three years trying to explain the Big Society and the Games Makers did it beautifully in just three weeks' (HM Government, 2012). Attempts by the government and the Mayor of London's office to build on the high profile of the London 2012 volunteering programme have included initiatives to offer volunteering opportunities under the Team London banner (Greater London Authority, 2014), events within the lottery-sponsored Join In legacy project which aim to encourage more sport-related volunteering (The Join In Trust, 2014) and projects under the Spirit of 2012 Trust which emphasise enabling disadvantaged people to volunteer (Spirit of 2012 Trust, 2014).

The concept of the Big Society has not been lacking in controversy. Announced in 2010 (Prime Minister's Office, 2010) and further explained in briefing documents (Cabinet Office, 2010a, 2010b), UK Prime Minister David Cameron claimed it to be about encouraging local initiatives, rather than about encouraging volunteering for the sake of it. Early worries that an emphasis on Big Society initiatives would threaten the policies and practices of the 'third sector' were expressed by Alcock (2010), while a later analysis by Bartels *et al.* (2013) suggests that volunteering of the type promoted by the Big Society is actually likely to decline when public spending decreases. Such (2012) highlights the need to consider people's availability of leisure time to fulfil volunteering duties, pointing out that this consideration is missing from Big Society discourse. Dawson's (2013) strongly worded critique uses a sociological underpinning to argue that, although the Big Society should be welcomed in its attempts to add a moral dimension to politics, its application could prove onerous to citizens, it could result in the expression of 'individual egoism' (2013:87), and more affluent areas could achieve their goals more easily, thus resulting in the intensification of economic inequalities.

Mega sporting event volunteering experiences and legacies

Green and Chalip (2004) point out the growing importance of volunteers to events, becoming vital for both the operation of the event as well as contributing to the demonstration of economic and social development. According to Baum and Lockstone (2007), relatively little is known about volunteers at mega sporting events, despite their large numbers and the extent of their contribution to these events. They suggest numerous avenues for further exploration, including how the experience of volunteering impacts the volunteers' working and personal lives, although appearing to miss calling for insights into impacts on the wider community.

Doherty's (2009) pre- and postevent study of the 2001 Canada Summer Games considers the ways in which the volunteers' experience of the volunteering at the event predicted their future volunteering, concluding that a sense of making a contribution to the community was a key factor. Ritchie (2000) drew on evidence from the Calgary Winter Olympics and Salt Lake City Olympics, finding that these events were providing long-term benefits by strengthening community volunteerism post-Games. An increase in interest or intentions to volunteer at further major events following a mega-event volunteering experi-ence was found by Doherty (2009), MacLean and Hamm (2007) and Twynam *et al.* (2002). Downward and Ralston's (2006) in-depth qualitative study of the 2002 Commonwealth Games discovered that volunteering enriched volunteers' lives and empowered them to make new choices.

Kodama *et al.* (2012) provide an auto-ethnographic account of the 'Olympic journey' of the first author's volunteering experience at the Vancouver Winter Olympics, from 'making the cut' as a volunteer to returning home after the event. Particularly notable in legacy terms is the feeling of prestige she experienced afterwards. This sense of prestige was long-lasting and further boosted by the chance to share it both socially and academically with others, provoking the sug-gestion that a further legacy could be its effect on others. Similarly, Kim *et al.* (2010) also feature pride as a key feature of the initial motivation to volunteer for a mega sporting event, as well as post-event, a factor which they suggest may influence the volunteer return rate to the same or similar events.

Theoretical framework

A variety of theoretical and conceptual models relating to the study of volunteer-ism have been generated, according to Hustinx *et al.* (2010), with different con-ceptual preferences evident across disciplines. The authors identify an emphasis on attempts to uncover predictors of volunteer participation, an approach which is evident within sports event volunteering. They suggest a need to examine vol-unteering through new conceptual lenses and also emphasise a need to highlight the negative as well as the potential positive outcomes of volunteering. However, their hybrid conceptual framework does tend to be biased towards why and how people volunteer, with less consideration of the framing of the outcomes of volunteering.

In his comprehensive review of the state of volunteering research, Wilson (2000) concluded that the study of the consequences of volunteering had only just begun. He suggests that a wider definition of citizenship, by including con-sideration of community organisations, is needed for outcomes research and also that more is needed on investigating the subjective well-being of volunteers.

The changing nature of volunteering is highlighted by Hustinx and Lammertyn (2003) who contrast the 'new' loose, irregular volunteering, termed 'episodic' by some (Macduff, 2004), with the 'old' community-based volunteering. They suggest that this new reflexive volunteering needs to be 'spectacular and enter-taining' and to address 'trendy' problems and 'hot issues' (Hustinx and Lammertyn, 2003:168) and that further empirical work on understanding and theorising contemporary volunteering styles is needed. Wilson (2012) agrees that these new types of volunteering need to be studied in order to avoid the social science pic-ture of volunteerism becoming outdated. This more recent review of Wilson's also includes a section on the consequences of volunteering, focusing on the impact on the individual.

It is, therefore, evident that there is no one overarching theory on volunteering, due to its variety of contexts, the different ways it is defined and its changing nature. A conceptual model which has found favour with volunteering researchers is the volunteer process model, developed by Omoto and Snyder (2002). A particular value of this model is the equal weighting it gives to the stages of the volunteer process, which it labels as antecedents, experiences and consequences. Further value is gained from the acknowledgement of three potential context levels: the volunteer recruitment agency, the individual volunteer and the social system. The consequences section of the model highlights the importance of considering the impacts of volunteering on individuals, organisations and communities.

Methodology

This study therefore builds on previous literature and conceptual approaches by providing further insight into the ways in which new types of volunteering impact the personal lives of the volunteers, as well as resonate within a wider community context. Inspired by the volunteer process model, it explores further the idea that volunteering may be seen as a progression involving before, during and after stages. The 'after' stage will be given particular emphasis with the aim of filling the gap in the knowledge about the outcomes of volunteering.

Giving the process model a further dimension in order to highlight the potential transformative effect of the London 2012 volunteer experience, this chapter is also underpinned by Van Gennep's (1960/1908) and Turner's (1969, 1982) three-stage rites of passage theory. The theory's links to the explanation of ceremonies and events make its application to the examination of volunteering at an Olympic event particularly pleasing. In the first phase of the rite of passage – separation – the individual detaches from his or her usual point in the social structure and sets off on a ritualistic journey. In the middle phase – transition – the individual enters a liminal state of ambiguity, when change or epiphany may take place, before reaching the final stage – incorporation – when they return to their community perhaps with new attributes and elevated social status. Consideration of Bakhtin's (1968/1965) concept of the carnivalesque, highlighting the ways in which everyday life is suspended while participants enjoy revelry and celebration, gives an added theoretical dimension to the middle phase.

The research question may, therefore, be defined as: 'to what extent and through what process did the London 2012 volunteering experience transform the volunteers into engaged citizens'? This empirical study explores the research question using two linked sets of data collected over several months. This longitudinal design enables the before, during and after volunteering phases of the Olympic volunteers' experience to be examined. To collect the first set of data, which covered the before and during phases, volunteers were asked to keep a diary, using the reflective learning cycle approach (Gibbs, 1988). They were asked to start their diary up to a month before the Games, as well as to continue making entries during the Games. This aimed to capture their 'here-and-now' evaluations of their day-to-day microexperiences as a volunteer and in the run-up to volunteering. The positive and negative feelings documented in their diary entries give insights into the immediate impacts of volunteering on the participants.

The collection of the second dataset, the semistructured interviews, took place 7 months after the end of the Games, thus covering the post-volunteering experience, as well as providing the opportunity to collect further insights into the before and during Games experiences. For these data, the participants were interviewed by telephone and asked to further reflect, looking back at the big picture across an interval of time. They were asked what they had learned about themselves, as well as whether or not they had been inspired by their experience to volunteer in their local community. Previous volunteering experiences were covered, and they were also encouraged to look forward to decide on whether their 'action plan', the final stage in the Gibbs cycle, might include further volunteering.

Findings

Pre-volunteering phase: volunteering status

The participants were asked during the interview about whether they had volunteered before the Games. Of the 20 interviewees, 13 had previous volunteering experience, with some of it being ongoing. The extent of this varied from Sarah's experience of stewarding at a university-related business event during her student years to extensive long-term volunteering. Neil, for example, had been involved in practical conservation work for the past 13 years, while Stella had volunteered as a youth worker for the previous 33 years. Sports-related volunteering also featured, with John and Jonas both being volunteer football referees, while Tessa regularly coached swimming and officiated at cycling events. Carol, Donna, Gayle and Sandy all volunteered to support others' well-being, with Carol having been a qualified first-aider and trainer for many years, for example.

Pre-volunteering phase: the lead-up

Pre-Games diary data highlight the mood of the volunteers as they prepared for the Olympics. A mixture of worry and excitement featured in diary entries, with mentions of uniform collection, pre-Games volunteer training and building familiarity with particular sports.

> I'm feeling nervous about it but kind of excited. It's very difficult to imagine what it's going to be like. I'm hoping I'll be able to cope with it all.
> (Louise, Paralympics Event Services, Olympic Park)

As the start of the Games drew nearer, diary entries showed that volunteers were thinking about the impending separation from their home life and wondering how they will feel as they embark on the volunteering experience:

This week I have realised how close it is to the time when I will start my duties as a Games Maker. I am making lists of things I need to do before I leave home and things I need to take with me. I have two part time jobs so I have to make sure that everything is up to date and in order before I go.

(Gayle, Communications, Cycling Races, London)

I'll be getting up really early and I think I will feel a little bit naff wearing my uniform for the first time, but then I'll get used to it.

(Kyla, Event Services, Wheelchair Basketball, North Greenwich Arena)

During the volunteering

As the Games got under way, the participants reported in their diaries on how much being an Olympic volunteer differed from their everyday life. Mentions in their diaries of the atmosphere of joy and celebration and of how unusual it was for people to talk to each other on the London Underground were made, as well as the presence of royalty (both pop 'royalty' and royal family) being accepted as the norm:

Going in between my shifts with my uniform on, people would smile at you, you'd be sat on the Underground and people would talk to you, which is really surreal – people talk to each other on the Underground! It was crazy!

(Sarah, Event Services, Paralympics Olympic Park)

Oh, we had royalty every day – one or other or several at once on the same day. So it was quite incredible. I remember distinctly one day when we had the Princess Royal and Paul McCartney in at the same time. Of course he was singing, and everybody was singing with him in the Velodrome.

(Simon, Event Services, Velodrome)

I loved it. Those two weeks, I mean, it was just like a holiday to me really, because it was just so different from what I normally do.

(Rosie, Event Services, Wembley and Olympic Park)

The atmosphere at the Games was mentioned by many of the participants, with the volunteers themselves playing a part in creating a buzz, as demonstrated in this example:

A huge highlight of working on Stratford Gate was during the evening egress as the Games Makers would form a high five line and the spectators loved it on their way out of the park. It really kept a buzz in the air all the way down the bridge. Everyone joined in from children running, being pushed in buggies and from their parents shoulders, along with adults, spectators on mobility scooters, wheelchairs and the Army.

(Sarah, Event Services, Paralympics, Olympic Park)

One of the participants noted the difference between her previous work as a waitress and being an Olympic volunteer, reflecting that the lack of payment did not matter in that situation: it was enjoyment which was the key.

> I've been a waitress in the past and, you know, you're there really for the money. But I think, when I was walking round Wimbledon and people were asking me for help and directions and I was really, really enjoying myself. And I wasn't, sort of, doing it for any, sort of, financial gain, I was being part of the Olympics.
>
> (Chloe, Event Services, Wimbledon)

Another participant did note in his diary that there could be downsides to being a volunteer, however, particularly if duties involved being stationed at one of the less busy entrance gates:

> Unfortunately, I met, in the Olympic Games, one young woman in her 30s was sitting in a quite depressed state up at the Eton Manor gate and just going, 'Oh, we are the lowest of the low'. She wasn't entirely explicit about why but I think it was the fact that we'd been sent to Siberia.
>
> (Neil, Event Services, Olympic Park)

A sense of the volunteers becoming immersed in their roles as they learnt more about the sports and their own roles could be identified in some diaries:

> I could hear people on the Tube all the way in talking about what tickets they'd got for the table tennis and don't know the rules. And I ended up going, 'Well, it's the second, it's the Bronze match this morning and then the Silver match this afternoon' . . . 'Oh, how do you know?' . . . 'Because I'm working there'. And then you end up talking to, like, people and they ask you loads of questions about why do you do it and where do you live. And that's good.
>
> (Christine, Table Tennis, ExCel)

Post-volunteering phase: immediate

Several of the participants mentioned in their diaries and interviews that they enjoyed being able to mention their volunteering to others afterwards:

> And the girls were, 'Oh, were you – ooh, I bet that was good, weren't it?' I said, 'It was brilliant'.
>
> (Donna, Transport Team, Old Trafford, Manchester)

> I definitely enjoyed being able to say afterwards that I had worked at the Olympics.
>
> (Alex, Venue Communications, Earls Court)

Post-volunteering phase: self-discovery

Participants also identified changes in themselves which they could link to their volunteering experience. These included gains in confidence, learning how to handle interpersonal relationships and increased self-knowledge. These three interview extracts illustrate some of these changes:

> It's made me a stronger person, it's made me a more confident person. I always thought I was quite confident but less confident to get out and do things. And I am now, I'm not going to hang around.
>
> (Kay, Event Services, Wembley Arena)

> I think what I did learn is how much further you get with people by being nice than you do by just being, sort of, aggressively in the right. Yeah, actually, which I think is a skill I should have learnt by now but it's interesting to see operate.
>
> (Tessa, Cycling Road Race Marshall, London)

> I guess some things were reinforced or made clearer to me from the experience. I've always had my friends telling me how much fun I am to be around or how funny I am. And, without even thinking about it or without even trying, I realised that I was entertaining the people in the queue while they were waiting to come in. I didn't mean to – I just, I was in the mood, I was just excited, I was just happy. So I guess some aspects of my personality became clearer.
>
> (Gina, Event Services, Basketball, Olympic Park)

One participant, in particular, was very clear that the experience had a profound effect on her:

> And, certainly, for me it was like an epiphany. I've found, in my whole life, that I actually found the last piece of the missing, of the puzzle. It really was that sensation.
>
> (Carol, Medical team, Test events, Olympics, Paralympics)

Post-volunteering phase: further volunteering

Almost all of the participants reported a new or extended interest in volunteering after their Olympic volunteering experience. Only two had not done any volunteering in the 7 months since the Games, and one of these did not rule out volunteering at some point in the future. The new volunteering included community-based volunteering, such as these four examples:

> Since then I've become a trustee for a special needs school in Andover.
>
> (Christine, Press Team, ExCel)

> We've got a social library we started up, that's once a month. I'm, sort of, one of the founding members of that.
>
> (Rosie, Event Services, Wembley and Olympic Park)

Well, since the Games, I've done some training in coaching disabled people in sport.

(Simon, Velodrome, Paralympics)

I've got an interview with the National Trust and I'm going to be doing some health walks with them.

(Stella, Event Services, Olympic Park)

Other participants reported volunteering at other major events, such as the World Police and Fire Games in Belfast and the Tour of Britain Cycle Race. Several mentioned applying to volunteer at the Commonwealth Games in Glasgow in 2014, and Jonas had been accepted as an assistant at the European Youth Olympic Festival in the Netherlands. Alex was interviewed via Skype for the Sochi Winter Olympics and, at the time of the interview, was waiting to hear if he had been accepted. Kay also reported that she and many of her fellow volunteers were intending to apply to volunteer for the Rio Olympics.

Charitable causes also received the benefit of former volunteers' increased urge to volunteer, such as John, who had been giving talks to community groups about being a 'Games Maker' in aid of a cancer charity; and Simon, along with 30 or 40 other former Olympic volunteers, was involved in the launch of the Enough Food If campaign with Save the Children, one of the charities involved.

Chloe's Olympic volunteering experience had encouraged her to start making enquiries about volunteering further afield too:

I've always, sort of, thought that I would quite like to go out to an African country and help out, I think. It was always something on my mind. But I never really seriously acted upon it, I think, until – cause I did have a really good volunteering experience, actually, at the Olympics.

(Chloe, Event Services, Wimbledon)

Aiming to broaden the 'Games Maker' influence even wider, Lynn and fellow former Olympic volunteers were involved in setting up the Spirit of London 2012 trust 'on the basis that we want to help people who were inspired by the impact of the Games Makers, to do something for others themselves'.

Many of the participants were continuing with their existing volunteering commitments, including Neil with his conservation work and Kyla who was continuing to support friends who were organising fashion events, for example.

The importance of building on the volunteering experience in the immediate aftermath of the Games was highlighted by Sarah's interview comment, when asked about post-Olympics volunteering:

Errm, no, probably not. I've thought about it, sort of, in the, when, straight after the Paralympics, when I was still in the little whirlwind. But since then nothing's happened, I've not, kind of, thought about doing it again.

(Sarah, Event Services, Paralympics, Olympic Park)

Post-volunteering phase – structural and material constraints

Although most were managing to volunteer in some context, several of the participants noted constraints on not extending their volunteering commitment. Neil, for example, would not be volunteering at the Rio Olympics, as he felt that at the age of 73 he would not be able to cope with the high temperatures there. The costs of volunteering at the Glasgow Commonwealth Games or Rio put off Rosie, and the distance from her home in Devon to Glasgow put off Sandy. Zadie, an international student based in London, would have liked to volunteer at Rio 'but very, very difficult, you know, since I still have the education thing going on, so I can't really leave London'. Donna found the prospect of regular community volunteering difficult to coordinate with her two part-time jobs, but was more easily able to volunteer periodically at events. However, Christine pointed out that her current family stage had actually enabled her to volunteer at the Games, as well as to continue volunteering: 'that was another reason for doing it, the fact that I could do it and wasn't tied down to having young kids or anything'.

Discussion

This analysis of Olympic volunteering data illustrates that the volunteers' experience of being a volunteer at the London 2012 Olympics and Paralympics may be divided into several stages. Omoto and Snyder's (2002) volunteer process model is, therefore, a useful model by which to structure investigations. As this study shows, it may be useful to subdivide the phases still further, and perhaps even add a further phase, as the consequences stretch out for an extensive period of time after the volunteering experience, as well as varying in type.

Although Omoto and Snyder's model is a good starting point for data organisation, its management-oriented emphasis does not, however, fully encourage the discovery of the emotion and experience of London 2012 volunteering which is evident in this case study. Sociological concepts which focus on the person and their place within the community, such as Van Gennep's (1960/1908) rites of passage theory, as well as Turner's (1969, 1982) further development of the middle or liminal phase, provide useful additional analysis tools.

Van Gennep's theory gives a sense of a traveller journeying from one state to another, with a key transition phase in the middle. The participants of this study demonstrate a clear sense of separating from their community in their preparations for being a volunteer. They then enter a liminal state, particularly emphasised by their volunteering taking place in protected and specially designated areas which are laden with Olympic and Paralympic symbols, myths and heritage. Even when en route to these venues, their uniform marks them out as special people who are currently immersed in the Olympic experience and there is evidence of the general public treating them differently. Bahktin's (1968/1965) concept of the carnivalesque, with its emphasis on celebration as well as difference from the everyday, enables the highlighting of the role of enjoyment in the encouragement of the volunteers' transformation.

Also striking is the effect of the volunteering experience on the participants, with examples of volunteers learning about themselves, and perhaps even experiencing the epiphany which is characteristic of Van Gennep's rite of passage. A sense of pride and newly acquired status was reported by many of the participants, again a key feature of the return of the 'traveller' to their community after their rite of passage.

Like Omoto and Snyder's model, Van Gennep's conceptual framework would also benefit from the addition of a further post-reincorporation phase which examines the period beyond the traveller's return. This study suggests that there is a further stage which involves the volunteer going out again beyond the community bolstered by their transformed identity and sustained by their enhanced status and newly acquired self-knowledge. The volunteers might also tackle new tasks within the community using these new skills.

Conclusions

The aim of this study was to discover how the London 2012 volunteers' experiences related to their post-Olympics community engagement. The study wanted to discover whether the Olympic experience transformed the volunteers into engaged citizens or enhanced the ways in which they contributed to their communities. The chapter was underpinned by the British government's hope that Olympic volunteering may be of help in the building of a 'Big Society' of selfless citizens.

There is certainly evidence here that volunteering at London 2012 enriched the volunteers' lives, even if it was not always a completely positive experience, although most seemed to find it enjoyable. There is also evidence of transformation in many of the participants' lives and sense of self, with some experiencing clear turning points or rites of passage. Community engagement appears to have been enhanced for this set of volunteers, although it is only a small sample and those who took part could have been more engaged than other volunteers. However, informal enquiries of other London 2012 volunteers since the study have not yet turned up any evidence to throw doubt on these conclusions.

The range of post-Olympics volunteering includes a very broad interpretation of community, from local (sports clubs and book clubs) to European (Youth Games) to Commonwealth (Commonwealth Games) to worldwide international events (Rio and Sochi Olympics). So if the Big Society is all about encouraging 'local' initiatives, then the impact of Olympic volunteering has not been confined to this result. It should be remembered, however, that the travellers returned to their communities and spread the word about their volunteering experiences, which may also have encouraged others to volunteer. So the effect of Olympic volunteering may be further magnified – that would be the topic of another study, however.

It should also be remembered that London 2012 was a one-off volunteering experience, enhanced by investment and reinforced by positive publicity. Very few volunteering experiences are quite that 'spectacular and entertaining', as Hustinx and Lammertyn (2003) put it. Olympic volunteers' subsequent volunteering experiences may even be disappointing as a result, which may in the long run decrease volunteering. However, there is no doubt that the London 2012 volunteers on the whole found the experience enriching and that many came away with increased confidence and self-knowledge, as well as new skills. It seems from the evidence of this study that the London 2012 volunteering experience could have increased community engagement in the widest sense and may have gone some way towards enhancing progress towards a Big Society.

References

Alcock, P. (2010) 'Building the Big Society: a new policy environment for the third sector in England'. *Voluntary Sector Review*, 1(3): 379–389.

Bakhtin, M. (1968/1965) *Rabelais and his world.* Cambridge and London: Massachusetts Institute of Technology.

Bartels, K. P. R., Cozzi, G. and Mantovan, N. (2013) '"The Big Society", public expenditure, and volunteering'. *Public Administration Review*, 73(2): 340–351.

Baum, T. and Lockstone, L. (2007) 'Volunteers and mega sporting events: developing a research framework'. *International Journal of Event Management Research*, 3(1): 29–41.

Cabinet Office (2010a) 'Big Society – frequently asked questions (FAQs)', available at: https://www.gov.uk/government/uploads/system/uploads/attachment_data/file/85850/Big_Society_FAQs.pdf (last accessed 15 May 2014).

Cabinet Office (2010b) 'Building the Big Society', available at: https://www.gov.uk/government/publications/building-the-big-society (last accessed 15 May 2014).

Dawson, M. (2013) 'Against the Big Society: a Durkheimian socialist critique'. *Critical Social Policy*, 33(1): 78–96.

Department for Culture, Media and Sport (DCMS) (2010) 'Plans for the legacy from the 2012 Olympic and Paralympic Games', available at: http://www.culture.gov.uk/images/publications/201210_Legacy_Publication.pdf (last accessed 13 May 2014).

Department for Culture, Media and Sport (DCMS) (2012) 'Beyond London 2012: the London 2012 legacy story', available at: https://www.gov.uk/government/uploads/system/uploads/attachment_data/file/77993/DCMS_Beyond_2012_Legacy_Story.pdf (last accessed 13 May 2014).

Doherty, A. (2009) 'The volunteer legacy of a major sport event'. *Journal of Policy Research in Tourism, Leisure and Events*, 1(3): 185–207.

Downward, P. M. and Ralston, R. (2006) 'The sports development potential of sports event volunteering: insights from the XVII Manchester Commonwealth Games'. *European Sport Management Quarterly*, 6(4): 333–351.

Gibbs, G. (1988) *Learning by doing: a guide to teaching and learning methods.* Oxford: Further Education Unit, Oxford Brookes University.

Greater London Authority (2014) 'Priorities: volunteering', available at: https://www.london.gov.uk/priorities/volunteering (last accessed 15 May 2014).

Green, C. and Chalip, L. (2004) 'Paths to volunteer commitment: lessons from the Sydney Olympic Games' in R. A. Stebbins and M. Graham (Eds.), *Volunteering as leisure/leisure as volunteering: an international assessment.* Wallingford, UK: CAB International.

HM Government (2012) 'Games makers win Big Society award', available at: http://www.number10.gov.uk/news/big-society-winner-pn/ (last accessed 15 May 2014).

Hustinx, L. and Lammertyn, F. (2003) 'Collective and reflexive styles of volunteering: a sociological modernization perspective'. *Voluntas: International Journal of Voluntary and Nonprofit Organizations*, 14(2): 167–187.

Hustinx, L., Cnaan, R. A. and Handy, F. (2010) 'Navigating theories of volunteering: a hybrid map for a complex phenomenon'. *Journal for the Theory of Social Behaviour*, 40(4): 410–434.

Kim, M., Kim, M. K. and Odio, M. A. (2010) 'Are you proud? The influence of sport and community identity and job satisfaction on pride of mega-event volunteers'. *Event Management*, 14(2): 127–136.

Kodama, E., Doherty, A. and Popovic, M. (2012) 'Front line insight: an autoethnography of the Vancouver 2010 volunteer experience'. *European Sport Management Quarterly*, 13(1): 76–93.

Macduff, N. (2004) *Episodic volunteering: organizing and managing the short-term volunteer program.* Walla Walla, Washington DC: MBA Publishing.

MacLean, J. and Hamm, S. (2007) 'Motivation, commitment, and intentions of volunteers at a large Canadian sporting event'. *Leisure/Loisir*, 31(2): 523–556.

Omoto, A. M. and Snyder, M. (2002) 'Considerations of community'. *The American Behavioral Scientist*, 45(5): 846–867.

Prime Minister's Office (2010) 'PM and Deputy PM's speeches at Big Society launch', available at: http://webarchive.nationalarchives.gov.uk/20130109092234/http://number10.ov.uk/news/pm-and-deputy-pms-speeches-at-big-society-launch/ (last accessed 15 May 2014).

Ritchie, J. R. B. (2000) 'Turning 16 days into 16 years through Olympic Legacies'. *Event Management*, 6(3): 155–165.

Spirit of 2012 Trust (2014) 'Our vision and aims', available at: http://www.spiritof2012trust.org.uk/about-us/ (last accessed 15 May 2014).

Such, L. (2012) 'Little leisure in the Big Society'. *Leisure Studies*, 32(1): 89–107.

The Join In Trust (2014) 'Join In', available at: https://www.joininuk.org/ (last accessed 15 May 2014).

Turner, V. W. (1969) *The ritual process: structure and anti-structure.* London: Routledge and Kegan Paul.

Turner, V. W. (1982) *From ritual to theatre: the human seriousness of play.* New York: PAJ Publications.

Twynam, G. D., Farrell, J. M. and Johnston, M. E. (2002) 'Leisure and volunteer motivation at a special sporting event'. *Leisure/Loisir*, 27(3–4): 363–377.

Van Gennep, A. (1960/1908) *The rites of passage.* Chicago: Chicago University Press.

Wilson, J. (2000) 'Volunteering'. *Annual Review of Sociology*, 26(1): 215–240.

Wilson, J. (2012) 'Volunteerism research: a review essay'. *Nonprofit and Voluntary Sector Quarterly*, 41(2): 176–212.

19 London 2012 and sport for its own sake

Andrew Calcutt

Introduction

In the years leading up to the thirtieth modern Olympiad, the official discourse of London 2012 was dominated not by athletics but by the prospect of urban regeneration in East London and by the possibility of mass participation in a community-building process. Under the terms of this discourse, the Olympiad would serve to re-engineer a regional economy characterised by lack of development and long-term, deep-seated deprivation. Meanwhile, the people of Britain, especially those living in the deprived areas of East London, would gain health and well-being from taking part in the preparations for the Olympiad, from entering into the community spirit of the whole enterprise and from volunteering for a supporting role during the Olympiad itself. Thus, London 2012 was invoked as the continuation of society by other means, reawakening economic development and rekindling conviviality – this in the absence of class-based solidarity, now defunct.

In this chapter, it is suggested that people in East London were never fully convinced of this rationale for London 2012. If there had been a local citizens' jury on the Games and their supposed benefits for East London, it would still have been out, even as the Olympic torch was brought in to the stadium to signal the commencement of the thirtieth modern Olympiad. Only a few days into Games-time, however, the popular mood had changed from widespread scepticism to vocal enthusiasm. What, then, had occurred during those few days to bring about this change of heart?

It is surely significant that once the Games were under way, the official discourse of economic regeneration and public participation was necessarily displaced by sport itself – by the stellar performance of athletes competing in events designed to test them to the very limit of their sporting prowess. Accordingly, although this chapter does not attempt to establish a causal link, it seems sensible to suggest a correlation between these two developments, i.e. the rise in popular enthusiasm for the Games and the temporary demise of official discourse about the Games, now supplanted by the Games themselves. In short, the Games seen in their own terms – as athletics – were readily embraced by the people of London, unlike the Games couched in terms of economic benefit and lifestyle improvement, which remained at some remove both from the lived experience of East Londoners and from the hearts and minds of the wider population.

Yet if there really was an inverse relationship between official discourse and popular enthusiasm, why did the proponents of London 2012 initiate and maintain their particular discourse, as described above? The chapter further suggests that London 2012's officialdom – a combination of politicians, policy people, managers and sports officials – did not credit the wider population with the level of discrimination required to appreciate the Games as the pinnacle of sporting achievement. Instead they made the assumption that most Londoners would remain consumed with self-interest, only supporting the Games if they thought that the Games were going to do something for them; moreover, something of economic or other tangible benefit. Conversely, London 2012's organisers underestimated the popular appetite for intangibles – for 'benefits' which may be sublime rather than measurable or 'evidence-based'. Thus, the front runners of the thirtieth Olympiad seem to have projected their own restricted view onto a population which thankfully does not adhere to such a diminished outlook.

Preparing the ground

On 6 July 2005, the International Olympics Committee (IOC) awarded the 2012 Games to London. In his speech to the House of Commons the following day, Foreign Secretary Jack Straw, MP, sought to explain how London's bid had won the Games – beating off strong competition from Paris and Madrid – and how London would gain from being the host city:

> London's bid was built on a special Olympic vision. That vision of an Olympic games that would not only be a celebration of sport but a force for regeneration. The games will transform one of the poorest and most deprived areas of London. They will create thousands of jobs and homes . . . One of the things that made the bid successful is the way in which it reaches out to all young people in two important respects: it will encourage many more to get fit and to be involved in sport and, whatever their physical prowess, to offer their services as volunteers for the Olympic cause.
>
> (Hansard, 2005)

Along similar lines, the Olympism chapter in London's candidate file, i.e. the section in the bid document which outlines how the putative host city aims to actualise the Olympic ethos, took as its text poet John Donne's observation that 'no man is an island' and promised 'an Olympic and cultural programme that will connect with the wider world' (London 2012, 2004:5). Ken Livingstone, Mayor of London at the time of the bid, welcomed the Games as a 'sword of Damocles' which would force the pace of urban regeneration by hanging over the heads of those in charge (Livingstone, 2006). Livingstone made this remark at the Thames Gateway Forum – the annual conference of those involved in regenerating the East London region and an event which had come to symbolise not only regional regeneration but also the frustratingly slow pace of its implementation.

In 2007, the Department of Culture, Media and Sport issued *Our Promise for 2012* (DCMS, 2007) in which it was said that hosting the Games would have the following beneficial effects:

- make the UK a world-leading sporting nation;
- transform the heart of East London;
- inspire a generation of young people to take part in local volunteering, cultural and physical activity;
- make the Olympic park a blueprint for sustainable living;
- demonstrate that the UK is a creative, inclusive and welcoming place to live in, visit and for business.

Mayor Ken Livingstone (2008) echoed this prospectus in a further set of 'legacy commitments': increasing opportunities for Londoners to be involved in sport; ensuring Londoners benefit from new jobs, business and volunteering opportunities; transforming the heart of London; delivering a sustainable Games and sustainable communities; and showcasing London as a diverse, creative and welcoming city.

These are only a few early examples of what came to be the official discourse of London 2012. Other contributions to this book will afford far greater insight into the nuances of this discourse. My purpose in rehearsing it here, if only in the barest outline, is to highlight what is NOT present within it, namely, recognition of the significance of sporting excellence of the highest order. Rather, in the promotion of London 2012, what is surely the defining element of each and every Olympiad – athletic prowess representing the furthest extent of human achievement – has somehow been demoted to the lowest rank; it is deprioritised to the point of being discarded.

Accordingly, in Foreign Secretary Jack Straw's speech, sport does receive a mention but it is not the centre of attention. Thus, London 2012 will 'not only be a celebration of sport', it will also be 'a force for regeneration'. This is to say, in effect, that sport is a given, requiring no further consideration; as Straw sees it, what makes the Olympiad worth talking about is its nonsporting potential, its capacity to act as midwife for the delivery of economic benefits and community development. Similarly, in the DCMS prospectus, London 2012 is commissioned to inspire a generation of young people to take part in physical activity, thereby catalysing their health and well-being. But in such documents, there is no understanding – nor even recognition – of what it is about elite sport which is capable of inspiring young people. Whatever such documentation was itself inspired by, it was not the prospect of sporting excellence.

Again, when Livingstone finalised his list of commitments less than 3 years after the Games were awarded to London, the term 'legacy' had already come to dominate the official discourse of London 2012. This in itself is a measure of how removed the focus was from sport. Whereas sport is actualised in the moment – as the sporting event is taking place – 'legacy' cannot but refer to the long-lasting outcomes of a process which is likely to have been equally long and drawn out – anything but momentary, in other words. Thus, by definition the key word in official discourse – 'legacy' – is antithetical to the essence of sport itself, which can only be momentary – occurring in and of the moment. In short, the discourse surrounding London 2012 encircled all kinds of social and economic benefits; conversely, the idea of athletics for the sake of athletics – sport for its own sake – was all but expelled from the conversation which politicians, policy makers and organisers sought to initiate with the wider public.

Their approach is summed up in a deliberately bold statement made by Sir Robin Wales, Mayor of the London Borough of Newham (one of London 2012's Olympic host boroughs). On 30 March 2006, at the start of his presentation to host cities, a conference on cities hosting the Olympics organised at the ExCel conference centre by the University of East London (UEL), Sir Robin declared that 'the Olympics has nothing whatsoever to do with sport'. He explained that 'it's about what it does for our community', adding 'that's the only way I can justify it' (Wales, 2006). According to Sir Robin, in the run-up to London 2012, the borough council's role was to 'build an Olympic community'. After only 9 months on the road to the Olympics, he ventured to suggest that such a community was already in evidence. Newham, he reported, experienced a drop in youth offending when London got the Games; the announcement had the effect of diverting kids from crime (Wales, 2006). Less than a year after the IOC announcement, already in evidence is a London 2012 discourse of 'regeneration', 'legacy' and 'community' which, with these as its priorities, also marginalised and even excluded mention of the activity at the core of every Olympiad – elite sport; indeed in Sir Robin's prognosis, 'the Olympics' was meant to have 'nothing whatsoever to do with it'.

The local view

The following section is in no way intended as a comprehensive survey of the popular response to London 2012 and its official discourse, but it will suffice to show (a) that in East London local people were equivocal in their response to London 2012, first in prospect and then in its development, and (b) that, whether for or against London 2012, their responses were often qualified by awareness of counter arguments and contrary opinion. In this respect, men and women in the streets neighbouring what became the Olympic park were often more nuanced than policy makers might have expected – or wanted them to be; moreover, in the long run-up to Games-time, their reactions were anything but unbridled.

Towards the end of 2004, UEL students Lennie Pothecary and Carly Crittenden canvassed local opinion on the 'Back the Bid' campaign launched by London Mayor Ken Livingstone. At Stratford station, which was to become the transport hub of London 2012, they spoke to a woman selling the *Evening Standard* newspaper who revealed that she was against London's bid on the grounds that clearing the putative Olympics site had already led to the loss of local jobs, e.g. in warehouses which she said had been demolished to make room for the planned Velodrome (Pothecary and Crittenden, 2005).

Pothecary and Crittenden (2005) found that the paper seller's scepticism was far from unique; most of the people they spoke to were reportedly unimpressed:

> None of them felt especially well-informed about the Olympic plans, about how things are being built and how building work might affect them in the coming months.

> Many said they hadn't read all of the leaflets they had received; one individual even denounced such material as 'a load of lies', pointing to a certain distrust of the media and the authorities.

> There was no 'type' who were expressing these kinds of opinions; it wasn't only a certain age group or a certain kind of person. Rather, negative opinion seemed rather prevalent among different kinds of people living near the Olympic site.

The student reporters observed that the largely negative character of the initial local response was markedly different both from the official view and from the recorded views of Londoners living further afield from the Olympic site.

In July 2005, around the time of the IOC meeting in Singapore at which London's host city status was announced, for the London East Research Institute, Phil Cohen and Iain MacRury carried out a series of focus groups on the bid and subsequently on the successful outcome of the bidding process. In their write-up of these focus groups, there is less evidence of outright opposition; rather, in a summary titled 'Hopeful or worried but not yet jumping for joy', Cohen and MacRury (2005) reported a range of mixed feelings on the part of local people. For example, various members of the focus group gave equally guarded responses to the pro-bid promotional video – *Imagine*:

> the film puts together all the best things but it doesn't really think about what's really going to happen'; 'the Olympic vision is marvellous, but all the squabbling to get it, and all the big business interests behind it, is against the ideal'; 'it dodges all the difficulties. Children take it all verbatim and of course they are excited by the potential of the Olympics. And rightly so. You must never stop young people dreaming, but it is irresponsible to encourage and trade off these dreams without being 100 per cent certain that they can be realized.

Almost before the bid was sealed, this focus group seems to have been attuned to many of the possibilities associated with London 2012, but also wary of official-dom making promises which it was in no position to keep.

Stratford-born Mitchell Panayis (2006), another UEL student, warned that 'billions of pounds will be spent on new stadia, transport and facilities, but outside this glitzy display, East London will be left to survive on scraps'. In the following year, student reporter Greg Pryke (2007) observed that 'when London got the Games' his initial reaction had been to 'jump for joy', but having interviewed a range of East Londoners on the advent of the Games, he could now see why many of them were doubtful of the benefits. One of Pryke's interviewees described the run-up to London 2012 as 'Catch 22'. Reporting on formerly unemployed, local trainees losing out on Olympics construction jobs for lack of previous experience, student journalist Kelly Handscomb (2006) went one better, describing their thwarted employment prospects as 'Catch 2012'.

Mixed opinions about London 2012 – hostile to hollow promises yet hopeful of new possibilities – remained very much in evidence all the way through to the opening of the Games in July 2012. Shortly before the Games were due to start, it emerged that G4S, the private company contracted to provide security, had failed to recruit enough security guards. Nick Buckles, the head of the company, failed to inspire confidence, and military personnel were brought in at the last minute. Some feared that this was only the start of an unsuccessful Olympiad in which British ineptitude would look especially inadequate next to the showcase of Chinese efficiency that was Beijing 2008.

Even Danny Boyle's opening ceremony met with a mixed reception initially. On the evening of Friday, 27 July 2012, to some contemporaneous observers the tableaux representing Britain's long-lost industrial past seemed unintentionally poignant, especially since this sequence was rehearsed in part of the Ford's Dagenham estate which is no longer used for car manufacture (the reduced scale of Ford's Dagenham is a by-product of the painful deindustrialisation of London and the South East). Meanwhile, as the opening ceremony continued to unfold, a Conservative MP tweeted his displeasure at 'leftie multi-cultural crap' (*Daily Mirror*, 2012). In the Olympic stadium itself, there were plenty of empty seats by the time Sir Paul McCartney stood up to conduct the final chord of 'Hey, Jude!' at 12.50 a.m.

The first line of response to the Olympiad's opening night seems largely in keeping with the mixed feelings – some positive, some negative, the one frequently qualified by the other – which local people had expressed towards London 2012 throughout the entire course of its long development. But the morning papers were unequivocally enthusiastic. Their upbeat tone seems to have been in tune with a mood swing away from ongoing doubts and continuing concerns, and Aidan Burley, M.P., was soon forced to explain that his tweets had been 'misunderstood' (*Daily Mirror*, 2012). Burley's tweets and his subsequent explanation were reported in the *Daily Mirror*, a tabloid newspaper with a mainly working-class readership. Also in the *Mirror* that day, columnist Tony Parsons suggested that although the organisers' track record of misjudgements might hitherto have alienated 'the Brit in the street', the time had come to 'celebrate' the Games – 'our Games', now that the athletes themselves were about to take the field.

'There have been mistakes galore', Parsons observed, citing 'traffic mayhem', because 'Olympic big shots' are 'staying in Mayfair, nine miles away from the Games'; 'security chaos'; and tickets being 'too expensive and too hard to obtain'. But Parsons went on to say that 'you would need a very small and very hard heart to not want to celebrate', since 'the next two weeks will be ablaze with the biggest names in sport, straining every sinew, pushing every muscle to the limit, striving for glory, making their bid for immortality'. Parsons was saying, in other words, not only that the athletes were taking the field but also that athletics could now take precedence, displacing the self-serving character of the official discourse and the associated state-sponsored process. On the day that Parsons' piece was published – 28 July 2012, i.e. the Saturday immediately following the opening ceremony on the night of Friday, 27 July, the public mood does seem to have changed in line with his recommendations. This is not to suggest that millions of *Mirror* readers acted in direct response to Parsons, taking his column to heart and implementing its core message; rather, that his column had drawn together and fleshed out what was already there, almost waiting to be drawn attention to.

In a general sense, Parsons was operating exactly as a columnist or commentator is meant to – formulating what readers, listeners and viewers are already on the point of thinking, even before they know it is in their minds. In this particular instance, Parsons was drawing attention to a key distinction which had been all but forgotten in the official discourse, namely, the distinction between London 2012 and the thirtieth Olympiad. In effect, he was reinstating, bringing back to the surface, what had remained dormant – largely forgotten but by no means eliminated – in the mind of every sports fan – the *separation* of sport and society.

Sport versus society

Whether for the ninety-plus minutes of a football game or the nine-plus seconds it takes gold medal winner Usain Bolt to sprint 100 metres, sporting events are removed from the rest of society. Each sport operates to its own rules, so that what is not permissible on track or field inside the stadium – e.g. handling a football or straying from a straight path – is perfectly acceptable behaviour in nearby Stratford station. The rules of the game serve to establish the borders between sporting events and the rest of our lives. But such boundaries are only a requirement because what goes on inside such events – the sport itself – is necessarily distinctive and different from everyday life.

Instead of being part of our day-to-day experience, each sport is an exception – an exception proved by its own particular rules – which offers rare insight into what we *could* be. The millions cheering on Jamaican sprinter Usain Bolt or Britain's gold medal–winning middle- and long-distance runner Mo Farah are willing these athletes to perform to their utmost – and at the same time calling on them to show the rest of us the utmost (in terms of physical prowess) that we human beings can be. What is higher, stronger and faster for athletes such as these is also higher, stronger and faster on behalf of everyone else – of interest to and in the interests of the whole of humanity. Thus, sport addresses our common humanity, presenting and extending it in the realisation of that incarnation of humanity – the elite athlete, which the mass of spectators readily identifies with.

This means that sport does indeed have a social role, but the role is realised primarily through the exceptional nature of sport and the special characteristics of elite athletes in whom the capacity to perform this role is most fully developed.

For those who follow it, sport becomes an integral part of who they are, because in its differentiation from the everyday, it transcends the banality of who they are obliged to be.

While this degree of separation is the *sine qua non* of spectator sport, at the other end of the spectrum sport is also connected to the timeless problem of man and nature. As from time immemorial humanity has been obliged to resist the arbitrary character of natural forces, so, from the Ancient Greeks onwards, sport has been a stage for dramatising the struggle to harness nature, including our own nature, for the betterment of humanity. In this sense, the arduous training programmes to which elite athletes subject themselves, along with the exertion and exhaustion entailed in all athletic performances, should be seen as the disciplined expression of humanity's tortuous relationship with nature.

In between the separation of sport from society and sport's connection to our continuous struggle with nature, there are a range of historically specific aspects in which sport and society have come to be reconciled. Note, however, that society's subsequent reconciliation with sport is predicated on that prior moment of separation without which sport as such could not exist.

For example, throughout the lifetime of the modern Olympics movement, i.e. since the closing stages of the nineteenth century, sport and society have been largely reconciled through *nation*. As capitalist society developed along national lines, so sporting activity tended to follow suit, hence the national league table of medal winners, which is as old as the modern Olympics. Moreover, when competition between advanced capitalist nations was at its most intense, i.e. during the twentieth-century era of interimperialist rivalry, so too was the animosity between nation-based support for rival medal contenders. By contrast, in the current period of unprecedented international cooperation – a key factor in the continuous extension of credit throughout the world economy – it is interesting to note the increased emphasis on host cities rather than on host nations, also what seems to be a growing readiness on the part of many sports fans to look beyond an athlete's country of origin. Thus, at different times, nationhood has played either a greater or lesser role in establishing the context in which sport events take place, not only in the relation between individual sports fans and their chosen athletes but also in regard to the reconciliation of sport and society.

Misreading elite sport, misreading the common people

During the nationalist era, right-wing public figures were particularly explicit in their attempted use of sport for political ends. In other words, they were quick to identify sport with society, often reducing the former to a function of the latter, and they made no apologies for having done so. Recently, the direction of travel has been reversed. With London 2012 as the case in point, readiness to reduce sporting events to a function of society has tended to come from the left or, more precisely, from politicians and policy makers whose characteristic way of thinking has its origins on the left. It is as if they have extended Lenin's aphorism that politics is the continuation of economics, so that sporting mega-events are deemed to be the further continuation of politics and economics, and sometimes a substitute for both.

Though it might be tempting to castigate this approach as an example of vulgar Marxism, this appellation would be doubly incorrect. First, in that subsuming sport within society in the forlorn hope of reconstructing society as a result is not even a bargain basement version of Marxism; it is wholly antithetical to the analytical tradition developed by Marx, Lenin and Trotsky, all of whom are equally insistent on the specificity of cultural forms, i.e. their separation and relative autonomy from politics and the economy. Second, if 'vulgar' is understood through its association with the Latin *vulgus* (common people), use of this term belies the extent to which the *vulgus* of London only fully engaged with London 2012 when the sporting character of the event finally came into its own. In effect, the people sided with Marx, Lenin and Trotsky on the relative autonomy of cultural forms; meanwhile they discriminated against the reductionism inherent in the outlook of Britain's political clique.

This is not just a conceit about method. The substantial point is that East Londoners remained largely unconvinced about London 2012 as a discourse in which sport was subsumed within politics and economics. Instead they held out until the real thing came along. Meanwhile, politicians and policy makers continued to address them in the only language which they thought that ordinary people could understand – the language of personal self-interest and local advantage. The popular response to the Olympics shows that this was a gross underestimation of the common people and their capabilities.

Apart from being an additional example of elite contempt for the masses, this episode also serves to suggest that, unlike the common people, at least some elements within the current political clique may have lost the capacity to think or act in anything other than instrumental terms. It was not popular pressure which prompted them to restrict their discourse to aims and objectives which had 'nothing whatsoever to do with sport' and no connection whatsoever with the potentially sublime character of sporting events. In which case, they can only have done so of their own volition.

At least there is no need to wait for future generations to indict today's ruling clique for its paucity of imagination. In their response to the Olympics – shunning official discourse and saving themselves for the transcendent capacity of sport itself – the people of East London have already done so, if only indirectly.

References

Cohen, P. and MacRury, I. (2005, August) 'Hopeful or worried but not yet jumping for joy: some emerging themes from a pilot study of the London 2012 bid', *Rising East Online*, 2.

Daily Mirror (2012, July 28) 'Blundering Tory MP Aidan Burley insists London 2012 opening ceremony Twitter swipe was "misunderstood"', available at: http://www.mirror.co.uk/news/uk-news/london-2012-tory-mp-aidan-1178770 (last accessed 19 May 2014).

Department of Culture, Media and Sport (DCMS) (2007) *Our promises for 2012*. London: DCMS.

Handscomb, K. (2006, May) 'Olympic construction: catch 2012', *Rising East Online*, 4.

Hansard (2005, July 6) 'House of Commons debates "London 2012 Olympic bid"'.

Livingstone, K. (2006, November 23) 'Speech to Thames Gateway Forum'.

Livingstone, K. (2008) *Five legacy commitments*. London: Mayor of London.

London 2012 (2004) 'Olympism', Candidate file, available at: http://www.london2012. com/news/publications (last accessed 17 March 2008).

Panayis, M. (2006, May) 'When the wow! Factor wears off', *Rising East Online*, 4.

Parsons, T. (2012, July 28) 'There have been mistakes galore but the true legacy of the Olympics is in the dreams of our children', *Daily Mirror*, available at: http://www. mirror.co.uk/news/uk-news/tony-parsons-on-london-2012-there-have-been-1174737 (last accessed 19 May 2014).

Pothecary, L. and Crittenden, C. (2005, January) 'Stressed out in Stratford', *Rising East Online*, 1.

Pryke, G. (2007) 'Mixed feelings' in A. Calcutt (Ed.), *Rising east review: East London and beyond 2005–2007*. London: London East Research Institute.

Wales, R. (2006, May) 'Olympics effects: the spirit of Newham', conference speech reported in *Rising East Online*, 4.

20 Looking back at London 2012

Recruitment, selection and training of Games Makers

Olesya Nedvetskaya, Rod Purcell and Annette Hastings

Introduction

The history of volunteer services for the Olympic and Paralympic Games is not new; it dates back to 1896 when 900 volunteers provided support for the Athens Games (Wei Na, 2009). The growing demands of the Games pressure Organising Committees to recruit and mobilise volunteers in increasingly large numbers, reaching 70,000 volunteers at the Olympic and Paralympic Games in London 2012. The London 2012 Games were referred to as the largest single mobilisation of a workforce in Britain since World War II. Volunteers were an indispensable part of this workforce. Their skills, enthusiasm and commitment helped afford an unforgettable experience for athletes, officials and spectators (Volunteering Strategy Group, 2006). However, large numbers of people involved in the Games also means an unprecedented scale of human resource operations and considerable managerial challenges.

One big issue faced by every Organising Committee is the recruitment of volunteers and their subsequent training and management. Each Olympic host city adopts its own volunteer recruitment strategy and methods, which range from central or government models (London 1948, Moscow 1980, Seoul 1988) to open recruitment (Barcelona 1992) and mobilisation of social organisations (Atlanta 1996) (Wei Na, 2009). Recently, some cities have attempted to use Games volunteering to achieve better event-related social impacts or 'legacies', of which London is the prime example. However, the empirical evidence of these impacts is scarce due to, among other things, the nature of these intangible impacts, the lack of details on the process and the short-term nature of the projects (i.e. Brown and Massey, 2001; Hall, 2001; Coalter, 2007; Smith and Fox, 2007; Clark, 2008; Wilson, 2000, 2012). This study intends to fill some of these gaps by examining the London 2012 Volunteer Programme.

Research focus

Being integral to the Games, the London 2012 Volunteer Programme consisted of three major phases: pre-, during and post-Games. This study is mainly devoted to the first vital phase of the programme: recruitment, selection and training of volunteers. This first stage is critically evaluated in terms of its structure, content, management and volunteers' experiences. It is argued that volunteers may have a very different volunteering journey based not only on personal attributes but also on the management style and organisational practices. Hence, illuminating the rules for roles planning, engagement activities, application, assessment, selection and training, as well as perceptions of volunteers, may shed light on the management approach and ultimately the quality of volunteer experiences and possible benefits they derived.

Methodology

The study adopted Omoto and Snyder's (2002) volunteer process model, which to our knowledge has not previously been applied to sport mega-event volunteering. However, it is immensely useful in analyzing the multidimensional and multilevel nature of volunteering. In this model, volunteering is approached as a dynamic process that unfolds over time through the 'life cycle' of volunteers reflected in three stages: antecedents, experiences and consequences. Although, to date, most of the empirical studies derived from the model have focused on individual and interpersonal levels of analysis, it serves as an excellent integrative framework allowing for organisational and societal levels to be included.

The following discussion is focused on the interaction between organisational and individual levels. At the organisational level, we were interested in finding out how the Volunteer Programme was set up and delivered within a broader organisational environment, e.g. objectives of the volunteering strategy, purpose and achievements of recruitment, selection, training and job assignment of volunteers.

At the individual level, the aim was to examine how the Programme was received by volunteers and whether the volunteers' experiences matched the stated objectives. This two-level analysis allowed for eliciting inconsistencies between the declared policy statements and the practice actually adopted, so that lessons can be learned from the London experience.

The methods used included participant observation by the lead author in volunteering before and during the Games; analysis of information available online, including the London 2012 official website, the Games Maker Zone (an online portal dedicated to volunteers), London Olympic and Paralympic Games Organising Committee (LOCOG) Volunteer Policy Games Time (LOCOG, 2011a) and My Games Maker Workbook (LOCOG, 2011b); documents, e.g. the official volunteering strategy (Volunteering Strategy Group, 2006); and interviews with participants, volunteers and managers of the LOCOG.

'Games Makers' programme makeup

According to human resource management literature (Cuskelly and Auld, 2000a, 2000b; Hoye *et al.*, 2006; Chellandurai and Madella, 2006), the process of acquiring volunteers begins with planning needs in terms of the numbers of volunteers and roles to be performed. LOCOG based their projections for the Volunteer

Programme on the Transfer of Knowledge data available from previous mega sport events, expected needs of various LOCOG functional areas and spectator numbers. About 70,000 Games-time volunteers to perform 3,500 roles were projected to be required for the Games. This number comprised 35 per cent of the total Games workforce of 200,000 members of staff, volunteers and contractors (Volunteering Strategy Group, 2006).

Recruitment

Recruitment of volunteers was set to begin 2 years before the Games. LOCOG aimed to attract people bringing passion and enthusiasm to the Games. To ensure consistency, quality and equity, a rigorous process of recruitment, application, interview and selection was set up. Successful applicants had to meet key criteria which were based on age, availability, eligibility to work as a volunteer in the UK and passing security screening and background checks.

In accordance with LOCOG values and principle, emphasis was placed on inclusion, transparency and diversity and a strong commitment to develop a more robust regional volunteering infrastructure. To this end, a fully devolved franchise model to nations and regions was recommended; however, LOCOG decided to utilise a centrally controlled recruitment scheme. Regionally based selection event volunteers (SEVs) were still allowed to tap into regional volunteering resources. Yet, ultimately, the centralised scheme limited inclusion and diversity that might have been otherwise created.

To build awareness, LOCOG utilised various means of engagement such as the media and recruitment agents. Multiple incentives were used, such as offering a chance to have a once-in-a-lifetime opportunity to be part of 'the most exciting event in the UK', develop skills, get free meals and an official uniform to keep. However, evidence from interviews suggests that those who had previously volunteered for mega sport events needed no incentives, while those who were new to volunteering would have liked clearer information on how and when to apply. This seems to contradict the objective of widening access to volunteering and deepening the level of engagement.

Application

The cut-off point for the applications was at the end of October 2010, followed by a lengthy recruitment process of almost 18 months. This suggests that LOCOG, being bound to internal deadlines, allotted substantial time for screening applications.

Based on the evidence, the Games Maker application was simple to fill out either online or on paper. People of various gender, race, sexual orientation, religious beliefs and disability were encouraged to apply. Apart from providing demographics and contact details, volunteers were asked about their skills and experiences as well as their availability for training and volunteering and their desire to be a team leader. Preferences in terms of functional areas could be indicated, but no guarantees were given. An assumption was that organisers needed specific skills for specific jobs, especially if volunteers wanted to be involved directly with certain events. Indeed, one of the interviewees restricted his choice to working with the football team in Manchester, which limited his options in the first place and left him frustrated of not having been given a chance to further take part in the selection process:

> I would have liked to have an interview; it was disappointing not to get [it]. I just felt like if you applied for a job and they just send you back a 'No thank you', it felt like that.
>
> (Bill, an unsuccessful Games Maker)

Applicants then gained access to a Games Maker Zone, which was personalised with the provided information.

Selection and screening

The selection process consisted of two stages: application forms and interviews. By the closing date, around 240,000 volunteers had expressed interest (LOCOG, 2012), with 40 per cent indicating that London 2012 inspired them to volunteer for the first time (DCMS, 2012). Given the scale and the complexity of the event, a task-based rather than preference-based approach to selecting volunteers seemed to be most efficient. Although LOCOG pledged to make every effort to take into account volunteers' interests, the primary concern was to provide an adequate workforce. As a result, those who had unique skills which did not meet the need criteria were not considered.

Using this selection process, LOCOG cut down the number of applicants to 100,000 eligible for interviews. The experience of the previous Games showed that some attrition is inevitable, which proved to be true for London 2012. Organisers needed to have leeway numbers of volunteers to choose from in order to fill 70,000 places. Eventually, 85,000 people were selected, of whom some were put on a reserve list. In fact, given the numbers that applied, LOCOG never faced any problems with recruiting the required numbers. The bigger challenge was envisioned in turning away those who applied unsuccessfully. In this case, the procedure was outlined in the volunteering strategy to notify each volunteer with a 'thank you' letter with an explanation of the reason for their unsuccessful application (Volunteering Strategy Group, 2006), which was not always the case. This suggests that LOCOG provided insufficient feedback.

Interviews were done in nine selection centers across the UK. International applicants and some specialist volunteers were interviewed via phone, although the vast majority, mainly generalist volunteers, went through a face-to-face interview. This was the preferred way of connecting potential volunteers to the organisation:

> A lot of emphasis was put on the experience of the volunteer . . . So they would have what they would call 'the volunteer journey'.
>
> (Andy, a LOCOG manager)

Around 2,000 nonpaid SEVs interviewed 100,000 potential Games Makers. They were recruited from among students and others who expressed interest. Successful SEVs were given a mandatory 1-day training designed by McDonald's, the official Games partner. The aim of the training was to equip SEVs with interview skills and techniques and familiarise them with LOCOG's values and principles.

In order to be successful, potential Games Makers needed to demonstrate the ability to speak and read English fluently, a commitment to the Games and the principles of the Olympic and Paralympic Movements and express appropriate personal behaviors (friendly, polite, outgoing and enthusiastic). They were encouraged to provide examples to illustrate their approach to managing conflicts, making a difference and 'going the extra mile'. The outcome of an interview depended on both the ability of the interviewee to express themselves and on the skills of the interviewer. For the most part, LOCOG relied on SEV's 'common sense' in using good judgement thereby putting a lot of responsibility on their shoulders.

Evidence from the interviews suggested that volunteers had mixed feelings about the selection process. Having no prior expectations helped some volunteers avoid the disappointment of not getting exactly what they wanted. Many had positive attitudes towards the interview and were generally satisfied. For instance, one retired interviewee mentioned:

> The interviews were fine; they were well organized, quite slick, impressive. They saw a lot of people, everything was quite specific, it was good. I liked that.
>
> (Jane, a Games Maker)

Those who could clearly see the connection between their prior work experience and a role allocated were particularly happy. Some credited previous volunteering experience with giving them a valuable Games Maker role. For example, Hazel did not have any managerial experience, but was allowed to have a team leader's role, which immensely enriched her volunteering experience:

> In the team leaders' course, there were 60 people roughly in the room and the training person said 'How many people here have managerial experience?' and nearly every hand went up. They said: 'How many people have got experience of being involved in a very important large sports event?' and there were five of us . . . that really opened my eyes.
>
> (Hazel, a Games Maker)

Yet, other interviewees stressed a mismatch between roles allocation and volunteers' interests and experiences, leading to dissatisfaction. Some respondents eventually decided not to apply at all as they felt that organisers were mostly concerned about recruiting large numbers to stage 'the show', without any substantial concern for volunteers:

> I just feel like the process isn't good enough . . . that people are not being matched enough to their skills so therefore if you were lucky enough to find

yourself volunteering somewhere that matched your skills and interests, then wow. Maybe you'd make some good contacts. But I think it's a lot of taking people's time.

(Lucy, a training camps volunteer in Manchester)

The time allocated for an interview was compared by some volunteers with a 'conveyor belt' of people coming in and out of an interview without enough time to express themselves. One experienced interviewee who was a team leader at prior sport events became upset with receiving the role of steward, which he felt did not utilise his skills:

I can only . . . put it [role allocation] down to the fact that the report he [SEV] did on me . . . didn't do me any favours . . . I was prepared to do more, I'd have found it more acceptable to pay for all the travelling, to be doing something . . . [commensurate to] my own capabilities.

(Bruce, a Games Maker)

It was a volunteer's choice to either accept the role offered or withdraw.

Thus, despite the fact that organisers took over a year to use the application and interviews to match volunteers to jobs, they did not always meet the expectations of volunteers or utilised those they chose to their full potential. This can be attributed to the way an interview was structured, conducted and evaluated that affected both role allocation and volunteer's satisfaction and productivity.

Thus, some volunteers complained about a standard interview procedure and the uncertainty of having no specific role understanding at the time of interview. Although intended to make the process more efficient, the likelihood of it leading to a proper match is doubtful. Alternatively, interviews tailored to specific jobs seem more appropriate to accommodate volunteers' preferences, as evidenced by a former Manchester 2002 Commonwealth Games volunteer:

We had questions to ask for specific jobs . . . and then we'd say 'There's this range of jobs on offer, which do you think would suit you best?' And if they wanted any more details, we'd explain it . . . If they didn't like what they were offered, they had a choice . . . to take something else within the organization . . . And they'd eventually get the job that they wanted.

(Daniel, a Games Maker)

However, it can be argued that a different approach at the Manchester 2002 Games was possible due to the much smaller scale of the event.

SEVs' professionalism was also questioned as well as the quality and intensity of their training. Despite the high standard set by LOCOG, the majority of SEVs were not trained as interview experts, which would have taken more time. The spectrum of people who became SEVs differed in background, age, experience and levels of motivation which influenced the quality of the interview. In particular, experienced Games Makers showed loyalty to the organisation but expressed a wish to have more experienced interviewers. Given the ultimate responsibility of SEVs in the evaluation process, this had an adverse impact on volunteers' satisfaction.

Some anxieties were also expressed that were related to inconsistencies in role allocations for the Olympics and Paralympics. Some volunteers applied for both but were chosen only to be either an Olympic or a Paralympic volunteer or were not chosen at all, or accepted but their roles vanished from the website. One 'side effect' of such cases was increased dropout rates. One of the respondents was allocated a role only at the Paralympics, although was happy to do both events; he eventually rejected his Games Maker role:

> I felt the communication wasn't very good . . . and in the end I decided it was going to be too expensive . . . I hope it's a great success . . . but I'm not sorry that I turned it down because I'm not happy with the organization.
>
> (Daniel, a dropped-out Games Maker)

From the management point of view, these instances seem to contradict the principle outlined in the volunteering strategy of having *One Games* via utilising the same volunteers for both the Olympics and Paralympics (Volunteering Strategy Group, 2006). This could have made the process more efficient, as one volunteer working at both events could have been trained only once for the same role.

Some volunteers expressed regrets that the organisers had the application process for Olympics and Paralympics in parallel rather than in series, which could have provided greater opportunities for those unsuccessful in the Olympics application to become a Paralympics volunteer. However, the whole process would have taken more than 2 years and the resources for interviewing and training would have been increased.

Training content and delivery

As outlined in the volunteering strategy, the provision of high-quality training for volunteers was considered important for ensuring the success of the Volunteer Programme (Volunteering Strategy Group, 2006). Training was intended to help volunteers carry out their roles safely and confidently, which would maximise volunteer experiences and make recruited volunteers 'the best qualified and most highly skilled of any recent Olympiad' (2006:35). The training programme consisted of five core elements: Orientation, Olympic and Paralympics, Health and Safety, Customer Focus/Care and Equalities and Diversity. Delivered through LOCOG educational partners, these elements were provided via three separate training sessions: orientation, role-specific and venue-specific. Team leaders had additional event leadership training.

Orientation

Orientation aimed at helping volunteers understand how they can contribute to the event and ideals of the Games (Volunteering Strategy Group, 2006).

However, in practice it was done in very broad terms. About 70,000 volunteers were gathered together at Wembley Arena in London, cheered on by famous sport stars and actors. It was organised to get volunteers into the spirit of the Olympics:

> It [Orientation] aimed at being fun and enthusing people . . . rather than hard-core learning . . . It was all done . . . with the volunteer experience in mind . . . so that they feel welcomed and part of the team.
>
> (Andy, a LOCOG manager)

The event was used for building team spirit which was considered key to the success of the Games. Particular attention was given to 'I Do Act' values – standing for being inspirational, distinctive, open, alert, consistent and part of the team. Volunteers were provided with an opportunity to learn new things such as the history and values of the Olympic and Paralympic Games, the history of the London 2012 bid, sports, athletes and venues (LOCOG, 2011b). Yet, experienced volunteers thought that both the content of the Workbook and the presentation at Wembley were poor, as they did not clearly outline practical things like location of venues, functional areas and roles, etc. Instead, an impression was of a 'big buzz' with too much PR and no substance.

The majority of the out-of-London volunteers incurred travel, accommodation and food expenses just to get to the orientation event, which was another point of criticism:

> I think it was expensive nonsense really, to have us all flocking down to London in 2 foot deep snow! . . . being given talks and then . . . a DVD with the whole thing on it and being sent away!
>
> (Mathew, a Games Maker)

Role-specific training

Role-specific training consisted of two parts; first, operational knowledge needed to perform the roles (LOCOG, 2011b) and training in customer service. The operational knowledge was delivered as a generic 90-minute session covering similar themes as the orientation event, e.g. LOCOG values, although more in-depth. It included information regarding discrimination, child protection, disability, etc., with a special attention given to cultural awareness:

> They were very straight on being respectful to minority backgrounds, gender, religions; it was good to see these at the forefront.
>
> (Glen, a Games Maker)

In order to perform their roles, volunteers needed to provide excellent customer service (Volunteering Strategy Group, 2006), which included skills such as strong verbal and nonverbal communication and conflict resolution skills, being able to identify customers' needs, handle customer's complaints and present oneself in a professional manner.

The second part of the training was planned to be more role-specific and lasted from several hours to several days. Volunteers were to be taught the specifics of their job, the scope of their responsibilities and the reporting structure. The evidence from the interviews, however, shows that volunteers had varied reactions to this part of the training.

Perhaps, the most fulfilling for interviewees was driver training in Manchester where volunteers had an opportunity to demonstrate that they were safe drivers. Those in that role were pleased with the quality of training and thought it contained all the information needed to perform their roles well.

Generally, younger and less experienced volunteers expressed positive feelings and found their training useful, especially in terms of learning team building, problem solving and customer service skills. They thought that the whole process was quite effective. Much information was delivered within a short period of time, and the trainers were friendly and knowledgeable. Being split into groups, volunteers were offered an opportunity to learn more about their teams, which was also well received:

> [It] was a helpful environment where everyone can rely on each other . . . I think this is the main asset of volunteering, the positive and the feel-good atmosphere . . . in which to work.
>
> (Glen, a Games Maker)

Yet, this group of volunteers mentioned that at times necessary details were omitted, and too much emphasis was given to the London Games, which made the learning not particularly transferable to other settings. Older and more experienced volunteers were more critical. Some of them did not learn anything new because of their previous volunteering experience:

> We've been through all this; it's very similar to what we did in Manchester.
>
> (Hazel, a Games Maker)

Yet others found the quality of training sessions to be poor. One interviewee noted that although the training gave her a bit more confidence, she was given too much irrelevant information, which can be explained by the requirement of complying with Games-time operational procedures:

> It covered lots of things that I never experienced . . . the health and safety stuff really didn't apply . . . different code alerts and dangerous situations . . . luckily there weren't any major problems.
>
> (Jane, a Games Maker)

Paradoxically, it was reported that role-specific training was lacking specifics. Eventually, volunteers learned jobs while on duty during the Games using common sense and help of others.

Venue-specific training

Volunteers had their venue-specific training where they worked, which seemed to satisfy volunteers' expectation to learn about the logistics:

> The venue training . . . was about getting to see the venues that were newly built and . . . learning the layout, but . . . it was also health and safety more than anything . . . where the fire exits were, what the procedures were.
>
> (Andy, a LOCOG manager)

Indeed, London 2012 was a very high-profile project where security and well-being for all were priority. Training was planned to help deliver secure Games. Based on Volunteer Policy Games Time (LOCOG, 2011a), the commitment was to be a leader in health and safety management and ensure that procedures were explained and followed. However, although in general the training was well received, frustration was expressed regarding poor information on *how* to solve issues when they arise, for instance, crowd control in the Olympic Park. Some felt that the training was rushed and lacked details:

> You've got a better idea of where we were going to be, and what we were going to be doing, that was obviously useful . . . but as I say, you couldn't really get to know the whole place until you'd been there for a few days. So I learned more on the job.
>
> (Jane, a Games Maker)

Event leadership training

Leadership training was set to equip team leaders with leadership and problem-solving skills (Volunteering Strategy Group, 2006), as they were given increased responsibility with regard to managing the tasks volunteers were supposed to perform, rotating them and trying to help them with issues they may encounter or escalate them to venue managers. Training was the same for the leaders of all functional areas.

Team leaders interviewed for this study expressed different levels of satisfaction with their training. One experienced volunteer felt that the pace of the training was slow and much content was duplicated. In contrast, a young and inexperienced volunteer found his leadership training helpful, especially the training on how to conduct briefing sessions (a) at the beginning of every shift to set the agenda for the day and provide an opportunity to meet new team members and (b) at the end of every shift for debriefing and to institute any necessary improvements. In practice, during the Games these sessions were highly important for the success of the Games and to give volunteers necessary feedback.

Training shifts allocation

Volunteer Policy Games Time (LOCOG, 2011a) stated that all training sessions must have been attended by all volunteers. Even one skipped training session or not collected uniform and accreditation could automatically disqualify a person from volunteering. Located in London, these sessions were scheduled by LOCOG on separate days and could not be merged or moved. This made the logistics difficult and expensive for out-of-London volunteers. Only one exception was made: local volunteers with a driving assignment in Manchester had their training in Manchester. Drivers driving in London still had to attend training and driving assessments in London. However, they received insufficient notification, which caused problems:

> They [organizers] should at least have had the decency to say 'We have now changed the system, you will no longer have need to come to London' which would give me ample time to get a refund on the railway ticket and the hotel.
> (Mary, a Games Maker)

There were instances when LOCOG cancelled at last minute a role-specific training due to insufficient numbers of people for that particular day. Again, neither prior notification nor explanation was given, and volunteers had to reschedule at their own expense. Changing dates for already allocated training was not straightforward either. The evidence below shows that not the needs of volunteers but the priorities of the organisation came first:

> I wanted to go to Australia . . . applied for the visa and suddenly I received an email asking me to the training . . . I asked them if I can delay my training and was waiting for about 20 days and they still haven't responded to me . . . So I changed my ticket and came back to take this training.
> (Lily, a Games Maker)

These cases indicate that LOCOG did not have a proper complaints procedure in place or enough skilled staff to handle these problems. Although this improved over time and venue managers were able to personally deal with problems with the smaller scale of the sites and numbers of participants.

Discussion

As stated, the main purpose of this study was to assess how the London 2012 Volunteer Programme was planned and delivered in terms of recruitment, selection and training and the extent to which it impacted Games Makers and the value of their experiences. The intentions of the organisers, analysed on the basis of publications, online documents and interviews with managers, were to improve learning and skills through volunteering opportunities and to develop more robust voluntary sector infrastructure by increasing the involvement of people from various backgrounds across the UK. However, during the course of the event preparation, operational demands put increasing pressure on the 'system' and changed stated priorities. Evidence provided here suggests that LOCOG seemed to follow a programme management approach (Meijs and Hoogstad, 2001) to volunteer management. This means that from the early stages of programme implementation, the major focus was on delivering the Games; everything else was subordinate to this target, placing management practices in conflict with volunteers' expectations.

Evidence from volunteers shows various degrees of satisfaction before the start of the Games. It was particularly interesting to interview unsuccessful Games Makers or those who dropped out to get insights otherwise not visible. Successful volunteers with no previous experience in volunteering and generally with less life experience were more pleased with the process and learned quite a lot. However, experienced volunteers did not find their training useful in learning new skills or having sufficient information to perform their roles successfully. For them many things were predictable, although some content was tailored to the London 2012 Games. In the same vein, those with a lot of work experience, albeit new to volunteering, were not particularly happy with the process. Although all volunteers were excited to see newly built Olympic venues during their training, it also lacked specifics on Games-time responsibilities. Albeit important, trainings was more about getting to know other participants, LOCOG procedures and potential situations that might arise, rather than learning the job. Perhaps, there is a reason for this. It was observed that training sessions were not successful in simulating the Games-time environment. It does not come as a surprise, then, that all interviewed Games Makers indicated that they learned how to do their job on their first shifts during the Games. It can be suggested that in order to make the training more effective, it could be done in smaller groups, specifically targeted at roles/tasks and enriched by the information available from previous Games.

Mismatch between skills and expectations of volunteers and roles allocated caused major dissatisfaction. While every job is important from an organisational point of view, volunteers unhappy with being allocated menial jobs, for example, considered this a failure of the organisation to meet their needs. Perhaps the scale of the event did not allow the 'system' to adopt an individual approach as 100,000 interviews needed to be processed to meet management priorities. This inevitably caused errors and inefficiencies such as a lengthy selection process, lack of proper communication and feedback, faceless management style and poor logistics. It can be argued that putting more effort into training of LOCOG staff and SEVs would have improved the process, and reimbursing volunteers' travel and accommodation costs would make Games Makers more satisfied. Yet, this would be more costly to the organisation.

Nevertheless, the majority of interviewed volunteers, regardless of their degree of satisfaction, did not drop out, but remained committed. They did so in order to stay true to themselves and to serve the organisation and community. However, this may not be the case with other events or those volunteers who are mostly concerned with fulfilling personal needs.

The acknowledged success of the Volunteer Programme and important contribution of the Games Makers to staging the Games were well publicised. However, it is claimed that if social objectives are to be achieved, the quality of volunteers' experiences should be a priority. The true challenge is to find a balance between strategic and operational demands and desires of volunteers – *if* the commitment is to make those who freely devote their time and effort feel valued – and hence to provide them with an array of opportunities and potential benefits. Yet, we will leave this question open as to whether this is attainable in the context of mega sport events – subject to the evaluation of the programme in action during the Games and the analysis of the post-Games volunteering legacy.

References

Brown, A. and Massey, J. (2001) 'Literature review: the impact of major sporting events. The sports development impact of the Manchester 2002 Commonwealth Games: initial baseline research, MIPC/MMU and UK Sport', available at: http://e-space.mmu.ac.uk/e-space/bitstream/2173/12509/1/brown%202001%20commonwealth%20games%202002.pdf (last accessed 20 July 2011).

Chellandurai, P. and Madella, A. (2006) *Human resource management in Olympic sport organizations*. Champaign, IL: Human Kinetics.

Clark, G. (2008) 'Local development benefits from staging global event, OECD publishing', available at: http://www.oecd.org/berlin/40514220.pdf (last accessed 17 June 2011).

Coalter, F. (2007) *A wider social role for sport: who is keeping the score?* Abingdon, UK: Routledge.

Cuskelly, G. and Auld, C. (2000a) *Volunteer management program – recruiting volunteers.* Brisbane: Australian Sports Commission.

Cuskelly, G. and Auld, C. (2000b) *Volunteer management program – retaining volunteers.* Brisbane: Australian Sports Commission.

Department for Culture, Media and Sport (DCMS) (2012) 'Beyond 2012: the London 2012 legacy story', available at: https://www.gov.uk/government/publications/beyond-2012-the-london-2012-legacy-story (last accessed 25 September 2012).

Hall, M. C. (2001) 'Imaging, tourism and sport event fever: the Sydney Olympics and the need for a social charter for mega-events' in C. Gratton and I. P. Henry (Eds.), *Sport in the city: the role of sport in economic and social regeneration*. London: Routledge.

Hoye, R., Smith, A., Westerbeek, H., Stewart, B. and Nicholson, M. (2006) *Sport management: principles and applications*. Oxford: Elsevier.

London Organizing Committee of the Olympic Games and Paralympic Games Ltd (LOCOG) (2011a) *LOCOG volunteer policy Games time, 2007–2011*. London: LOCOG.

London Organizing Committee of the Olympic Games and Paralympic Games Ltd (LOCOG) (2011b) *My Games Maker workbook, 2007–2011*. London: LOCOG.

London Organizing Committee of the Olympic Games and Paralympic Games Ltd (LOCOG) (2012) 'London 2012', available at: http://www.london2012.com (last accessed 25 October 2010).

Meijs, L. C. P. M. and Hoogstad, E. (2001) 'New ways of managing volunteers: combining membership management and programme management'. *Voluntary Action*, 3(3): 41–61.

Omoto, A. M. and Snyder, M. (2002) 'Considerations of community: the context and process of volunteerism. *American Behavioral Scientist*, 45(5): 846–867.

Smith, A. and Fox, T. (2007) 'From "event-led" to "event-themed" regeneration: the 2002 Commonwealth Games legacy programme'. *Urban Studies*, 44(5/6): 1125–1143.

Volunteering Strategy Group (2006) *The London 2012 Olympic Games and Paralympic Games volunteering strategy.* London: LOCOG.

Wei, N. (2009) *Experience, value, influence: a research report on the volunteer work legacy transformation of the Beijing 2008 Olympic Games and Paralympic Games.* Beijing, China: Renmin University Press.

Wilson, J. (2000) 'Volunteering'. *Annual Review of Sociology*, 26: 215–240.

Wilson, J. (2012) 'Volunteerism research: a review essay'. *Nonprofit and Voluntary Sector Quarterly*, 41(2): 176–212.

21 The Olympic regeneration of East London in the official discourse

Preconditions for the construal of public space

Antonio Desiderio

Introduction

As Mike Raco (2012) argues, the Olympics are not exceptional events whose analysis can be circumscribed within the narrow boundaries of the literature on mega-events. They need instead to be considered in relation to the current forms of urban politics and contemporary capitalism. Such forms are characterised by the shift from government to governance, which is turning representative democracy into a 'second-level indirect representative democracy – citizens elect representatives who control and supervise "experts" who formulate and administer policies in an autonomous fashion from their regulatory bastions' (Levi-Faur, 2005:13).

Raco's work focuses on the framework of contracts and agreements between public authorities and corporations that shape the process of policy making, planning and the *delivering* of London 2012 (Raco, 2014). This chapter goes back to the preconditions for the formation of such a structure of governance. It focuses on the discourse, in Foucauldian terms, of laws, acts, plans and development strategies that construe a specific *knowledge* of urban public space – a knowledge that, I believe, shapes and enables the actual policies being enacted. This chapter aims, therefore, at understanding how the official discourse of laws, acts, plans and development strategies work in creating the preconditions for the formation of East London's public space. As the focus is on the knowledge of public space (*publicness*) rather than on public space itself (on the *how* rather than on the *what*), the question is how the dominant discourse shapes the concept of public space in East London urban regeneration.

As the notion of public space involves a number of diverse and even contrasting meanings that cannot be synthesised into a single definition (Habermas, 1992), we need to outline what might be called an ideal model against which to evaluate the *publicness* emerging from such discourse. The basic features of this model must be identified since defining these makes it possible to establish how and why urban space may be called public. Drawing on Hannah Arendt's reflections on democracy and the public sphere (Arendt, 1998), the conceptual element I assume as essential to any definition of public democratic space is plurality: the dialectical interaction between differences arising in the social realm. This chapter addresses the extent to which the idea of *publicness* that is construed by contemporary official discourse differs/corresponds to an interpretation of the public sphere based on the idea of plurality – Arendt's precondition for democracy. As democracy and public space are discursive construals, the methodological approach I use is critical discourse analysis (CDA). CDA aims to understand and question the dominant assumptions and representations present in the social realm. As far as this analysis is concerned, such assumptions and representations consist of the worldviews, ideas and interests that shape the official discourse of the Olympic-inspired regeneration of East London.

The chapter divides into two parts. Starting from Hannah Arendt's discussion on politics, the first elaborates on the notion of democratic public space. Here, I also draw upon Robert Dahl's (2002) interpretation of plurality and Colin Crouch's (2004, 2011) analysis of 'post-democracy' – his term for the current phase of capitalism's development. The concept of postdemocracy helps to put into critical perspective the progressive elimination of plurality, and hence democracy, from within the processes of policy and decision making and from its expression in the competition between different economic actors in the marketplace. The second part focuses on the discourse presented in a number of key texts that have provided the framework for policy making in London: the Greater London Authority (GLA) Act 1999, the London Plan 2011, the London Implementation Plan 2011, the Deregulation and Contracting Out Act 1994, the CH 2 M Hill, Laing O' Rourke and Mace (CLM)-Olympic Delivery Authority (ODA) contract and the Mayor's Cultural Strategy.

The chapter concludes that the preconditions for the physical materialisation of public space (*construction*) are set out in structures of governance and legal frameworks (*construal*). Such structures of governance and legal frameworks constitute discursive practices that reflect social relations of power and define the nature of public space itself (*publicness*).

Public space: a definition

There is no single definition of public space. The concept spans, as Claudio De Magalhães explains, from all nonprivate realms of social life to all those spaces that perform public functions – no matter whether they are publicly or privately owned (2010:561). The discussion reflects the wider debate on the public sphere, which Jürgen Habermas (1992) analysed in relation to the development of state institutions since the Greek *polis*. In order to understand the publicness of East London's urban space in the official discourse of laws, acts, plans and development strategies, we need to identify some core principles to provide a definition of public urban space. The starting point for this discussion is Hannah Arendt's idea of politics. The relevance of Hanna Arendt's work is that it focuses on the conditions for politics rather than on politics itself (Canovan, 1998:vii). An important example is *plurality*, which is 'not only the *conditio sine qua non*, but *the conditio per quam* of all political life' (Arendt, 1998:7). Despite sharing a common nature, men are different from one another. *Action* in *speech*, that is to say politics, is where differences are revealed. Plurality is, therefore, the condition for the existence of politics, while the *polis* and public space are where such plurality is expressed and practiced; each cannot exist without the other. This implies an immaterial notion of *polis*, whose possibility does not rely on its physical location, but on the acting and speaking together of people (Arendt, 1998:198). That brings to the fore the concept of *entelechia*: Aristotle's idea of things developing out of an internal reason. According to this principle, Arendt explains, the means to achieve the end 'would already be the end; and this "end", conversely, cannot be considered a means in some other respect, because there is nothing higher to attain than this actuality itself' (1998:206–207). The implication for public space is that its purpose is nothing more or less than the existence (and permanence) of public space itself. For public space is where plurality, and hence democracy, is exercised.

In his attempt to identify a pure model of democracy against which to evaluate actual forms of government and political organisation, Robert Dahl argues that plurality (which he calls *polyarchy*) is a necessary requirement for democracy. Apart from free elections (which are a necessary but not sufficient condition for democracy), one of the essential requirements of representative democracy is to guarantee all citizens equal possibilities to engage in political activity, to take part in and affect the processes of policy making within political parties, unions, associations, interest groups and other civic associations (Dahl, 2002). From a critical standpoint, Colin Crouch shows how one of the consequences of increasingly closer relationships between governments and corporations in the form of the contracting out of services and functions is the progressive reduction of both public control and accountability in policy making and of economic competition in the market. The antidote to such a reduction of democracy is seen in the strengthening of civic society – the plurality of forces, institutions, organisations and actors constituting the societal world. Plurality and *entelechia* are necessary preconditions for the creation of democratic urban space. As I shall discuss later in this chapter, insofar as culture and urban space are no longer ends in themselves and become means to attract tourists and investors' money, the democratic mechanisms of discussion and negotiation between different social forces, groups and subjects are turned into the bureaucratic management and implementation of top-down strategies. Such strategies constitute, in turn, the preconditions for the degradation of the civic and for the formation of an undemocratic public space.

The formation of a democratic or an undemocratic space has an intrinsic discursive nature, for it is enacted through consultation, law making, public discussion and the media (Habermas, 1992). As I argue elsewhere (Desiderio, 2013), far from being something immaterial, discourse plays a central role in shaping the societal world in its physical form. By enacting policies, the discourse of laws, acts, plans and development strategies also shapes the form and the practices of urban space. As Norman Fairclough, Simon Pardoe and Bronislaw Szerszynski explain, discourse can be interpreted as a combination of *discourses*, *genres* and *styles*. 'Discourses: ways of *representing* the world from particular perspectives. . . . Genres: ways of *acting* and *interacting* with

other people, in speech or writing. . . . Styles: ways of *identifying*, constructing or enunciating the self, including both social and institutional identities'
(Fairclough *et al.*, 2010:418–419). The discourse framing the regeneration of
East London (in which urban space becomes an asset – a means to achieve the
accumulation of capital in various forms) entails a specific genre, a specific way
of acting and interacting in space. One such genre is shopping, which becomes
the principle of a planning policy envisaging London as a place for lifestyle.
In this context, culture is no longer an end in itself but a complex of marketing
strategies aimed at attracting more tourists and investment. Such discourse and
genre imply in turn style – a specific way of being of urban space in terms of
form and practices – which also entails the construction of individual and
collective identities.

Such discourse also reflects the shift from government to governance as
described by Colin Crouch (2011) and David Levi-Faur (2004, 2005). The shift is
characterised by the contracting out of public services to big corporations – whose
aim is to freeze competition in the marketplace by securing exclusive relations
with governments and public authorities. Such 'privatisation of the market' – as
Crouch calls it – reflects the privatisation of decision-making processes and the
weakening of the mechanisms of public accountability and control. By assuming exclusive control of public services, firms and corporations are not, in fact,
accountable to taxpayers, voters and citizens but to their clients and are judged by
their capability to fulfil the terms of the contract. The elimination of politics at the
level of law making by this process of privatisation is reflected in the elimination
of plurality at the level of the forms, uses and practices of space.

The GLA Act 1999

The organisation of the London Olympics 2012 is characterised by a shift from
deliberation to *delivery* (Raco, 2012), which entails a change in the policies, practices and interpretation of democracy. This is an important shift, as it marks the
difference between democratic government – where the possibility of discussing
issues from different perspectives and approaches is guaranteed – and nondemocratic governance – where institutions focus on the delivery of a product. The key
principles of such nondemocratic urban governance, as Raco (2014) explains, are
to 'get things done' and deliver 'on time' and 'to budget'.

The discourse of the Olympics is composed of words and concepts such as
change, priorities, delivery and strategy. Accordingly, social practices and services such as urban planning and culture become *strategic sectors* – elements
of a wider strategy aimed at delivering a product. I take as a starting point for
this discussion the GLA Act 1999 – the act that establishes the Greater London
Authority and its functions (GLA 1999). The Mayor's prerogative and actions
are defined in this legislation in terms of 'strategy' – 'The Mayor's strategies',
'General Duties of the Mayor in relation to his strategies', 'The Mayor's Spatial
Development Strategy', 'Culture Strategy and Tourism', 'The Cultural Strategic
Group for London' (GLA 1999:25–44).

The word strategy originates from the ancient Greek *strategós*: general, commander, literally army leader. *Strategema* is the Greek word for war trickery, stratagem, ploy. The verb *strategeo* means 'I employ a stratagem', 'I manoeuvre in order to', 'I deceive somebody'. Strategy has, therefore, an intrinsic military dimension; planning and culture are not the domain of specific policies aimed at improving London's public sphere but instruments to make London attractive to investors and tourists.

Culture strategy and tourism

The discourse of strategy implies the discourse of delivery and vice versa. Both of them need to be considered in the context of the progressive reduction of democracy from decision-making processes. The creation of independent agencies with contracting out powers and the complex of contracts and agreements establishing the relations between public authorities and contractors are meant to deliver projects without going through the processes of political discussion and control. As culture is part of the Mayor's strategic plan for London, the act establishes the Cultural Strategy Group for London, whose task is to 'formulate and submit to the Mayor a draft strategy containing policies with respect to culture, media and sport in Greater London' (section 376:450–452). The questions are: Why does culture need a strategy? How is the concept of culture articulated?

I shall answer the second question first. Culture here is a key investment sector to maintain and increase London's status as a global city. As Frederic Jameson suggests, in late capitalism the concept of culture exceeds more traditional meanings such as knowledge or, say, civilisation and comes to include the disparate elements of spectacle and consumerism so that the boundaries among, for example, art, history, shopping, food, music, tourism and sport blur. The GLA Act 1999 reflects this dynamic as culture is conceived as part of a strategy of urban development along with media and sport (the title of Part 10 Chapter 1 of the Act is 'Culture Strategy and Tourism'). That also answers the first question. Since culture is a key element in London's image as global capital and, as Andrew Calcutt suggests, finance's twin sister, it becomes an asset (2012:67). It is turned into a product to be traded on the market on the basis of calculations about its capacity to produce more capital. The implication of this is that governance, for culture's development, cannot be left to the free play of different social actors in society.

The GLA Act sets out the conditions for such a form of governance. The Cultural Strategy Group for London is currently composed of 23 members who are appointed by the Mayor (in 2014, Boris Johnson) and are selected from a number of public and private institutions. The official page of the group reads:

> [the] primary role is to develop the Mayor's Culture Strategy – maintaining and promoting London as a world-class city of culture. Members represent regional cultural agencies and key institutions across London, acting as the

voice of the cultural sector, to monitor and present to the Mayor the ongoing challenges and needs of the sector.

(http:// www.london.gov.uk/priorities/arts-culture/
london-cultural-strategy-group)

These few lines present the reader with some of the claims characterising, according to Norman Fairclough (2010a), contemporary political discourse. Changes in the way that states are governed are deemed as necessary to answer the challenges of global financial capitalism, which means that states and cities need to compete against each other to secure a privileged position on the map of global capital. Since in the current economic and political discourse to gain such a position has become an unquestionable priority, as a result the traditional distinctions between 'right' and 'left' blurs (Fairclough, 2010a:172). By the same token, general consent is sought for policies and projects deemed to answer the requirements of global financial markets, so that any opposition to such policies and projects is silenced. The Olympics as catalyst for urban regeneration and culture and as a complex of strategic policies are to be understood in this context. They become, in other words, an instrument for 'maintaining and promoting London as a world-class city of culture'; that is to say, London's status as a city for tourism, lifestyle, investments and consumption.

As culture becomes a key asset, cultural strategy has to be delivered without any political interference. The GLA Act provides the conditions for the elimination of politics. The Act establishes the right for the group to 'enter into arrangements with any other person or organisation for or in connection with the carrying on by that person or organisation of any activity which the Authority has power to carry on' (GLA 1999, section 378, 3d:234). According to the Act, the planning of cultural activities is a top-down process enacted by the Cultural Strategy Group, whose decisions can in principle rely on the knowledge of experts and organisations which may have the right to elaborate and enact policies on behalf of the group. Despite being contracted by public funds, these experts and organisations would not be accountable to representative bodies such as London's Assembly or the Parliament, for they act on the basis of contracts and agreements signed with the group, which is the only authority they need to answer to. Thus, culture in London is not a horizontal and independent practice but is turned into a privatised business aimed at making the city an attractive place for tourists and investors.

The London Plan 2011 and the London Implementation Plan

The London Plan 2011, also known as the 'Mayor's Spatial Strategy', turns the discourse of delivery into a planning strategy. The first objective of the strategy is to retain and build upon its world city status as one of the three financial centres of global reach. It must be somewhere that people and businesses want to locate, with places and spaces to meet their needs. This economic dynamism is vital to ensuring the prosperity Londoners need, to maintaining the world-beating innovation increasingly needed to address global challenges and to secure the highest quality development and urban environments (GLA 2011:6). These introductory lines are characterised by the same semiotic elements that characterise the Cultural Strategy Group's statement. The Mayor recontextualises the language and meanings of the global financial economy discourse in creating guidelines for 'his' planning policies. This entails specific linguistic strategies operating on both the macro and the micro level.

The dynamics at work in global financial capitalism are represented as self-sustaining, as historical and necessary forces whose existence is independent from human agency. In so doing, such forces become unquestionable: natural facts that 'we' all have to adapt to in order to prosper. As Fairclough explains, the 'we' = the government as opposed to 'they' = past governments and/or political opposition. The characterising narratives of identities are turned into a 'we' = the country. In the Mayor's discourse 'we' is identified with Londoners and the rest of the UK. 'We = the Londoners and the rest of the UK' embraces the entire political, ideological and cultural spectrum, so that the existence of any political, ideological and cultural opposition is denied. This is reflected in verb modality, which indicates what 'must' and 'needs' to be done in order for London: (1) to maintain its status as 'world city and one of three business centres of global reach'; (2) to be 'somewhere people and business want to locate'; (3) 'to ensure the prosperity of Londoners' (GLA 2011:6). It is significant that the Plan is limited to the provision of guidelines, without indicating any specific policies or the means by which they will be enacted. To put it simply, the Plan provides a very generic 'what' without providing the 'how', for the how is contained in the contracts and agreements between public authorities and private contractors. The Plan thus becomes an open and flexible instrument to allow the enactment of specific policies formulated and framed by contracts and agreements.

The Olympics are said to be 'providing a global showcase for the capital' and to constitute a 'unique opportunity to secure and accelerate the delivery of many elements of the Mayor's strategies, and for this reason it is the Mayor's highest regeneration priority for this period' (GLA 2011:24). 'Deprivation' is a key concept. Once East London is classified as a 'priority', the adoption of 'special policies' is urged. The second chapter of the Plan, in fact, 'sets out special policies for areas of London facing particular needs or with distinctive parts to play in the capital's development over the period to 2031, particularly using the legacy of the 2012 Games to regenerate the Lower Lea Valley' (GLA 2011:34). From a theoretical perspective, discourse is not limited to the realm of mental representations, but becomes materialised into 'real' practices and policies, which in turn shape the physical transformation of urban space. The implication of the discourse of 'special policies' and 'delivery' in terms of democratic control and accountability is that the processes of policy and decision making rest, as Mike Raco demonstrates, on a complex system of contracts and agreements that determine the exclusive relations between the client (the government, the Mayor) and the contractor (private companies, corporations) – to the exclusion of the mechanisms of participatory democracy.

As the Cultural Strategy establishes the Cultural Strategy Group, so the London Plan establishes the London Implementation Plan. The latter is designed to 'support and facilitate the implementation of the Plan's policies' (GLA 2011:278) and 'set out how the policies of the London Plan will be translated into practical action' (2013:5). The Implementation Plan in turn establishes the Implementation Group, whose aims are to:

> a) assist in providing the Mayor with data or potential sources of data required for the development and updating of the Implementation Plan; b) assist in providing the Mayor with advice and analysis; c) suggesting and delivering actions for inclusion in the Implementation Plan; d) assist in making policy recommendations to the Mayor on matters relating to implementation and infrastructure planning for possible inclusion in the London Plan and/or other strategies. The Implementation Group is chaired and managed by GLA officers. Representatives are drawn from delivery agencies covering different types of strategic infrastructure. Local authority officers and community representatives as well as other key stakeholders involved in infrastructure planning are also represented.
>
> (GLA 2013b:6–7)

It might be argued that such discourse does not preclude the exercise of a form of democratic control, for, as we have just read, local authority officers and community representatives are, in fact, involved. The issue at stake, however, is not the disappearance of democratic institutions and instruments, but that they are deprived of their content, and hence disempowered, since the Plan establishes a discourse which sets out the preconditions for the 'privatisation' of the processes of decision and policy making. No matter that the principal agent enacting such discourse is a public authority, the publicness that is entailed lacks in plurality – plurality meaning the variety of civic organisations and social actors that should be involved in the processes of policy and decision making and the wider regime of economic competition.

In this document, the concepts of strategy and delivery are in fact employed to reinforce the image of states, governments and public finance as incapable of undertaking and managing projects as big and demanding as the Olympics. The emphasis is on the importance of the private sector in financing and delivering the strategy (see, for instance, paragraph 2.19), the relevance of tools such as Business Development Districts (see paragraphs 2.7 and 2.14) and the reference to 'significant constraints on public expenditure' (paragraph 4.3). This needs to be read in the context of a more or less explicit critique of public institutions. The Implementation Group's role in supporting the implementation of the Plan is important, as it affirms, 'in the light of the demonstrated complexity of implementation planning and the lack of capacity of public sector planning staff in this area' (GLA, 2013b:75, paragraph 5.13).

The Deregulation and Contracting Out Act 1994 and the CLM-ODA contract

The Deregulation and Contracting Out Act 1994 enables the reduction of democratic control and accountability within the decision-making processes involving public and private sectors. The Act establishes restrictions on disclosure of information whenever 'a contractor is authorised to exercise any function of a Minister, office-holder or local authority' and whenever 'the disclosure of relevant information, in or in connection with the exercise of the relevant function or a related function, is restricted by any enactment or by any obligation of confidentiality' (Deregulation and Contracting Out Act 1994:120). It regulates the disclosure of information between public authorities and contractors and between the contractors themselves. No mention is made of public disclosure, as disclosure is only conceived between contracting parties and as long as it is 'necessary or expedient for the purpose of facilitating the exercise of the relevant function' (Deregulation and Contracting Out Act 1994:120–121).

Such criteria informed the contract between the ODA and its delivery partner CLM. Section 70.1 clearly states that 'each party does not disclose information to any third party without the other Party's prior acceptance; does not use information it receives from the other except for the purpose of this contract; does not copy information it receives from the other except to the extent necessary for it to use information for the purpose of this contract' (ODA, 2005:40). Furthermore, the contract established that the delivery partner has the right to disclose information 'to its employees and Sub-consultants only to the extent necessary for them to undertake their duties to provide the services; and is treated in confidence by them and not disclosed without the Employer's prior acceptance or used by them otherwise than for the purpose of providing the services' (ODA, 2005:40). As Raco explains in relation to ODA's information policy (Raco requested a copy of the CLM-ODA contract on the basis of the Freedom of Information Act), while the ODA says that there is a public interest in obtaining information about important processes of decision and policy making; it also says that disclosure of information is restricted to protect CLM in relation to competitors. Since CLM acts on behalf of a public authority – the ODA – restrictions on the release of information are justified on the basis of public interest itself, as it may be prejudicial to it. Large parts of the CLM-ODA contract were for this reason redacted and classified as 'commercially confidential' (Raco, 2012:456–457).

The concept of 'ambush marketing' is in this regard significant. Ambush marketing, the contract reads:

> means any activity, commercial or non-commercial, undertaken by any person or entity, whether public or private, that creates, implies or refers to a direct or indirect association of any kind (including an association in the minds of members of the public) with any Games Body or the Games (including by reference to the City of London and the year 2012), which has not been authorised by the LOCOG or any other Games Body.
>
> (ODA, 2005:40)

At stake here is what may be called the 'privatisation of language'. Such privatisation of language exceeds the realm of spoken and written language and involves the realm of mental associations. How is it possible to establish which words and/ or images prompt an association with the Games, the Games bodies, the City of London and even the 2012 in people's mind? How is it possible to establish how such an association works? The CLM-ODA contract reflects the reduction of plurality (competition) within the marketplace, as it establishes the exclusive relations between them, but there is more at stake here. The fundamental issue is the shift of judicial and legal frameworks from an instrument for the enactment of the bourgeois public sphere in the eighteenth century (the division between public authority and the public sphere within which a space arises where private owners independently and 'freely' engage in economic exchange – the classic liberal model of laissez faire capitalism); to a founding principle for the capitalist relations of production of the late nineteenth/early twentieth century (in which the state actively engages with the sphere of economic exchange to secure the conditions for their reproduction) (Habermas, 1992); to an instrument for the top-down regulation of the public sphere by regulatory frameworks in which the state, the market and society are no longer distinct entities (the 'closing down' of public sphere) (Levi-Faur, 2005:14). Such contemporary regulatory frameworks rely on a complex process of contracts and agreements written by 'experts' and specialised firms (Raco, 2012, 2014), which are aimed at mitigating 'negative externalities through "social regulation" (or the regulation of risk)' (Levi-Faur, 2005:14). The function of law is, therefore, to protect the exclusive commercial relations between the public authority and private contractors and subcontractors, rather than guaranteeing competition in the marketplace and the mechanisms of democratic participation in the processes of policy and decision making.

The Mayor's Cultural Strategy

Culture and planning constitute strategic elements of a wider strategy, 'Cultural Metropolis. The Mayor's Cultural Strategy – 2012 and Beyond', which involves a number of 'strategic' sectors such as education, jobs, skills, transport and infrastructure. Culture here indicates a complex of economic and productive strategies that need to be managed and cannot be left to the spontaneous play of social actors. By the same logic, the Olympics become a means to revitalise an economic system whose capacity to create and absorb surplus value has much decreased over recent years (Poynter, 2012). The regeneration of East London provides the space for the production and the absorption of such new capital (Harvey, 2006), while the materialisation of culture as lifestyle in a 'real' urban space is what enacts the process of production-absorption-reproduction of capital.

All this implies the concepts of 'priorities' and 'prioritisation'. 'The role of the GLA and the Mayor is to work in partnership across the cultural sector and its myriad organisations in order to set priorities, provide leadership and deliver long-term improvements. The cultural sector is large, complex and highly interdependent. Therefore, this strategic role is crucial in helping make better use of existing resources, develop innovative solutions and link culture to other strategic areas of importance in the capital. A key responsibility of the Mayor is 'to advocate the importance of culture, ensuring it is supported with appropriate investment and remains free from unnecessary bureaucracy and interference' (Mayor of London, 2012:155). Culture and cultural activities are not considered as ends in themselves, as they are ranked, and hence financed, out of their supposed capacity to produce profit. To free policy making from 'unnecessary bureaucracy and interference' means to bypass politics and the mechanisms of public control and accountability. In this way, 'culture' becomes the realm for the bureaucratic management of an asset rather than the realm for the free interaction of different social actors and ideas.

Conclusions

This chapter analysed how the official discourse of laws, acts, plans and development strategies that framed the decision-making process of the city and, in particular, the Olympics and the urban regeneration of East London creates the preconditions for public space formation and how the language of such discourse works in defining the nature of public space (publicness). It employed a deductive approach, which proceeds from the identification of a pure idea of democracy, public sphere and public space and goes on to compare this idea with the kind of publicness emerging from the analysis of texts. The element informing such an ideal type (the element without which it is not possible to refer to urban space in terms of democratic public space) is Hannah Arendt's concept of plurality, which is to be understood in terms of the free play of differences (in visions, perspectives, values, ideas, identities and economic actors) in the social realm. Democratic public space is, therefore, a space that provides the conditions for such differences to emerge and interact. The opposite of democratic public space is the imposition of one single vision, perspective and identity reflected in its reduction to a competition between different economic actors in the marketplace.

The kind of publicness of East London's public space has been analysed against the three interrelated dimensions of legislation, culture and governance. The legislation to be found in the complex of laws, acts, plans and development strategies establishes the content of a politics of space that is mainly articulated in terms of *strategy* and *culture*, or of *cultural strategy*. Culture comes to indicate a strategic sector for the management and transformation of space as a site for leisure, tourism, investments and consumption, rather than as a site for the free play of different social-economic actors. This implies the construction of a system of governance (Raco, 2012, 2014) to deliver such strategies 'on time and to budget' and regulate risk ('social regulation') (Levi-Faur, 2005). This form of governance in turn entails the reduction of politics (and the 'risks' connected to it) within the processes of policy and decision making and, hence, the curtailing of democracy.

Such a dynamic needs to be placed in the context of the transformation of the public sphere. As Jürgen Habermas explains, with the rise of the market economy, the separation of the public sphere from public authority – the separation of the space for political action and economic exchange between private owners from the state – was substituted at the end of the eighteenth/beginning of the nineteenth century by the concentration of political and economic power in territorial states (Habermas, 1992:141). This brought about a different kind of separation between the public and the social – the former taking over powers of political and economic administration, the latter being limited to the intimate sphere of the family and culture consumption. In the current phase of late capitalism, another shift occurred, which did not cause the separation of the state from the economy in the form of deregulation but, as Levi-Faur shows, resulted in an even stronger relationship among the state, economy, politics and society in the form of regulatory capitalism (Jordana and Levi-Faur, 2004; Levi-Faur, 2005). Regulatory frameworks are required that limit the risks of competition in the global market and adjust social change to the needs of capital so that political and social opposition is restrained. A shift occurs 'from representative democracy to indirect representative democracy. Democratic governance is no longer about the delegation of authority to elected representatives but becomes a form of second-level indirect representative democracy – citizens elect representatives who control and supervise "experts" who formulate and administer policies in an autonomous fashion from their regulatory bastions' (Levi-Faur, 2005:13).

However, it would be simplistic to say that urban, social and economic processes of transformation and change are solely economy-led. The economy is part of a wider structuring dimension in which I regard discourse as a site for political action. Legislation, culture and governance construe a precise knowledge of space and the societal world that is enacted through texts. Such a discourse, which implies specific social relations of power, sets out the preconditions for the construction of physical 'public' space and defines the content of publicness itself. The implication is that no matter how many people use space, no matter whether space is publicly or privately owned, no matter whether the ultimate agent of regeneration is a public authority, public space does not necessarily equal democracy, for democracy and 'publicity' are not intrinsic qualities of the contemporary urban order. They can only exist if they arise from plurality – the precondition for challenging the contemporary 'post-democratic' narrative that dominates London's strategies for urban renewal.

References

Arendt, H. (1998) *The human condition.* London: The University of Chicago.

Calcutt, A. (2012) 'Finance and culture: Twin Towers in London's lightness of being' in G. Poynter, I. MacRury and A. Calcutt (Eds.), *London after recession: a fictitious capital?* Farnham, UK: Ashgate.

Canovan, M. (1998) 'Introduction to Hanna Arendt' in H. Arendt (Ed.), *The human condition.* London: The University of Chicago.

Crouch, C. (2004) *Post-democracy.* Cambridge: Polity Press.

Crouch, C. (2011) *The strange non-death of neoliberalism.* Cambridge: Polity Press.

Dahl, A. R. (2002) *Intervista sul Pluralismo.* Roma-Bari: Laterza.

De Magalhães, C. (2010) 'Public space and the contracting-out of publicness: a framework for analysis'. *Journal of Urban Design*, 15(4): 559–574.

Desiderio, A. (2013) 'Branding Stratford: social representation and the re-making of place'. *Architecture_MPS. Architecture_Media_Politics_Society*, 2(3), available at: http:// architecturemps.com

Fairclough, N. (2010a) 'A dialectical-relational approach to critical discourse analysis in social research' in R. Wodak and M. Meyer (Eds.), *Methods of critical discourse analysis.* London: Ashgate.

Fairclough, N. (2010b) *Critical discourse analysis: the critical study of language*. London: Longman.

Fairclough, N., Pardoe, S. and Szerszynski, B. (2010) 'Critical discourse analysis and citizenship' in N. Fairclough (Ed.), *Critical discourse analysis: the critical study of language*. London: Longman.

Greater London Authority (GLA) (1999) 'Greater London authority act', available at: http://www.legislation.gov.uk/ukpga/1999/29/contents (last accessed 3 June 2013).

Greater London Authority (GLA) (2011) 'The London plan. Spatial development strategy for Greater London', available at: http://www.london.gov.uk/priorities/planning/london-plan (last accessed 3 August 2013).

Greater London Authority (GLA) (2013a) 'London implementation group draft terms of reference', available at: http://www.london.gov.uk/priorities/planning/implementation-plan/implementation- group (last accessed 3 August 2013).

Greater London Authority (GLA) (2013b) 'London implementation plan', available at: http://www.london.gov.uk/priorities/planning/publications/london-plan-implementation-plan (last accessed 3 August 2013).

Habermas, J. (1992) *The structural transformation of the public sphere*. Cambridge: Polity Press.

Harvey, D. (2006) *Limits to capital*. London: Verso.

Jordana, J. and Levi-Faur, D. (2004) 'The politics of regulation in the age of governance', in J. Jordana and D. Levi-Faur (Eds.), *The politics of regulation: institutions and regulatory reforms for age of governance*. Cheltenham and Northampton: Edward Elgar.

Levi-Faur, D. (2005) 'The global diffusion of regulatory capitalism'. *Annals of the American Academy of Political and Social Science*, 598: 12–32

Mayor of London (2012) 'Cultural metropolis. The mayor's cultural strategy – 2012 and beyond'.

Olympic Delivery Authority (ODA) (2005) Contract with CLM, released under Freedom of Information Request, Reference Number RF100526.

Poynter, G. (2012) 'Introduction: a fictitious capital?' in G. Poynter, I. MacRury and A. Calcutt (Eds.), *London after recession: a fictitious capital?* Farnham, UK: Ashgate.

Raco, M. (2012) 'The privatisation of urban development and the London Olympics 2012'. *City*, 16(4): 452–460.

Raco, M. (2014) 'Delivering flagship projects in an era of regulatory capitalism: state-led privatization and the London Olympics 2012'. *International Journal of Urban and Regional Research*, 38(1):176–197.

UK Government (1994) 'Deregulation and Contracting Out Act', available at: http://www.legislation.gov.uk/ukpga/1994/40/contents/enacted (last accessed 12 April 2015).

22 Portraying Britain's past

English national newspaper coverage of the 2012 London Olympic ceremonies

Jack Black

Introduction

In commenting upon the decline of the British Empire, historian Brian Harrison noted:

> Although between 1970 and 1990 the winding up of the British empire was almost complete, the story did not end there. The empire, having grown by evolving from informal influence to formal control reverted in its decline from formal to informal – retaining many of its original cultural, economic, and demographic features. . . . The empire's relatively peaceful demise ensured that its slowly fading cultural palimpsest persisted long after formal imperial structures had vanished.
>
> (2010:46)

In accordance with Harrison's (2010) remarks, this chapter will explore how the former British imperial 'imagination' can provide a valuable insight into mediated constructions of Britain.[1] Specifically, this will be achieved by examining how the English national newspaper coverage served to construct, frame and represent 'Britain' during the 2012 London Olympic ceremonies.[2] While notions of imperial prestige have formed an important part of British identity and British society, they have also shaped its postimperial decline (Darwin, 2012; MacKenzie, 1998, 1999, 2001; Thompson, 2005). By locating contemporary newspaper discourses within a historical context, critical examinations of the national press can expose how representations of Britain, during the 2012 Olympic ceremonies, were constructed and (re)constructed within a historical conjecture that served to discursively frame Britain in relation to its imperial past. Before this, however, the following section will consider how the historical significance of the nation forms an important part of the mediated sporting spectacle.

The mediated sporting spectacle: representing the host nation

Although some have argued that national cultures are undermined by processes of globalization (Appadurai, 1996; Featherstone, 1990; Hardt and Negri, 2000), others have examined how the mediated sporting spectacle stands as part of a complex interplay between the global and the national (Lee and Maguire, 2009; Maguire and Falcous, 2005). While the hosting of international sporting events is coordinated in order to provide compelling significations of the host nation (Hogan, 2003; Panagiotopoulou, 2010a; Tomlinson and Young, 2006), such events take shape within a particular 'space where nationalisms, internationalisms, and trans-nationalisms interact in complex and frequently potent and emotive ways' (Silk and Falcous, 2005:450). While the Olympic Games operate under a global rhetoric of peace, humanitarian ideology and international unification (Tomlinson, 1996; Panagiotopoulou, 2010b), at the same time, embodiments of nationalism remain a prevalent part of the Games presentation, organisation and associated media coverage[3] (Hargreaves, 2002; Lee and Maguire, 2009).

Consequently, for the host nation, the Olympic Games present a valuable opportunity to represent the nation and its national identity to a global audience (Price and Dayan, 2008). Indeed, the prospect 'of a rite of passage into a certain "elite" of nations' (Dayan, 2010:30) offers the chance for nation-states to garner unprecedented world attention, both positive and negative (Collins, 2011; Curi *et al.*, 2011; Tomlinson and Young, 2006). One important opportunity to achieve such attention is during the Olympic Games opening ceremony. Aside from the athletic competition, the opening ceremony stands as a 'symbolic space' (Silk and Falcous, 2005) through which the host nation's culture, identity and history is theatrically presented across a series of choreographed performances (Tomlinson, 1996).

For example, Hogan (2003) illustrates how the opening ceremony for the 2001 Salt Lake City Winter Olympics provided American patriotism an opportunity to pay homage to the 11 September terrorist attacks through layered performances of sound (choir) and symbolism (the use of the World Trade Center American Flag). Acting as 'a global nationalist forum' (Lee and Maguire, 2009:6), the presence of presidents – both national and sporting – along with members of the American services added to a sequence that powerfully represented the triumph and resolution of the United States to an international media audience (Silk and Falcous, 2005). Similarly, the 1992 Olympic Games afforded Barcelona the opportunity to internationally promote Catalonian pride, culture and commerce (Hargreaves, 2000).

Particular attention can be paid to how the Olympic Games act as a powerful signifier of national prestige for the host nation (Giffard and Rivenburgh, 2000; Price and Dayan, 2008). For example, Wood argues that 'a drive for supremacy at the Olympics games and staging China's own in Beijing exemplify a relentless obsession with national prestige' (2014:11). Similarly, desires for national prestige can be allied with claims for political legitimacy and national revival. In commenting upon the 1936 Berlin Olympic Games, former president of International Olympic Committee, Avery Brundage, stated:

> We can learn much from Germany. We, too, if we wish to preserve our institutions, must stamp out communism. We, too, must take steps to arrest the

decline of patriotism. Germany has progressed as a nation out of her discour-
agement of five years into a new spirit of confidence in herself.

(Mosco and Mahoney, 1985:xiv)

Certainly, Brundage's acknowledgement of the 'new spirit of confidence' within
Germany coalesced with the Nazi's attempts to use the Berlin Olympic Games as
an opportunity to portray a 'New Germany' (Keys, 2006:135).

The successful hosting of a sporting mega-event may encourage a sense of
national pride within the host nation (Ismer, 2011; Tomlinson and Young, 2006),
and such a desire may prove to be particularly important for nations that have
witnessed a decline in their global status. Norbert Elias (1996, 2010) emphasised
how a nation's decline from global power can often take a long time for the nation
to come to terms with their diminished status and the 'consequent lowering of
their self-esteem' (Elias, 1996:4). In such instances, nations may seek to claim
national prestige 'by invoking a purported greatness of the past' (Wood, 2014:13).
An important part of this process relies on linking the national past and present
and constructing important national occasions with historical meaning (Zerubavel,
1997). Collective social memories, ideas and symbols from the past are (re)
constructed in daily practices and media discourses[4] (De Cillia *et al.*, 1999;
Maguire, 1999; van Daalen, 2013; Wood, 2014). Journalists and newspaper editors play an important role in representing the national 'imagined community'
(Anderson, 2006).

Nonetheless, efforts to represent the nation and its history are open to critical
discussion and can form part of a wider debate regarding the contemporary character of the nation (Ismer, 2011; Silk and Falcous, 2005). While the global mediated sporting spectacle may provide an opportunity for the host nation to celebrate
its national culture and historical past, in the case of Britain, such attempts remain
somewhat contradictory (Falcous and Silk, 2010; Gott, 2011; Owen, 1999). The
following section aims to briefly highlight how Britain's own 'continuing history
of imperialism, colonialism and immigration' (Rowe *et al.*, 1998:123) forms an
important and, indeed, contested part of contemporary Britain.

'An imperial people': the British Empire and British identity

There is not the potential to do justice to the full history of the British Empire in this
chapter. Yet, in order to understand contemporary media constructions of Britain,
'there is a need to look not just at comparatively recent developments, alignments
and pressures, but also at much longer and deeper histories' (Colley, 2014). Ho
(2013) has argued that the London Olympic Games provided a notable opportunity
to assess the effects of Britain's colonial history, both within Britain and the former
colonies. In order to pursue this opportunity, however, a 'brief' understanding of the
development of the nation-state in Western Europe is required.

Diaz-Andreu (2004) notes, 'From the 1830s to the 1870s the criteria that
defined a successful nation were transformed' (227); notions of 'Civilisation'

became a dominant expression among the Western European states and were closely aligned to imperial projects (Dunning and Hughes, 2012; Kumar, 2003):

> It increasingly became crucial not only to be an instituted, large state and have a long-established cultural elite with a literary and administrative tradition in the vernacular language, but also . . . to have the capacity for conquest, to be an *imperial people*.
>
> (Diaz-Andreu, 2004:227; italics added)

In the wake of the Seven Years' War, Britain's capacity to become 'an imperial people' (Diaz-Andreu, 2004:227) was largely secured, emerging from the war as the triumphant imperial power (Anderson, 2000; Bumsted, 2008):

> Its achievement as the main shaper of the modern era was manifested in naval and trade predominance. Indigenously, that encouraged pride and self-assurance; exogenously, it stimulated awe, admiration, fear, envy and, for some, a heightened, antagonistic national feeling.
>
> (Wood, 2014:6)

Consequently, despite the loss of the 13 colonies during the American Revolution (1775–1783), Britain's political and economic agendas were largely imperial both in their outlook and administration (Colley, 2005; Reid, 2013). Here, the relationship between Britain and its empire was fundamental to Britain's sense of self as well as to its constitutive nationalisms (Dawson, 2006; MacKenzie, 1999, 2001; McGregor, 2006).

After 1945, the British Empire – and, more importantly, its significant control over large areas of the world – was undermined by a new world order based upon the 'super-powers' of the United States and the Soviet Union. Indeed, over the course of the twentieth century, the governance of the Commonwealth Secretariat, led by Canadian diplomat Arnold Smith, sought to distinguish itself as independent of Britain and the former British Empire (Porter, 2007). Correspondingly, while 'Britain disentangled from the entrails of Empire' (2007:439), new relations were being forged with Europe (Harrison, 2010).

Despite Britain's closer alignment with Europe, a history of imperialism had 'resulted in a diverse comingling of "British" national culture and identity with other cultures' (Maguire, 2011:989). Indeed, this movement of people from the former British territories did not decline during the postwar period. 'Despite the demise of the Empire – and the crisis of identity that this itself presented – this movement of people continued. . . . citizens of Britain's former colonies not only visited, but stayed and made Britain their home' (Maguire, 2011:989). In such instances, Britain's postimperial decline remained closely entwined with the former British Empire, revealing particular insecurities in the English/British identity (Kumar, 2003).

By the end of the twentieth century, Britain's former empire was a Commonwealth of Nations and its own internal state structure was being redefined through devolution. The (re)establishment of the Scottish Parliament in 1997 and the opening of the Welsh assembly provided the national cultures of Scotland and Wales political legitimacy (Finlay, 2001). Later, in 1998, the Good Friday Agreements signaled a growing move towards 'peace' in Northern Ireland. For England, however, its own political governance would remain tied to the British parliament in Westminster. It seems to be against this system that calls for Scottish Independence, led by the Scottish National Party, have served to highlight the growing disillusionment with the political status quo within Britain (Perryman, 2009). Such disillusionment has often been reinterpreted through questions related to what it 'means' to be 'British'.

Thompson (2005) argues that Britain's cultural, structural and institutional explanations of decline can all be said to have an 'imperial' component (2005:6). Subsequently, while opinion remains divided on the merits of the British Empire (Ferguson, 2012; Gott, 2011; Owen, 1999), Britain's postimperial decline has been marred by problems with the welfare system, a persistently precarious economy and a lack of confidence in a political establishment that is perceived to be out of touch with the British electorate (Harrison, 2010; Richards, 2014). Amidst a global recession and a Euro-zone debt crisis, continuing security concerns and the prospect of an Independent Scotland, the pre-Olympic media coverage remained skeptical about London's hosting the 2012 Olympic Games. It is against this backdrop that the following sections examine how the English national press served to draw upon British history in their construction of Britain during the 2012 Olympic ceremonies. Attention will be paid to how the empire served as a form of historical prestige but also as a lingering reminder of the imperial decline of Britain.

'What kind of nation are we anyway?'

The postwar image of Britain as a nation beset by decline and 'where nothing works' (Freedland, 2012a:1) was frequently drawn upon in reports before the opening ceremony.[5] Indeed, uncertainties regarding Britain's ability to host the games were seen as a reflection of the British 'national malaise' and characteristic of its contemporary problems (Hayward, 2012:S2). According to Freedland, such problems conveyed a similarity with Britain's recent history and its 'troubled political past':

> Even up to the last minute, in the final days of preparation, the question of whether Britain can actually pull this off has seemed in doubt. A wearily familiar narrative is already in place: the Britain of the Daily Mail and Crap Towns, the Britain where nothing works any more. If it wasn't the failure of G4S to provide security staff, it was the threat by the PCS to call border guards out on strike. One an incompetent company made rich by privatisation, the other a militant-led trade union, the two seemed to spell out twin aspects of our troubled political past: Thatcherism and the winter of discontent uniting to ruin the Olympics.
>
> (2012a:1)

Similar sentiments were expressed by Hayward (2012) who made a clear distinction between Britain's 'past' and 'present'. For Hayward, Britain was 'a country that has always imposed its view on the world, *through imperial adventure*, culture and commerce' (2012:S2; italics added), however:

> *now* the Games open in east London in an age of mass insecurity and collapsed assumptions, stemming from last summer's riots, the Leveson inquiry, double-dip recession and the banking scandal, which has shaken all our senses of what Britain really is.
>
> (Hayward, 2012:S2; italics added)

Hayward's portrayal of a nation that once 'imposed its view on the world, through imperial adventure' was *now* characterised by a number of recent crises and scandals. Consequently, 'the story of a nation in decline' was one that was often contrasted with Britain's former imperial status (Paxman, 2012:11). Here, the decline of the British Empire was compared with Britain's lack of sporting achievements, a narrative which for Paxman 'fitted comfortably into the story of a nation in decline, a country that has lost an empire and failed to find the goal net' (2012:11). Bradley argued, 'Where once British identity was about feeling superior, there is now perhaps something of an inferiority complex, allied to a culture of low expectations, an acceptance of the second-rate and a lack of drive and dynamism' (2008:63).

However, whereas Bradley's (2008) remarks allude to concerns regarding the British sense of self, correspondingly, such concerns were closely aligned with anxieties about its 'place in the world':

> these Olympic weeks will offer answers to a clutch of questions that have nagged at us since the last time London hosted the Games in 1948. *What exactly is our place in the world? How do we compare to other countries and to the country we used to be? What kind of nation are we anyway?*
>
> (Freedland, 2012a:1; italics added)

Freedland's remarks reveal how concerns about the national self were closely allied with Britain's wider global position and the belief that Britain was a country that 'used to be' *something* (2012a:1). Such remarks correspond with Ward's (2004) assessment that Britain's 'world position' formed an important part of its identity. As a result, the subsequent decline of Britain post-1948 had clearly affected the British sense of self ('What kind of nation are we anyway?') and its place within a global order of nation-states ('What exactly is our place in the world?') (Freedland, 2012a:1).

Determining exactly *who* the British are proved to be a prominent feature of the press' discourse; Lott noted, 'over the past several generations we have been a nation obsessed with "who we are"' (2012:42). This was shared by Adams, who argued that 'the Games . . . would be an opportunity for *us* to tell the world what *we* were about' (2012:2; italics added). Here, it is evident that for the English press a decline in British self-respect and its location within a global order of nation-states had resulted in an uncertain understanding of who the British were.

Despite examples of British decline and insecurity, recollections of Britain's past could also serve another important function within the press' discourse. While popular and theatrical representations of the nation serve to glorify the national past 'through a shared sense of descent and destiny' (Rivera, 2008:622), such representations can also be used to provide 'evidence of a country's superiority' (622). (Re)-constructions of British history provided a powerful reminder of Britain's former global hegemony. References to the former British Empire provided a notable example of what Britain *could* achieve:

> From the moment we knew that the Olympics were coming to our shores, there was a symphony of self-loathing. It would be rubbish compared to Beijing. They would be too expensive. London would grind to a humiliating halt. The poor old British can no longer organise a drink-up in a brewery. Wrong, wrong, wrong. *The British ran an Empire covering the world for three centuries – why the hell did we ever doubt that we could run a sporting event for two weeks?*
>
> (Parsons, 2012:10; italics added)

Evidently, the empire was chosen as a particular period where British achievements were at their greatest and its global power was at its zenith. Wood has highlighted how a sense of imperial prestige provided Britain the ability 'to govern a vast, far-flung network of colonies' (2014:2). In the above examples, however, this sense of 'imperial prestige' continued to command both a historical and contemporary importance. *The Independent on Sunday* echoed such sentiments when it cited a *New York Times* article, which had stated that 'Britain offered a display of humour and humbleness that can only stem *from a deep-rooted sense of superiority*' (2012a:41; italics added). Here, Britain's history and global influence acted as a powerful signifier of its established position within the world:

> We dislike being instructed on how to behave by people wholly unqualified to offer such instruction. It is one of our oldest and most endearing traits. In any case, our history has earned us the right to exercise our own choice on these matters. Again, it is central to who we are.
>
> (Collins, 2012:S9)

Similarly, Phillips noted:

> We recognised our history with pride and unashamed acceptance that it has made us the country we are today, a country still able to put on such an extraordinary event with style and to welcome visitors from around the world with open arms and with open minds.
>
> (Phillips, 2012:9)

Such accounts were closely tied to a 'British system of national beliefs [which] had, since time immemorial, legitimated their claim to superiority at least partially through Britain's service and achievements for others, for humanity and civilisation' (Elias, 1996:348). *The Mail on Sunday* argued:

> We have no need to assert ourselves. These small islands have influenced the world in countless ways for centuries. No other capital has hosted the Games three times, or is likely to do so.
>
> (2012:31)

Such positive sentiments were echoed in reports of the opening ceremony, which according to Reade served to highlight '*our* genius, tolerance, humour, and all *we* have given to the world' (2012a:2; italics added). Indeed, representations of what Britain had 'given to the world' were clearly evoked in the opening ceremony depiction of the Industrial Revolution as well as more recent cultural icons, such as the Beatles and popular children's literature (Brown, 2012; Gibson, 2012; *The Sunday Telegraph*, 2012). In regard to the closing ceremony, Gibson highlighted how the set featured 'London landmarks covered in newsprint bearing quotations from Shakespeare, Dickens and other luminaries', adding that 'the show was a camp, joyous romp through pop culture' (2012:3). Accordingly, references to Britain's history and its culture served as a notable reassurance of its prominent role in global popular culture (Mangan *et al.*, 2013). In contrast to all 'the doom-mongers who said it was all a costly distraction' (Reade, 2012b:2), Reade added:

> That's what sport, music and culture is all about. We've reminded the world, and more importantly ourselves, that we are still blessed with wealth in all those fields.
>
> (2012b:2)

Underlying Reade's remarks was a sense that despite its decline from empire, Britain could still maintain a global role, not as an imperial power but as a dominant figure in global popular culture. Mangan *et al.* note that whereas 'Britain, . . . had once been called an "Empire on which the sun never sets", arguably in a very different way, it was still an "Empire" as an innovator in the contemporary global popular culture industry' (2013:1848).

'A spirit regained' or 'another kind of Britain'?

References to Britain's past proved to be a prominent part of the press' framing of Britain (Conboy, 2006). Indeed, while recollections of British history served to underlie concerns regarding its sense of self and its political, cultural and economic instability (Freedland, 2012a, 2012b; Hayward, 2012; Paxman, 2012), paradoxically, Britain's global influence was predicated on a history that served to remind the British of its continuing global importance (Parsons, 2012; Phillips, 2012; Reade, 2012a, 2012b; *The Mail on Sunday*, 2012). With the Games success,

Lawton (2012) noted:

> We came so fragile and, let's be honest, fearful into the 30th Olympic Games that ended here last night with all the poignancy of the sweetest parting. Already it seems like an impossible stretch of memory but it is true and it is why the closing rites were filled with so much pride and emotion and, maybe above all, a feeling not so much of a job well done but a spirit regained, a sense of ourselves and the world around us that might just defy, for a little while at least, the bleakest forecasts.
>
> (2012:8)

The sense of a 'spirit regained' posited a poignant 'reminder of what Britain [could] still achieve, even in the most testing times' (*Daily Mail*, 2012:14). In these instances, echoes of Britain's past were once again drawn upon in order to contextualise Britain's newfound confidence. The former British athlete Sir Roger Bannister expressed similar feelings when he stated, 'how thrilling it is that I can see again today, on the Olympic track, the spirit that I recall from another era' (2012:28). Britain's renewed 'spirit' was entwined with a belief that contemporary Britain had reconnected with a Britain 'from another era' (Bannister, 2012). Accordingly, while the success of the Olympic Games was represented as reconnecting Britain with its past, references to Britain's postimperial decline were also reframed as a particular 'turning point' (Lott, 2012:42). Lott noted:

> For me, the Olympics feels like a turning point, a moment in which for the first time since our decline from empire, we felt genuinely self-confident. For the first time I can remember, we like ourselves.
>
> (2012:42)

Consequently, 'no longer was Britain casting itself as the imperial power, which once came to the countries of others, determined to shape their futures' (Freedland, 2012a:1); instead the Olympic opening ceremony 'celebrated modern Britain, a post-imperial nation, still half in and half out of Europe but surprisingly comfortable with its role' (*The Independent on Sunday*, 2012:41).

Elsewhere, Falcous and Silk observed how 'contemporary concerns' can be superimposed 'onto reconstructed versions of the past' (2010:175). Indeed, they argue that 'these narratives are mythologies that point to the capacity of the media to tell us stories about ourselves' (Falcous and Silk, 2010; see also Barthes, 1972). However, as highlighted in the above examples, media discourses could also serve to reveal discontinuity with the national past, especially with regard to those examples that sought to highlight that Britain had traversed its postimperial decline in order to present a united and largely confident depiction of its present self (Lott, 2012; *The Independent on Sunday*, 2012a, 2012b). It was during the Olympic Games that 'we got a glimpse of another kind of Britain' (Freedland, 2012b:32). *The Independent on Sunday* stated:

We may not be galvanised by the Olympics into suddenly transforming the economy or curing the ills that tainted our streets last summer. But we'd like to think that more than a passing feel-good factor has been generated by London 2012 – not just the immediate luster of gold, silver and bronze, but *the knowledge that this was a triumph not of old Britain, but new*: competitors in their teens or fifties, black, white and shades in between; ageing rockers, young rappers; women, contributing nearly half the glory and more than their shares of the smiles; volunteers from every background; the witty, the imaginative, the accomplished. The knowledge of that, the confidence to be drawn from it, could be the real legacy of these Games.

(2012b:41; italics added)

In these examples, it was the transference from an 'old' to a 'new' Britain which served to characterise the press' discourse. Via discourses pertaining to Britain's imperial history, historical 'time' served to reconnect contemporary Britain in both positive and negative ways. Indeed, while Britain's present problems and sense of decline were highlighted, the relative success of the 2012 Olympic Games heralded contemporary Britain as one 'from another era' (Bannister, 2012:28). Such sentiments were echoed in Sandbrook's declaration of a 'rekindling of Britishness itself' something that had been 'in danger of dying out' (2012:16). In these instances, legacies of the past served to be (re)constructed in accordance with the present.

Conclusion

This chapter analysed how the national media coverage of sporting mega-events seeks to discursively construct the host nation in relation to its national history. The English national press coverage of the 2012 London Olympic Games was considered to examine how constructions of British history were related to contemporary constructions of Britain. Britain's imperial history afforded the press 'a set of meaning-producing practices' (Pietsch, 2010:426) that formed part of, and were related to, the wider social, cultural and historical context of the event. Indeed, it is through such practices and in such contexts that interpretations of the past can have an important role in shaping contemporary mediated constructions (De Cillia *et al.*, 1999).

   This analysis of the English national press reconfirmed this importance, yet at the same time provided an alternative perspective on the use of national history in mediated discourses. While examples of 'continuity' with the national past were identified, corresponding examples of 'discontinuity' could also be found (cf. Alabarces *et al.*, 2001; Falcous and Silk, 2010; Mihelj, 2008). While national memories and histories are based upon the historical continuity of the nation (Alabarces *et al.*, 2001), operating as a form of 'orientation' (Sindbaek, 2013), for a changing or fragmenting society they can also reveal moments of 'disorientation' (Boyle and Monteiro, 2005; van Daalen, 2013). This was exemplified in those examples that questioned 'who' the British were (Adams, 2012;

Collins, 2012; Freedland, 2012a; Lott, 2012; Phillips, 2012) and what 'they' had subsequently become (Freedland, 2012b; Lott, 2012; *The Independent on Sunday*, 2012a, 2012b).

By exploring how Britain's 'imperial history' was used within the press' coverage, it was possible to see how constructions of Britain stood precariously 'between two identities – the imperial and the post-imperial' (Colls, 2011:111). While the English press served to frame Britain in relation to its imperial decline (Hayward, 2012; Paxman, 2012), the subsequent success of the Games revealed discourses that reflected (Bannister, 2012; Lawton, 2012; Lott, 2012), reinvented (Sandbrook, 2012; *The Independent on Sunday*, 2012b) and reimagined (Freedland, 2012b; Reade, 2012b) Britain's past within the present (Healey, 1997).

Based on the examples presented, it is evident that the mediated framing of the nation's past remains an important feature of international sporting mega-events. Indeed, examinations of these discourses expose how recollections of the nation's past can act as both a facilitator of national unity and pride but also foster feelings of decline and anxiety. Critical consideration of the ways in which the nation's history is discursively constructed as well as contested will continue to be of relevance for understanding a 'British' sporting future.

Notes

1 For further work on the relationship between Britain and its imperial history, see Darwin (2012), Howe (2008, 2010), MacKenzie (1998, 1999, 2001), Maguire (1993), Owen (1999), Pocock (1975), Thompson (2000, 2005) and Wilson (2006).
2 A qualitative thematic content analysis method was used to analyse the English national newspapers (Mayring, 2000). In total, six national newspapers were chosen (broadsheet) *The Daily Telegraph*, *The Independent*, *The Guardian*, *The Observer*; (tabloid) *The Daily Mail* and *The Mirror*. Sunday editions and sporting supplements were also included. Articles with an 'S' before the page number refer to a sporting supplement. Newspapers were collected on the day prior to, the day of and the day following the Olympic opening and closing ceremonies. Accordingly, the data ranges were: opening ceremony – 26, 27, 28 July 2012 and closing ceremony – 11, 12, 13 August 2012.
3 Similarly, Panagiotopoulou highlights how a 'compulsory [Olympic] program' is given 'a specific national interpretation' by the host nation (2010a:240).
4 Conboy highlights how for tabloid newspapers in Britain – in particular England – the Second World War continues to be 'particularly important to popular historical memory as . . . [it] coincide[s] with the lived experience of a significant number of people, directly or vicariously, through the many popular cultural re-imaginings of this period' (2006:71).
5 In regard to the referenced articles by Freedland (2012a) and Hayward (2012), note that these were released on the morning of 27 August 2012. The opening ceremony began at the carefully chosen time of 08:12 p.m. (20:12) of 27 August 2012.

References

Adams, T. (2012, July 29) 'Cycling dream fails but London still smiles on Olympic opening', *The Observer*, p. 2.
Alabarces, P., Tomlinson, A. and Young, C. (2001) 'Argentina versus England at the France '98 World Cup: narratives of nation and the mythologizing of the popular'. *Media, Culture & Society*, 23: 547.

Anderson, B. (2006) *Imagined communities: reflections on the origin and spread of nationalism* (3rd ed.). London: Verso.

Anderson, F. (2000) *Crucible of war: the seven year's war and the fate of empire in British North America, 1754–1766.* New York: Vintage Books.

Appadurai, A. (1996) *Modernity at large.* Minneapolis: University of Minnesota Press.

Bannister, R. (2012, August 12) 'These remarkable Games have filled my heart with pride. It is as if the golden age of my youth had never gone away', *The Mail on Sunday*, p. 28.

Barthes, R. (1972) *Mythologies.* New York: Hill & Wang.

Boyle, R. and Monteiro, C. (2005) 'A small country with a big ambition: representations of Portugal and England in Euro 2004 British and Portuguese newspaper coverage'. *European Journal of Communication*, 20: 223.

Bradley, I. (2008) *Believing in Britain: the spiritual identity of Britishness.* Oxford: Lion.

Brown, M. (2012, August 13) 'Two weeks of unbelievable spectacle that surpassed our wildest dreams', *The Daily Telegraph*, p. 2.

Bumsted, J. (2008) 'The consolidation of British North America, 1783–1860' in P. Buckner (Ed.), *Oxford history of the British Empire companion series: Canada and the British Empire.* Oxford: Oxford University Press.

Colley, L. (2005) *Britons: forging the nation, 1707–1837.* New Haven, CT: Yale University Press.

Colley, L. (2014, January 5) 'We need new solutions for governing this disunited kingdom', *The Guardian*, available at: http://www.theguardian.com/commentisfree/2014/jan/05/solutions-governing-disunited-kingdom-break-up-uk-ireland (last accessed 7 January 2014).

Collins, P. (2012, July 29) 'Anthems fiasco is an own goal by the patriotism police', *The Mail on Sunday*, p. S9.

Collins, T. (2011) 'The invention of sporting tradittion: national myths, imperial pasts and the origins of Australian rules football' in S. Wagg (Ed.), *Myths and milestones in the history of sport.* Basingstoke: Palgrave Macmillan.

Colls, R. (2011) 'The lion and the eunuch: national identity and the British genius'. *The Political Quarterly*, 82(4): 574.

Conboy, M. (2006) *Tabloid Britain: constructing a community through language.* London: Routledge.

Curi, M., Knijnik, J. and Mascarenhas, G. (2011) 'The Pan American Games in Rio de Janeiro 2007: consequences of a sport mega-event on a BRIC country'. *International Review for the Sociology of Sport*, 46(2): 140–156.

Daily Mail (2012, July 27) 'Now let's make these Games the greatest', p. 14.

Darwin, J. (2012) *Unfinished empire: the global expansion of Britain.* London: Penguin.

Dawson, M. (2006) 'Acting global, thinking local: "liquid imperialism" and the multiple meanings of the 1954 British Empire & Commonwealth Games'. *The International Journal of the History of Sport*, 23(1): 3–27.

Dayan, D. (2010) 'Beyond media events: disenchantment, derailment, disruption' in N. Couldry, A. Hepp and F. Krotz (Eds.), *Media events in a global age.* London: Routledge.

De Cillia, R., Reisigl, M. and Wodak, R. (1999) 'The discursive construction of national identities'. *Discourse & Society*, 10(2): 149–173.

Diaz-Andreu, M. (2004) 'Britain and the other: the archaeology of imperialism' in H. Brocklehurst and R. Phillips (Eds.), *History, nationhood and the question of Britain.* Basingstoke: Palgrave Macmillan.

Dunning, E. and Hughes, J. (2012) *Norbert Elias and modern sociology: knowledge, interdependence, power, process.* London: Bloomsbury Academic.

Elias, N. (1996) *The Germans: power struggles and the development of habitus in the nineteenth and twentieth centuries.* Cambridge: Polity Press.

Elias, N. (2010) *The loneliness of the dying and* humana conditio. Dublin: University College Dublin Press.

Falcous, M. and Silk, M. (2010) 'Olympic bidding, multicultural nationalism, terror, and the epistemological violence of "making Britain proud"'. *Studies in Ethnicity and Nationalism,* 10(2): 167.

Featherstone, M. (1990) *Consumer culture and postmodernism.* London: Sage.

Ferguson, N. (2012) *Empire: how Britain made the modern world.* London: Penguin.

Finlay, R. (2001) 'New Britain, new Scotland, new history? The impact of devolution on the development of Scottish historiography'. *Journal of Contemporary History,* 36: 383.

Freedland, J. (2012a, July 27) 'Time to find out who we are', *The Guardian,* p. 1.

Freedland, J. (2012b, August 11) 'We've seen a glimpse of another kind of Britain, so let's fight to keep hold of it', *The Guardian,* p. 32.

Gibson, O. (2012, August 13) 'Athletes steal the aftershow', *The Guardian,* p. 3.

Giffard, C. and Rivenburgh, N. (2000) 'News agencies, national images, and global media events'. *Journalism & Mass Communication Quarterly,* 77(8): 8–21.

Gott, R. (2011) *Britain's Empire: resistance, repression and revolt.* London: Verso.

Hardt, M. and Negri, A. (2000) *Empire.* Cambridge: Harvard University Press.

Hargreaves, J. (2000) *Freedom for Catalonia? Catalan nationalism, Spanish identity and the Barcelona Olympic Games.* Cambridge: Cambridge University Press.

Hargreaves, J. (2002) 'Globalisation theory, global sport and nations and nationalism' in J. Sugden and A. Tomlinson (Eds.), *Power games.* London: Routledge.

Harrison, B. (2010) *Finding a role? The United Kingdom 1970–1990.* Oxford: Clarendon Press.

Hayward, P. (2012, July 27) 'A very British party as the planet comes to London', *The Daily Telegraph,* p. S2.

Healey, C. (1997) *From the ruins of Colonialism: history as social memory.* Cambridge: Cambridge University Press.

Ho, G. (2013) 'Reconnecting colonial imagination? Hong Kong people's attitude towards the London 2012 Olympics'. *The International Journal of History of Sport,* 30(18): 2209–2222.

Hogan, J. (2003) 'Staging the nation: gendered and ethnicized discourses of national identity in Olympic opening ceremonies'. *Journal of Sport and Social Issues,* 27: 100–123.

Howe, S. (2008) 'Empire and ideology' in S. Stockwell (Ed.), *The British Empire: themes and perspectives.* Oxford: Blackwell.

Howe, S. (Ed.) (2010) *The new Imperial histories reader.* London: Routledge.

Ismer, S. (2011) 'Embodying the nation: football, emotions and the construction of collective identity'. *Nationalities Papers: The Journal of Nationalism and Ethnicity,* 39(4): 547–565.

Keys, B. (2006) *Globalizing sport: national rivalry and international community in the 1930s.* Cambridge: Harvard University Press.

Kumar, K. (2003) *The making of English national identity.* Cambridge: Cambridge University Press.

Lawton, J. (2012, August 13) 'A gold medal to the athletes and the audience', *The Independent,* p. 8.

Lee, J. and Maguire, J. (2009) 'Gobal festivals through a national prism: the global national nexus in South Korean media coverage of the 2004 Athens Olympic Games'. *International Review for the Sociology of Sport,* 44(1): 5–24.

Lott, T. (2012, August 2012) 'We have surprised ourselves – and our potential is unlimited', *The Independent on Sunday*, p. 42.

MacKenzie, J. (1998) 'Empire and national identities: the case of Scotland'. *Transactions of the Royal Historical Society*, 8: 215–231.

MacKenzie, J. (1999) 'The popular culture of empire in Britain' in J. M. Brown and R. Louis (Eds.), *The Oxford history of the British Empire (Vol. IV): the nineteenth century.* Oxford: Oxford University Press.

MacKenzie, J. (2001) 'The persistence of empire in metropolitan culture' in S. Ward (Ed.), *British culture and the end of empire.* Manchester: Manchester University Press.

Maguire, J. (1993) 'Globalization, sport and national identities: the empire strikes back?' *Loisir et Societe*, 16(2): 293–322.

Maguire, J. (1999) *Global sport: identities, societies, civilizations.* Oxford: Polity.

Maguire, J. (2011) 'Globalization, sport and national identities'. *Sport in Society: Cultures, Commerce, Media, Politics*, 14(7–8): 978–993.

Maguire, J. and Falcous, M. (2005) 'Making touchdowns and hoop dreams: the NFL and the NBA in England' in J. Maguire (Ed.), *Power and global sport: zones of prestige, emulation and resistance.* Abingdon, UK: Routledge.

Mangan, J., Ok, G. and Man Kwak, Y. (2013) 'East reflects on west, east meets west! South Korean media responses to London 2012'. *The International Journal of the History of Sport*, 30(15): 1834–1853.

Mayring, P. (2000) 'Qualitative content analysis'. *Forum: Qualitative Social Research*, 1(2), available at: http://www.qualitative-research.net/index.php/fqs/article/view/1089 (last accessed 10 May 2010).

McGregor, R. (2006) 'The necessity of Britishness: ethno-cultural roots of Australian nationalism'. *Nations & Nationalism*, 12(3): 493–511.

Mihelj, S. (2008) 'National media events: from displays of unity to enactments of division'. *European Journal of Cultural Studies*, 11(4): 471–488.

Mosco, V. and Mahoney, E. (1985) 'Introduction' in V. Mosco and J. Wasko (Eds.), *The critical communications review (Vol. III): popular culture and media events.* Norwood: Ablex.

Owen, N. (1999) 'Critics of Empire in Britain' in J. M. Brown and R. Louis (Eds.), *The Oxford history of the British Empire (Vol. IV): the twentieth century.* Oxford: Oxford University Press.

Panagiotopoulou, R. (2010a) 'Sports events: the Olymics in Greece' in N. Couldry, A. Hepp and F. Krotz (Eds.), *Media events in a global age.* London and New York: Routledge.

Panagiotopoulou, R. (2010b) 'Greece: the Olympic torch relay in ancient Olympia – an ideal showcase for international political protest'. *The International Journal of the History of Sport*, 27(9–10): 1433–1451.

Parsons, T. (2012, August 11) 'These Games revealed the true nature of our people. All of our people. London 2012 reminded the British of who we were, who we are and everything that we can be', *The Mirror*, p. 10.

Paxman, J. (2012, August 12) 'Who thinks Britain is rubbish now?' *The Sunday Telegraph*, p. 11.

Perryman, M. (2009) *Breaking up Britain: four nations after a union.* London: Lawrence & Wishart.

Phillips, A. (2012, July 28) 'History class that dan us all so proud', *The Mirror*, p. 9.

Pietsch, T. (2010) 'A British sea: making sense of global space in the late nineteenth century'. *Journal of Global History*, 5: 423–466.

Pocock, J. (1975) 'British history: a plea for a new subject'. *Journal of Modern History*, 4: 601–624.

Porter, J. (2007) 'Empire to Commonwealth – a cultural dimension'. *The Round Table*, 96(391): 435–446.

Price, M. and Dayan, D. (Eds.) (2008) *Owning the Olympics: narratives of the new China*. Ann Arbor: University of Michigan Press.

Reade, B. (2012a, July 28) 'Unpredictable and inventive as the British themselves, it was the people's opening ceremony', *The Mirror*, p. 2.

Reade, B. (2012b, August 13) 'That was Great Britain', *The Mirror*, p. 2.

Reid, I. (2013) 'Shinty, nationalism and national autonomy in Scotland, 1887–1928'. *The International Journal of the History of Sport*, 30(17): 2098–2114.

Richards, D. (2014) 'A crisis of expectation' in D. Richards, M. Smith and C. Hay (Eds.), *Institutional crisis in twenty-first century Britain*. Basingstoke: Palgrave Macmillan.

Rivera, L. (2008) 'Managing "spoiled" national identity: war, tourism, and memory in Croatia'. *American Sociological Review*, 73: 613.

Rowe, D., McKay, J. and Miller, T. (1998) 'Come together: sport, nationalism, and the media image' in L. Wenner (Ed.), *Media sport*. London and New York: Routledge.

Sandbrook, D. (2012, August 11) 'Rebirth of Britishness', *Daily Mail*, p. 16.

Silk, M. and Falcous, M. (2005) 'One day in September/a week in February: mobilizing American (sporting) nationalisms'. *Sociology of Sport Journal*, 22: 447–471.

Sindbaek, T. (2013) 'A Croatian champion with a Croatian name: national identity and uses of history in Croatian football culture – the case of Dinamo Zagreb'. *Sport in Society: Cultures, Commerce, Media, Politics*, 16(8): 1009–1024.

The Independent on Sunday (2012a, July 29) 'A very British show', p. 41.

The Independent on Sunday (2012b, August 12) 'The days of our lives', p. 41.

The Mail on Sunday (2012, July 29) 'It's our chance to be the best in the world', p. 31.

The Sunday Telegraph (2012, July 29) 'What an inspiring achievement', p. 27.

Thompson, A. (2000) *Imperial Briton: the empire in British politics, c. 1880–1932*. London: Pearson Longman.

Thompson, A. (2005) *The empire strikes back? The impact of imperialism on Britain from the mid-nineteenth century*. London: Pearson Longman.

Tomlinson, A. (1996) 'Olympic spectacle: opening ceremonies and some paradoxes of globalization'. *Media, Culture & Society*, 18: 583–602.

Tomlinson, A. and Young, C. (2006) 'Culture, politics, and spectacle in the global sports event – an introduction' in A. Tomlinson and C. Young (Eds.), *National identity and global sports events: culture, politics, and spectacle in the Olympics and Football World Cup*. New York: State University of New York.

van Daalen, R. (2013) 'Classroom preoccupations: the shadow of the past in Dutch vocational training'. *Human Figurations*, 2(3), available at: http://hdl.handle.net/2027/spo.11217607.0002.304 (last accessed 10 February 2014).

Ward, P. (2004) *Britishness since 1870*. London: Routledge.

Wilson, K. (2006) 'Old imperialisms and new imperial histories: rethinking the history of the present'. *Radical History Review*, 95: 211–234.

Wood, S. (2014) 'Nations, national identity and prestige'. *National Identities*, available at: http://dx.doi.org/10.1080/14608944.2014.897315 (last accessed 29 May 2014).

Zerubavel, Y. (1997) *Recovered roots: collective memory and the making of Israeli national tradittion*. Chicago: University of Chicago Press.

23 Conclusion

A London model?

Valerie Viehoff

Introduction

London's Turning is the title of a book that captured the spirit of the moment in 2008, when ambitious plans were being discussed to 'shift the unequal balance of London's development from the generally affluent west to the relatively deprived east of the city and its region' (Cohen and Rustin, 2008). The subject of discussion was the *Thames Gateway Plan for Sustainable Communities*, one of the UK's largest urban regeneration projects ever undertaken, yet only one in a long line of projects aimed at regenerating East London since the establishment of a metropolitan government for the London region in 1888 (Mann, 2008).

The latest project, only discussed tangentially in the abovementioned book, was of course the Olympic and Paralympic Games to be held in London, more precisely in East London, in 2012. While it might have been just another project in the long line of 'interventions' targeted at London's East End, it was a project of a different kind; it was a mega-event.

And, as urban sociologists suggested more than 20 years ago, for cities faced with the double pinch of insufficient public funding and fierce international competition for private (foreign) investment, mega-events might be the hoped-for *deus ex machine* able to solve the problem of funding for urban development or regeneration projects, because they are 'Subventionsumlenkungsmaschinen', that is, vehicles for the diversion of (public) funding (Häußermann and Siebel, 1993:16). The authors contend that strategic and long-term urban planning is being replaced by a policy of festivalisation and a festivalisation of urban planning where efforts are spatially, temporally and thematically focused on large events or mega-events. Drawing on a range of examples from Europe and North America, they propose the following characteristics as defining this new form of 'planning by mega-event': (a) the sheer size of the project (e.g. with regard to the surface area, the financial investment or the number of visitors) making it a 'landmark' in the physical space of the city and in its media representation while at the same time necessitating public backing to mitigate the risk connected to a project of this size; (b) the preferred site for such mega-event projects being brown field sites or other perceived gaps in the post-industrial city's urban fabric; (c) their delivery via newly created bodies (e.g. development corporations) operating outside the existing public governance structures;

(d) the sidelining of public bodies as one partner among others, for instance within public–private partnerships or their total exclusion; (e) a predominant concern with 'delivery' often reflected in organisational structures that integrate all dimensions of the project (e.g. planning, managing, marketing) in the hands of one single entity; and finally (f) a belief that the main role of urban planning and development is to promote the city internationally to attract foreign investment (Häußermann and Siebel, 1993:9–10).

This book has been interested in how these two narratives – of the mega-event and the renewal of London's East End – have been brought together in the case of the London Olympics. It offers a kaleidoscope of perspectives, from inside and outside, including practitioners and civil servants who were involved in East London's regeneration at one time in its long history, academics from around the world and from (East) London. The contributing authors, drawing upon a wide range of disciplines and professional backgrounds, have provided analysis and evaluations and suggested lessons to be learned and models to be derived from the London 2012 Olympic and Paralympic Games.

Given the range and breadth of perspectives, any attempt at summarising the insights would necessarily be reductive. Instead, this final chapter will indicate some cross-cutting themes and issues regarding the legacies of mega-events identifiable across the chapters of this collection before concluding with a discussion of the potential role model character of the London Olympics.

The first thematic strand that runs through several chapters is concerned with how we can define, measure, analyse, research and evaluate the elusive term 'legacy' and what the difficulties and limitations are in doing so. Approaching the topic from a philosophical perspective, Shane Kerr and P. David Howe, for example, discuss the difficulties of defining (Paralympic) legacy. Drawing on Wittgenstein, Bourdieu and McFee, they contend that the ongoing debate over the definition of 'legacy' is an important contest in itself, further complicated by the fact that legacy is a multifaceted concept. In more practical terms, Judith Grant Long argues in chapter 7 that, while 'urban development aspirations' are becoming an increasingly important factor in cities' bid decisions, it is actually more and more complicated to assess and evaluate the (urban) impacts and legacies of the Games due to their growing complexity and sheer scale. Based on her comparative research of infrastructures built for Olympic Games 1896–2016, she reminds us that, although London might be lauded as a new role model for using the Olympics to achieve long-term (legacy) urban development plans, replacing Barcelona 1992 as most coveted model, the Los Angeles Games in 1932 and the 1936 Games in Berlin already featured purpose-built Olympic sport complexes, and Rome 1960 was in fact the first city to use the Games to realise an 'ambitious urban development agenda'.

The second recurring thematic cluster addresses the (contested) meaning bestowed to the Games and/or the legacy, the discourses surrounding legacy and the instrumentalisation of mega-events and legacies for various (political) purposes. In chapter 14, Andrew Hoolachan, for instance, investigates the (in)compatibility of the narratives of Localism and sustainable legacy. He positions the

London 2012 Olympic Games within a complex network governance and planning of different scales from the neighbourhood to the nation-state and questions the reconcilability of, on the one hand, the coalition government's policies that favour the local neighbourhood level as enshrined in the 'Localism Act' and, on the other, the delivery of the promised 'Sustainable Olympic Legacy'. His chapter reveals the false assumptions that underlie these localist policies, as they assume the one scale (the local) to be 'naturally' more democratic or effective at decision making than any other. Mark Purcell has called this 'the local trap' (Purcell, 2006) and has argued strongly against assuming that local initiatives will per se result in more democratic, sustainable or just cities. 'The local trap equates the local with "the good"; it is preferred presumptively over non-local scales' (Purcell, 2006:1924). Yet, scales and the relationships between them are always produced through social struggle (Smith, 1993; Swyngedouw, 1997; MacLeod and Goodwin, 1999; Marston, 2000; Brenner, 2001; Purcell, 2003), making the question of scale 'a fundamental (but under-examined) element of democratic politics because it goes to the heart of the eternal tension between particular and common interests' (Purcell, 2007:202).

As Hoolachan shows, in the context of the sustainability legacy of London 2012, the different and contradicting interpretations of 'sustainability' at different scales result in a 'fragmented vision for East London'. While the local authorities of the former Olympic host boroughs predominantly focus on the issue of convergence, in other words, a levelling out between East London and other parts of London with regard to a wide range of socio-economic (but not environmental) indicators, the Queen Elizabeth Olympic Park under planning regulation of the London Legacy Development Corporation (LLDC) seems like 'an island of high-quality urban design centred on carbon neutrality', i.e. an interpretation of sustainability focused entirely on its environmental component.

Another contested discourse in relation to the London Olympic and Paralympic Games and their legacies is the role of national identities and their showcasing as discussed, for example, by Jack Black in his chapter 'Portraying Britain's Past: English National Newspaper Coverage of the 2012 London Olympic Ceremonies'. He demonstrates that, while Olympism is founded on rhetoric declarations of peace and internationalism, nationalism still plays an important role both in the presentation and organisation of the Games as well as in the associated media coverage.

A third thematic strand is concerned with the role of London 2012 as best (or worst) practice and potential role model. Ralph Ward (chapter 8) argues, for instance, from his insider perspective of a former government advisor for Olympics and Olympic legacy that, although it might not be possible yet – or ever, due to the problem of the unknown counterfactual – to assess in detail the effectiveness and legacies of the Olympic interventions in East London, it is very likely that some positive outcomes will accrue, because of the enormous amounts of public money sunk into a relatively small area. He suggests that the key lesson to be learnt from the London Olympics is that the legacy plans for urban regeneration are more likely to be successful when a site is chosen that – like the site of the new Queen Elizabeth Olympic Park in East London – 'really had a legacy future' thanks to its inherent potential for development resulting from its favourable, yet hitherto undervalued geographical location in close proximity to the city of London and the new financial district of Canary Wharf.

From a more critical perspective, Guy Osborn and Andrew Smith argue in chapter 10 that mega-events are essentially part of a general project of rolling out neoliberalism, which is realised via, among other elements, the promotion of greater urban entrepreneurialism and the commoditisation of culture, time and space. Using the concept of 'brandscapes' they focus on the commercialisation of public space during and after the Games as one essential element of this project. They conclude that the Olympic Games have become 'an agent of urban commercialisation', initiating a legacy of commercialised public spaces through a process of 'legislative creep', whereby 'the next edition of the Games learns from previous legal mappings and redraws its legal framework in the light of this experience'. This final theme, namely the extent to which London provided a model of the mega-event city, is what this conclusion will now turn to.

London 2012 as model?

On the day after the end of the Olympic Games in August 2012, the US ambassador to the UK, Louis B. Susman, congratulated London and the UK in an open letter 'for staging what will doubtless be remembered as the greatest Olympic Games ever'. He then concluded, 'London has raised the bar for other cities around the world seeking to host the Olympic Games. 2012 will be a tough act to follow' (Susman, 2012). The ambassador might have felt obliged to use some hyperbolic praise to compensate for the offence caused earlier by Mitt Romney, the presidential candidate of the Republican Party, who on a visit to the UK just before the opening of the Olympics had questioned London's readiness for the Games. Yet, the US ambassador was not the only one impressed with the perfect Games that London had delivered. International Olympic Committee (IOC) president Jacques Rogge, short of calling the Games the 'best Games ever', praised them as 'happy and glorious Games' in his speech at the closing ceremony and later elaborated further: 'We encourage future Games organisers to innovate and expand on what they learn and ultimately improve upon the best practices of their predecessors. London managed to do exactly that in preparing for and delivering the Games of the XXX Olympiad. It may still be too soon to call them the greatest Games ever, but ask the same question again in 20 years and you might just get a "yes"' (2012).

The point made by Jacques Rogge is important, especially from the IOC's point of view, because it reflects the recent shift away from expecting every Olympic host city to deliver 'the best Games ever', towards an expectation that, in addition to putting on a great show for two weeks, the city should deliver the best legacy outcomes in the long term.

'Legacy', as synonym for long-term benefits, has accrued its position as *the* dominant rhetoric in the promotion of the Olympic Games, especially with regard to the Games effects and impacts on the host city, because the promise of

'Olympic legacies' provides the ephemeral two-week sporting circus with a justification beyond the short-term entertainment and spectacle. The 'spin' of legacy[1] serves as justification for enormous public investment by the host city and nation and it provides a boost to the Olympic brand, which had been ailing after allegations of corruption and a growing critique of its over-commercialisation (see also MacAloon, 2008).

And London seems to have nailed it: delivering the Games on time, putting on a great show without any major incidents or disruptions and also delivering an astonishing legacy.

London 2012 has become a new role model on par or even replacing Barcelona 1992 as the most coveted model of Olympic urban regeneration. For the IOC, London 2012 serves as a role model to inspire future host and candidate cities and to measure them against (Rogge, 2013). For the UK government the 'London model' is a success story and advertisement to promote 'UK plc', the fictitious community of shared commercial interests of everyone in the UK.

For instance, the Olympic Delivery Authority (ODA) is promoted as a model institution, from which other mega-event organisers could learn with regard to its excellent track record in the field of sustainability, health and safety, project and programme management. To capitalise on the ODA's success, a 'Learning Legacy' programme was created to 'share the knowledge from the construction of the Olympic Park to help raise the bar within the sector and act as a showcase for UK plc' (ODA, 2011).

Tessa Jowell, former Olympics minister, claimed that the construction of the Olympic park was a 'model for public-private partnerships', showing that 'it is possible to make public money work harder in the public interest' (Gibson, 2012). And Ian Watmore, former Cabinet Office Permanent Secretary and former chair of the Major Projects Authority Board overseeing the Olympics, retrospectively lauds the London 2012 Olympics as a 'shining success' and as a model of how the public sector can successfully complete major projects on time if 'political meddling' and 'hasty deadlines' are avoided (Watmore, 2014).

At the same time, critical voices like the London-based researcher Anna Minton have pointed out that many of the new developments in East London (e.g. Westfield Shopping Centre and the Olympic Park) are based on the return to 'an undemocratic model of land ownership', where 'councils decide to hand over swaths of land to private ownership' thereby 'reducing democracy to an optional extra' (Minton, 2012).

'The London model' from a critical perspective

Parallel to the rise of London 2012 as a world renowned model of best practice in delivering a mega-event plus legacy, a growing literature from a wide background of disciplines (including geography, planning, architecture, political and social sciences) is trying to dissect and analyse what exactly the 'London model' might be, how it functions and what its implications and consequences are for the future.

Put in simple terms, the London model could be described as the combination of two inherently 'good things': on the one hand a mega-event (i.e. the Olympic and Paralympic Games) that captures and potentially inspires global audiences and brings together visitors and elite athletes from across the world; and on the other 'city building' (i.e. the promised legacies for East London) as a project aimed at providing, among others, infrastructure upgrades and new housing/neighbourhoods (Poynter, 2013). The problem lies in how these two elements are brought together. The particular (governance, legal, political, social) arrangements of this 'London model' with its bold promises of delivering a great event and a positive lasting legacy for East London affect the way in which urban regeneration is planned and implemented and, consequently, they influence who benefits from the (intended) process of revalorisation of the land after extensive injection of public expenditure. Poynter's research on the 'London model' reveals (a) 'the increased dependency of the private sector upon the technocratic state as a source of profitability', whereby public bodies provide the higher risk initial investments and act as stabilising influence, and (b) the fact that the urban policies implemented have so far not only been inefficient in improving the life of the socially disadvantaged local communities but will ultimately be to their detriment (Poynter, 2013).

Mike Rustin (2009) identified a closely related element of the London model, namely that such technocratic models of Games organisation and urban regeneration derive their perceived efficiency in 'delivering' from excluding any disturbances that might stem from 'politics', especially the politics associated with city building.

Grabher and Thiel (2014) suggest that London 2012's heterarchic project ecology was one of the key elements contributing to the success of the 'London model' of mega-event delivery. Based on the assumption of structural analogies between mega-events and (large-scale) disasters, adaptability becomes the key to successful project delivery. Adaptability is achieved not via strict hierarchies but via ambiguity, redundancy and loose coupling, three elements of *heterarchy*, that is, a 'system with multiple, tangled and shifting hierarchies' (Grabher and Thiel, 2014:531). Yet, while heterarchies increase the ability to cope with all sorts of 'contingencies, disruptions and shocks', they also resulted in inflation of the cost of the project. Furthermore, although staff moving into new prominent positions after the Games might distribute the lessons learned (e.g. a more mindful management style) to a variety of public and private bodies, these positive effects were mainly witnessed at the national and global scale and were paralleled by a brain drain at the level of local authorities (Olympic host borough). Allowing for ambiguity can also provide opportunities for passing on responsibilities:

> By assigning the responsibilities for short-term (the event) and long-term (the legacy) objectives to different organizations, the temptation to externalize the costs of the own activities to other organizations arises. In London, for example, the massive public spending prior to the Olympic Games through the ODA had to be partly recovered by a different organization, the LLDC,

charged with generating as much revenue as possible from selling the land on the Olympic site (LM1).

(Grabher and Thiel, 2014:540)

And the final caveat of this 'London model' of hierarchic project governance is that one particular group of players 'will definitely receive the lion's share of the symbolic profit: the global consultancies which actively contributed to the London Games and which now act as global carriers of "shockproof" Olympic Games' (Grabher and Thiel, 2014:543).

Mike Raco has investigated in detail the role of the global consultancies mentioned by Grabher and Thiel and he has traced the creation of the legal, political and governance frameworks that have been implemented 'to enable experts to get on with the task of getting things done' (Raco, 2013:172). He defines the London 2012 governance model that has been created, partly based on the input of the same global consultancy and development companies that stand to reap its benefits, as a 'transferable delivery-focussed governance model' (172) and he demonstrates that its 'efficiency' comes at the price of severe democratic deficiencies (Raco, 2013, 2014a, 2014b). Raco identifies, for instance, the following three issues for urban politics that derive from this model:

(a) Any form of 'politics' is considered potentially disruptive to the most important 'delivery-focussed and profit-making activities' and hence 'institutional barriers are put in place to insulate public and private elites from democratic demands' (Raco, 2013:173).
(b) Economically, this model is very lucrative for the few top consultancy, advocacy and construction experts who are able to provide the necessary (legal) advice, e.g. with regard to the drawing up of contracts, but it comes at enormous costs to the funding body of the project, which in the case of the London Olympics was the public purse.
(c) The overriding focus on delivery paired with the reliance on private expertise and contractual arrangements has important political implications, because, in effect, vast parts of the project are removed from public scrutiny and not accountable to any democratically elected body.

For Raco (2014a, 2014b), the governance arrangements of the 'London model' are not noteworthy for their exceptionalism, but rather they are archetypical for the UK's present system of 'regulatory capitalism' (Braithwaite, 2008; Levi-Faure, 2005), an ideological belief in contractual arrangements with serious consequences for urban politics.

Levi-Faur defines the 'new order of regulatory capitalism' as relying heavily on 'rules and rule enforcement' and characterised by the following five criteria:

(1) a new division of labour between state and society (for example, privatization), (2) an increase in delegation (remaking the boundaries between the experts and the politicians), (3) proliferation of new technologies of

regulation, (4) formalization of inter-institutional and intra-institutional relations and the proliferation of mechanisms of self-regulation in the shadow of the state, and (5) the growth in the influence of experts in general and of international networks of experts in particular.

(Levi-Faur, 2005:27)

According to Raco, the governance structures of the delivery of the London 2012 Games and their legacy are rooted deeply in the concept of 'regulatory capitalism' and its contradictions. On the one hand, urban politics and urban development have been marked by a rhetoric of citizen empowerment, devolution of (planning) decisions to the local level, 'participatory practices', empowered citizens, good governance, while '[t]op-down state bureaucracies that seek to reduce the risks faced by citizens are characterized as outmoded and of a bygone era' (Raco, 2014a:180). On the other hand, cities are increasingly embarking on mega-events, flagship projects and large-scale infrastructure developments in the hope of attracting the 'creative class', trigger investment and stimulate economic growth. Because these mega-projects are of 'enormous technical and regulatory complexity' (Raco, 2014a:180), they usually require public backing to turn them into attractive low-risk investment opportunities for private investors.

Concluding thoughts

Why does it matter? Why should we spend any effort on dissecting, analysing and understanding the London Olympics? The answer is, we as critical researchers need to understand the 'London model' and its implications, because this model is being used as a blueprint that is promoted as 'best practice' worldwide with (normative) implications both for the organisation of other global mega-event worldwide and for urban planning, policies and politics in the UK in general.

Raco's conclusions chime with the conclusions drawn by Häußermann and Siebel, who suspected in 1993 that mega-event urbanisation circumvents established forms of public politics and instead relies on a combination of populism (drumming up public support) and corporatism (serving the needs of multinational corporations). The 'fatal paradox' of the combined politics of mega-events and the festivalisation of (urban) politics is, they contended, that while they appear to be the only solution to achieve urban regeneration or development in the face of an 'erosion of the collective basis for democratic governance', they contribute even further to the erosion of this collective:

> The intermediary levels of government are being weakened; the impact and influence of democratic civil organisations are reduced and, in the long-term, institutionalised and established forms of self-regulation in democratic societies are being hollowed out.

(Häußermann and Siebel, 1993:30)

It is to be expected that, with the worldwide mobility and diffusion of 'best practice', many cities bidding to host future mega-events, vying for global attention and investment or simply trying to deliver an urban regeneration or development project, will emulate the 'London model', which despite the tensions and contradictions alluded to above still seems to demonstrate the capacity to balance the demands of the event with those of a longer term programme of urban renewal.

Note

1 See also Michael Rustin's closing comments on 'spin' with regard to who will, in reality, profit from the London 2012 Olympics versus who is made to believe to be the beneficiaries of the Games (Rustin, 2009:20–21).

References

Braithwaite, J. (2008) *Regulatory capitalism – how it works, ideas for making it work better*. Cheltenham: Edward Elgar.

Cohen, P. and Rustin, M. J. (Eds.) (2008) *London's turning: the making of the Thames gateway*. Aldershot: Ashgate.

Gibson, O. (2012, June 15) 'Tessa Jowell lauds Olympic Park as model for public–private partnerships', *The Guardian*, available at: http://www.theguardian.com/sport/2012/jun/15/tessa-jowell-olympic-park-blueprint

Grabher, G. and Thiel, J. (2014) 'Coping with a self-induced shock: the heterarchic organization of the London Olympic Games 2012'. *Social Sciences*, 3: 527–548.

Häußermann, H. and Siebel, W. (Eds.) (1993) *Festivalisierung der Stadtpolitik. Stadtentwicklung durch große Projekte*. Wiesbaden: Springer.

Levi-Faur, D. (2005) 'The global diffusion of regulatory capitalism'. *Annals of the American Academy of Political and Social Science*, 598(1): 12–32.

MacAloon, J. (2008) '"Legacy" as managerial/magical discourse in contemporary Olympic affairs'. *International Journal of the History of Sport*, 25(14): 2060–2071.

Mann, W. (2008) 'One hundred and twenty years of regeneration, from East London to the Thames gateway: fluctuations of housing type and city form' in P. Cohen and M. J. Rustin (Eds.), *London's turning: the making of the Thames gateway*. Aldershot: Ashgate.

Minton, A. (2012, June 11) 'We are returning to an undemocratic model of land ownership', *The Guardian*, available at: http://www.theguardian.com/commentisfree/2012/jun/11/public-spaces-undemocratic-land-ownership

Olympic Delivery Authority (ODA) (2011) 'Learning legacy: Lessons learned from the London 2012 construction project', available at: http://learninglegacy.independent.gov.uk/about

Poynter, G. (2013) 'Value creation in the Olympic city' in P. Cardullo, R. Gupta and J. Hakim (Eds.), *London: city of paradox*. London: University of East London.

Purcell, M. (2003). Citizenship and the right to the global city: reimagining the capitalist world order. *International Journal of Urban and Regional Research*, 27(3): 564–590.

Purcell, M. (2006) 'Urban democracy and the local trap'. *Urban Studies*, 43(11): 1921–1941.

Purcell, M. (2007) 'City-regions, neoliberal globalization and democracy: a research agenda'. *International Journal of Urban and Regional Research*, 31(1): 197–206.

Raco, M. (2013) 'Governance as legacy: project management, the Olympic Games and the creation of a London model'. *International Journal of Urban Sustainable Development*, 5(2): 172–173.

Raco, M. (2014a) 'Delivering flagship projects in an era of regulatory capitalism: state-led privatization and the London Olympics 2012'. *International Journal of Urban and Regional Research*, 38(1): 176–197.

Raco, M. (2014b) 'Sustainable city-building and the new politics of the possible: reflections on the governance of the London Olympics 2012'. *Area* (online, n.p.).

Rogge, J. (2012, November 23) 'Was London 2012 the best Olympics ever?', *The Guardian*, available at: http://www.theguardian.com/commentisfree/2012/nov/23/london-2012-olympics-best-ever

Rogge, J. (2013, July 27) 'IOC President Jacques Rogge: London 2012 Olympic Games the model for future hosts', *The Telegraph*, available at: http://www.telegraph.co.uk/sport/olympics/athletics/10203571/IOC-president-Jacques-Rogge-London-2012-Olympic-Games-the-model-for-future-hosts.html

Rustin, M. (2009) 'Sport, spectacle and society: understanding the Olympics' in G. Poynter, and I. MacRury (Eds.), *Olympic cities: 2012 and the remaking of London*. Farnham, UK: Ashgate.

Susman, L. B. (2012, August 13) 'London 2012: a tough act to follow', *The Guardian*, available at: http://www.theguardian.com/sport/2012/aug/13/london-2012-tough-act-follow

Watmore, I. (2014, September 17) 'Opinion: Ian Watmore on the Olympics', *Civil Service World*, available at: https://www.civilserviceworld.com/print/2259

Index

eBooks
from Taylor & Francis

Helping you to choose the right eBooks for your Library

Add to your library's digital collection today with Taylor & Francis eBooks. We have over 50,000 eBooks in the Humanities, Social Sciences, Behavioural Sciences, Built Environment and Law, from leading imprints, including Routledge, Focal Press and Psychology Press.

Free Trials Available
We offer free trials to qualifying academic, corporate and government customers.

Choose from a range of subject packages or create your own!

Benefits for you
- Free MARC records
- COUNTER-compliant usage statistics
- Flexible purchase and pricing options
- All titles DRM-free.

Benefits for your user
- Off-site, anytime access via Athens or referring URL
- Print or copy pages or chapters
- Full content search
- Bookmark, highlight and annotate text
- Access to thousands of pages of quality research at the click of a button.

eCollections

Choose from over 30 subject eCollections, including:

Archaeology	Language Learning
Architecture	Law
Asian Studies	Literature
Business & Management	Media & Communication
Classical Studies	Middle East Studies
Construction	Music
Creative & Media Arts	Philosophy
Criminology & Criminal Justice	Planning
Economics	Politics
Education	Psychology & Mental Health
Energy	Religion
Engineering	Security
English Language & Linguistics	Social Work
Environment & Sustainability	Sociology
Geography	Sport
Health Studies	Theatre & Performance
History	Tourism, Hospitality & Events

For more information, pricing enquiries or to order a free trial, please contact your local sales team:
www.tandfebooks.com/page/sales

www.tandfebooks.com

For Product Safety Concerns and Information please contact our EU
representative GPSR@taylorandfrancis.com
Taylor & Francis Verlag GmbH, Kaufingerstraße 24, 80331 München, Germany

www.ingramcontent.com/pod-product-compliance
Ingram Content Group UK Ltd.
Pitfield, Milton Keynes, MK11 3LW, UK
UKHW021623240425
457818UK00018B/708